POLITICAL
ANALYSIS

Series Editors:
B.Guy Peters, Jon Pierre
and Gerry Stoker

Political science today is a dynamic discipline. Its substance, theory and methods have all changed radically in recent decades. It is much expanded in range and scope and in the variety of new perspectives – and new variants of old ones – that it encompasses. The sheer volume of work being published, and the increasing degree of its specialization, however, make it difficult for political scientists to maintain a clear grasp of the state of debate beyond their own particular subdisciplines.

The Political Analysis series is intended to provide a channel for different parts of the discipline to talk to one another and to new generations of students. Our aim is to publish books that provide introductions to, and exemplars of, the best work in various areas of the discipline. Written in an accessible style, they provide a 'launching-pad' for students and others seeking a clear grasp of the key methodological, theoretical and empirical issues, and the main areas of debate, in the complex and fragmented world of political science.

A particular priority is to facilitate intellectual exchange between academic communities in different parts of the world. Although frequently addressing the same intellectual issues, research agendas and literatures in North America, Europe and elsewhere have often tended to develop in relative isolation from one another. This series is designed to provide a framework for dialogue and debate which, rather than advocacy of one regional approach or another, is the key to progress.

The series reflects our view that the core values of political science should be coherent and logically constructed theory, matched by carefully constructed and exhaustive empirical investigation. The key challenge is to ensure quality and integrity in what is produced rather than to constrain diversity in methods and approaches. The series is intended as a showcase for the best of political science in all its variety, and demonstrate how nurturing that variety can further improve the discipline.

POLITICAL

 ## ANALYSIS

Series Editors:
B.Guy Peters, Jon Pierre
and Gerry Stoker

Political Analysis Series
Series Standing Order
ISBN 0–333–78694–7 hardback
ISBN 0–333–94506–9 paperback
(*outside North America only*)

You can receive future titles in this series as they are published by placing a standing order.
Please contact your bookseller or, in the case of difficulty, write to us at the address below with
your name and address, the title of the series and one of the ISBNs quoted above.

Customer Services Department, Macmillan Distribution Ltd, Houndmills, Basingstoke,
Hampshire RG21 6XS, England, UK

Doing Political Science and International Relations

Theories in Action

Heather Savigny

and

Lee Marsden

© Heather Savigny and Lee Marsden 2011

All rights reserved. No reproduction, copy or transmission of this publication may be made without written permission.

No portion of this publication may be reproduced, copied or transmitted save with written permission or in accordance with the provisions of the Copyright, Designs and Patents Act 1988, or under the terms of any licence permitting limited copying issued by the Copyright Licensing Agency, Saffron House, 6–10 Kirby Street, London EC1N 8TS.

Any person who does any unauthorized act in relation to this publication may be liable to criminal prosecution and civil claims for damages.

The authors have asserted their rights to be identified as the authors of this work in accordance with the Copyright, Designs and Patents Act 1988.

First published 2011 by
PALGRAVE MACMILLAN

Palgrave Macmillan in the UK is an imprint of Macmillan Publishers Limited, registered in England, company number 785998, of Houndmills, Basingstoke, Hampshire RG21 6XS.

Palgrave Macmillan in the US is a division of St Martin's Press LLC, 175 Fifth Avenue, New York, NY 10010.

Palgrave Macmillan is the global academic imprint of the above companies and has companies and representatives throughout the world.

Palgrave® and Macmillan® are registered trademarks in the United States, the United Kingdom, Europe and other countries.

ISBN 978–0–230–24586–0   hardback
ISBN 978–0–230–24587–7   paperback

This book is printed on paper suitable for recycling and made from fully managed and sustained forest sources. Logging, pulping and manufacturing processes are expected to conform to the environmental regulations of the country of origin.

A catalogue record for this book is available from the British Library.

A catalog record for this book is available from the Library of Congress.

10   9   8   7   6   5   4   3   2   1
20   19   18   17   16   15   14   13   12   11

Printed in China

To Simon, Sam and Gill

Contents

List of Illustrative Material

Acknowledgements

There are many people, both friends and colleagues, who have played an extremely important role in shaping this book and to whom we would like to extend our gratitude. To Henry Allen, Earl Gammon, Simon Gerrard, Mike Gough, Stephen Greasley, Peter Handley, Colin Hay, Nicola Pratt and Mick Temple we would like to say thank you for taking the time to read, comment and engage with what we have done here. We would particularly like to thank the series editor Gerry Stoker and the reviewers, Cathy Gormley-Heenan and Jonathan Moses, whose detailed, constructive and critical (not to say prompt!) comments have been very much appreciated. We hope we have made this a better book for your thoughts and observations.

We would like to thank all at Palgrave Macmillan, particularly Helen Caunce, Keith Povey and Stephen Wenham. And, finally, we feel that this book simply would not have been possible without the insight, encouragement and engagement of our publisher Steven Kennedy – and to whom we would like to say a massive thank you!

HEATHER SAVIGNY
LEE MARSDEN

On a personal note, Sam was ill for a long period while this book was in preparation, and there are so many people that I wish to acknowledge for their friendship and support. I would, however, particularly like to extend thanks to Simon Gerrard and David Vaughan, Catherine Ball, Steve Davies, Luke Garrod, Ann and Pat Gerrard, Barbara Goodwin, John Greenaway, Gina Irving, Nicola Jervis, Lee Marsden, Matt Olczak, Jean Savigny, Hazel Savigny and Catherine Waddams for their kindness and support. And thank you to Chris and Linda, Steve and Paula, Pam, Benito, Carl, Connor, Fern, Jenny and Nick, Sarah and Solay whose friendship was (and still is) everything.

H.S.

Introduction

What is it that we 'do' when we engage in Political Science or International Relations? Clearly, we study the world of politics, but what does this activity entail? The aim of this book is to provide an understanding of what it means to be a political scientist/analyst; that is, to demonstrate what it is that we as students or analysts of politics do, and how we do it. In this book we reflect upon the different ways in which we might go about: tackling a particular question or political problem; analyzing an issue or event; discussing the potential for political and/or social transformation; or challenging dominant interpretations of the political world. Our central argument is that the 'doing' of political analysis is an active, and interactive, process of critical evaluation and application of theory, and it is this skill which we hope to shed some light on in the pages that follow.

This book is designed as a new kind of introduction to Political Science and International Relations (which we will refer to by its abbreviation – IR). We focus in particular upon the different ways in which we might analyze a similar issue or problem in both disciplines. Of interest to Political Science and IR are questions such as: why do states go to war? Is world peace politically possible? Why are some societies more unequal than others? In whose interests does the political system work? Is a solution to climate change possible? These questions are all concerned with issues, problems or events which affect and transcend both the domestic and international levels of politics. The disciplines of Political Science and IR provide differing theoretical explanations as a means to analyze or seek to provide answers to these questions. With this in mind our book has a particular focus on the existence of a wide range of theoretical perspectives and shows how they might be applied. We also suggest that just as political questions and issues cross-cut domestic and international boundaries, so our analysis needs to do the same.

Our book has three starting assumptions: first, that the 'doing' of political analysis is theoretically informed; second, that there are several different ways that we can approach our studies, all of which are legitimate; and, third, that the disciplines of Political Science and International Relations are not discrete but overlap, asking similar questions, albeit with a slightly different vocabulary and a slightly different focus of enquiry. In part these differences stem from differences in subject matter – a disciplinary divide. In part these differences stem from approaches, or ways that we carry out our analysis; there is also a methodological

1

divide. Political Science and IR both ask important questions about our contemporary environment. They might explore the way history or economics shapes our understandings of today. Both disciplines also enable us to reflect upon and analyze the complexity of the 'real world' of politics and the possibilities of changing it. Nevertheless, this reflection is shaped not only by what we see in the 'real world' of politics, but also by the way in which our disciplines have developed and have taught us what are regarded as legitimate areas of enquiry. That is, the important point here is that debates centre around not only what we study, but *how* we study it.

The debate over how we study is an important one, but one which can be incredibly complex and confusing. Our aim here is to simplify this debate through illustrating that there are different ways to address similar political questions and issues. We might have intuitive thoughts about what the answer to a particular political problem is. What we are trying to do in this book is show how these intuitions can be systematically and logically developed, to enable us to do coherent and rigorous analysis. We are seeking to demystify some of the vocabulary that is used within our disciplines, and give labels to those intuitions which lie behind the analysis that we do.

We might have particular views about what the political world is like, or what it should be like. These views translate into differing ways in which we undertake our study. Our first example of how these differences manifest themselves can be found in the title of this book. While this book is entitled 'Doing Political Science and International Relations' there are two key contentious issues here that are worth briefly reflecting on. First, to term the study of politics 'Political Science' reflects a set of assumptions about the way in which the discipline can and should be studied – as a science. For us this definition provides only a partial account of what the analysis of politics entails (the debate over whether Politics may be considered a 'science' will be explicitly addressed in the following chapter and is a theme which runs throughout the book). Second, the title acknowledges the existence of a disciplinary split between Politics and IR, but another aim of the book is to suggest that this is somewhat limiting. What we are seeking to do here is to reflect upon these divisions which we do through a series of substantive topics.

We proceed in the introduction by giving a short discussion of the terminology which will be used to describe the two disciplines, and a brief overview of what is conventionally regarded as their legitimate areas of enquiry. As the need for theory to show us how we 'do' what it is we do is a key theme of this book, the main part of the introduction provides an overview of why theory is crucial in our analytical 'toolkit'.

A brief note on terminology: Politics and International Relations

It is easy to get confused about the terms IR, Political Studies and Political Science, and whether they refer to the world 'out there' or the study that we do. Conventionally, when referring to the discipline, the words begin with uppercase – Political Science/ Political Studies and International Relations. However, given our assumption that these divisions are arbitrary and limiting, we use the word Politics as an overarching umbrella term to include the whole field of Politics/Political Science/International Relations. We also assume an overlap of methodologies in both disciplines and so we use the term 'political analysis' to refer to the activity engaged in by both disciplines.

What is Politics (Political Science and International Relations)?

So what is it that we study when we analyze politics? For some people, politics is about war. For others, war is the consequence of a breakdown or failure of politics. For some politics is about government and the institutions of the state, whereas for others, notably, but not exclusively, politics is not only what happens in public life but is played out in private lives too through the politics of family relationships. For some politics is what happens on the news, while for others politics characterizes what happens in popular culture, where we are taught values of citizenship and political identities outside of a formal news setting (see, for example, Street, 1997).

Arguably, politics is also about the allocation of scarce resources, asking Laswell's (1936) famous question: who gets what, when and how? Related to this is the idea of collective bargaining, the interests of which might then be represented in public policy. Political study can also be about political behaviour, for example of politicians or the electorate. For some politics is about class conflict and the way in which this forms the basis of systems of exploitation. Politics can also be about the possibility of social transformation and as such provides an opportunity through which this is possible. Politics can be about challenging the status quo and envisioning alternative ways in which society can exist and operate.

Underlying this diversity of content, Leftwich (2004) suggests, are two broad approaches to defining the study of politics. First is the 'arena' approach, which suggests politics is something which takes place in a certain site, or set of institutions within certain kinds of societies, and is linked to the idea of states. Second, Leftwich suggests, is a 'procedural' approach, which is concerned with the processes of politics. That is, politics is not confined to geographic location or formal institutions, but takes place between people and is a process. Feminists, for example, argue that the 'personal is the political'. In their definition politics does not only occur in public life, but also in the private lives of citizens. Feminism is interesting as it blurs the boundaries of Leftwich's definitions and shows us how politics becomes a process of interaction, yet can also be embodied in institutions (so can combine a processural and arena account). However, arguably what underpins these definitional debates, and both disciplines, is a concern with power. Who has it or where is it located? How is it used and with what effects? Whose interests does it operate in? While these questions may not always be explicitly addressed in the work that we read, they do inform and shape the kind of questions that we ask about what we study. Given the centrality of the notion of power for understanding both how politics in the 'real world' works and in understanding how we, as analysts, formulate our research, power is discussed in more depth in Chapter 2. However, the study of politics isn't simply about the topic, it is also about the approach that we adopt, that is *how* we study our area of enquiry. We make a series of assumptions before we even begin our analysis, and so it is useful, and provides for much better analysis, if we are aware of our theoretical predispositions before we begin.

What are we trying to do as analysts of politics?

When considering what it is we do when we analyze politics, we need to think first about what it is that we are seeking to do. Are we seeking to provide causal explanation of phenomena? Are we aiming to uncover statistically measurable regularities and generate general unifying laws in order to provide both explanation and the possibility of predictions? Or are we trying to understand a set of phenomena through reference to its historical and cultural context? Do we need an awareness of the actions and intentions of the participants and the meaning they attach to them? These questions are related to one of the most fundamental questions that underpins Politics: can it be conceived of as 'scientific'? There is an enormous debate around this issue within the disciplines and given its importance in shaping the way in which we approach the study of politics, this will be addressed in more detail in the following chapter.

How do we 'do' Politics (Political Science and International Relations)?

In short, in this book we argue that the way in which we 'do' Politics is through the application of a theoretical framework to a particular political phenomenon, question, issue, process or event. Our argument is that theory provides a mechanism through which we can make sense of the world, but also we need to reflect on this. We also need to be aware of the limitations and strengths of our theories. That is, the way we use theory enables us to *critically evaluate* the world, but we should also *critically evaluate* our theories. This is a skill which we learn and refine and the aim of this book is to introduce the differing ways in which we might do this.

When we do our political analysis we might begin by looking at a particular problem or issue and think about how we might resolve it, such as: why are some tax regimes more progressive than others? How might participation in universities be widened? Why are ideas about neo-liberalism dominant and largely unchallenged? How can wealth be redistributed to address problems of inequality? Or we might have a particular question that we want to answer, such as what caused World War II? Why was a decision taken by the UK and US to invade Iraq? We may want to ask how we can address problems of social inequality, or how we can bring about political change. However, before we can apply theoretical frameworks to address these kinds of questions, we need to think about the assumptions that we are making about what is real, what we can know about reality and how we can find out about it.

Before we do any kind of analysis we have already made a set of assumptions about what the political world looks like and how we can know about it. This discussion about our ability to know about political reality reflects a complicated debate which we engage in throughout our lives as political analysts. We give an overview of this debate in the next chapter as it is crucial in helping us think about the way in which we analyze Politics. One reason we need to think about this issue is that it informs the theories that we adopt and a key argument in this book is that critical use of theory is central for us in doing our political analysis. We now turn to discuss why.

The importance of theory

The way in which we analyze politics and international relations is through the use of theoretical frameworks. Much like a mechanic needs a toolkit to do his/her job, so in order to do our job – to analyze political phenomena – we need a toolkit. However, the toolkit of the political analyst is not made up of spanners and screwdrivers; rather it comprises theoretical frameworks which provide us with a means through which we can analyze, explain, understand and potentially change the world.

Theory is crucial for a number of reasons. First, what makes political analysis different from journalism, or the kind of conversations we might have in the pub, is that theory is employed not only to describe events or issues but also to look for causation. It allows us to ask how and why particular events have happened, and to enable us to think about the likely implications of particular outcomes and observations. Theory helps us establish what we are looking for and why what we are looking for is relevant. When we analyze politics, we can collect stylized 'facts', but how do we put them together to make a coherent story or argument? It is not enough to establish what is (and so provide a descriptive analysis); we need to establish *why* something might be the case. Why do a certain set of 'facts' appear as they are? To ask these 'how' and 'why' questions, we need to use theory. Theory provides the framework through which we can understand or at least analyze why a certain set of 'facts' or a certain set of behaviours link together in the way that they do.

Second, theory provides us with a way to simplify the world so that we can analyze it. Political phenomena are inherently messy and so theory enables us to identify the key features, which are significant in analysis and so providing for understanding or explanation, and this would seem intuitively appealing as, *ceteris paribus*, we tend to be attracted to parsimony. However, this already raises complications. The more simplified a theory is the more abstract it is from what is happening, or what is being observed or analyzed, so it may miss important factors. But, at the same time, the more complex theory becomes the more difficult it is to identify the cause or conditions which produce that observation. So, getting the balance between simplification and reflecting the complexity of political life is crucial. Third, relatedly, through a critical evaluation of the theory we are using, we are able to see what is missing from our analysis – are there other factors which we should pay attention to? This then enables us to engage in theory building, to provide for more sophisticated analysis in later work. As we set out below, one of the key differences in the development of International Relations as a discipline was its atheoretical approach, its lack of theory. This led to a series of failings and weaknesses within the discipline (such as its inability to predict the outbreak of World War II or the collapse of communism). Although, this is discussed, and widely accepted as a 'failure' of the discipline, it raises the question: is it possible for any theory to make such a prediction? Whether the function of theory is to produce predictions or to help us to make sense of the world is something which we need to reflect upon when we do our analysis. Today the leading IR journals focus on publishing theoretical work, which aim to build and develop theory, not just for its own sake, but to provide us with more comprehensive 'tools' with which to do our job.

Fourth, for those who adhere to a scientific approach to politics, theory is also used to ask 'what if' questions. That is, theory is used to generate hypotheses to be tested. This can be used to explore counterfactuals (e.g., if A happens, then B *might* happen). Counterfactuals explore what might have happened or what may have been the case given certain conditions (for example, whether there would still have been a Democrat president if Hillary Clinton had won the nomination, or whether the UK would not have gone to war on Iraq if Blair had not been prime minister). Theory can also be used to establish causal relationships (e.g., if A happens, then B *will* happen) and can be also be used to make predictions about what happens if certain conditions are fulfilled. For example, there has been a great deal of research which has argued that the reason we voted for whom we did was related to our socio-economic background. A causal theory of voting behaviour was premised upon the following: in the UK, if you were middle class you were likely to vote Conservative; working class, you would vote Labour. Therefore, we would not need to observe someone in the ballot box, it is enough to know their social class and we would be able to predict their likely voting behaviour from that. Theories of voting behaviour, such as this, provide a simplification of reality. Using this theory, it is possible that we could have explained why the Conservatives might have won seats at election time if there were a high number of middle-class voters in the constituency. While this argument has been subject to much debate (as summarized in Denver, 1994/2003) the point to be made here is that the theory has been used to simplify reality so that predictions can be made, and an explanation and account of political reality can be offered. In this way, theory shows us where to look, and what is important for our analysis. For those who adhere to a 'scientific' approach it also provides the opportunity to offer a causal explanation.

Fifth, theory can also provide us with a way in which we can generate social and political transformation. For critical theorists, the use of theory enables us to reflect upon how we can challenge the existing order, through analysis of how it operates. This in turn provides us with the basis from which we can explore alternative conceptions of our social and political world.

Sixth, and linked to the previous point, theory provides us with a way to problematize the world. That is, it may not necessarily produce a definitive solution to a political problem or issue, but it provides us with a means through which we can understand the complexity of a political issue. Crucially, it helps us to understand the questions that we need to

Box I.1   Summary: the role of theory in political analysis

- Distinguishes the discipline from journalism in providing the opportunity for rigorous analysis
- Helps us to know what to look for and why this is relevant
- Simplifies the world to help us try and make sense of it
- Enables us to ask 'how' and 'why' questions
- Makes it possible for us to recognize the existence of different 'worldviews'
- Allows for a critical consideration of implications and possible outcomes
- For scientific approaches it provides for the possibility of predictions
- For critical accounts it provides a way to think about possibilities for social and political change
- Helps us to formulate the questions that we need to ask
- Theory also provides a language for communities of scholars, giving us terminologies to engage in dialogue

ask. Seventh, theory also gives us a language, a community with which to share that language, and a set of terminologies and 'labels' which we can use to define our intuitive and logical responses or thoughts about topics. It also gives us a vocabulary through which to discuss issues with other scholars in the community.

To be aware of differing theoretical perspectives enables us to understand that not everyone sees the world in the way that we do and so theory draws our attention to differing perspectives and ways in which people understand the political world.

Using theory enables us to think about what we should look for and why that particular aspect is relevant to our analysis. One of the ways in which theory does this is through the 'framing' of underlying issues or concerns. That is, what is it that we look at through a theoretical framework, what do we use theory to tell us? There are a number of issues which underpin all our theoretical frameworks both prior to and during our analysis. Some of these are discussed in Chapter 12, and below we draw out three of the key concerns that we need to be aware of: what is the level of analysis; what is the relationship between structures and agents; and are we accounting for/describing or explaining continuity or change? Our answers to these questions inform the way in which we approach our topic and influence the kind of outcomes we may produce. A brief account of these issues is outlined below.

Spatial levels of analysis

Something which theory has done much to highlight is the issue of 'levels of analysis'. That is, what is it that we look at when we analyze politics? Do we look at the actions of politicians, such as prime ministers and presidents? Do we look at the actions of nation-states? So, do we analyze the individual or an individual unit? Or, do we look at the systems or structures that are in place? Should we focus attention on the anarchic structure of the international system, the structure of capitalism, or the regulatory structure within states? To some the study of the international arena is macro level, where the domestic state is seen as a micro-level actor. Yet at the domestic level, the state can also be viewed as a macro-level actor, with political actors/individuals regarded as micro-level units of analysis. As this suggests we not only use theory to help us identify what we are looking for; it also helps us to think about the positioning of what we are looking at. An awareness of this enables us to reflect upon both what we are explaining or accounting for, and what we are missing.

Structure and agency

This levels of analysis debate focuses our attention on the geographical location that we may look at the international arena, the workings of the domestic state apparatus, or, as is being recently discussed in IR, the role of cities. However, is it enough only to think about the physical location of politics? Our argument is that it is not. We need also to think about the individuals who take part in the political process and the historical and institutional structures which shape and influence their behaviour. The interaction between the two has been widely debated across the social sciences, and has been labelled the 'structure/agency' debate. For some this debate is framed as a problem, which implies the need for a solution. However, philosophers have debated this issue throughout history and a solution has yet to be found. We prefer to go with the notion of the interaction with structure and agency not as a problem requiring a solution, but as a means to problematize the world. That is, through reference to the interaction between structure and agency, we can see what issues need to be addressed.

The tensions between structure and agency are inherent in both disciplines and there is a wealth of literature surrounding this theoretical issue (see, for example, Giddens, 1984; Hay, 2002, McAnulla, 2002; Wendt, 1987). This is also important because it influences what we might study and what we might miss in our theoretical frameworks. For example,

Marxist accounts will draw our attention to the way in which the world is shaped by capitalism (so providing an account which privileges the role of structures in explaining events); whereas elitist accounts would look at the role of leaders (so thereby privileging the role of agents, or individuals). We would endorse the argument that we need to reflect upon the role of both structures and agents to understand politics. That is, we cannot understand how structures operate, without understanding the role of individuals within them, at the same time, we cannot look at individuals divorced from their context. While this may seem a fairly obvious statement, many of the theoretical frameworks we explore through this book will (often implicitly) privilege one over the other.

An understanding of the underlying interaction and tensions between structures and agents in whatever theoretical framework we adopt is useful in that it reminds us of the complexity of the social and political world. It also enables us to reflect upon what is missing from our analysis. For example, if we explain the political world in terms of capitalist structures, are we missing the role that individuals (such as politicians, businessmen/women and bureaucrats) play in shaping those structures? If we explain the world in terms of individuals within it, are we missing the wider structures which constrain or facilitate our behaviour? In economic recession it may seem wise for the individual to be careful with their hard-earned cash – in this case the level of analysis would be upon the individual and the benefits to them of this frugal behaviour. However, if every individual chooses to behave in this way, then the sum total of this behaviour is a lack of money in circulation and so recession deepens. Analysis here might then instead focus upon the economy as a whole in recession, which misses the role of individuals (collectively) acting within it. Combining an analysis of structures and agents in this example would suggest that what is needed within a recession is government intervention to facilitate greater spending within the economy, by providing individuals with the means (i.e., jobs and wages) to make this interaction possible. The aim of this example is thus to illustrate that it is useful to consider the role of both structures and agents in our analysis. It is worth noting, however, that the choice to introduce this level of complexity contains a trade-off: if we study both structures and agents we may increase the complexity of our analysis at the expense of parsimony.

Change or continuity?

The other way in which we use theory is not just to look at static phenomena, but also to understand why things are the way they are, how they have come to be a particular way. The point being that we are not simply concerned to describe what is the case, but our aim is to seek to understand *why* something has come to be the case. What particular set of circumstances has facilitated this particular event, issue or outcome? We are not only looking to understand or explain what is, but more importantly we are seeking to understand why things are the way they are. To do this we need to be able to understand why things change and why they don't. So, when we are seeking to understand or account for events, or resolve particular problems, what is it that we are looking for? Are we looking to explain or understand why things have changed, why change happens? (For example, why are voters in contemporary society less likely to vote according to their socio-economic class compared to 50 years ago?) Or are we seeking to understand why things stay the same? (For example, why is capitalism so enduring?)

Each of the theories that we look at throughout this text includes assumptions about what the level of analysis should be when explaining or analysing political phenomena. The theories we use are also under-pinned by assumptions about the relationship between structure and agency. These may not always be explicitly spelled out within the theoretical frameworks, but an awareness of this is important for understanding what it is the theory is doing and what it is missing. Likewise, it is important to reflect upon the issue of continuity and change, as this enables us to think about the role that theory is playing in our analysis. Is our theory providing for a description of what is? Or does it enable us to understand why particular issues or events or problems are framed the way they are? Does this theory provide us with an opportunity to reflect upon the political world differently? This is important for two reasons. First, if we want to understand why things are the way they are and, second, because a more critical analyst of politics, again to paraphrase Marx, is not simply seeking to observe the world but seeking to change it too. In this way, theoretical frameworks provide us with an opportunity to reflect upon how things may be different. Second, the theory we adopt influences the outcomes available to us, be those outcomes ones which reinforce the status quo or those that bring about change. However, given the way in which theory shapes what it is possible to establish, we need to have this critical awareness of the assumptions that we make before we begin.

In summary, we argue that the way in which we 'do' political analysis is that we apply a particular theoretical framework and evaluate political phenomena against it. This enables us to simplify political phenomena, look for key aspects which we may use to explain events, or answer particular questions, to understand why and how something has happened, consider an alternative and possibilities of change and, depending upon our standpoint, address 'what if' questions. These issues are of concern to all students of Politics and given our suggestion that the disciplines are closely linked, we now turn to provide a brief overview of how the disciplines have been separated and what unites them.

What is the difference between IR and Politics and how are they connected?

Disciplinary contexts

Politics and IR have developed as separate disciplines. For some this is strange, as the subject area of enquiry for both disciplines is often similar (e.g., political institutions, ideas and behaviour, differentiated only by spatial levels of analysis). Moreover, if we look closely we can see a lot of similarities, not only in what is studied, but also in the way in which political phenomena are studied. The next section gives a general overview of how the two disciplines have developed historically and then draws out some of their similarities. It is important to draw attention to what may be one of the dangers of providing such a brief disciplinary history, in that this neglects the influence of broader disciplines, such as communications and media studies, gender studies, as well as psychology and, more recently, neuro-science. The aim here, however, is to illustrate how the two disciplines have emerged independently of each other, and yet to also highlight their shared approaches and concerns. In addition, we argue against the demarcation of the two disciplines, which a) may prevent insights into the other and b) while these boundaries may facilitate parsimony in analysis we believe that political life is inherently more complex than the superficial boundaries suggest.

This brief overview is not intended to suggest cohesion within the disciplines (and, indeed, there are debates about the historical development of the disciplines; see, for example, Schmidt, 2008; Adcock and Bevir, 2005; Savigny, 2010). Rather, the aim is to suggest that while Politics and IR may have had differing starting points, there are two main areas of agreement. First, as suggested earlier in this introduction and as reflected in the substantive chapters of this book, there are overlaps in terms of subject matter. Second, both disciplines are united in containing a number of divergent views upon how we actually proceed in analyzing the content matter.

Politics

Politics as a discipline was established in the late nineteenth/early twentieth century across Europe and in the US (although its roots in Europe – for example, in Sweden – date back to the mid-nineteenth century).

Historically, in the US and UK, the emphasis was upon political philosophy and normative political theory, although more recent variants have to varying degrees been informed by the natural sciences and economics. Politics as a broader discipline, concerning the study of ideas, institutions and interests, in the UK was formally established in the 1950s. Theoretical development more recently moved beyond philosophy and, in the US, Political Science has tended to focus upon quantitative approaches and formal modelling, strongly influenced by work from economics, and institutions. The 'scientific' quantitative approach still dominates the pages of the leading US journals. British Political Science (also referred to in the UK as Political Studies) has tended to be more qualitative, with a focus upon political philosophy (also known as normative theory), history and institutions, while European Political Science tended towards humanities, particularly history and sociology (for discussion of its contemporary character see special issue of *European Political Science*, e.g. Savigny (and other papers) 2010). Historically, the study of politics was concerned with normative issues such as the nature of (good) government. The behavioural 'revolution' meant an increasing focus upon the behaviour and workings of political systems, and analysis focused on voters and electoral outcomes. More recently the challenges came from a group of political analysts who are referred to as the *perestroika* movement. They sought to challenge the mainstream status quo and their emphasis is upon the need for a wider remit of methods and approaches. Nonetheless, Political Science has also tended to be dominated by white males, and written as a reflection of their interests. In recent years greater prominence has been achieved by feminists and female writers and we have sought to mainstream their approaches within this text.

In recent years, as noted above, challenges have also come from outside, although still within academia, from, among others, economics, media and communications and psychology. However, Politics as a discipline has also had to respond to 'real world' events which challenge the primacy of the nation-state (Politics' original focus of analysis). Political processes, issues and structures, such as globalization, climate change and the European Union, have meant that the discipline has had to rethink, or at least re-evaluate, what is studied and how it proceeds. One way this can be seen is through the increasing number of academic articles and papers. In recent years we have seen a proliferation of specialist journals, and sub-fields within the discipline (Taggart and Lees, 2006), which reflects not only a widening of remit of subject matter, but also increasing influence from other disciplines and a recognition of changes in the real world of politics.

International Relations

Historically, the main concern of IR was *policy relevance*. The primary motivation for the emergence of IR was to analyze the events that had led to war, with a view to preventing its reoccurrence. The main focus of scholars in this tradition was to ensure their work had *policy relevance*, and to advise decision-makers how to avoid war. Scholars in this school of thinking were referred to as Idealists and in the early twentieth century they were concerned explicitly with the *policy relevance* and application of their work. There was also an important normative aspect, in that scholars sought to prescribe to policy-makers. In this way, IR developed as a distinctly empirical, practical atheoretical and historically focused prescriptive discipline. Idealism largely collapsed with the outbreak of World War II and realism came to take its place as the dominant organizing paradigm (and this is discussed in more detail in Chapter 3).

IR's subsequent historical development was also shaped by theoretical innovations, again, which can be characterized by cultural differences. In Germany, IR was a sub-discipline of Political Science, and although theoretical developments occurred within the field between the 1960s and 80s, this was largely in the area of peace research and was aimed at international audiences (Waever, 1998: 705). In France IR did not develop as a separate discipline, and where it is studied it is largely practical rather than theoretical, with a key focus on Area Studies. In the UK, the 'English school' developed (usually associated with the work of Martin Wight and Hedley Bull). In the UK, IR was not originally considered part of Political Science but a field which drew on many disciplines (sociology, history, law, political philosophy) (Waever, 1998). As with American IR, in the UK the development was a response to foreign policy, an aim to influence policy-makers in the postwar period.

As with Political Studies/Political Science, IR's analysis traditionally began with the state, although, in contrast, it assumed the state was a unitary actor. However, IR has also been faced with the same challenges as Politics (e.g., globalization, climate change and interconnectivity of markets, to name but a few), plus a recognition that issues transcend the domestic and international divide. For example, security (one of the key concerns of IR) is no longer only concerned with military issues and the balance of power in the international arena, but also with the security of individual citizens within states. In this way, the boundaries between IR and Political Science/Studies, in terms of their 'real world' subject matter, have become increasingly blurred. At the same time, the influences of economics and natural science have been as significant in IR as Politics. Like Politics, IR has also been dominated by Western white men. Feminist IR theory has achieved increasing prominence in

Box 1.2   Disciplinary boundaries

These serve to demarcate what counts as a legitimate area of concern within a particular discipline. For some, though, these boundaries are socially constructed and serve to obscure debates, prevent insights being realized (Wilson, 1998). It could also be suggested that the boundaries are constructed through institutional developments and the separation of learning into departments within universities. These boundaries are also reinforced through the existence of specialist journals within disciplines. This is less pronounced in the natural sciences, where there are a number of leading journals which transcend disciplinary boundaries. The top journals are *Science* (in the US) and *Nature* (in the UK). In the social sciences, however, the equivalent does not exist.

the discipline, and done much to challenge the dominant orthodoxy, providing for both fresh insights into the discipline and possibilities of emancipation for women across the globe.

The broader context

It is also important to remember that while the shaping of disciplines is identified within particular schools of thought (which are discussed in more detail in the following chapter), these did not emerge in a vacuum. Rather they are reflective and constitutive of a wider environment of ideas, not only in terms of what is happening in the 'real' world of politics, but also in terms of how knowledge is gathered and studied, and how this is institutionalized within universities and research communities, through the construction of disciplinary boundaries.

One of the main problems in thinking about IR and Politics as separate disciplines is that it leads us to downplay the importance of factors usually regarded as the preserve of the other discipline. It may also lead us to neglect particular theoretical insights which may be of use in our analysis.

Similarities and differences

The earlier atheoretical development of IR has in some ways been one of the dividing features between the disciplines. However, as noted above, 'real world' events, such as the inability of IR to explain or predict the collapse of communism has led to an increased emphasis upon the role of theory. Indeed, now both disciplines have strong theoretical components to them and both are characterized by disagreement over what constitute legitimate fields of enquiry. For example, should the study of globalization or the European Union occur within Political Science or IR? Should the environment be studied in terms of its domestic impact, or in terms of the effect it has internationally and, if studied internationally, does this absolve people within states from any kind of responsibility to act? Should war be discussed only in military terms, or should the effects upon civil society within states also be the concern of political science? Do domestic women bear the adverse costs of internationally pursued war?

The separation of the domestic from the international characterizes much of what is taking place in the two disciplines at present. However, should we not consider both international and domestic elements in our analysis? Might we not benefit from discussing the interrelationship between individual human action, the action of individual states and the impact this has on the global climate, necessitating global solutions as well as individual ones? Should we not think about both the effects of war upon the international community and its impacts upon citizens and civilians who live in those war zones? Our argument in this book is that these questions, while separated by disciplinary boundaries, are inherently interlinked. We argue that the disciplines overlap in subject matter and, in turn, need to be considered together.

Despite debates over the legitimate areas of study within the disciplines, and differences in historical development, what we have seen more recently has been a move to broader debates around methodology. That is, both disciplines have become increasingly concerned with how they proceed and how analysis should be done. The big methodological debate is centred around whether Politics may be conceived of as 'scientific' and given the significance of this not only for how we understand the development of the disciplines we are in, but also the implications this has for how we study; this issue is addressed in the following chapter.

Cultural factors have also played an important role in the development of the disciplines and both are characterized by a strong US dominance in their respective fields. Many of the 'top' journals are located in America; for example, *American Political Science Review* and *International Organization*. While this may provide some cohesion to the disciplines, what this can also mean is that significant variables in analysis may be missed.

Recognizing the significance of culture can enable us to reflect upon questions such as: is liberal capitalist democracy something which is possible in all states across the globe? Or are other forms of democracy possible and more 'workable' given a particular cultural context? Happily, in our disciplines, physical violence is less likely to be a response to the issues; however, crucially, failure to discuss these cultural differences in the 'real world' may well lead to conflict and war.

The aim here has been to provide an overview of the differing ways in which both disciplines have developed and to suggest that the disciplinary boundaries between them may serve to obscure rather than enhance

Box 1.3 Journals

Journals are an important source of up-to-date scholarship in the field. There are generalist journals such as *American Political Science Review* and *International Studies Quarterly*, which give an overview of the shape of the discipline, and also more specialist journals such as *British Politics* and *Journal of Middle East Studies*. While journals are often available electronically, these are not to be confused with other internet sites. Articles published in academic journals go through a peer-review process; this means the information contained within these journals may be considered authentic and authoritative in a way in which information published elsewhere on the web may not (for example, on sites such as Wikipedia).

opportunities for political analysis. Awareness of the historical development of the disciplines can enable us to understand why politics is studied in the way that it is today and can also provide us with a basis from which to move both the disciplines and our analysis forward.

Layout of book

In this book our aim is to encourage reflection upon how we 'do' Politics. We argue that the way in which we undertake political analysis is principally through the application of theoretical frameworks to a particular area of enquiry. The following chapters are by no means an exhaustive account of the topics of interest for students of politics. What they are intended to do, however, is to address some of the central areas of study within our disciplines and show how we use the theory within each area. One of our main aims is to highlight the contingent nature of political analysis; that is, there is not one, but competing ways in which to 'do' the study of politics and this issue is discussed explicitly in the next chapter, and reflected throughout the book.

Chapter 2 provides a discussion of a central concept in the study of Politics: power. While the study of power could be said to define and underpin the disciplines, its own definition is considerably more difficult. A contested concept, power can mean differing things depending upon our definition of power and our starting point. Clearly, where we look for power influences where we might find it. If we think power is something which belongs to politicians, then the likelihood is, we will analyze the behaviour of politicians to establish the nature of the power relationship. Suppose, though, that politicians are not the only sources or sites of power. Consider the notion that the actions of politicians are limited by their positioning in a liberal democratic capitalist system. This suggests we would need to have an awareness of this system: we may not necessarily be able to see the system, but it may be powerful in influencing how politicians, states and others behave. Alternatively, suppose we think that power is located in the ideas which shape our society – analysis then might begin by exploring the role of a particular set of ideas (such as neo liberalism) and how they inform behaviour within a political context.

The background of the Introduction and Chapters 1 and 2 then sets the context for the substantive chapters which deal with topics of interest to both Political Science and IR: the state; public policy; institutions; representation and participation; the media; security; globalization; political economy; and the environment. While it is not possible to cover all areas which fall under the remit of Politics, the intention is to highlight that while debates occur within the disciplines over what the legitimate area of study is, simultaneously within those areas of study there are also debates about how and what should be studied. The intention is also to show that Politics is broadly defined and fluid, characterized by 'grey' areas, and that reflexivity is a key component in analysis. Each of the substantive chapters is structured in the same way to reflect the differing ways in which political analysts may approach the same issue or problem. Consistent with our view that there is an overlap in Political Science and IR, we introduce the dominant theories, not by their disciplinary split, but with reference to the things which we think really divide them, their ontological and epistemological positions.

Much of Political Science, and to a lesser degree IR, is dominated by positivist approaches (cf. Marsh and Savigny, 2004). We are not seeking to deny the contribution of positivism to the discipline; however, we are aiming to challenge its dominance. By dividing the frameworks according to their underlying claims to knowledge, we are seeking to reinforce the idea that, to paraphrase Marsh and Smith (2002), there is more than one way to "do" Political Science (and IR). Each chapter is divided into three sections which broadly reflect the assumptions that are made within the discipline about what the real world is like and how we find out about it. (These are labelled: foundationalist/positivist; foundational critical realist; and anti-foundational interpretivist – and as they reflect quite complex debates, we discuss their definitions in the following chapter). Within each section we then apply approaches and theories from within these positions to an example where Political Science or IR is likely to analyze or ask questions. Our point is that, when faced with the same problem, differing explanations and outcomes are possible depending upon the assumptions which we make prior to our analysis.

Each chapter illustrates these differing analytical processes and outcomes through reference to a case study. It then summarizes the key features and compares differing theories and approaches, drawing out not only their differences but also their similarities. A set of reflective questions and seminar activities is also provided at the end of each chapter.

Clearly, these chapters do not exhaust the potential topics which we might analyze, so the final chapter (12) provides a discussion of the wider considerations that we need to make when we do our own political analysis. One of the driving assumptions of this book is that theory plays a crucial role in helping us analyze political reality. The wider aim of the book is thus to encourage a critical reflection upon the way in which we use a theory or approach, its purpose, assumptions and the implications that flow from it.

Conclusion

Our aim and arguments in this book are threefold. First, we argue that to 'do' political analysis we must be theoretically informed, meaning that that we use theory to structure and guide our analysis. However, we need also be aware of the underlying assumptions that those theories or approaches make (more widely discussed in Chapters 1 and 12). Second, we have sought to challenge the dominant forms of theorizing about politics by 'mainstreaming' alternate approaches in each chapter. This means we have given equal weighting to different positions in each topic. Third, we have sought to highlight the parallels between Political Science and IR. The socially constructed division between the disciplines, we argue, means that operating solely within one discipline means that we miss an awareness of the insights of the others. In short, we argue that political analysis is an active process. We need to be critically evaluating our assumptions both prior to and throughout our analysis so that we can produce coherent, rigorous and potentially emancipatory political analysis.

Reflection

Do you think the following should be studied by Political Science or IR?

Water scarcity

GM foods

Social mobility

'Honour' killings

War and peace

Do you think we should we look at the individuals who are affected by these issues? Or the individuals who cause them? Or the systems they take place in?

Can you think of a topic or issue that can only be studied by Politics or IR?

Do you find the division useful or unhelpful?

Seminar activities

Identify five journals in the disciplines of Politics and IR (perhaps one from the UK, one from the US, one from Europe and from the fields of both Politics and IR).

What issues do they discuss?

What is the difference between the articles in the Politics journals and those in the IR journals?

What are the differences between the European, UK-specific and US journals?

Why do you think these differences exist?

Can you identify theory in these articles?

What purpose has it been used for, what is the theory 'doing'?

What difference has the theory made to what is being studied?

Why do you think there are these differences?

Evaluation of electronic sources

A lot of the information we gain these days is via electronic means, but there is a wide variety of quality and problems of authenticity in some of these sources.

Having identified the journal articles above:

What is the difference between an article in an e-journal and that on Wikipedia?

How can we identify reliable and credible online sources?

Why is this important to producing coherent political research?

Why should we not rely upon sources such as Wikipedia?

Chapter 1

Themes and Issues in Political Science and International Relations

Introduction

As we identified in the introduction, one of the biggest debates within Politics is about how we actually go about doing our analysis: how do we actually 'do' Politics? How do we decide what it is we are looking at? How do we find out what the real world of politics looks like and how can we find out information about it? How do we decide what questions to ask? How do we decide what theoretical position to adopt and which theory to apply? Once we start to think about these questions, we realize that there are bigger issues at stake; we don't simply randomly pick what it is that we analyze. Rather we make a series of assumptions and judgements about what it is that is important, what it is we are seeking to do. These assumptions may often be implicit in the work of some of the scholars that we read, but it is important to be aware of them. Why? Because it enables us to recognize the strengths and limitations of the work we are analyzing and to enable us to be more rigorous in our own work. Awareness of these assumptions also enables us to be able to reflect upon differing positions and contributions of other approaches and enables us to make a decision about why that particular perspective provides the most useful account. It also provides a vocabulary through which we are able to articulate to others why we see the world in the way that we do.

The aim of this chapter is to introduce some of the debates around how we decide what it is we are looking at when we look at the world of politics, and how we can access that information: these are centred around ontology and epistemology. We begin by reflecting upon the nature of reality, and the assumptions that inform our analysis; that is we start with a discussion of ontology. The next issue we need to consider when beginning analysis is how we can gain access to that reality. How can we have knowledge of it? This leads us to introduce a brief discussion about epistemology. As such, we introduce one of the key debates in our disciplines; that is, can we know about the political world through the assumptions and methods of the natural sciences? Can we have a 'science' of Politics? What can this tell us about the way in which we can know about the 'real world' of politics? This debate is crucial to our studies.

We should point out that we see the 'doing' of political analysis as very much a learned skill. It is a skill which we continually refine and think about throughout our academic lives and the aim of this book is to reflect upon how we acquire this ability. As one of the reviewers helpfully observed, when we began our studies we had no idea what an ontological and epistemological position was, and it was something that we learned about (and we very much agree with this point). What we are seeking to do here is to demystify the vocabulary and processes that we engage in when we do Politics. That is not to say, however, that once we grasp the basics we stop learning or thinking about what we do. Rather like learning a musical instrument, once we master the basics we continue throughout our lives to practise, reflect, improve and refine.

Having introduced the philosophical issues that inform our work, the second part of the chapter is concerned to give an overview of the different approaches we may adopt when studying Politics. There is a number of different perspectives, but we will focus our attention on some of the main ones within the discipline: behaviouralism; rational choice theory; Marxism; feminism; poststructuralism; and constructivism. When discussing these approaches we also show how their differing ontological and epistemological assumptions are important in shaping what they focus on. Throughout the rest of the book each of the theoretical frameworks that we introduce makes assumptions about ontology and epistemology and is also informed by one of the approaches detailed below.

A note of caution!

The debates outlined in the first half of this chapter are incredibly complex and have generated vast discussion throughout the history of philosophy. We are not seeking to reconcile those debates here! Nor are we seeking to suggest that they can be reconciled. Rather we argue that they are a means for understanding why people do Politics in different ways. What we are seeking to do here is give a brief, simple and accessible introduction to these issues, the positions outlined below represent a starting point. Rather than a definitive attempt to demarcate rigid boundaries, we argue that the borders around these positions and approaches are fluid and open to contestation (as we have hoped to illustrate in Figure 1.1 and Table 1.1). Much like the way in which theory is used to simplify the world, our aim here is to simplify these debates so that we can understand the starting points. Thereafter, further reading (beyond this book) is useful to understand some of the greater complexities of these debates.

The first section of this chapter draws substantially on the work of David Marsh and Paul Furlong (2002). We should note that their arguments have been subject to criticism (for their presentation of these positions as having tightly defined boundaries [see, for example, Bates and Jenkins, 2007]) and more critical accounts reflecting the 'fuzziness' of these boundaries are offered by Hay (2002) and in later work (Marsh 2010). However, we believe that in order to engage in these debates we need to understand the basics. Much like building a house, we begin with a few basic building blocks and it is only once we start to lay these foundations that we can see the different forms that may be available to us. We are simply aiming to provide those basic building blocks.

Underlying philosophical issues

Ontology and epistemology

As we have suggested, before we begin our analysis we have already made a series of assumptions about what we think political reality looks like, what it is possible to know and how we can find out about that reality. At first glance this might seem a quite straightforward idea, but consideration of this is crucial for our analysis. The assumptions that we make about what the real political world looks like and how we can know about it inform all the analysis that we will go on to do. More specifically for us as political analysts it enables us to ask: what does the real world of politics look like? How can we know what is really happening in the world of politics? These, then, are questions of ontology (the former) and epistemology (the latter). Because there are a variety of ways in which we can answer these questions, it is useful to have the language to do so and we use the terms ontology and epistemology to discuss these ideas and issues. Ontology and epistemology are philosophical positions, but they also provide us with a vocabulary with which to talk about the assumptions that we make about what is real, what is out there to discover and how we can discover it.

Ontological and epistemological positions

Articulating responses to questions of ontology is often done through reference to two main positions: foundationalism and anti-foundationalism. Once we have established our ontological position this then informs our epistemological position (although this ordering has been challenged; see, for example, Hay, 2002), and we continue with an overview of some of their key features. Our view that ontology underpins epistemology is illustrated in Figure 1.1.

Ontology: foundationalism and anti-foundationalism

When we think about what is out there in the world, we make assumptions about what it is we think exists. For some people (foundationalists) the world exists as a reality out there and is largely independent of us. It is possible to establish a truth about this world. For others (anti-foundationalists), it is the way that we interpret and interact with the world that is important, so in this way we are intimately involved in the creation of reality. As people interact differently with the world out there, so different realities are created. For anti-foundationalists there is not one truth about the real world, but competing truths and interpretations.

Think of the age-old question that confounds philosophers and scientists alike. If a tree falls in the woods, and there is no one there to see it, does it make a sound? Foundationalists would argue with some certainty that the answer is yes. Every other tree that has been observed falling has made a sound, and therefore it can be said with conviction, that yes, that tree made a sound. This is because the world is thought to exist independently of us, and crucially our understanding of how the world works is not dependent on us being there to interpret it. In contrast, anti-foundationalists would say we cannot be sure. Rather, trees may have fallen noisily elsewhere at other points in time, but this particular tree, which no one observes, may well have fallen silently. Indeed, it is the act of hearing the noise that brings noise into existence, rather than the physical event itself.

This debate may seem abstract; however, what it does do is highlight that we need to be sure of the assumptions that we make when we do political analysis, as the differing ways in which we think about what the real world looks like can lead us to make different assumptions about how it is possible to know about the 'real' world. It is important to be aware of the assumptions that we make prior to our analysis because this not only informs the positions that we adopt when we do our analysis, but also shapes what is possible for us to find. These positions are summarized in Figure 1.1 and are discussed below.

Epistemology: positivism, interpretivism, scientific/critical realism

So how can we know about the real world? This question can be discussed through reference to epistemology, and one way in which epistemological issues present themselves to us as students of Politics is through the debate around science. Is it possible to have a science of Politics? By this we mean is it possible to adopt the methods of science? Is it possible to generate predictions about political behaviour? Is it possible to establish universal covering laws, in the way that we are able to do in the natural sciences? (For a much more detailed discussion of this, see Moses and Knutsen, 2007.)

The issue, in part, is informed by the assumptions that we make about the kind of knowledge we think it is possible to have about the political world. If we believe a science of politics is possible, then we are likely to adopt a scientific methodology. From this vantage point the way in which we can know about the political world is through empirical investigation. This would suggest that we can gain knowledge of the political world through that which is available to our senses: sight, sound, taste, smell and touch. Observations which flow from these are assumed to be measurable and can subsequently be quantified. Adherence to a scientific methodology and the assumptions that inform it also enable us to make scientific claims to knowledge about the political world.

Juxtaposed to this scientific perspective is the view that the subject matters of natural and social science are fundamentally different and therefore the methods of natural science are deemed simply inappropriate. In this view, the study of Politics is about the study of human beings, who simply do not behave in predictable ways, like numbers and atoms. Moreover, unlike the subject matter in natural science human beings also have subjective values, which raises the question: can we ever be value-neutral in the analysis of our subject matter? For example, it is possible to say that Hitler and Nelson Mandela were powerful leaders given that they were able to mobilize vast numbers of people in support of their aims. But, normatively, would we want to equate the two? Would we not want to differentiate between the 'rightness' or legitimacy of their actions? Some would argue that a science of Politics is just not possible, in part because of the normative aspects, which are an inherent part of our analyses which simply do not feature in the natural world.

The issue of whether we can have a science of Politics is reflected through debates around how we can know what we do about our political world. These debates are enormously complex and we have sought here to simplify and introduce them. (For much greater depth, see Hay, 2002; Stoker and Marsh, 2002; Marsh and Furlong, 2002; Agger, 1991.) These debates are often presented as polarized around two mutually exclusive positions, positivism and interpretivism, of which we give a brief overview below. We then move to outline a position which draws from both and provides for a kind of middle ground between the two, scientific or critical realism. We also illustrate and summarize the key points of each position in Figure 1.1.

Positivism

Positivism is the dominant perspective in contemporary political analysis. Many of the articles and books we read are underpinned by the assumptions of positivism. It is beyond the scope of this book to discuss why positivism is dominant (and this has been done elsewhere; see, for example, Marsh and Savigny, 2004), but what we do here is give a brief overview of what its main assumptions are.

Positivism is underpinned by a foundational ontology. It assumes that there is a singular real world out there, which is available to be discovered though recourse to the senses. This is informed by empiricism as derived from the work of Comte, which assumes that all that we can know can be counted and empirically measured and states that we can discover and establish regular relationships between phenomena. This school of thought seeks to apply the methods and thinking behind the natural sciences to the subject matter of the social 'sciences'. Through observation and measurement of the 'real world' we are able to establish laws and certainties like those established in the natural sciences. For example Michels' (1911/1959) Iron Law of Oligarchy states that society will always be dominated by elites. This relationship was established by observing regular patterns in elite and societal behaviour. A generalization and covering law was then proposed, which could be empirically tested, akin to the testing of hypotheses in the experiments of the natural sciences. Underlying this notion of covering laws is the wider aim of providing causal explanation.

Informed by the methods and assumed certainties provided by science, positivists are concerned to establish the cause of an event or phenomena, to explain why something happens. Cause and explanation are two words strongly associated with positivism. For example, consider the statement – 'female voters are more likely to vote Democrat'. This statement would form the function of a hypothesis which would be tested against empirical evidence. If the outcome confirmed the hypothesis then gender may be used as an explanator of electoral success for a candidate like Obama. This may then provide an explanation of why people have voted for Obama (because they are women) and also establishes a causal link between gender and political preferences.

Finally, positivism also claims to be able to separate facts and values. Positivists argue they analyze facts and that their goal is not to address normative questions. They view this separation as legitimate and possible. The argument is that because scientific method is assumed to have no content it therefore has no politics (Villmoare, 1990: 150).

Objective knowledge can be generated through this value-free approach. Positivists, in their academic research, are only concerned with empirical questions about what the case is, rather than the legitimacy, or rightness or wrongness of an issue. For example positivists may measure the rate of inequalities of income between rich and poor (as has been evidenced in both the UK and US). However, they would not seek to make normative judgements about the legitimate or illegitimate nature of that inequality.

Interpretivism

Interpretivism can be usefully contrasted with positivism. Interpretivism is generally viewed as anti-foundational as it assumes that there is more than one way in which reality can be understood. Rather than seeking universal laws and to establish regularities in relationships, interpretivists seek to provide understanding of a particular issue or event. They argue that facts and values cannot be separated as the nature of the enquiry (human beings) is inherently value-laden. That is, as human beings we all make judgements, from the seemingly simply judgement about what is fashionable to wear (although once considering the ethics of the producers of clothing, debates become more complex) to establishing responsibility for societal inequalities. Interpretivists reject the notion of causation; rather they seek to provide understanding of, or the meaning of, a given context of political issue. Interpretivists would seek to explore the context which gave rise to a set of political conditions, so they may not argue that a change in the tax regime *caused* an increase in social inequality. However, what they would seek to explore would be the conditions that made this possible; in so doing they may also seek to transform these conditions. In this way interpretivists might look at the ideas and social structures that are dominant in society. They might look at the discourses which informed and shaped the creation of tax reduction legislation. They may draw attention to a political discourse which emphasized entrepreneurship and, more importantly, the role of individuals, over the existence of society (think about Thatcher's infamous (mis)quote – there is no such thing as society!). In this way then we can start to understand the role that ideas and discourse may play in enabling us to understand present political conditions.

The important point to note is that interpretivists draw attention to the contingent nature of social reality and, rather than providing explanation, they seek to provide understanding. This is informed by the assumption that there is no one overarching truth about the 'real world' out there. Rather, they suggest, there are a series of competing truths which are dependent upon our interpretation of the world and if we are to understand this we need to move analysis beyond only what is available to the senses. All action is meaningful, and our role as analysts is to uncover that meaning. Moreover, rather than assume that analysis is value-free, they highlight the value-laden nature of social and political analysis (so their work may be explicitly informed, for example, by particular ideas of what a just society should look like).

Scientific/critical realism

Scientific realism or, as it is also referred to, critical realism offers something of a middle ground between positivism and interpretivism. While it accepts the possibility of causality in explanation and can aim to make predictions (a feature of the scientific approach), it also admits interpretivist features into its analysis with its assumption of unobservable layers of reality.

Scientific/critical realists argue that there are differing layers of reality which comprise the real world out there. They claim that we cannot see all these layers, but we know that they exist because we can see causal consequences. For example, capitalism is a layer of reality, and we know that capitalism exists. We cannot see it but we know that it exists as it has causal consequences which we can observe. For example, we might take some money into a shop and exchange it for a product. This is an outcome and a causal consequence of the underlying mechanism of capitalism. Capitalism determines the value of both the product and the money that we hand over in exchange for the good. Here we see influence from the positivist approach, that it is possible to establish causal explanation. However, as noted, this position, also admits from the interpretivists that there are influencing features which we cannot see; there is a reality which exists beyond that which our physical senses can access. Indeed, there is also argued to be a difference between reality and appearance (see, for example, Hollis and Smith, 1990). So, in the example of capitalism, we know there is this reality called capitalism, but what we see is not capitalism itself; rather we see evidence of the existence of capitalism, in the transaction which takes place in the act of consumption.

The idea of unobservable, underlying causal mechanisms, means that critical realism tends to be associated with Marxism. Similarly, it is also a position within feminist analysis. For example, patriarchy can be argued to be an underlying causal mechanism; we cannot see 'patriarchy' but we can see its effects (as we will see through some of the frameworks we use within the book). (It should be noted that this discussion about the layers of reality in scientific/critical realism has led to debate as to whether it represents an ontological or epistemological position. We recognize this debate; however, for the purposes of providing a starting point into these debates we begin by accepting the more widely held view that it is more epistemological in its positioning than ontological.)

Figure 1.1   *Summary of epistemological positions and their underlying ontologies*

Positivism	Critical / scientific realism	Interpretivism
A science of politics is possible (and desirable)

Focus upon empirical observation and measurement

Causal explanation can be provided

Analysis is objective and value-free | A science of politics is possible, as is causal explanation

Draws from anti-foundationalism and admits unobservable layers of reality into analysis

Has a strong normative component | Rejects scientism

Highlights contingent nature of reality and draws attention to unobservable features such as norms, values and identities

Is normative and aims to be emancipatory

Political analysis is value laden |

◄——————— **Foundationalism** ———— **Anti-foundationalism** ———————►

Assumes a real world exists independently of what we can know about it and that the establishment of a single truth about reality is possible

There are competing interpretations of reality and these are contingent upon our interaction with it

Approaches

The ontological and epistemological assumptions that we make subsequently inform the approach that we adopt when we come to do our political analysis. These assumptions, positions and approaches underpin many of the theoretical frameworks that we may use (as we will see in the substantive chapters that follow). This in turn can lead us towards some outcomes and close off other possibilities. This is one reason why we need to be clear about our prior assumptions. Another is so that we can maintain logic, rigour and consistency in our analysis whichever approach we adopt. We now turn to give an overview of some of the main approaches within the disciplines.

Behaviouralism

Behaviouralism has been one of the dominant schools of thought in Politics during the twentieth century. It emphasizes the explanation of behaviour (in reaction to the normative philosophical approaches which had gone before). Behaviouralism emerged in the 1920s/1930s and was consolidated by the 1950s/60s. Its development was influenced by psychology, is committed to the methods of the natural sciences and as such it is highly empiricist and positivist in its approach. Behaviouralism is foundationalist in that it assumes that there is a world that exists independent of our knowledge of it. Behaviouralists focus upon observable behaviour (in contrast, for example, to Marxist accounts which suggest unobservable features may influence our behaviour). Behaviouralists also assume that any explanation of behaviour can be subjected to empirical testing or verification (for more detailed exposition, see Sanders, 2002/2010). For example, behaviouralists might argue that we can explain the outcome of the 2008 US election through reference to the voting behaviour of US citizens (rather than, for example, because of the campaigns run by the politicians, the economy or the personality of the politicians themselves). A behavioural approach to voting behaviour would observe who voted for Obama and who voted for McCain (through the use of methods such as opinion polls). They would then categorize these people into groups (which have traditionally been around race and class). While the techniques for categorizing voters become more sophisticated, they rely on the assumption that we can observe certain characteristics. Once data has been gathered behaviouralists would argue they can then generate knowledge as they are able to offer analysis which enables them to make predictions about the likely behaviour of voters and, in turn, this would lead to predictions about outcomes of future elections. We not only see this kind of analysis in the academic literature, but also more publicly in opinion polls.

In this view, to understand political phenomena behaviour needs to be observed. From this data can be gathered and hypotheses generated and tested. For example, using these observations we could hypothesize that if your income is below \$x then you are more likely to vote for Obama (H1). From here, then, we could hypothesize that if your income exceeds \$x then you are more likely to vote for McCain (H2). Testing these assumptions against the data gathered means that in future elections we could make predictions about the likelihood of a particular class of the electorate and their likelihood to vote Democrat or Republican.

With this adherence to 'science' also goes the assumption that it is possible to separate facts from values, and the possibility of objective, value-free political analysis arises. So, for example, we may be able to observe what different classes of voters do, and how they behave, but we would not be able to make any normative statements about how they should behave, or about what is desirable for them. This may seem intuitively appealing; however, we highlight within this book that many scholars conflate normative and observational statements. For example, Dahl's work on pluralism (that we discuss in Chapter 3) is a classic piece of behaviouralism in that he focused upon decisions made in government, and used this as a means to describe how government worked. However, his work was not entirely objective, as this was underpinned by a normative proposition: not only was this how government worked, he argued, but this was how government should work. This brief illustration suggests that the separation of facts and values, while in principle may seem a laudable objective, becomes problematic, in large part because of the subject matter of the discipline (as noted above; this issue is also discussed in more depth in Chapter 12).

Rational choice theory (RCT)

The next approach we consider is rational choice theory (RCT, sometimes known as public choice theory). This came to prominence during the 1980s partly as a response to, and partly because of its influence upon, the wider political conditions at the time (Thatcherism and Reaganism). Rational choice accounts, like behaviouralism, are foundational and positivist. They assume a truth exists about the political world and this can be discovered and measured. For RCT adherence to the 'scientific' method is derived from the influence of economics.

The rational choice approach (which is also sometimes referred to as a method) argues that individual choice is the basis of action (and inaction). Directly informed by theorizing and models drawn from economics, rational choice accepts a series of starting assumptions. First, that individuals are the unit of analysis, and that they are assumed to be rational; that is, individuals will pursue rational strategies to maximize their utility. We are able to chart these courses of actions and choices that are made, through reference to other information and assumptions we make about behaviour. Rational choice also assumes that an individual has a fixed set of preferences which they have identified, can express and rank order. Behaviour is assumed to be means–ends without specification of what the ends are or should be and rational behaviour is pursued to achieve a specific end (see, for example, Elster, 1986). As such, to be able to establish the choices that individuals will make, we simply need to identify their preferences. Once we know these preferences, we are then able to make predictions about the behaviour of that individual, as we assume that they will seek to maximize their utility. (Rational choice is sometimes referred to as formal political theory, or as a form of political economy, and will be discussed in more depth in Chapter 9.) For the purposes of this section, however, suffice to note the basic assumptions. Analysis focuses attention upon the criteria for rational action, so assumptions are made and the method suggests that if we accept those assumptions then particular outcomes, or courses of action will follow. These assumptions of rationality are then used to construct models, again so we can make predictions about how individuals will behave. For example, a rational choice model of voting will assume that rational individuals will look at both/all candidates in an election and chose the one which best satisfies their preferences (which are identifiable and expressed). Therefore, in order to predict election outcomes, we can simply establish voters' preferences and then match that to candidates' policies.

Again, we can see there are problems here not only in the separation of facts and values (as above), but also in the way in which we separate the individual from their wider context. In the voting example, can we really say that individuals approach the voting booth as a 'blank sheet', without reference to their personal history and experiences, and to the society within which they live, which may also influence how they decide to vote? In this sense, we need to reflect upon what we gain by adopting these parsimonious assumptions (i.e., simplicity of explanation) and what we miss (the complexity of motivations for individual behaviour and the social context in which it takes place).

On a methodological note, we may also see that just as behaviouralists have conflated normative and observational claims, so rational choice theorists have implied normative statements. (For a fascinating critique of rational choice theory as individualism, see Taylor, 2006.) The purpose of models and modelling is to simplify behaviour, so we can isolate key features which in turn facilitate the possibility of predictions. However, when we do this, we abstract from reality; models are used to simplify reality so we can try to understand it. Models do not provide a template for how reality should be (a normative claim). What became evident during the 1980s was that the works of rational choice theorists (such as Niskanen, 1971; Buchanen and Tullock, 1962) were used not only to describe the nature of politics, but also to make prescriptive (and normative) claims about how it should operate.

Marxism

Marxism as an approach is unusual in that it combines aspects of positivism and interpretivism, which tend to be viewed as mutually exclusive. Marxism does have a foundational view of the world, seeks to establish truth through scientific methods and enables us to make causal statements, which links into positivism. However, it also acknowledges the role of intangible and unobservable features (for example, ideology) in shaping the real world around us, and so Marxism can be located in the epistemological 'middle ground' and tends to be associated with scientific or critical realism (as noted above) (for an extension of this, see Marsh, 2002).

Marxism draws attention to the class basis of social and political relationships and the way in which this basis results in exploitative relationships of power. For some Marxism is a political doctrine – communism, and it has been expressed through the political actions of Stalin, Lenin and others. For those who view Marxism through its manifestation as a regime, the collapse of these political systems may suggest Marxism has little left to offer. However, it is not simply the political systems that Marxism informed that matter to us as political analysts, but the tools that Marxism provides. Here, Marxism is able to expose and offer an opportunity for us to question existing power structures within society. Through doing so we can make sense of inequalities within our society. This enables us not to simply consider them as immutable and therefore unchangeable, but also to understand them as a consequence of the way in which society has developed, allowing us to play a role in changing them. Marx, in *Theses on Feuerbach* (1845/1969:15), draws attention to those who have sought to gain knowledge and offers a critique: 'The philosophers have only interpreted the world, in various ways; the point is to change it.' In this sense, Marx also introduces an explicit normative aspect to his work; that we are not only, or merely, to interpret what happens in the world, but we can, or indeed should, use this to attempt to effect change.

Marxism is often criticized for its structuralism: its over-emphasis upon the role of structures as guiding behaviour, and downplaying the role of individuals who are, critiques suggest, powerless, like automatons, with very limited room for manoeuvre within these structures. Despite this criticism, Marxism does draw our attention to the role of ideas, in particular, the importance of ideology which functions to ensure that the proletariat accept their role in the system. Marxism highlights the structural basis of inequality in our society, which for Marx is located in the economic divisions that exist in the class divisions which form the basis of our society (between the bourgeoisies and the proletariat). These find expression through the mechanisms of capitalism, which in turn is reliant upon and reinforces inequalities (while primarily economic, these are also intimately linked with political and social inequalities). Rising levels of economic and social inequality in contemporary capitalist Western societies (see Barry, 2005; Sandel, 1982/1998) suggest that Marxist analysis still has much to offer.

Feminism

Feminism is perhaps the most methodologically unusual of approaches as it straddles the epistemological spectrum. There are a number of differing strands of feminism. The central feature within feminism is to draw attention to the role of women and gender within society, and feminism(s) is/are overt about its/their normative positioning. It seeks to achieve equality and emancipation for women, but differing episte-mological assumptions and positions within feminism lead to this being manifested in very different guises.

For example, positivist feminists may argue that in order to understand equality for women, we need to look at the role of women in public life. To establish if women have achieved equality in the workforce, for example, we can know this through reference to observable features we can measure, such as pay scales, or counting the number of women in public life (for example, those who hold senior positions such as judges, or are in office in such bodies as Congress or Parliament, see, e.g., Childs, 2008; Lovenduski, 2005). Feminism may also draw attention to the masculine nature of political systems and the way in which women's rights are subsumed and seconded to ideas of how political systems should operate. For example, the 2009 elections in Afghanistan were largely supported by the West, irrespective of the retrograde legislation which had been recently introduced which downplayed women's' rights in the home and relegalized rape within marriage. This focus upon the observable position of women in formal political systems means that some feminism can be located within the positivist position.

Alongside this positivist account, critical feminists argue that under-standing the role of women in society is about understanding relationships of power, which are gendered, and we need to consider why it is that we observe that which we do. Here the concept of patriarchy is crucial and, in this discussion of deep-rooted underlying unobservable structures with causal effects, means that some critical feminism can be located within the scientific/critical realist position. For example, in this perspective feminists highlight the way in which patriarchal societies have constructed a gendered division of labour, where women's work was traditionally thought of as being tied to the home, male work the public sphere of the workplace. The slogan 'the personal is the political' encapsulates the idea that to understand women's role within contemporary society we need to explore the way in which society constructs personal relationships as well as those located in formal employment.

Constructivist and/or poststructuralist feminists tend to be located in the interpretivist position and, in contrast, draw attention to the way in which the role of women in society needs to be understood through reference to the way in which their roles are articulated. For example, the common reference to an abstract person as 'he', suggests that the 'norm' is male and in turn society privileges the expectations of the 'norm'. Natasha Walter's (2010) recent book refers to the way in which social practices (supported through legislation) have constructed a very narrow public perception of what it means to be a woman (see also Mulvey, 1975). In this way, Walter suggests, far from achieving the equality and empowerment that 'first-wave' feminist fought for, while women may have suffrage, the way in which society teaches women to behave is through a dominant male view of what women should be like, rather than one which reflects parity between men and women. This suggests then that the position of women in society is something which we need to understand through recognition of underlying unobservable structures, or with reference to language and social practices.

Feminism takes a variety of forms and is largely subject to internal critique; so while liberal feminists might argue we need to look at numbers of women in the workplace, feminist critical theorists might argue we need to look at the structural conditions which defined their opportunities (or lack of) to engage in the workplace. Constructivist feminists might draw attention to the way in which women are socially constructed and their roles defined through dominant discourses, prevalent at work, in the media, in government and in everyday life.

Constructivism

Constructivism is widely debated and contested, and as with feminism and poststructuralism, it is not an overarching approach, rather it takes a variety of forms. A uniting feature is that it highlights the importance of norms and values in analysis. However, this manifests itself in different ways, and here we are concerned with how constructivism draws our attention to the contingent nature of the world around us. The way in which we present constructivism here is anti-foundational and linked to interpretivism. This suggests that to understand the world around us we need to understand the way in which it has been constructed according to particular norms and values. In this perspective, our interpretation and articulation of the world around us plays a role in the way in which it is constructed. For example, we can say that education exists. But what is this thing called 'education'? We can see features which serve to support the idea of education, such as schools, colleges and universities, but the notion of education itself is something that we cannot see, we cannot touch; but it is something which we, as a society, consider to be important (albeit to varying degrees). But that we discuss education, its purpose and how we might engage with it, in short, that we articulate the notion of education, from this perspective, plays a role in its construction and so its existence. In this view, education exists through our experience of and our interaction with it.

Constructivism has had varying degrees of influence within the disciplines, and has been much more successful in becoming part of the orthodoxy in IR than in Politics. Therefore, throughout this book we highlight that we are much more likely to see fully formed constructivist theories in IR.

Constructivism has been criticized for its focus upon the specific and its lack of ability to make generalizations. However, constructivism provides a significant challenge to the positivist view of scientific ways through which to understand the world. Moreover, crucially it draws our attention to the role of ideas and norms in structuring processes and social and political relationships. In this way constructivism as an approach is concerned to explore and evaluate social patterns and relationships rather than making a set of specific claims or hypotheses about interactions or relations in world or domestic politics. In order to discern these processes and values constructivists have drawn from critical theory and provided compelling critiques of existing power relationships.

Poststructuralism

As with constructivism, poststructuralism is also linked to anti-foundational interpretivism and is subject to similar criticisms. Finlayson and Martin (2006: 155) suggest there is no single version of poststructuralism, but what it does is provide a challenge to the dominant Enlightenment view and draw attention to some of the problems associated with the Westernized scientific (and liberal) worldview. Here, then, poststructuralism proceeds not quite as an alternative to the positivistic accounts detailed above, but as a discipline which draws attention to the existence of competing truths about the social and political world. In contrast to approaches which assume that the subject matter of social science (human beings) can be understood in the same way as the subject matter of social sciences, poststructuralism does not assume a uniform behaviour of individuals. Rather it highlights that individuals are reflexive, reassessing their activities and behaviour, not only in the context of that behaviour but also within the context or system of meaning that they are situated in. This system of meaning is characterized by cultural and ideological norms. Thus, the way to understand individual behaviour is not simply through reference to that behaviour, but through an understanding of the system of meaning within which that action takes place. For example, we may witness an individual place an X on a sheet of paper, but we cannot establish the meaning of that action without recourse to the context within which it takes place. If that action takes place in a polling booth then we understand the action through reference to our understanding of the function of elections in society. As such, we cannot understand what is going on without reference to concealed meanings and contextualization (for detailed discussion of the philosophers whose thinking informs this approach, see Agger, 1991).

But how is this system of meaning constructed? Here poststructuralists draw attention to the ways in which many actors and institutions negotiate and organize these systems of meaning so that political claims are legitimated, making particular actions seem normal or inevitable. In order to understand the 'rules of the game' one must be conversant in the particular language game which is being played or used. For example, we cannot understand why someone would kick a ball in a net, unless we understood the language game associated with football, which suggests that the side who kicks the most balls in the net is the winner. These language games and systems of meaning also function as a mechanism to include and exclude certain options, ideas and possibilities. In this way, in order to understand power relations, we need to understand how systems of meaning are constructed. To do this, poststructuralists explore the role of discourse in institutionalizing norms and behaviours. A discourse is an 'historically, socially, and institutionally specific structure of statements, terms, categories and beliefs' (Scott, 1988: 35). That is, it moves beyond language and text, and explores the processes, interactions and social relationships which embed meaning. Crucially, poststructuralists alert attention to the notion that there is not one system of meaning, rather there are competing interpretations, which may clash. As such, at the heart of this is contestation and political struggle; through recognition of which comes the opportunity to challenge the dominant order and effect transformation.

The differing approaches we are using within this book, and outlined above, are summarized in Table 1.1. We have sought to highlight that the boundary between each approach is not fixed. Each approach may be predominantly associated with a particular ontology and epistemology, but that is not to suggest that their boundaries are fixed. As theoretical work progresses the boundaries between approaches can become blurred. This is most evident within feminisms, which can adopt differing ontological and epistemological positions while having shared and overlapping concerns.

A word on method: quantitative and qualitative approaches

The approaches detailed above also inform the method, or methods that we may adopt. A discussion of the reflection of the method that we use is called methodology, and so when we reflect methodologically we think about not only the methods that we actually use, but also the assumptions that inform those methods. We argue that the boundaries around these positions and approaches are not discrete, but fluid and open to contestation (as we noted earlier). One of the ways this fluidity

Table 1.1 *Overview of differing approaches informed by their underlying positions (note: all boundaries assumed to be fluid rather than fixed)*

Foundational positivism	*Foundational scientific/ critical realism*	*Anti-foundational interpretivism*
Behaviouralism	**Marxism and critical theory**	**Constructivism**
Empirically testable theory	Accepts scientism in that it provides for universal laws (such as capitalism)	Analysis focuses around the way in which norms are constructed and guide behaviour
Assumes a real world exists and that knowledge of this is empirically accessible	Seeks to make predictions and causal explanations	
Aims to generate causal explanation, predictions and general laws	Makes foundational assumption of a real world out there, but draws from anti-foundationalism in admitting unobservable features into analysis	Highlights the contingent nature of reality and the social construction of meaning
Political analysis is and should be objective and value-free	Political analysis is normative and can be emancipatory	Political analysis is inherently value-laden
Rational choice theory		**Poststructuralism**
A method which adheres to scientific principles		Reflexive behaviour of subject of analysis
Seeks to generate predictions and general laws		Competing truths about the political world available
Assumption of individual rationality		Aims to challenge dominant power relations
Political analysis is (and should be) objective and value-free		Political analysis value-laden but has emancipatory potential

◄──────────────Feminism──────────────►

Liberal feminism	**Critical feminism**	**Poststructural feminism**
Institutional and reformist	Systemic inequalities reflected in patriarchy	Challenges dominant gendered power relations
Focus on public role of women		
Observation of behaviour	Overtly normative and aims for emancipation	

between ontology and epistemology is reflected is in the division over method. Quantitative and qualitative methods are often juxtaposed and have tended to be treated as mutually exclusive. Over recent years, however, there has been an increase in methodological triangulation – or combining methods (see, for example, Tashakkori and Teddlie, 1998). What is briefly summarized here is how the differing methods (categorized as quantitative or qualitative) are linked to the ontological and epistemological positions outlined above.

Foundational and positivist assumptions tend to lead to quantitative methods. These are often (but not always) statistical methods. But as suggested by the scientific approach, they are concerned with counting and observing what is available to our senses. The key here is empirical observation and the way in which it can be quantified. This is often through the use of statistics: for example, 66 per cent of new voters voted for Obama in the 2008 election (www.bbc.co.uk), which suggests targeting new voters was crucial to securing Obama's electoral success. Here, then, positivists would focus upon observable and quantifiable behaviour and make a claim to knowledge on the basis of their empirical evidence.

In contrast, anti-foundational interpretivist approaches tend to adopt qualitative methods such as discourse analysis that would draw attention to the importance of language, such as the symbolism invoked by Obama's continued campaign rhetoric of 'change' and 'hope' which suggests electoral victory was about the mobilization of ideas. This approach would thus emphasize the contingent nature of political reality and that, while slogans such as these depicted above may have mobilized support, we might also look at the way in which the campaigns were symbolic and reflective of a clash or conflict of wider political interests.

The methods that we adopt are informed by the meta-theoretical decisions we make, the approaches that we adopt and the theories that we use. Our aim here is not to discuss these methods (as this has been comprehensively done elsewhere, see, for example, Burnham *et al.*, 2004; Bryman, 2008); rather our aim is to discuss what assumptions we make and how this might influence the way in which we do our analysis.

Adjudicating between competing perspectives

As becomes clear, the choice of which theory to adopt in order to do political analysis is not straightforward. So how do we decide which approach to use? This simple question belies a complex set of thought processes and assumptions that we make, and while we are not concerned with the psychology of how we choose, we think it is important that we understand and are able to reflect upon the consequences of what we choose.

It might be that we choose a particular position because of the audience we want to influence; for example, if we were trying to influence policy-makers we may choose a more 'scientific' approach. If we were seeking to get an article published in the *American Journal of Political Science*, then we may be well advised to choose a method that enables us to use sophisticated econometric techniques. If we were trying to engage a lay audience a narrative approach might be more useful. Considerations of our audience may form one part of our decision as to which approach or position best serves our purpose. However, we argue that, less instrumentally perhaps, what we consider to be important is to acknowledge that it is the assumptions that we make about the world prior to our study that will influence the theoretical framework which we adopt. As we have discussed in this chapter, if we believe that all that we can know about the world is based upon what is available to our empirical senses, then we are likely to adopt a positivist approach to our study. If we believe that there are structures which, although we may not be able to directly observe, still may shape or inform our behaviour, then we are more likely to adopt a scientific/critical realist approach. If we believe that ideas play an important role in shaping our approach to understanding the world, then we are more likely to adopt an interpretivist approach. We argue that our response to these issues then tends to inform how we choose the theoretical framework that we adopt.

This may raise the following questions. Can we not have a theory which does everything? Why do we have separate theories? While some have attempted to discover a general theory of politics, the main reason that this doesn't happen is twofold. First, because political reality is so inherently complex that it would be impossible to find a theory which was able to explain every detail of behaviour at all times. Second, because of the competing ways in which people think that it is possible to do Politics and, while there are blurrings of these boundaries, at the same time their aims and fundamental assumptions are incommensurate.

Some argue we need to adopt an epistemological position and stick to it (Marsh and Furlong, 2002). Others suggest that different theories capture different aspects of the world and thereby we choose theory accordingly; we need to acknowledge that differing epistemologies can capture differing aspects of reality. Our objective here is not to resolve these debates (indeed, these debates reflect hundreds of years of philosophical discussion). Rather our aim is to suggest that these are not issues which need a solution. Instead we see these debates like a prism which we call 'Politics'. Depending upon the perspective that we adopt, we shine light on a particular angle of a puzzle, issue or problem. In this way, we are using these debates to problematize issues, and to reflect upon their causes and the likely consequences, rather than to provide solutions to them.

Conclusion

The aim of this chapter has been to introduce the different philosophical assumptions and the dominant approaches that we use to inform our analysis of the real world of politics. It is important to stress that these are not the only approaches; indeed, as we are very aware, our narrative expresses a particular view of what political analysis is that reflects the roots of these approaches – that is, these are very Western-centric. Our aim here is not to give an exhaustive account, but to introduce some of the dominant assumptions and approaches, so that when we engage with other readings and research within Politics we can understand how other scholars and students may come to the conclusions that they do. In short, we have aimed to give a brief summary of the some of the ways in which we 'do' political analysis. The following chapters now apply these assumptions and approaches more explicitly by introducing a range of theoretical perspectives and illustrating how they tell us about the world of politics.

Reflection

Do you think the political world is characterized by a 'clash of civilizations'?
Do you think we have seen the 'end of ideology'?
Do you think that women are more likely to vote for left-wing candidates?
Do you think war is inevitable?
How do you know these things?
Is it possible to establish them scientifically?
What do you think are the key components of the political world?
What do you think exists? Can you draw or map the political world?
How do you know what is in there?
Do you think you are a positivist, critical/scientific realist or interpretivist?
Can you give reasons for your answer?
Do you think your position may change?
Can you see what the position you adopted enables you to do?
Can you see what it misses or its limitations?

Seminar activities

Identify one journal article from the field of Politics and another from an IR journal.

What is the article about?

Do the authors assume explicitly or implicitly (this is more likely) that a science of politics is possible?

What assumptions are they making about what the world of politics 'looks like'? (Again, this assumption is likely to be implicit.)

Can you identify the authors' epistemological position?

How did you do this?

What are the differences or similarities between the approaches in the articles?

Which do you find the most credible and why?

What are kinds of questions are they asking?

Can the questions they ask be categorized as either Politics or IR or do you think the boundaries around the subject matter are blurred?

Chapter 2

Power

Introduction

Open any book on Politics and we do not have to turn too many pages before seeing the concept of power discussed. Indeed, the pursuit and exercise of power is traditionally presented as the very cut and thrust of both domestic and international politics, and theorists go to great lengths to conceptualize and contextualize this power. Politicians go into politics to be able to exercise 'power' in order to achieve their personal and party political objectives; electorates may be said to exercise power when they choose who governs them. Power can also be exercised in the suppression or expression of a particular political debate or issue. Power might be the property of individuals, or might be located within systems. Power may be a 'thing' or it may be a process. So what do we really understand by the concept of power? In seeking to do political analysis for ourselves how should we approach the subject of power? There will certainly be questions that need addressing such as: what is power? Who has it? Where is it located? How is it exercised? In whose interest does it operate? The ontological and epistemological approaches we adopt will also largely determine how we explore 'power'. Because of the assumptions that we make prior to our analysis about what is possible to establish, our theoretical perspectives emphasize different facets of power. Indeed, so important is the concept of power to Politics that in each of the subsequent chapters we address the implications for, and the impact of, power on each of the topics covered. In locating the sources, exercise and consequences of power we are able to analyze and interpret how individuals, states and systems operate in domestic and international spheres.

In this chapter, we seek to provide an overview of the different ways in which power is conceptualized. Using Steven Lukes' seminal text *Power: A Radical View* (1974) as a starting point, we examine his three dimensions of power to discover how such understandings of power can serve as an analytical tool. In doing so, we explore pluralist, elitist and Marxist

43

approaches to power and how these fit into theories of power that have grown up within Political Science and IR. We consider: realism, in its classical and neo-realist variants; liberal institutionalism; neo-Marxism; world systems theory, with its global stratification of class; feminism; constructivism; and poststructuralism. Through outlining these different approaches, we highlight the contested nature of power. Indeed, a number of these theories reject the very idea that they are concerned with power, arguing that they are about cooperation or identity, providing an antidote or a different way of looking at the world other than through the prism of power relationships. We argue, however, that the way in which power is studied is crucial in all aspects of Politics. In short, what this chapter seeks to do is to discover what power is and how we can study it.

Three dimensions of power

In 1974, Steven Lukes produced a small book entitled *Power: A Radical View* which neatly encapsulates three different approaches to power: the one-dimensional behaviouralist view pioneered by Robert Dahl (1957, 1958, 1961), a slightly more critical two-dimensional view championed by Peter Bachrach and Morton S. Baratz (1970) and Lukes' own three-dimensional view, which criticizes the behavioural focus of the first two dimensions. Robert Dahl's work has been heavily influential in a school of thought known as pluralism. Dahl studied the behaviour of political elites by examining all the decisions taken in the policy-making process in New Haven, Connecticut. During the period of his study he observed who initiated, vetoed or proposed alternatives and who had their initiatives turned down and by whom. A positive and negative ratio recording defeats and successes was tabulated, which, according to Dahl, was sufficient to determine who had most power or influence (Dahl, 1961). (The terms 'power' and 'influence' are often used interchangeably by pluralists.) The underlying normative assumption held by Dahl (as with other pluralists) is that government's role is to mediate between differing interests. Power or influence is assumed to be located in political actors (we can establish this assumption, as this is who Dahl observed, and, following observation of their behaviour, went on to make claims about their power). For pluralists, then, the amount of power that political actors have can be determined simply by observing who gets what, when and how, in the decision-making process.

In Dahl's formulation power can be defined as A having power over B to the extent that A can get B to do something they would not otherwise do (Dahl, 1957; Lukes, 1974: 11–12). This view of power has been the most influential approach to understanding power because of its simplicity. This one-dimensional view of power focuses on the behaviour of political actors who are involved in decision-making; it prioritizes the key issues and looks for observable conflict. Participation in the political process reveals interests as policy preferences (Lukes, 1974: 25). Dahl's formulation relies on overt observation, which is readily available in the public domain. But what about those decisions that are not observable, which take place outside formal decision-making structures?

Bachrach and Baratz argue that power has two aspects – Dahl's one-dimensional view *and* Schattschneider's (1960) 'mobilization of bias'. They posit that political scientists should not just be concerned with observable behaviour but also with that which takes place beyond public scrutiny. In particular, who, what, why and how is it determined what is to be included or excluded from decision-making? For Bachrach and Baratz personal or group power is manifest to the extent 'that a person or group – consciously or unconsciously – creates or reinforces barriers to the public airing of policy conflicts' (Bachrach and Baratz, 1970: 8). In distinguishing between overt and covert faces of power, where those exercising power are able to determine what is included or excluded from discussion, Bachrach and Baratz challenge Dahl's assumptions of an open and democratic process. They argue that the mobilization of bias determines what is included and excluded from the decision-making process. In this way the vested interests of individuals or groups are able to control policy agendas. In short, power is still assumed to be identifiable through the observation of the behaviour of individuals (as with Dahl's formulation). However, power in this view lies in the capacity to determine which decisions get made and, crucially, which don't (non-decisions). Power is the ability to 'set the agenda'. For example, there is no longer discussion in the UK about unilateral nuclear disarmament, which, within this perspective, would represent power being exercised by political elites (and the nuclear industry?) in their ability to keep this issue from the public agenda.

Those who determine such decisions or non-decisions are policy elites who can mobilize through:

> A set of predominant values, beliefs, rituals, and institutional procedures ('rules of the game') that operate systematically and consistently to the benefit of certain persons and groups at the expense of others. Those who benefit are placed in a preferred position to defend and promote their vested interests. (Bachrach and Baratz, 1970: 43–4)

Whereas Dahl and other pluralists predetermine what are, or are not, political issues through insisting on observerability, Bachrach and Baratz also try to discover those political issues that non-decision-making prevents from taking place, thereby wholly or partly excluding people from the political system (Lukes, 1974: 19–20). Lukes describes this position as a two-dimensional view of power, which includes a qualified critique of behaviouralism and focuses on decision-making and non-decision-making, issues and potential issues, overt and covert observable conflict, and policy preferences or grievances defined as interests (Lukes, 1974: 25). Here, then, we can see that power is still assumed to be observable and the property of individuals.

Lukes challenges the two-dimensional view outlined above, arguing there is a third dimension to power. Power has structural features, he suggests, and, while the two previous approaches highlight the exercise of power as located at a site of conflict, in the structural view, power in the third dimension is the prevention of conflict emerging in the first place. Power is thus more than just conflict; it is also about manipulation and authority (Lukes, 1974: 23):

> Decisions are choices consciously and intentionally made by individuals between alternatives, whereas the bias of the system can be mobilised, recreated and reinforced in ways that are neither consciously chosen nor the intended result of particular individual's choices. (Lukes, 1974: 21)

Lukes argues that it is not enough to simply examine open conflict or consider what is and is not discussed (as suggested by the first two dimensions); we also need to recognize that 'the most effective and insidious use of power' actually prevents conflict even happening (Lukes, 1974: 23). Herein lie the seeds of latent conflict where the real interests of the people represented are diametrically opposed to the interests of their representatives. Lukes warns that just because there might appear to be an absence of grievance it is not necessarily the case. Indeed, a grievance consensus can be reached by a 'false or manipulated consensus' (Lukes, 1974: 24). By this Lukes does not imply a Marxist false consciousness of privileged access to truths but rather the 'power to mislead' people (Lukes, 1974: 149). Lukes critiques behaviouralist approaches to power and instead focuses on decision-making and considerations of who controls the political agenda, which is not always through decisions being taken. For Lukes, both the issues and potential issues are important. He is concerned about observable conflict but also latent conflict, and not simply subjective interests but also real interests (Lukes, 1974: 25). Lukes widens Dahl's formulation that *A has power over B to the extent to which A can get B to do something B would not otherwise do* to *A exercises power over B when A affects B in a manner contrary to B's interests* (Lukes, 1974: 34).

Approaches to power

Pluralism, elitism and Marxism

The discussion above has focused on Lukes' three dimensions of power. In this next section, we briefly reprise the key aspects of pluralism and elitism before introducing Marxist approaches to power. Pluralism takes both a positivist and subjectivist approach to power in which the subject discovers power relationships and seeks to identify who prevails in decision-making. The decisions, which are taken, involve real and observable conflict, the outcomes of which determine whether or not there is a ruling elite. Power is about consciously made and articulated decisions (or preferences) resulting in conflict. For the pluralist, preferences are always articulated, observable and actors are always aware of their own interests without being mistaken (Dahl, 1958: 463–9; Lukes, 1974: 13–14).

Bachrach and Baratz's neo-elitism is somewhat softer than the approach of C. Wright Mills or Lasswell, for example, who saw a powerful elite existing in the United States, where the holders of power use it to advance their own interests and prevent others achieving their objectives (Wright Mills, 1956; Lasswell, 1936). For elitists, power is a permanent feature of political life and even human existence (Dunleavy and O'Leary, 1987: 148). Classical elitists and ruling-class theorists including Pareto, Mosca and Michels would subscribe to this position. A key criticism of both elitist and pluralist theories, with their common subjectivist core, is that they only consider one form of power and are unable to account for social change (Therborn, 1982: 229–30). Dahl, Bachrach, Baratz and Lukes, despite different emphases, are all subjectivists and concentrate on interrelationships to the exclusion of other aspects of power. The key question for them is the study of power 'in' society rather than power 'over' society. They want to know who governs in society, whether it is an elite or competing leadership groups, and how stable such groupings are:

> What they have been debating is whether there is an *interpersonal* relation between the different moments of power in society; Is there a cohesive elite which unites the different exercises of power by making the decisions in different areas? (Therborn, 1982: 230)

This rather narrow perspective on power, about who governs in any given polity, is expanded considerably by Marxist approaches that question the focus of pluralists and elitists. Why should the study of society be so restricted when it could, and they would argue should, also include the process of reproduction. Therborn argues that in adopting this approach, the key question now becomes: 'What kinds of society, what fundamental relations of production, are being produced?' (Therborn, 1982: 232).

Marxist approaches emphasize that the relationship to the means of production determines class relationships based on exploitation and domination. The two key classes within capitalism are the bourgeoisie and the proletariat: those who control the means of production and those who are exploited. While pluralism and elitism focus on the subject holding or exercising power, Marxist approaches are more concerned with relationships to the means of production and the way in which the ruling class is organized to maintain and develop capitalism (Therborn, 1982).

The perpetuation of domination and exploitation sets the basis for class rule in which the given social structure and the individuals who occupy positions within it are reproduced, thereby enabling capitalism to develop (Therborn, 1982: 233; Poulantzas, 1973a: 49). Some neo-Marxists, such as Althusser (1967, 1969) and Poulantzas (1967), analyze the structures which support the exercise of power in society, arguing that the way society is organized is itself a power relationship. Domination and exploitation, in this understanding, are built into societies' 'social structures and practices' (Joseph, 1988: 49). Pluralist, elitist and Marxist approaches, which we have discussed from a Political Science perspective, also resonate within the field of IR and in the next section we will seek to develop these themes.

Realism

Realism purports to describe the world as it really is, to get to the basics of how the world actually operates, how countries interact with one another and what their role and purpose is. In brief, classical and neo-realists (also known as structural realists) are united in their identification of statism, survival and self-help as the way the world operates. Statism highlights states as the key international actors, even in a globalized world with international organizations and transnational actors. States in this view operate as rational and autonomous actors in pursuit of their own national interest. In an international system, unlike domestic systems, there is no overarching authority and sovereign states must compete for power and ensure their survival in an anarchical world. In the last resort, states have to rely on themselves to ensure their survival.

Realists are the power theorists in IR. Drawing on a classical literature that dates back at least as far as Thucydides' history of the Peloponnesian wars (431–404 BCE), and includes Sun Tzu's *The Art of War*, Niccolò Machiavelli's *The Prince* (1532) and Thomas Hobbes' *Leviathan* (1651), realists form a particular worldview through the prism of power. Classical realists emphasize human nature as a main driver for international relations. They adopt a pessimistic view of human nature that suggests that if there is no overarching authority then humans will pursue their own interests, selfishly and to the detriment of others. In other words, they will seek to maximize their own power. In a world in which every state is compelled to act in the same way, the most successful will be those with most power. The greater the power the state has, the greater its prospects of survival.

When realists talk of power, what they really mean is military power, the ability of the state to achieve its objectives and ensure its survival because it has the military capability to do so. Clearly, power is not evenly distributed and states will be involved in an ongoing competition for greater power. Pecking orders are established and either accepted or contested based on power distribution. States are 'powerful to the extent that they affect others more than others affect them' (Goldstein and Pevehouse, 2010: 45). Realists expect states to behave in certain ways based on their interpretation of human nature, which Hans Morgenthau, describes as 'the desire to live, to propagate, and to dominate' (Morgenthau, 1955: 30). Powerful states in such thinking are obliged to act in such a way that maximizes their power and prevents challenges emerging. Thucydides depicts the Peloponnesian wars as a conflict in which Sparta and Athens are both obliged to go to war, the former to avoid domination by Athens and the latter to preserve its empire. Further down the pecking order, the islanders of Melos are given a salutary lesson in the realist worldview when caught up in the war between Sparta and Athens and given an ultimatum to surrender by the Athenians:

> you know as well as we do that, when these matters are discussed by practical people, the standard of justice depends on the equality of power to compel and that in fact the strong do what they have the power to do and the weak accept what they have to accept. (Thucydides, 1954: 360)

For realists, power and justice are a matter of a capacity, which do not just depend on the size, quality and preparedness of the military and its weaponry, although this is crucial, but also on a state's ability to attract allies, its diplomacy, the size of its economic strength and territory, its geographical terrain and location, and natural resources. Weaker states will need to appease or satisfy the interests of stronger states in order to survive or form alliances with rival strong states, thus balancing the power of opposing stronger states. Alternatively, weak states could choose to ally with the strongest state, or hegemon, to promote national interests as far as possible within prescribed limits. States constantly have to adapt to the changing configurations of power that occur within international politics. Realists tend to divide the world up into great, middle and small powers and focus on military polarity to describe world order. In this view, we can see how the multipolarity of the nineteenth- and early twentieth-century great powers gave way to the bipolarity of the Cold War era and subsequent unipolarity, with the United States as global hegemon (following the fall of the Berlin Wall).

Structural realists, inspired by Kenneth Waltz during the Cold War, agree with classical realists that international politics is all about the struggle for power but rather than emphasize that this is due to human nature, argue that it owes more to the anarchic structure of the international system and the relative distribution of power within it. Waltz argues that anarchy creates an international environment in which each state has to protect its own interests and seek to maximize its own security. While all states have different capabilities we can only understand international outcomes through recognizing those differences, the number of great powers that exist and the rank order of each of them. For Waltz, power is simply a means to the greater end of achieving security for the state. Indeed, power maximization might be counterproductive by persuading other states to join forces to counterbalance against the power-maximizing state (Waltz, 1979, 1989).

> The opportunity and at times the necessity of using force distinguishes ... the balances of power that form inside a state ... The balance of power among states becomes a balance of all the capabilities, including physical force, that states choose to use in pursuing their goals. (Waltz, 1959: 205)

For Waltz, the most stable form of world order is one based on bipolarity where nuclear weapons and the threat of mutually assured destruction equalize military power and therefore maximize security. John Mearsheimer, however, rejects this defensive premise and adopts a structural realism that emphasizes offensive capability. He argues that, in an uncertain world, it is impossible to second guess rivals' intentions and therefore states need to maximize their military might. There can be no satisfied or status quo states but each must seek to increase their relative power against other states. Rather than seeing bipolarity as ideal, Mearsheimer looks to a global hegemon as the most stable world order, albeit one that is continually tested by great power rivalry (Mearsheimer, 2003).

If we return for a moment to Lukes' three dimensions of power, then a realist understanding of power in its various classical, defensive and offensive structural guises lies within the approach adopted by Robert Dahl: power and security maximization both involve state A persuading state B to do what it would not otherwise do. The extent to which it is successful in doing so indicates the power that the state has within the international system. We can know this takes place based upon our observation of behaviour of political actors (for realism these are states).

Realists argue that there are fundamental differences between hierarchical domestic politics, where the state imposes order on its citizens, and anarchical international politics, where there is survival of the fittest or most powerful. As a result, realists argue that domestic and international politics need to be considered independently. Realists are largely unconcerned with politics at the domestic level, considering that they have little bearing on decisions taken at the international level. Given the dominance of realism in IR in the post-war era, we can perhaps also understand why within IR it sees itself as distinct from the remit of Political Science.

Epistemologically, the realist claim is to objectivity: through empirical observation they argue that the social scientist standing outside events is able to record the world as it actually is. In this perspective 'the evidence' reveals an international system where states are forced to maximize power and/or security. States behave the way they do because, as rational actors who make an ontological assumption of the existence of an anarchical world order, they cannot do anything else.

Realists deny that their approach is overtly normative. Faced with accusations that their worldview is amoral, or even immoral, realists argue that international morality consists in the survival of the state to enable it to continue to pursue domestic politics. Such a position, however, does have significant normative implications, laying realists open to the charge that in seeking to maximize security and/or power and reifying the state, they promote a world order in which such thinking becomes the norm and a conflictual world order a self-fulfilling prophecy.

Liberal institutionalism

Liberal views of world politics tend to be rather more optimistic about human nature and seek to emphasize cooperation and interdependence rather than antagonism and power maximization. Whereas realism separates domestic and international politics, liberalism considers that international politics develop from the domestic realm. John Locke's three *Letters Concerning Toleration* (1689–92), *Two Treatises on Government* (1690) and *An Essay Concerning Human Understanding* (1690) underpin subsequent liberal thinking. Locke advances a theory of government within states and good governance between states and their peoples. Good governance consisting of order, liberty, justice and tolerance at the domestic level is the blueprint for an international order based on those same values. As Tim Dunne would have it: 'In a sense, the historical project of liberalism is the domestication of the international' (Dunne, 2008: 110).

Immanuel Kant develops this theme in his *Perpetual Peace: A Philosophical Essay*, arguing that a peaceful world order could exist among like-minded states, which were republican and liberal. For a 'perpetual peace' to exist Kant (1795) insists that nine points must be established, which he summarizes in six preliminary articles:

1. 'No Treaty of Peace Shall Be Held Valid in Which There Is Tacitly Reserved Matter for a Future War
2. No Independent States, Large or Small, Shall Come under the Dominion of Another State by Inheritance, Exchange, Purchase, or Donation
3. Standing Armies (miles perpetuus) Shall in Time Be Totally Abolished
4. National Debts Shall Not Be Contracted with a View to the External Friction of States
5. No State Shall by Force Interfere with the Constitution or Government of Another State
6. No State Shall, *during* War, Permit Such Acts of Hostility Which Would Make Mutual Confidence in the Subsequent Peace Impossible: Such Are the Employment of Assassins (percussores), Poisoners (venefici), Breach of Capitulation, and Incitement to Treason (perduellio) in the Opposing State.'

Three Definitive Articles provide a foundation on which a lasting peace could be established and perpetuated:

1. 'The Civil Constitution of Every State Should Be Republican
2. The Law of Nations Shall be *Founded on* a Federation of Free States
3. The Law of World Citizenship Shall Be Limited to Conditions of Universal Hospitality.'

Whatever the merits of Kant's claims, what is apparent here is that such thinking represents a radical departure from realist thought. Kant's premise that domestic governance has international implications and application is anathema to realists. The rejection of unjust treaties and contracts, domination, the ending of standing armies, non-interference in the internal affairs of other countries fly in the face of all that realists hold dear. Here, Kant presents a world that is interconnected and interdependent, where power is of secondary consideration to cooperation and mutual benefit. Woodrow Wilson took up and developed these themes during and after World War I. Wilson's *Fourteen Points* found expression in a League of Nations that substituted balance of power politics for collective security and, in principle, the right of self-determination. Power, in its military context, when it is used is to be exercised collectively in defence of maintaining peace. The failure of this liberal experiment, resulting in a second world war, ushered in the dominant realist paradigm in international relations. This paradigm is inspired by E. H. Carr's forensic analysis of the failings of liberalism to prevent war and the necessity to see the world as it really is, rather than how it ought to be in an ideal world (see Carr, 1946).

Liberalism refuses to be restricted to realism's prioritization of military and strategic power. Trade and commerce are also of importance and states develop organizations and rules of conduct to facilitate this. Greater interaction will encourage best practice between states in terms of governance and promote peace through the reciprocal benefit of trade. Liberal institutionalists argue that rational actors are able and willing to forgo short-term gains for longer-term benefits and that what matters are not relative gains but absolute gains benefiting all states involved in transactions. The risk of cheating or resort to violence can be overcome through institutionalizing processes of trade and other international relations in international institutions. International institutions and international law enable states to develop confidence in the good faith of other states while acknowledging that it is in each national interest to cooperate. The rules and expectations, which facilitate cooperation, become embedded and normalized.

Although the international system is still anarchic the worst and most violent excesses can be ameliorated by working together in permanent institutions such as the World Bank, International Monetary Fund, or the World Trade Organization. For liberal institutionalists the realist problem of state survival has largely been overcome through participation in security regimes such as the United Nations, NATO or the European Union. In this new world, it is transnational actors, transnational corporations and international non-governmental organizations rather than states as such that are increasingly important (Keohane and Nye, 1972, 1977). When states act, they should use more tools than are available in the realist box, including soft power, the power to attract rather than naked aggression (Nye, 2004). For liberal institutionalists, institutions are actually an antidote to power and the way forward for a more pacific world (see Keohane, 1984).

Liberalism overtly rejects the military associations of power, rather than power per se. Liberalism focuses its attention on the actions and behaviour of key political actors, NGOs and organizations. Power, in this perspective, is exercised through the facilitation of cooperation at elite level. Power is observable and in the hands of elite-level actors, with shades of both pluralism and elitism characterizing this perspective, as outlined in Lukes' first two dimensions of power.

Although liberal institutionalists seek to distance themselves from realist or military power, with their emphasis on interdependence, they nonetheless perpetuate power relationships through 'the control actors exercise indirectly over others through diffuse relations of interaction' and the 'behavioural constraints and governing biases of institutions' (Barrett and Durrell, 2005: 43, 52). E. H. Carr castigates the claims of those who present international institutions as an antidote to power as mere hubris. He contends that the idea that these institutions represent a gain for all parties is deceitful and that they introduce a new set of power relations of dependency and exploitation that leads to domination as surely as military power. This is achieved through those dominated submitting to their own domination through a false consciousness that the international system operates for mutual benefit (Barrett and Durrell, 2005: 68; Carr, 1946).

Neo-Marxism

Marxist approaches to power in international relations have their origins in Lenin's *Imperialism, the Highest Stage of Capitalism* (1917). Lenin argues that as capitalism reached its highest state of development in the industrialized countries of Europe, monopoly capitalism developed, which in order to generate sufficient profit necessitated exporting excess capital abroad. In order to control this, the major powers acquire and seek to maintain colonies with the super-profits generated returned to them. European capitalists and skilled labourers are financially rewarded, reducing the latter's revolutionary potential. Lenin concludes that the new proletariat in this developing world, such as Russia, possessed greater revolutionary potential at capitalism's weakest point. The revolutionary fervour of the new proletariat, he argues, would then spread to the developed world. Power resided with the monopoly capitalists of the colonial powers, but this would be taken from them by proletarian revolution.

Lenin, along with all Marxist theorists, sees society, and indeed the world, as divided by class. In an international system where there is an uneven distribution of capital and resources, not only do class relationships of exploiter and exploited prevail, but also the proletariat is divided between developed and developing states and the idea of harmony of interests among all workers is lost. The nature of capitalism necessitates that the world system is considered in its entirety to determine who has power and how these power relationships work out. What can be observed is that class relations now exist around the world and the total accumulation of the surplus value produced by labour moves from poor developing countries to the rich developed ones. If the developing countries of the global South retain their surplus they would be considerably better off and yet neo-Marxists would argue they are constrained from doing so by false consciousness and the constraints of an international system based on the needs of global capitalism. This suppression of interests is also articulated in Lukes' third dimension of power, to which Marxist approaches are often linked.

The basic unfairness of the capitalist system and its attendant power structures are evident in all modern societies and yet Marx's prediction of workers rising up and casting off the chains that bind them has largely failed to materialize. Antonio Gramsci (1971) rejects traditional Marxist teaching that emphasizes state violence, politically and economically coercive practices, as an inadequate or incomplete explanation of why the masses fail to rise up. Instead, he presents a conceptualization of power that introduces the concept of hegemony. Here, it is not so much coercion as consent that determines working-class passivity. Consent is produced and reproduced by societal institutions such as the media, the education system, third-sector organizations and religious institutions, which are at least partly autonomous from the state (Hobden and Wyn Jones, 2008: 150).

Whereas traditionally Marxists consider that the base of socio-economic relations is the dominant aspect in explaining power relations, Gramsci insists that the superstructure of political and cultural practices is more significant. The interaction of the base and superstructure is the key to understanding hegemony. The 'mutually reinforcing and reciprocal relationships' between socio-economic relations, culture and ideology serves to strengthen the existing capitalist order (Hobden and Wyn Jones, 2008: 150). Rather than coercion, the working class cooperates in their own subjugation by absorbing and reproducing bourgeois values and aspirations. Ruling-class values become normalized and, if unchallenged, maintain the existing status quo. The only antidote to this ruling-class hegemony, Gramsci suggests, is to build a counter-hegemonic struggle leading to the creation of an alternative power bloc. Given the international character of global capitalism, IR and international political economy, theorists in the Gramscian tradition, argue that the counter-hegemonic struggle needs to take place at the level of national and international civil society. The anti-globalization, solidarity, global justice movements and international labour organizations with emancipatory agendas fit within this Gramscian tradition.

Robert Cox has emerged as one of the leading thinkers in linking Gramsci's hegemony within individual capitalist states to the international sphere (see Cox, 1981, 1983, 1987). Cox argues that dominant powers in the international system have shaped the world for their own benefit using both coercion and consent. The most successful, like the United States, are able to reproduce systems and values that advance their hegemony. The universal norms of world hegemony are established in part by international organizations. Cox describes the features that express this hegemonic role:

> (1) the institutions embody the rules which facilitate the expansion of hegemonic world orders; (2) they are themselves the product of the world order; (3) they ideologically legitimate the norms of world order; (4) they co-opt the elites from peripheral countries; and (5) they absorb counter-hegemonic ideas. (Cox, 2010: 222)

International organizations and institutions are established and exist to perpetuate and advance dominant social and economic forces throughout the world. The rules are set by the hegemonic state with the cooperation of a hierarchy of other states – for example, the United States in the Bretton Woods Agreements. The international institutions perform an ideological role shaping a discourse and universal norms that reinforce a dominant consensus, which reflects the interest of the core countries. Talented members of elites in the developing world are co-opted into the organizations, reducing the prospects for a counter-hegemonic movement (Cox, 2010: 223).

Where Gramsci identifies workers absorbing ruling-class values Cox identifies developing nations' acceptance of free trade, which operates in the interest of developed countries. For Cox, traditional theories of IR perpetuate and seek to legitimate the existing world order. Realism and structural realism in particular present a worldview that is not subject to change because either human nature or the international system will always serve to maintain inequalities of power. Realists reinforce the status quo which favours ruling elites in the industrialized world and perpetuates the subordinate status of the global south.

Cox rejects the notion of a scientific, value-free, positivist approach to international relations, insisting that '[t]heory is always for someone, and for some purpose' (Cox, 1981: 128). The theoretical impulse to solve problems actually masks an agenda that maintains the existing order. Instead, critical theory (which is derived from Marxist thought) has emancipatory potential to understand the existing system and its unequal power relationships and how those dynamics can be transformed to create a fairer world. Cox is clear though that the existing structure of the world order cannot be changed by international movements or wresting control of international institutions. A new historic bloc can only emerge through building up a national socio-political base for change (Cox, 2010: 224).

Another way of understanding power relationships in a global capitalist system, which has its origins in Marxist thought, is world system theory. World system theorists expand the class struggle within states and use a global analysis to project regional class divisions. For IR scholars such as Immanuel Wallerstein (1974; 1980; 1989), the most important class divisions are those between regions of the world. Wallerstein identifies developed manufacturing states as constituting the core region. This core uses its power, derived from its wealth, to concentrate surplus from the poorer countries in what he terms the periphery. While Lenin foresaw developed capitalist nations exporting capital to their colonies, world system theorists believe the failure to do so perpetuates regional inequality. The manufacturing regions in the core have greater capital, higher wages and a more highly skilled workforce than the peripheral nations situated in the global south. The periphery is an extraction region defined by agricultural economies with raw materials, low-paid and low-skilled workers.

When conflict occurs among the great powers, as it did during the two world wars and the Cold War, such conflict is the result of competition among the core states for the right to exploit the periphery. Between the core and the periphery a buffer zone of semi-peripheral regions exist, which have some manufacturing and capital accumulation. States in the periphery cooperate in this system through not only the coercion of core states but also the assimilation of norms and a system, which is flexible enough for peripheral states to become semi-peripheral or core. The prospect of progression to the core keeps disaffected states in the periphery from rebellion against the overall system. Understandings of core, semi- and periphery are not confined to nations but are also found within them. The power relationship is based on relationship to (and access to) the means of production.

Feminism

So far, our discussion has been concerned with power relationships that consider states, institutions or classes. We now turn our attention to those based on gender relations. Feminist theorists have tended to be marginalized in disciplines that have been largely dominated by privileged middle- and upper-class white men. In Martin Griffiths' book *Fifty Key Thinkers in International Relations* (1999) it is not without significance that only four of those selected were women (three of whom specialized in gender). However, gender is beginning to play a far more significant role in providing an alternative lens to mainstream IR approaches and a critique to norms of unequal gendered power relations. Although there are a number of different feminist approaches, all are united in using gender to highlight inequalities in the power relationships between men and women and seek to increase women's visibility as actors within international relations.

A critique of realism, the dominant paradigm in IR for much of the second half of the twentieth century, tends to be the starting point of feminist understanding in IR theory. Realism's separation of domestic and international politics reflects the division between the public and private sphere that traditionally consigned women to the role of supporting actors in a man's world. The social and cultural construction of gendered identities with masculinity associated with power, authority, aggression, rationality, calculation and an assumption of leadership in public roles fits into a realist perception of how states should and do behave (Viotti and Kauppi, 2010: 378). Femininity, on the other hand, stereotypically defines women as passive, submissive, nurturing, sensitive, caring and more focused on the private realm. Therefore, according to the implied assumptions in realism, for women to play a part in international politics they are required to assume a masculine role, which incorporates power, balance of power politics, coercive diplomacy and a willingness to act unilaterally.

This assumption is embodied in the following examples. Margaret Thatcher, UK prime minister during the Falklands conflict, and Secretaries of State Madeleine Albright and Condoleezza Rice personified this masculine approach to international relations. Albright infamously declared that the death of half a million Iraqi children, through the imposition of sanctions in Iraq during the 1990s, was a 'price worth paying' to contain Saddam Hussein, and Rice was George W. Bush's national security advisor and as such a leading proponent of the decision to invade Iraq in 2003. Difference feminists have adopted an essentialist approach and argued that men and women are equal but different and that promoting women to leading positions within the military and foreign policy-making hierarchy would substantively change the course of international relations. Others, citing the actions of women when placed in positions of power, suggest that the international system is masculine and this is what needs to be radically overhauled to end the imbalance in gendered power relationships. This is equally true of neo-liberal theorists who adopt masculinist assumptions about the interactions of autonomous actors (Goldstein and Pevehouse, 2010: 136–48).

Radical feminists are far more concerned about the referent object in international relations and security. While realist and liberal scholars emphasize states or the system as the referent object, radical feminists such as Cynthia Enloe (1989) and Sandra Whitworth (1994) highlight the individual. In order to understand power relationships we need to consider who and what are omitted as much as are included. Enloe's study of what goes on in and around military bases demonstrates previously ignored issues of gendered domination and exploitation. The patriarchal role of the military is portrayed in traditional theory as selflessly protecting 'good' women – that is, wives, mothers, sisters and daughters – while simultaneously overlooking or exploiting the contribution of other women and ethnic minorities that sustain the system by providing cooking, cleaning and sexual services.

Radical feminists, including constructivists, critical theorists, post-modernists and post-colonialists reject positivist assumptions and argue instead that the underlying assumptions of traditional IR need challenging. While there are clearly differences in perspective between these different theoretical positions, they each challenge the claims to truth adopted by traditional approaches. Post-colonialists reject the notion that females can be categorized as a homogeneous entity and highlight the imbalance in power relationships resulting from race, class, sexuality and history. Postmodernists and constructivists challenge the notion of femininity and masculinity as socially constructed and seek to deconstruct those taken-for-granted assumptions. They see such a revised discourse as emancipatory in seeking to challenge prevailing norms in IR by providing visibility to the role of women as both referent objects (the focus of academic attention) and actors in IR.

Constructivism

Constructivist thinking also emerged as a result of a critique of structural realist thinking. Alexander Wendt's seminal article 'Anarchy is What States Make of It' (1992) and subsequent book *The Social Theory on International Politics* (1999) attempted to present a different reality ignored by neo-realism. For Wendt, the ontological depiction of power-maximizing autonomous actors seeking to survive in an anarchic world order becomes a self-fulfilling prophecy. Instead, what is needed, according to Wendt and fellow constructivists, is an appreciation of how and why states act in the way they do: how do identity and ideas actually shape the foreign policy options that are pursued? For constructivists, norms and new ideas drive state action rather than naked power interests. Constructivists are therefore concerned to examine how debates are framed and ideas and identities constructed to determine which issues are securitized and the discourse used to shape those identities.

> To analyze the social construction of international politics is to analyze how processes of interaction produce and reproduce the social structures – cooperative or conflictual – that shape actors' identities and interests and the significance of their material contexts. (Wendt, 1995: 79)

Constructivist accounts of domestic and international politics demonstrate how social movements, non-governmental organizations and international organizations each play their part in helping shape identity and norms of appropriate behaviour. While rejecting the inevitability and permanence of existing power relations, constructivists are not necessarily part of an emancipatory project in that examining how ideas and identities form and how they shape behaviour at individual, state and system level does not mean that relationships can or should change. Power is not the raison d'être of constructivist theory, but in examining identity and norm formation power can be seen to reside with those who construct those norms and identities.

Poststructuralism

Poststructuralists, inspired by philosophers such as Michel Foucault, Jean-François Lyotard, Jacques Derrida and Jean Baudrillard, seek to go beyond the structuralist claims of neo-Marxists such as Althusser and Wallerstein and positivist approaches to politics. They reject the idea that structure takes precedence over agency and express a commitment to analytical principles that deconstruct texts, explore subtexts and seek out omissions in discourse on issues as diverse as race, class, gender and individuals to reveal the meanings underneath what we say and mean. Poststructuralism is both normative and critical in that it deconstructs traditional interpretations of reality, especially those that would posit a grand theory of the world or a linear approach to human progress. They reject notions of a single objective truth or value-free science and turn their attention, following Foucault (1979, 2002), to the three key areas of identity, power/knowledge and representations/interpretation (Jørgensen, 2010: 165).

For Foucault power is located everywhere, in all relationships, in institutions and is 'rooted in the whole network of the social' (Foucault, 2002: 346–7). We all operate according to rules and power relationships that we have no control over. We all live out roles that are constructed rather than innate, and determined by power relationships that may change from one role into another. Power and the subject are indivisible and, once a role is constructed, that construction defines how we act and what we say (Smith, 2009: 44). Foucault is particularly interested in 'projects of docility', about how society is disciplined and controlled by processes of surveillance through a combination of 'supervision, control and correction' (Foucault, 1979, 2002: 345). Rather than coercion Foucault, like Gramsci (1971), believes that socialization – the acceptance of values and norms by society – comes about through discourse rather than material structures. While the state increases its power and control over daily life, Foucault contends that all power relationships are resisted and, along with identity, contested (Foucault, 2002: 345).

Conclusion

Power is one of the defining characteristics of the study of Politics. Some theories such as pluralism and elitism seek to locate power in individuals or agents, through examining the behaviour of different actors. Others, such as Marxism and some feminists, suggest that power is located in the political, economic and social system that we operate within. In this chapter we have discussed some of the different facets of power and sought to highlight how the way in which we view power is shaped by our perception of the world. The study of politicians' behaviour favours an agency over a structural approach to power. Individual or group political actors identified by pluralist and elitist approaches are assumed to have power because of the decisions they take or do not take and what is and is not discussed or placed on policy agendas.

In contrast to the above emphasis upon individual elite level behaviour, Marxist and neo-Marxist writers have taken a more structural approach and argued that agency, when it is exerted, is exerted by the bourgeoisie or ruling class. In this way, power has systemic features. The individuals are interchangeable but capitalism operates exclusively in the interest of the ruling class nationally and internationally. Globalization extends class domination and exploitation to the developing world in the periphery and semi-periphery of world regions. Gramsci and Cox suggest that no longer does this exploitation involve coercion, but through rewarding working-class elites, and rulers in developing countries cooperate in their own exploitation by consenting to prevailing ruling-class norms. We have seen how realists have reduced the power relationship in IR to power maximization in a system based on statism, survival and self-help in which the powerful states maintain their privileged status and dominate the weaker. Liberal institutionalists consider that the world is far more interconnected and has the potential through increased cooperation to be more pacific. In emphasizing the democratic peace and international institutions as overcoming anarchy, liberal institutionalists actually situate power within the status quo of the developed nations.

Feminists insist that traditional approaches to Political Science and IR theory ignore the role of women and perpetuate gender inequality throughout the world. They draw attention to patriarchal systems that promote a masculinist worldview, reinforcing exploitative social systems and relationships. We also considered constructivist approaches that highlight the importance of identity and ideas in establishing norms of behaviour, which serve to highlight that power resides with those framing and talking the debate. Poststructuralists who deconstruct texts, subtexts and omissions from dominant narratives in order to expose dominant power relationships and challenge that which is taken for granted also develop this approach.

When it comes to doing Politics, we need to consider which approach is best suited to explain whatever issue we are seeking to explore. Many theorists will make use of one approach to explain every area they research, while others will use a combination governed by the issue concerned. If a theorist argues that that class or gender is the most important issue and that this discourse underpins everything else, they will necessarily see every aspect of the private and public realms as being governed by power relationships reflecting this. In examining power relationships, it is necessary to inject a final note of caution. By their very nature power and influence are very difficult concepts to prove. As we have seen, power consists in assumptions and is as much about what is unseen as what is seen, about consent as much as coercion, about structures and agency; but the key question is: how do we prove power and influence? The counterfactual argument must always occupy our attention: would anything different have occurred if this hypothesized power relationship did not exist? Over the remainder of the book we consider power as one aspect among many as we examine substantive issues at the heart of Politics.

Reflection

Why do you think power is so important in the study of Politics?

What are the weaknesses of Robert Dahl's pluralist approach to power?

Lukes identifies three dimensions of power; which do you think is the most convincing and why?

Can you think of other dimensions of power?

What are the similarities and differences between Political Science and IR theorizations on power?

How effective are pluralists and elitists at accounting for political change?

Which do you consider more important – military or economic power? Why do you think this?

Do you agree with Robert Cox that 'theory is always for someone, and for some purpose'?

How important are class relationships today and what, if anything, can they teach us about power?

Is Foucault right to suggest that all power is resisted and identity contested?

Seminar activities

Examine the lead political story in today's newspaper. Consider and discuss the importance of power in the story.

What evidence is there of power at work?

How can we tell?

Who is exercising power and for what purpose?

Does the story provide us with enough information to make a judgement?

If not, what other information would we need?

Which theory best explains the use of power within the story?

Are there other explanations that would explain power as well?

Chapter 3

The State

Introduction

The state is often assumed to be the starting point of analysis in the traditional study of Politics. This dominance has been challenged in recent years by empirical phenomena (and subsequent theoretical debates) around issues such as globalization and the perceived move away from government to governance. Some scholars have argued that there has been too little focus upon the state and that it needs to be brought back in to our analysis (Skocpol, 1985). Given the importance of the state for understanding our discipline(s), even if in our later work we come to reject its centrality, we need to begin with an understanding of what it is and how it operates. We do this by asking questions such as: what role does the state play in society? Is the state powerful? How can we understand what happens within and between states? We give an overview here of some of the different ways in which political scientists/analysts and IR scholars have sought to address these questions.

There are different ways in which we can conceive of 'the state' and this depends upon our ontological positioning. Foundationalists might conceive of it organizationally and conceptualize it as an institution, a cohesive unit in its own right; or it may be viewed as a sum of its individual parts – such as government, bureaucracy and individuals within state organizations (as behavioural and RCT accounts might suggest). It can also be viewed functionally, in terms of its objectives, and/or its outcomes and capacity to act (as with Marxist and some IR theories). It can be viewed as a set of rules and procedures, and an outcome of political action. Anti-foundationalists might suggest that it can be viewed not as an object, or a thing, but as a set of practices which normalize and institutionalize social and political relations (as interpretivist approaches might suggest).

It is important to note that this chapter gives only a brief overview of some of the main ways in which the state is theorized. Within each

64

approach are a series of internal debates, although space prevents us from discussing them in greater detail. This has also been excellently and comprehensively done elsewhere (see, for example, Baylis and Smith, 2004; Dunleavy and O'Leary, 1987; Hay *et al.*, 2006; Smits, 2009) and this work is drawn on to provide an overview of the dominant theories of the state or state behaviour in the field of Politics and IR. Examples of each position are provided through reference to the recent financial crisis.

Power

Analyzing the state as an institution, as an actor, or as a set of practices involves differing conceptions of power, its location and role in the political process. Those approaches which view the state as functional and define it in terms of its capacity to act tend to focus upon the observable outcomes of state behaviour, so the assumption is that when the state chooses to act, or not to act, it is exercising power. We can know this because we can observe evidence of action or inaction.

If, however, we view the state not as an outcome but as a series of practices and a site of political contestation and negotiation, we might view power as lying within the discourse surrounding the state. Why do we accept the state as powerful? Is it because it is supported by a series of legislative instruments, and actions and decisions or deciding not to take a decision, made by agents of the state (such as politicians and bureaucrats) which we can observe and witness taking effect? Or do we do this because of a set of norms which teach us how to behave? Is power rooted in the broader structures which underpin our states? Is the state autonomous or does it serve a particular set of interests? For example, it might be suggested that the state functions to protect and enhance the accumulation of wealth; in this way power is rooted in the system of capitalism. What we cannot do, however, is observe the existence of capitalism; but just because we cannot see this 'thing' called capitalism does not mean it does not exist. We can know of its existence, however, because we can see the effects of capitalism (for example, in the form of legislation by the state which seeks to promote the interests of capital).

Alternatively, if we view the state as a site of contestation and negotiation of political practices which establishes dominant norms as to how we should behave within states, then we might view power as located within the language used to define the reach and remit of the state. The theories below all are reliant on differing conceptions of power, which in turn is important in understanding how these theories work and what this might mean for our analysis.

Box 3.1   Case study. The 'Credit Crunch': the privatization of profit and the socialization of loss?

This case study forms the basis for analysis from the differing perspectives presented within this chapter.

The 9 August 2007 marks the beginning of the period in recent financial history known colloquially as the 'Credit Crunch'. This signalled a massive shift in the transition from a period of previously reasonable prosperity in the financial markets. In prosperous times it is assumed that borrowers feel wealthy and are seeking to increase that wealth through speculation and borrowing; lenders support this borrowing in the belief that assets will rise, making loans safe. However, this bubble burst, a large number of loans went 'bad', and this has been widely presented as a consequence of the collapse in the housing markets in the US, UK and in parts of Europe (for a comprehensive account see Gamble, 2009).

Consumers in the UK and US had been granted loans on relaxed criteria, irrespective of whether those loans were repayable, and had become increasingly unable to repay those debts. At the same time lenders had been mixing both poor- and good-quality loans together and selling on these packages of debt in a process called 'securitization'. Warnings had come from the IMF, the Bank of International Settlements, the Bank of England and elsewhere of the potential difficulties ahead, but securitization was based upon the assumption that any short-term problems would be eased by strong property markets. However, as borrowers in the subprime mortgage market began to default on their loans, the US housing market began to collapse. Mortgage-backed securities lost their value and the markets began to suffer from lack of confidence.

Foundational positivist approaches

Pluralism and neo-pluralism

Pluralism is foundational in its approach in that its focus is upon the observable nature of the political world. Like elitism it has a strong normative strand. This overt normative positioning is unusual in positivistic accounts, which tend to deny the significance of normative questions (so here already we see a blurring of boundaries). Pluralism's emphasis, however, upon empiricism, combined with its attempt to establish causation and explanation, locates it clearly within a foundational positivist framework.

Pluralism is one of the dominant perspectives in Political Science and some of its assumptions also inform behavioural theories in IR. Pluralism is both a normative and a descriptive theory; that is, it not only describes what is taking place, but it also provides an ideal of how things should be.

Borrowing became much more difficult and expensive as banks stopped lending to their customers and each other. Banks and businesses began to collapse and governments were called in to bail out financial companies such as Freddie Mac and Fannie Mae (in the US), while others, such as Lehman Brothers went into administration. Bank collapse also has an enormous impact upon financial markets, which are premised on norms such as confidence and trust. Loss of confidence in banks and financial companies, economists and financiers argue, mean that credit stops flowing and markets seize up. While this began in the US, the global interconnectivity of finance meant that soon banks across the world were reporting massive losses. The financial markets reacted and stocks and share prices fell. Policy-makers began to respond, in conjunction with large-scale financial institutions. In a bid to inject confidence into the markets, and to get capital flowing again, the European Central Bank and the US Federal Reserve injected cash into financial markets. Governments in the US, UK and across Europe stepped in with deals from the public 'purse' to try and shore up banks and restore faith in the financial markets.

For some on the right, the financial crisis was a political issue, a consequence of the politicization of the housing market or over-regulation of banks; for those on the left this was driven by the private sector, and insufficient regulation (Coates, 2010). For radical accounts crisis is a feature of the capitalist system, and an inherent part of the process of capital accumulation and renegotiation of the state's role in this process (Burnham, 2010). The willingness of governments to intervene and support the financial markets (in a way that states have not been willing to do in other sectors in society, such as manufacturing), has led some to argue that the banks became 'too big to fail' (see, for example, Sorkin, 2009) and arguably, the outcome has been the privatization of profit and the socialization of loss.

These two features do not necessarily have to be linked. We can be normative pluralists while doing analysis from other perspectives. For example, we can offer a Marxist account of state behaviour, and at the same time advance the argument that the world should work in a different (pluralistic) way. Pluralism (as Marxism) does not provide a theory of the state per se, although the basis of pluralism lies in its critique of state monism. As with the other theoretical approaches outlined below, there is some disagreement as to what constitutes pluralism (see Smith, 2006). The aim here, however, is to provide a starting point.

The philosophical basis and roots of pluralism lie in the works of Madison's Federalist Paper no. 10 (Dahl, 1956) and de Tocqueville's *Democracy in America* (1956), which were concerned with the nature of the relationship between state and civil society. Premised upon the assumption that individuals seek to maximize power, clashes are thought to be inevitable, therefore institutional checks and balances need to be in place. Another way this could occur would be through the articulation and expression of interest through groups, who would compete to have their interests heard. The role of groups representing competing interests are seen as significant in preventing absolute power being held within the state.

As a theoretical position, pluralists adopt positivist and behavioural approaches to the analysis of the workings of the state. Bentley and Truman sought to develop an empirical theory that reflected the reality of the workings of the state (see LaVaque-Manty (2006). Pluralism came to prominence in the 1950s and 1960s and can also be seen as embodied in the work of Robert Dahl (1961), who described the workings of the political decision-making process. Here Dahl argued that the political process was open and fluid. There were checks and balances on state power and these took the form of pressure (or interest) groups.

Dahl's approach was a consequence of his empirical observation of the decision-making process in New Haven. From this, operating with an implicit agency-centred view of power (as we discussed in Chapter 2), he argued that, while conflict was an inherent part of the political process, differing groups could be successful in differing policy areas, and as such, he claimed, power was dispersed. His work was characterized by methodological individualism, and assumed that the behaviour of individuals revealed their preferences. By extension this suggests that if there is no observable behaviour, then there are no preferences. If groups don't mobilize to support a particular interest then it is assumed that there is no interest in that particular issue (which of course denies any awareness of the problems of group mobilization [see Olson, 1965], and assumes that individuals are able to identify their own interests in contrast to the Marxist account of false consciousness).

Adopting a behavioural approach (which means a focus upon observation and description), pluralism describes how democracy works and, crucially, is also used to support the normative proposition that this is how democracy should work. The central focus is upon the existence of representative government, elections and interest groups within a state. The existence of representative government alone, while a necessary condition of democracy, is assumed to be insufficient to ensure and protect democracy. As a result, party competition and interest groups are crucial in reflecting the diversity of interests within the polity. Interest groups provide governments with more information about the preferences of the citizens than can be established through the act of voting in elections. Here the state is assumed to be a mirror of civil society, or neutral, acting as an arbiter of competing interests. In Easton's (1953) terminology it is a 'black box', which does not contain or exhibit any interests of its own. Pluralist accounts also assume that different groups can be successful in different areas, but no one group dominates. The ability of interest groups to get their voices heard means that power is assumed to be fragmented and dispersed. This dispersal of power is also used to support normative claims of the democratic benefits of pluralism. Power is also assumed to be observable and was assumed to lie in the hands of those who were making decisions (as in Lukes' first dimension, see Chapter 2).

Lindblom (1977) and Dahl (1982, 1985) provide the foundation to a revised form of pluralism: neo-pluralism. This emerged as a response to both the observations in the 'real world' of policy-making, and to the critiques of pluralism which came from other theoretical perspectives, such as Marxism. Here they highlight the role of capital and the dominance of business interests in the policy process, which provides for less of an equal dispersion of power. Focus remains upon the observable and is the property of individuals, located with those who made the decisions.

Elitism

Alongside pluralism, elite theory has a normative aspect to it (which distinguishes them both from 'harder' scientific approaches within this broad school of thought). However, elitism is an approach which sits

---

Box 3.2 The Credit Crunch: a pluralist view

The emphasis for pluralists is very much upon description of the observable. For pluralists, bankers act as an interest group, seeking support from a neutral state in order to enable them to pursue their interests. Policy-making is open and transparent. While business interests dominate the policy agenda on this particular occasion, on other occasions, and in different policy issues, it is equally likely that alternate interested parties will dominate. Neo-pluralism draws attention to the privileged role of business in this process and, while acknowledging that on other policy matters and debates other interests may be represented, it becomes more likely that business will also play a role, and have their interests recognized. The state in this process is reasonably neutral, responding as an arbiter of demands from pressure groups. While customers withdrew their savings from banks on the brink of collapse, they did not formally organize, and so the assumption within pluralism would be that there was not sufficient support for a particular interest beyond the function fulfilled by representative government (in this instance customers) and therefore groups did not mobilize (although there are critiques of this point, see Olson, 1965). Power is assumed to be located with decision-makers who consider competing demands of interested parties. The focus here is very much upon what can be observed and the role of individuals (agents).

easily in a positivist perspective. Classical elitism has also sought to provide unifying causal laws, akin to the universal laws provided within natural sciences. An example of this is Michels' Iron Law of Oligarchy, which predicted that the emergence and existence of elites was almost inevitable. This he premised upon his empirical investigation into political parties (1911/1959). He argued that leaders may stir the masses out of apathy, but, once organized, the masses will revert to enabling leaders to pursue their own interests, rather than those of the masses.

As with pluralism, elite state theory draws attention to the role of individual actors within a state. There are two strands to elite theory. The normative classical view (derived from Pareto, Mosca and Michels) argues that society should be ruled by a small body of elites; the modern account describes how society operates, rather than how it should operate. Like pluralism, elite theory offers an empirical, behaviouralist and positivist account of the world. In this way, again, focus is upon what can be observed to support a theoretical position. Observation is of particular individuals, or groups of individuals, but the emphasis, as with pluralism is upon description. Elitism provides a direct critique of pluralism (and Marxism), as it highlights the inequalities between the differing ability of groups to influence the policy process (some may have more influence than others).

Elitism rejects the idea that power is diffused (as with pluralism) or that the state is an instrument of the ruling classes (as in Marxism); rather classical elitism argues that power is located within individual elites and is distributed unequally in their interests. The lack of diffusion of power is most notably reflected in the 'non-decision-making' (Bachrach and Baratz, 1962) or second face of power (Lukes, 1974) (see Chapter 2). This is echoed by Schattschneider's (1960) phrase 'mobilization of bias', wherein some interests are organized, and some simply don't reach the agenda in the first place. Elite theorists focus attention upon political leaders and their roles within the state. For C. Wright Mills (1956) there was a 'power elite' of the president, the military and business, with whom decision-making power lay. Throughout their accounts, however, power was located in the hands of individuals and asserted, expressed through their actions and embodied in the state.

Public choice

Public choice theory is a variant of rational choice theory (RCT, see Chapter 1) and as such, with its underpinnings economics, viewed as a 'hard science'. With its emphasis upon empirical observation, causality, explanation and prediction, it can be located firmly within the positivist school of thinking. While pluralism and elitism adhere to a scientific

Box 3.3 The Credit Crunch: an elitist perspective

In the elitist view, we would focus attention upon the role of individual actors, such as political leaders, Bush, Brown, Sarkozy and Merkel, alongside central bank governors and City elites, and their respective roles in investing and seeking to restore faith in the financial markets. As with pluralism, preferences are assumed to be revealed through observable action and attention would also be drawn to the negotiations of those political actors, with other key leaders such as the heads of banks and finance companies such as Northern Rock and Freddie Mac. Attention here is very much on the role of political and business elites acting in concert, and pursuing their own interests. Power is assumed to be concentrated in the hands of these individuals, rather than dispersed as with pluralist accounts. Civil society, and the impact of elite behaviour, is largely neglected in these accounts. In turn, what this means is that the interests of the unemployed or those who have lost their homes and jobs as a consequence of this crisis are organized out of the agenda.

view of the social sciences, the difference between them and public choice is largely in their methodology. While pluralism and elitism tend to focus upon observation and empirical description, rational choice moves away from empirical observation and focuses upon modelling based upon assumptions drawn from economics about individual behaviour. From here, predictions can be made about how individuals will behave in given conditions (this can often mean that, like economics, theories can be modelled in mathematical formulae in order to test what will happen). In the same way that economic theory had been used to account for market 'failure', it was assumed that this form of modelling behaviour could account for 'state failures'.

Public choice as a school of thinking about the state emerged as response and a critique to pluralism in the 1960s; the 1980s saw not only its development as a method of modelling, but also its implementation as a political project and it is usually associated with the new right political agenda. For public choice theorists the state is a source of inefficiency and as a result governments see the state as 'overloaded'. Leaders such as Thatcher and Reagan influenced by this thinking began to seek mechanisms through which the state could be 'rolled back'.

This approach has its roots in classical economic theory. Adam Smith's (1776) *Wealth of Nations* provides an account of competition which starts from the self-interest assumption as the ultimate guarantor of economic prosperity. Smith assumes that self-interest will manifest itself as an 'invisible hand' which guides the market, as, if there is competition, producers will respond by lowering prices, improving quality, in order to satisfy their own profit maximizing self-interest. State intervention, Smith argued, would threaten the functioning of the invisible hand and undermine prosperity. Accepting the assumption that individuals seek to maximize their self-interest, the role of the state, for public choice theorists, is (and should be) one of minimal intervention. In this way, not only is it assumed that the market functions effectively and promotes economic prosperity, but that this is also imbued with political values. For public choice theorists individuals interacting in the market are assumed to be empowered as they are free to enter or exit a market as they so choose. The focus in this approach is the intentional actions of the individual who is assumed to be autonomous; indeed, only a very minimal context is assumed (the market). Given this focus, power is implicitly assumed to be agency-centred.

Bureaucracy was also viewed as an impediment to market efficiency, inefficient and unwieldy (Niskanen, 1971). One of the reasons for this was that bureaucrats within governmental organizations could also be analyzed according to the principles of public choice theory. So, the logic was extended which suggested that just as self-interested individuals would maximize profits in a market, bureaucracies, and more specifically the bureaucrats within them, would seek to maximize their own utility through increasing their departmental budgets, in order to wield greater influence within and across government (Dunleavy, 1991).

Clearly, one of the key difficulties in this approach is the idea that individual behaviour can be modelled in this way and from these starting assumptions. If we assume, for example, that all individuals operate in their own self-interest, then how might we account for acts of kindness and altruism (such as giving to charity)? Moreover, there is a further methodological difficulty, in that rational choice theory was just that: a theory. It was a simplification of the world, rather than a normative statement about the way in which the world should work. One of the difficulties with the public choice approach to politics is that it strips politics of all its political properties; for example, it fails to incorporate ideas about justice and equality (we discuss this in more detail in Chapter 12).

Realism and neo-realism

Realism and neo-realism are both foundational and positivist. Their focus is upon the real world and an attempt to provide a realistic account of it (hence the term 'realism'). It assumes that there is a real world out there available for us to discover through recourse to empirical observation. Realism sought to develop as an explicitly scientific approach generating causal laws and a universal science of politics, although this was challenged by the behaviouralist school of thought. However, despite

Box 3.4 The Credit Crunch: a new right perspective

For the new right, economic crises are linked to inefficiencies of government where government was compared with private businesses. Government intervention is only necessary to ensure the smooth functioning of the market; light touch regulation is all that is required to provide for a solution. The injection of cash into the markets by governments and institutions should stimulate markets, but extra regulation is not a requirement. For the new right the problem lay with politicians seeking to provide home ownership for those who could not afford it. The aim to increase home ownership was seen as a politically motivated move, rather than an economic one. For the new right, the problem was inherently political: politicians were trying to bring about outcomes that the markets simply would not sustain.

In this view, financial markets are assumed to view banks as more credible than politicians; they will 'reward' banks who start to lend to each other to stimulate the market. Politicians are assumed to be self-interested vote maximizers and, with this motivation in mind, likely to introduce a series of measures designed to encourage voters to spend money (such as a reduction in VAT) and to encourage the banks to lend to each other (such as state guarantees) to avoid further bank collapse and loss of voters' investments. The action of politicians, however, is assumed to be motivated by the desire to maximize the votes which will be cast for them in the next election. (For an alternative rationalist account of these events, see Minford, 2010.)

In this account, then, power is firmly located with individual decision-makers, but this differs from pluralism as this is derived not from observation about behaviour, but from a set of economic assumptions made about the motivations of individuals.

differences over methodology, this debate took place within a positivist paradigm.

Realism in IR emerged in the late 1930s/1940s as a result largely of the failings of Idealism. Idealism developed after World War I and sought to promote peace based on harmony of interests between states and institutionalized in the League of Nations. However, the failings of the League, evident in its inability to deter the Italian invasion of Abyssinia, Japanese invasion of Manchuria and German rearmament and aggression leading to World War II, challenged idealist orthodoxy. The failure of idealism was ruthlessly exposed by E. H. Carr (1939/1946) in *The Twenty Years' Crisis*. Carr lampooned idealism as 'utopian' and criticized its worldview based on harmony of interests. For Carr, the world was based not on harmony but realistically on privilege, conflicting and competing interests where 'have-nots' seek to overturn the status quo and the powerful seek to preserve and advance their own interests, ultimately with recourse to violence.

Following the outbreak of World War II, realism rose to prominence as a descriptive alternative, which seemed to characterize world events; it not only replaced idealism, but also remains one of the dominant theoretical approaches within IR. Morgenthau's (1955) *Politics Among Nations* was one of the founding texts, and was premised upon a Hobbesian view of human nature; that human nature was essentially selfish. For realism, state behaviour can be read from this assumption. States are regarded as the central actors in politics, and it is the self-interest of states, in the pursuit of power, which motivates behaviour. Morgenthau's view was scientific, in that he assumed that politics was 'governed by objective laws that have their roots in human nature' (1955:4) and this suggested, first, the existence of 'laws' of politics and, second, that to understand politics we need to understand human nature, which was reflected in the behaviour of states. As with public choice theories (above) realism starts from the assumption of individual (states) maximizing self-interest. While rationalistic in its approach, it also has a strong normative element, in that it asserts that this is how states should behave given these 'laws' of behaviour. While noting the existence of an anarchic international system, with no overarching authority, states are considered the key actors, indeed autonomous actors, who seek to maximize their power base.

While previous approaches we have discussed in this chapter seek to explain influences upon the state, realism assumes that this state is a unified actor. Power is assumed to be observable and defined in terms of military capabilities (and given the historical context of this theorizing, and its focus upon observable 'real world' events, it is not difficult to understand why).

However, building from this base, structural or neo-realists argue that, while we can understand behaviour on the world stage through reference to states, it is insufficient to look at them alone. Rather, it is the structure of the international system itself that determines how states behave. Concerned with the scientism that informed realism, Kenneth Waltz (1979) argued that if we want to understand why states behave the way they do, we need to look at the arena in which they are pursuing their self-interest; that is, a world stage which is characterized by a lack of central authority and anarchy. He suggests that in order to understand behaviour we need to understand the system as a whole and therefore we also need to look at interstate behaviour. While initially, this implies all states are at the same starting point (for Waltz, all states were 'like units' in that they are sovereign and therefore comparable units of analysis), the way in which we can understand outcomes is a consequence of the unequal distribution of capabilities (or power) of sovereign states.

Power, then, is viewed as a mechanism to provide states with security in an anarchic system. States are assumed to rationally pursue power-maximizing strategies to maximize their own security, in order to maintain their survival. As a consequence of this, states must pursue power to protect their own interests; indeed, this is viewed as a rational outcome of the system in which they operate. This, therefore, is a structuralist account which focuses upon the interstate system (or structure) itself to explain behaviour. For realists, power is an end in itself defined through primarily military capabilities, and the capacity to coerce other states. For neo-realists power is slightly differently defined, in terms of the way in which it positions a state and its position in the international order; it is this positioning which in turn affects and shapes a state's behaviour.

The lack of central authority in the global arena is viewed in this perspective, as a key difference between national and domestic politics, as is the greater likelihood of the use of violence at the international level for states to ensure their survival in an anarchic system. As states seek to increase their own security, so in turn this is assumed to fuel insecurity in other states. This is termed the 'security dilemma' and can account, for example, for the arms race during the Cold War. Faced with the perception of threat from the other, both the US and the USSR sought to maintain their position in the international arena and, more significantly, ensure their own survival. Expanding (military) power, while

Box 3.5 The Credit Crunch: a realist/ neo-realist perspective

What we can see from a realist or neo-realist perspective is that states are seeking to maximize their own security and survival in financial terms. The human nature assumption leads us to understand that states are inherently self-interested and so will impose measures (such as support for failing banks) which will benefit themselves, and maintain their position in the international system. While there is a lack of central authority to impose solutions upon states, a series of interventionist measures have been taken by successive states, in their own interest. This might occur through mechanisms other than military power, but states are aware that their position is supported and backed up by the threat of violence if they perceive their security (in terms of survival) to be significantly threatened. While the threat of violence or use of military force has not been used (as with the realist perspective), the position of states within the international system has in part structured their response to the crisis. Historically, the inter-war years provide an account of the difficulties posed by states working individually in their own interests to address severe economic problems of deflation and unemployment. What a realist account might show is how to problematize the current situation and the potential difficulties which may lie ahead. The underlying emphasis upon science also suggests that we may be able to make predictions and provide causal explanations or accounts of state behaviour.

potentially enabling each state to feel more secure, generated insecurity in the other and vice versa.

For realists, states are the central 'units' or levels of analysis: they are the actors which 'count'. However, critics draw attention to the role of non-state actors, such as the role of non-state institutions (the World Bank), transnational corporations and movements or networks (such as terrorist organizations) in shaping world politics. For critics, challenges to state sovereignty and authority also arise from issues or events such as globalization and climate change, which do not respect state borders or sovereignty.

Neo-liberal institutionalism and internationalism

The other main approach to studying the state in the international arena, so allowing for the state to be seen as a micro-level actor, comes in the form of neo-liberal institutionalism and internationalism. Implied within this approach is, again, the importance of observable and measurable phenomena, and, as such, there is an implicit commitment to a behavioural and positivist framework. In its contemporary form it has come to be referred to as neo-liberalism (although this is not to be confused with the political project of the same name), the umbrella term for its two main variants, liberal institutionalism and liberal internationalism, which retain a commitment to the values of liberalism.

Neo-liberalism accepts the neo-realist premise of an anarchic system, but stresses that this should foster cooperation, rather than provide for the possibility of conflict. Neo-liberals also downplay the significance of military as a measure of power. In this view (and in critique of realism), states should surrender some of their sovereignty in the wider and mutually beneficial interests of economic growth, or to address regional issues (such as with the creation of the European Union). While accepting the rationalist assumption of the pursuit of self-interest, in contrast to realists, neo-liberals emphasize cooperation. Liberals argue that the dominance of sovereign states is also being challenged by the existence of increasingly powerful transnational actors, but that states can achieve their goals by working with other states and non-state actors in order to achieve mutually beneficial outcomes. The debate between neo-realists and neo-liberals (known as the neo-neo debate) became one of the key theoretical debates within IR (Nye, 1988).

Offering a critique of neo-realism, liberal institutionalists draw attention to possibilities for cooperation in the international arena, and their focus is upon relationships and institutions (such as the UN) which facilitate this. While sharing with realism a focus upon the self-interest of states, liberal institutionalism acknowledges that states are not the only actors in the international arena. Institutions are viewed as a mechanism through which cooperation can be achieved. Still under the umbrella of neo-liberalism, the liberal internationalists recognize the need and opportunities for cooperation, but also focus their attention upon the interdependence between states, particularly at the level of trade/economics. Here we see the concept of complex interdependence admitted into analysis. What this means is, given the interconnectivity of states and non-state actors in the international arena, when changes take place in one part of the system this is likely have an impact elsewhere (Keohane and Nye, 1977). So, rather than change impacting on a single state, changes which impact upon one state are likely to have a ripple effect elsewhere (and this can be seen with the Credit Crunch example given below). The emphasis in the neo-liberal framework though is upon regimes and institutions as a means of enabling cooperation so that states may secure their interests, but that this can be mutually beneficial, rather, than at the expense of another state, as in the realist view.

Both realism/neo-realism and liberal institutionalism/neo-liberalism focus their attention on anarchy in the international system, but view its

Box 3.6 The Credit Crunch and neo-liberal institutionalism

With a focus upon the observable, neo-liberal institutionalist approaches would draw attention to the role of institutions in addressing the 'Credit Crunch'. Here then attention would be focused not only on the behaviour of states, but also the role of institutions, such as the IMF and World Bank in facilitating that cooperation. Neo-liberal internationalists would also draw attention to the complex interdependence which characterized the Credit Crunch. First, we can see the effect of this economic interdependence through the way in which the crash in the US housing market exerted extreme pressure, the effects of which spread well beyond the borders of that state. Given the interconnectivity of the financial markets and institutions which were implicated in the housing market crash, the fallout from this went far beyond the United States. Transnational corporations are also significant actors. For example, the collapse of Lehman Brothers not only affected its host country, the US. Losses were felt also, first, in the loss of jobs in countries were Lehman Brothers had offices, such as the UK. Second, the collapse of a bank sent shock waves through the financial markets. The effects of this were not localized to US markets, but the perception of instability and insecurity in the financial system was felt in stock markets across the world, with share prices tumbling on the Nikkei in Japan, the FTSE in London and the Dow Jones in the US. This economic interdependence, then, requires not simply localized, state-based solutions to secure their own interests; neo-liberals would look to international financial institutions such as the World Bank and the IMF to support and/or provide cooperative solutions in the interests of all states involved.

impact in differing ways. What this means is that attention becomes focused upon states and, while liberal institutionalists admit non-state actors, the assumption is still made that politics takes place at the level of the state. This negates or at least downplays the role of identities, the relationship between the state and civil society, and political culture. Critiques also point to the elitist nature of these institutions, which arguably reinforce existing power capabilities of states. For example, critics point to the World Trade Organization as representing the interests of global corporations, which with an adherence to free market principles fail to fully address issues such as human rights. Further, neither of these approaches asks critical normative questions about the distribution of power to the extent that this may lead to severe inequalities both between and within states.

Foundational critical/scientific realist approaches

Marxism

Marxism accepts that there is a real world 'out there', but, crucially, in contrast to the earlier approaches we have looked at, Marxism also assumes that there are underlying structures that exist that we can't necessarily observe. Despite our inability to see them, we know that they exist because we can see their effects. Marxism is located in the critical/scientific realist position as it accepts a degree of scientism in that it does provide for universal laws (such as within capitalism). It also, however, draws from anti-foundationalism and so, while we might be able to make predictions and establish the existence of causal relationships, what is critical here is that we cannot observe the source of these causal relationships. (For example, we all know that capitalism exists, because we see its effects, but we cannot see or touch this thing called capitalism per se.) In contrast to the approaches we discussed earlier, Marxism provides us with accounts of the state both as a micro- and macro-level actor and the overview below reflects these two differing levels of analysis.

Marxism in Political Science

Marxism provides a critique of capitalism and liberal democracy. While Marxism as a method of government is no longer evident, Marxism is still able to provide a powerful analysis of capitalism which is the dominant economic order in the international, as well as domestic, system today. For Marxist theorists any attempt to understand events within the international arena needs to be premised upon an understanding of global capitalism. Underlying structures shape and influence outcomes and these structures are those of capitalism. We may not be able to see capitalism but we can see its effects. The historical materialism which characterizes Marxism means that we need to understand historical development as a reflection of economic development within society. Here the central tension is between the means of production (such as labour) and the relations of production (such as the technological and industrial relations combined with the broader structures, such as that of wage labour and private property) which serve as an economic base for society. Legal, social and political institutions reflect this economic base in a superstructure (the superstructure is largely the focus of critical theory approaches). Marx provides an account of conflict based upon the tensions between those who control the means of production (who in turn have the opportunity to shape the economic base and therefore the superstructure which governs all aspects of life) and the workers.

In Marxism the class conflict is the starting point of analysis. As Hay (2006c) observes, there is no one or unified theory of the state within Marxism, but there are common themes. First, that the existence of class conflict is central to analysis and, second, that the role of the state is to secure the long-term interests of capital. In this way, understanding the state provides a mechanism through which the interests of the ruling classes are advanced. Governments and institutions develop to advance and support capital accumulation. While there is divergence within Marxist theory the dominant view is that the state is instrumentalist; the state is viewed as an instrument of the dominant or ruling class, meaning that there will be some state intervention into economic affairs in order to secure the long-term interests of capital. Power is located structurally, within the capitalist system. It is not necessarily observable, but its effects can be identified. This structural reading of the location of power, however, downplays the intentionality of individuals in the process (in contrast to elitism and pluralism). Political and economic changes and adaptations can be understood through revealing the contradictions within the structures, rather than through the actions of individuals.

There is debate about the character of the state itself and the extent to which the state itself is capitalist (Poulantzas, 1969) or a reflection of a capitalist society (Miliband, 1969). For Miliband, power lies with the personnel of the state (so has an approach which highlights the role of individual agents within the state), whereas for Poulantzas it is the state, rather than its personnel, which is engaged in the reproduction of economic relations. However, whether or not the state is contingent upon its personnel, the state, in Marxist theory is the site through which class conflict is negotiated, reproduced and provides the conditions through which the long-term interests of capital are secured. As such, in order to understand crises in capitalism, we need to reflect upon the role of the state as economic regulator.

The work of Marx was influenced by philosophical idealism and the role of ideas is picked up in this tradition by Gramsci and his notion of hegemony. Here the ruling classes are able to dominate not only through the existence of the state apparatus, but through the existence of a set of ideas, a set of ideological societal norms that are constructed as common sense. The success of this ideological project means that however much people may feel alienated from the prevailing societal order, at the same time an alternative is inconceivable (and this is discussed in more detail in Chapter 9).

Marxism and global capitalism (an IR approach)

Marxism provides a theory of conflict (in contrast to theories of cooperation as proposed by neo-liberals above) and draws attention to exploitation as a means of understanding how and why the world operates in the way that it does.

In Marxism a number of different approaches have emerged at international level; focus here will be upon world systems theory. In the Marxist tradition, Immanuel Wallerstein (1974; 1980; 1989) argues that we need to understand the international arena historically, in order that we can account for change. We can understand the international

---

Box 3.7 The Credit Crunch: a domestic Marxist perspective

The state intervenes to prop up the banks in order to secure the longer-term interests of capital, to maintain the system and ensure its longer-term survival. In this way Marxism shows us that we need to look beyond that which we directly observe. Financial crises, in this approach, are bought about by the inherent contradictions of capitalism; that is, the need to maximize profit (and thus, in this example, extend borrowing) to the extent that workers can no longer afford to consume. If workers are not consuming/purchasing, capitalists are unable to realize their profits. It is this contradiction which accounts for the emergence of the crisis, and within these periods of crisis opportunity emerges for agency to be exhibited.

The hegemonic aspect is revealed in that, despite the economic crisis, the global nature of which can be argued to have revealed a fundamental contradiction in the contemporary capitalist system: state responses have been to attempt to rebuild the system, rather than consider an alternative. For example, the Green New Deal has posed an alternative solution, faced with the three crises – finance, world peak oil and climate change – yet successive governments still seek solutions within the existing capitalist system to restore the economic system to its pre-crisis state.

arena in terms of time (history) and space. The spatial dimension draws attention to the economic roles played by different actors in the world economy. Here Wallerstein draws a core–periphery distinction. The periphery – states in what was then called the Third World and is now referred to as the global South – plays an important counterbalance to excessive demands on wage pressures in the core of industrialized states. This also affects both regions in terms of labour sources and in terms of geographical location for industries, which may be more probable to the core, but are now located outside of the core (think, for example, of call centres located internationally). As wealth is drained to the core from the periphery, the core is reliant upon the periphery to maintain its position, and an exploitative relationship becomes entrenched. This approach denies the significance of states as unitary actors, and draws attention to the system as a whole: in the form of the economic interdependence of the global economy underpinned by global capitalism.

The other aspect Wallerstein draws attention to is the temporal component, and here, in order to account for change (rather than stasis), he draws attention to the cyclical trends of expansion and contraction within the economic system. These cyclical trends, combined with the inherent contradictions and instability of capitalism, mean that every so often there is crisis. What crisis means, though, is not a reversion to the status quo; it can mean not only crisis, but also an opportunity for actors to exert more autonomy when the system is functioning smoothly, and change the structure. Here, power is assumed to be systemically located, shaping economic and subsequently social and political relations.

Box 3.8 The Credit Crunch: Marxism and global capitalism

The kind of excessive lending in pursuit of profit, which characterizes the Credit Crunch, can be seen historically in the international arena, where Western banks lent excessively to developing/Third World regimes. These countries found themselves unable to repay debts and turned to the IMF (heavily controlled by Western countries). Third World countries were required to implement neo-liberal policies which would further entrench the core–periphery relationship ensuring a continuation of capital accumulation by the core (West). Simultaneously, while the Credit Crunch may represent a crisis for the core, what Marxist analysis highlights is that very little has changed in terms of the global structures of capitalism; indeed, the core is still reliant upon exploitation of the periphery. And so, while contractions may manifest themselves within the core (as noted in Box 3.3), global capitalism remains unchallenged as the same underlying capitalist processes are in operation. This exploitation continues to be necessary for the system to maintain or regain equilibrium. In this sense, the Credit Crunch represents little change to the established order of exploitation.

Anti-foundational interpretivist approaches

The two following perspectives provide a critique and alternate positions to some of the mainstream theorizing detailed above. Here the assumption is that there is not necessarily one real world out there; rather there are competing truths and interpretations of the way in which we can understand them. In order to reflect upon how our social world is constructed, we cannot simply focus upon that which is observable and measurable; rather we need to be aware of contingent factors which may shape social and political relationships (such as ideas and identities). Methodologically the ways in which this can be accessed are, first, through the acceptance that these factors may play a role in our analyses and, second, that a way in which we can uncover these is critique. Crucially, these approaches highlight the way in which power is contested and negotiated, rather than existing as 'given', as assumed by the positivist accounts.

Social constructivism

Social constructivism is a relative latecomer to IR theory, in that it emerged in the 1980s as a response to the IR theories noted above, but grew in prominence following the end of the Cold War. Constructivism focuses attention upon the role of ideas, discourse and the way in which identities and interests can shape behaviour. Developed as a critique of the neo-realist/neo-liberal debate and drawing upon critical theory, constructivism draws attention to the way in which ideas and identities might construct how states perceive their interests (rather than factors that earlier debates had defined materially, such as power, geographic and systemic location). Here the work of Ruggie (1983) challenged Waltz's view of the state system. In order to understand state interaction and behaviour, we needed to understand the international, interstate, transnational and domestic levels of interaction. Following on from this, Ashley (1984) argued that we cannot simply accept concepts such as sovereignty as a given, but that we need to recognize that this is something which is socially constructed for a purpose: to enable states to pursue their own objectives. Against the individualism of realism, he argued that society can shape the individual, and from this we can see how history plays a role in shaping the interests, identities and capabilities of states. Here then constructivists draw attention to the existence of norms, which guide and influence behaviour, and the way in which they are constructed.

In contrast to earlier accounts, social constructivism highlights the interaction between agents as playing a role in constructing the social and political world. Here agents are not simply automatons, but are acknowledged as being imbued with values and ideas. These ideas and values inform behaviour and in turn agents construct institutions which reflect identities and values, while at the same time these institutions reflect and shape individuals' behaviour and identities through the presence of certain norms. As such, recognition of these processes can enable us to understand why change occurs.

Poststructuralism

For poststructuralists the state is not a cohesive unit (as implied by some of the earlier approaches we have looked at), rather it is a site of contestation, and series of interactions and processes within defined systems of meaning. The state is not a thing, but a set of processes and practices. Power is not observable in the way pluralists and elitists, for example, would view it. Rather power is bound up with knowledge. Here a Foucauldian view of power would draw attention to the way power is dispersed throughout society which encourages particular forms of behaviour and discourages others (see Chapter 2). State power is derived through control of these practices and the generation of norms of behaviour. However, we are reminded in poststructuralism that the state is not a monolithic entity; rather the state embodies a range of agencies and practices generating a variety of mechanisms of control and types of knowledge which in turn mean that areas of social and political life become available for political intervention or governmental action (Finlayson and Martin, 2006: 167).

In this approach, the focus is upon the way in which meaning can be understood and actions need to be understood through reference to those social meanings. Beliefs and norms are studied as they are manifested within institutions and frame actions. What this perspective illustrates is that we cannot understand behaviour simply as a consequence of the assumptions we are making about individual motivation (as, for example, public choice theory does). As such, narratives are another way in which we can understand meaning. Accounts can be given of political action by discussing practices and institutions, how they are and how they came to be preserved. In short, social and political action can only be understood through reference to the framework of meaning within which it is situated.

Rather than providing us with a theory of state behaviour as with foundational approaches, what this perspective encourages us to consider is that there may be alternate discourses and competing conceptions of the role of the state (indeed, even the possibility of the non-existence of the state) in contemporary society. Poststructuralists draw attention to the way in which concepts are constructed to support the existence of the state (for example, sovereignty) and the way in which these concepts

Box 3.9   The Credit Crunch: a poststructural and constructivist perspective

In most of the other approaches to understanding the Credit Crunch, we looked at material factors in analysis. Here, social constructivism and post-structuralism draw attention to the discursive practices employed in this scenario and the way in these embody a set of norms which become institutionalized and normalized. From this perspective we can see that the Credit Crunch was constructed as a financial crisis. The word 'crisis' has negative connotations, requiring the need for action. Here, then, the way in which the Credit Crunch was framed as a 'crisis' necessitated state action, as this was not simply about the collapse of a number of companies, but was presented as a threat to the existence of our social order. What these approaches enable us to reflect upon is the narrative and discourses within which this event took place. Governments began to refer to the Credit Crunch as a global financial crisis. Thus we see clear attempts by governments, to disassociate themselves with the financial markets (which had been deregulated by them). Where banks have been nationalized, governmental discourses have positioned the public as stakeholders, yet there is no opportunity for publics to intervene and influence the running or control of the banks. The public have been constructed as a 'silent partner' benefiting the interests of capital. The state provides a site of contestation, where this 'crisis' takes place and is played out. In an era of internationalization of economies and the notion of globalization – which for some, has weakened the remit and relevance of contemporary states – the Credit Crunch provides an opportunity for the state to reassert itself in the face of 'crisis'. These perspectives would highlight the construction of this event as a financial 'crisis' as something which threatened our very way of life, the stability of our systems, as a mechanism which enabled finance to continue the pursuit of their own interests, legitimated by the support of governments.

arc 'loaded' as mechanisms to justify and legitimate the behaviour of states. By unpacking these discourses we can reveal and understand the operation of power which therefore provides opportunity to challenge its dominant power relations.

Comparison of theories and approaches

The theories presented above are split by their approaches to what they view as legitimate areas of enquiry. If we discard that boundary between national and international we can see that both IR and Politics theories share similarities and draw attention to areas which we may not have previously considered. Moreover, while some of them have differing areas of analysis, what does not make them amenable to each other is their differing methodologies. For example, realists will be unable to reflect upon the role of capitalism (as identified by Marxism) because their analysis is simply focused around that which can be observed and quantified (which capitalism cannot be). The similarities and differences between the two disciplines are thus drawn out below.

Both realists and elitists assume there is a coherent unit of analysis. For realists this is the state, and this is where power is located, for elitists power is located within a group of elite actors. Power is concentrated rather than dispersed, and elites, like realists, pursue strategies to maintain their own survival. What is different here then is the 'level' of analysis. Elitists and realists downplay the existence of structures as a shaper of behaviour, and both have sought to establish scientific 'laws' (Michels' 'Iron Law of Oligarchy', and the realist view that there are 'laws' derivable from knowledge of human nature governing politics). Yet, what realist theories miss is the role of elite actors in driving state behaviour. State leaders may have a powerful role because of their positioning in the international arena, but at the same time, strong state leaders may enhance state power, and so state power becomes contingent upon both the nature and role of elites as well as positioning within the international system. The shared methodology of these approaches, in terms of their scientific adherence and their focus upon the observable, means that it is relatively straightforward to integrate and combine theoretical approaches. This in turn can provide for a more complete analysis combining the roles of agents within structures. However, in privileging the state as an actor and/or state actors, both these approaches downplay the importance of non-state actors and the actions of those outside the state. For this we turn to neo-liberalism and pluralism.

Liberal institutionalists also share with pluralists an assumption that power is observable and the property of states, but also non-state actors or individuals. The implicit assumption in both approaches is that power is dispersed, and that no one interest dominates, whether within the state or in the international arena. Liberal institutionalists, with their focus upon regimes and institutions, miss the role of interest groups, which act not only on a domestic level, but also internationally (think, for example, of the presence on the international stage of organizations such as Amnesty International and Greenpeace). However, the emphasis upon cooperation in neo-liberal accounts is commensurate with the assumption of lack of conflict in the pluralist view. These two accounts focus their attention upon the role of individuals. And, both neo-realists and neo-liberals share with new right theories an assumption of rationality, in that states are assumed to rationally pursue their interests, in the way that individuals within states are assumed to do. The differences between the two lie first in their differing levels of analysis (neo-realist and neo-liberal focus upon the state, new right theories focus upon actions within the state). Second, new right state theories are largely thought of as agency-centred (given the focus upon individual actors), whereas neo-realist theories account for behaviour as a consequence of the structure states find themselves in.

What is lacking from these theories is an awareness of the role of ideas and the broader context within which agency is displayed – in this example, the broader context of the financial crisis. Here, Marxist accounts provide a useful tool as they draw attention to the ideological climate and underlying unobservable structure (capitalism); while we cannot see or observe it directly, its effects are palpable. Thinking back to the structure/agency debate, we might then be able to understand why states or state actors behave the way that they do. However, one of the difficulties with Marxist analysis is it tends to privilege the role of structures as the drivers of change. This gives limited autonomy to individual actors (states or elites) to be able to radically effect change.

What is interesting to note with all these theoretical accounts, is that despite their similarities, they perform a very specific function, in that they are used to analyze either behaviour within a state or behaviour by states. What they do not do is transcend the two to consider how behaviour within states might shape the behaviour of states in the international arena, and vice versa.

Adjudicating between perspectives

What we see, then, are similarities in approaches between Political Science and IR – distinguished by empirical and analytical levels of analysis in that IR theories focus upon the state as an individual-level actor, and Political Science approaches tend to focus upon individuals within states. Yet IR theories are able to contribute to understandings of domestic political behaviour and vice versa. This then raises the question: how do we decide between competing claims and theories? This is discussed in more depth in Chapter 1, but, in short, the answer is that adjudication between competing positions may depend upon the epistemological position we adopt. If we adhere to the notion that politics can be conceived of as a science, that, for example, laws of politics are possible, then our standpoint might be that of a positivist leading us to adopt, maybe, the approach of an elite theorist, or a neo-realist/neo-liberal. If we think that while we might be able to observe effects, rather than their causes then we might adopt a critical/scientific realist position, leading potentially to a Marxist approach. In the example given above, is it important that we understand inequality (as Marxists would suggest), is this something that we should be concerned with understanding and explaining? Or should our focus be upon the way in which political decisions are made? Should we see politics as conflict or cooperation? As we cannot see this should we be concerned with something that we can observe, such as elites making political decisions? The point here is that the theoretical position we adopt is underpinned by a certain set of assumptions as outlined in Chapter 1. Recognizing these assumptions enables us to reflect upon what it is in analysis that is important and, more importantly, it enables us to understand and justify why that is the case and the same is true for each topic we discuss throughout the book.

Conclusion

There are many different ways to theorize the state both within Politics and IR and this is not an exhaustive account of how this might be done. However, what this chapter has sought to illustrate is how applying different frameworks sheds light on different aspects of the same issue. Positivist accounts have focused our attention upon observable behaviour with the aim of providing causal explanation as to why governments and states have responded to the Credit Crunch in the way that they have. The focus is upon the observable actions of political actors and, in political science, this is concerned with influence upon the state. Pluralist and elitist frameworks have been used to describe why bankers have been able to influence governments. For positivist accounts in IR, realist/neo-realist accounts have enabled us to problematize and think historically about state behaviour as reaction to financial crisis in the past, while neo-liberal accounts offer potential solutions to the crisis through cooperation and the role of institutions. However, here the state is assumed to be a unitary actor, with clearly defined interests. For critical realists, the aim is to provide causal explanation but with recognition of the existence of unobservable factors which influence outcomes. For Marxists within this perspective, we might understand why this crisis might have occurred through reference to the inherent contradictions in capitalism and while political science has traditionally focused upon the domestic effects, in IR Marxism highlights to us the continuation of exploitation and the systemic inequalities which continue in order for global capitalism to function. Interpretivists suggest that reality is contingent and dependent upon our articulation of it. Thus, constructivists in IR point to norms which govern state behaviour and possible responses, whereas poststructuralists in political science, would focus upon the state as a site of negotiation and contestation between competing interests and the wider discursive environment within which this takes place.

Reflection

Which perspective or approach does the best job of explaining or accounting for the Credit Crunch?

Why do you think this is the case?

Do you think that to understand why the Credit Crunch occurred we need to look at the observable behaviour of political and economic elites?

Do you think that the Credit Crunch is simply part of capitalism, and its real success is in preventing us from thinking of an alternative system of political, social and economic organization?

Do you agree with the argument that dominant discourses depoliticized the Credit Crunch, enabling political leaders to distance themselves from it, and thus prevent themselves from being held responsible and accountable?

How can insights from Political Science and IR help us analyze and understand the Credit Crunch, or prepare us for the next one? What are the reasons for your answer?

Seminar activities

What does the state look like and how do we know this?

Is the state the same or different in Politics and IR?

Why do you think these differences exist?

Do these differences add or detract from our analysis?

What are the key areas of analysis in pluralist, elitist, Marxist, new right, realist/neo-realist and neo-liberal theorizing of the state?

How do they differ from one another?

How are they similar?

What is missing from each approach?

Which do you find the most convincing analysis of the Credit Crunch and why?

Using a variety of newspaper sources (e.g., tabloids and broadsheets representing different political persuasions and from different countries) consider one of the main stories of the day in relation to state behaviour. Analyze the story from each of the competing theoretical perspectives discussed above.

Which one works best?

Why is that?

Are there any which don't work?

What claims are you able to make as a result of your analysis?

Which perspective does your answer fit most closely with and why do you think this is the case?

Chapter 4

Policy

Introduction

Public policy impacts upon our lives every single day, both in our private lives (affecting the things that we do at home) and public lives (for example, at work). Public policy isn't only directed at us but is created to regulate the way in which individuals, organizations or states interact with each other in domestic polities and international society. As such, a fundamental area of investigation in Political Science, and to a lesser degree IR, is the way in which public decision-making takes place, and how the outcomes of those decisions are implemented. One of the ways in which we do this is through policy analysis.

Broadly speaking, policy analysis concerns the interaction of the state with public officials. Policy is viewed as important as it can be seen as a tangible feature of what politics is about; it is one of the main ways that we can see the 'real' world of politics put into practice. But behind this seemingly simple observation is a series of questions. What exactly is it that we look at when we study policy? Do we study how policy is made, the policy process? Or do we look at the outcome of policy – so what it looks like once it has been agreed? Is policy an event or a process? Or do we look at the way in which policy is implemented, and try and understand how that may be the same or differ from what policy-makers intended? Underpinning the study of policy are some fundamental questions: how and why does policy succeed or fail? How democratic is the policy-making process? Within this we then may need to think about why some policies change and some don't. Why are there variations between policy outcomes (in sectors or between countries, e.g., in defence and education or between France and the US)? There is a wide debate within the academic literature about what it is we do when doing policy analysis (see, for example, Parsons, 1995 for an excellent summary). Here, however, we are principally concerned with introducing theories and approaches which offer us opportunity to undertake analysis of the policy process (rather than in, or for, the policy process [cf. Parsons, 1995: xvi]). We also intend to focus upon how policy is made, rather than how it is implemented (although again for an excellent integration of these, see Parsons, 1995).

As with the other chapters in this book, rather than give a detailed and extensive discussion of the theories and approaches, the aim here is to give a brief overview of some of the differing ways in which policy is analyzed. The chapter also shows how these differing perspectives can be used to analyze our chosen case study of climate change, with the aim of illustrating how differing perspectives have different foci and therefore offer differing forms of analysis. Most policy analysis is avowedly empirical and, while theoretical development has occurred, this has been largely dominated by positivist accounts. Sabatier's (2007) call for 'better theories' includes a social constructivist account (Ingram *et al.*, 2007) and research on deliberative public policy is beginning to emerge (Hajer and Wagenaar, 2003; Fischer, 2003). However, in the main, policy analysis is no different from most of the other topics we are presenting in this book in that it has been dominated by positivist and behavioural accounts, and so below we have sought to introduce alternative approaches and ways in which we can do policy analysis.

What is also interesting for us is that the distinction between Politics and IR is less overt, largely, we suggest, as both disciplines implicitly seem to assume that policy is the preserve of the state and it is actions of and within the state which are viewed as significant in analyzing public policy. The disciplinary distinctions between Politics and IR simply reflect the differing levels of analysis. So, foreign policy analysis, being principally concerned with policy beyond the nation-state, tends to be treated as the preserve of IR, whereas all other forms of policy tend to be treated as domestic policy and hence the preserve of Political Science (which is assumed to be primarily concerned with the internal working of the state). What happens though when there is a need for policy agreement at the international level, which has domestic implications? This is why we have chosen the case study of climate change, an issue which does not respect the geographical or socially constructed boundaries of the nation–state, meaning that policy responses need to reflect both national and international levels of engagement.

Power

Underpinning analysis of policy, and often implicit in much of the work we read, are assumptions about power (as we discussed in Chapter 2). The assumptions that we make about power lead us to look at a problem or an issue in a particular way. Much of the mainstream literature on policy analysis positions itself as empirical and sees little need for explicit discussions of power (although an exception can be found in the community power debate, see Hunter, 1953; Polsby, 1970). However, we argue that policy-making and implementation are political activities and thus inherently bound up with discussions of power. Therefore, to fully understand what is taking place in the policy process we also need an awareness of the underlying power relationships. We might ask questions such as: where is power located? Is it located with individual politicians (public officials) who propose policy to the legislature? Or does it lie with the executive in their transformation of legislation into policy? Is power located much earlier in the process, with those who are able to influence what the policy looks like? Or is power the capacity to get policy proposals onto the agenda? In this way power would be located still with individuals, but with particular interests such as pressure groups, businesses or lobbyists who attempt to influence policy-makers into shaping policy to fit their vested interests.

Alternatively, is power located with the people who are required to implement policy? For example, civil servants (also public officials) at senior level may have different views of what policy means and how it should work. This is known as the 'implementation gap' (Pressman and Wildavsky, 1973) and is used to refer to the distance between what a policy-maker envisions and the reality of the practice. The policy process may also be subverted by 'street level bureaucrats' (Lipsky, 1971) – those people on the ground, in the front line of public services (also public officials) who have conflicting goals or targets and, again, this may influence the way in which policy is implemented. Thus far, however, we have suggested that power is located with individuals who act politically, and is expressed, crucially, that we can observe individuals holding this political power, when they interact with the political system. More recently, there has been an attempt within public policy to develop an empirical account of power (Dowding, 1996). Power here is located systemically, in a similar vein to Marxist accounts. However, that is where the similarity ends. In this empirical view power is recognizable simply as 'luck'. Individuals may be at a point in the system where their interests and those of the system coincide, but this is considered systemic luck, rather than individual positioning, or the system protecting vested interests (as with Marxist accounts). Alternatively power may lie within networks, or communities (Jordan, 1990; Marsh, 1998). Yet this implies that where we look and what we observe is correlated with the existence of power.

On the other hand, power may be less directly observable. For Marxist and critical accounts, power may also be regarded as systemic; however, its location and outcomes are different from the empirical account of

Box 4.1   Case study. Climate change and the Copenhagen Accord

Climate change is one of the most pressing political issues of our time. There have been attempts to address the issue at both domestic and international levels. While there is a chapter later in this book which addresses ways in which we analyze the environment and environmental issues (see Chapter 10), the aim here is to give an example of the way in which international policy on climate change can be analyzed (given it has both domestic and international implications).

Self-evidently, climate change is an issue which does not respect the geographically imposed boundaries of the contemporary system of nation-states. It is an issue which requires both national and international cooperation to address. As such political actors have a role to play in formulating policies, in providing the frameworks, through which the world as a whole and individual nations can aim to address the problem. While individual states may (or may not) have explicit climate policies, transnational organizations (such as the Intergovernmental Panel on Climate Change [IPCC] and the UN) have played a role in bringing states together in order to try to address climate change collectively, promoting a series of world discussions with the aim of generating an international policy.

The most recent of these discussions took place in December 2009 at Copenhagen when delegates and leaders from 192 countries met to

→

power above. For critical and Marxist accounts power is located in the socio-economic system and comes prior to the political system, leaving political actors very little opportunity for influence, other than to reinforce the needs and demands of the socio-economic system. For poststructural accounts power may also be located systemically, but in systems of discourse, reproduced and legitimated through language and symbolism, and daily practice. Below we give an overview of some of the competing approaches in policy analysis but before we do so we begin with a brief overview of the case study, to which we will be applying our approaches and theories.

Foundational positivist approaches

Behaviouralism

Peter John suggests that the study of public policy 'seeks to explain the operation of the political system as a whole' (1999: 1–2). He goes on to discuss the ways in which the issue of climate change could be addressed. One of the original aims of the talks was to find a way to agree to reduce emissions significantly (by around 80 per cent by 2050) to prevent a rise in temperature this century to any more than 1.5°C (originally 2°C, see Chapter 10). There was, however, no legally binding agreement achieved (despite the aim of the previous summit at Kyoto that one should be produced). Rather there was an Accord, a voluntary, non-legally binding agreement to which signatories agreed (and by the end of the session not all countries had agreed to the process). At the time of writing c. 107 countries had agreed to be covered by the Accord, and, in March 2010, China and India also signed up.

One of the difficulties that faced the delegation is that the UN has no authority over the behaviour of nation-states. Realist accounts will draw attention to the sovereignty of nation-states and the UN's lack of ability to enforce agreements. Liberal institutionalists point to the possibilities of cooperation and the notion of the Accord, it may be argued, may be understood through these two frameworks. What realists and liberal institutionalists miss, however, and what policy analysis illustrates, is the translation of the demands of states and recognized interests, (such as Greenpeace) and less publicly recognized interests in the policy process (such as lobbyists for the oil industry) into agreements or politics with domestic and international implications. More critical accounts also draw attention to the role of dominant interests and their reliance upon systems of exploitation.

suggest that the focus is upon outputs – that is, what comes out of the political system. Each policy goes through a complex sequence of nego-tiations – for example, between interest groups, bureaucrats, politicians and the general public – and the focus here is upon what emerges at the end of that process.

Within behavioural political analysis, there are a variety of differing approaches to policy analysis; however, the starting point are those which are sequential, or suggest that policy analysis can be understood in stages. But there are two different foci: one draws attention to the role of individuals, the other to the role of institutions. In both, the emphasis, as with other behavioural approaches in political science, is upon measur-able and observable phenomena. That is analysis-focused attention upon those who propose and formulate policy. Behaviour is observed and measured against outcomes – for example, the successful creation of a policy. This perspective implicitly accepts pluralist assumptions of power. It suggests that we can see decisions being made, and we can see the outcomes of those decisions in the form of policy and therefore power is observable and located in the hands of those who make the decisions.

The first approach assumes that there is a relationship between citizens, politicians and bureaucrats. In this focus the work which has been undertaken is largely empirical and, rather than adopting an explicit theoretical framework, describes the policy process as taking place in a series of stages, which can be observed and measured (see, for example, Sanderson, 1961; Hogwood and Gunn, 1984). It is assumed (and this can be seen through the description of the process) that citizens advise politicians of their policy wishes through electing them to office, and by voting for their policy platforms. Sometimes, in consultation with interest groups, politicians generate policy and pass this to bureaucrats to implement. As is clear, there are a series of other assumptions made here (about the reasons, for example, why people vote, and that bureaucrats carry out politicians wishes without distortion). However, this approach suggests that by understanding the inputs (wishes of politicians and citizens) into the policy process and comparing them to the outputs (e.g., implemented policy) we are able to gauge how a policy emerges and the extent to which it is a success or failure. Here, then, there is a clear line, or a clear sequence of events; policy has a beginning, middle and end, all of which can be observed, defined and measured. The assumption is also implicitly made that power is located with the people who make the decisions and we can observe the different stages and measurement of outcomes.

In contrast to this overt emphasis upon individuals, David Easton's (1953) systems model draws attention to the role of institutions underpinning the stages, rather than individuals per se. This type of analysis focuses attention upon the way in which the legislature and executive respond to demands from society and then bureaucracies apply policy to generate policy outcomes. Again, the focus is upon the process of inputs and outputs which can be observed. What these approaches don't do, however, is enable us to understand the role of the state, or indeed, what happens when decisions are made. The state is assumed to be a 'black box' into which inputs go and outputs emerge, but we do not know what happens in between.

The systems model approach has been largely superseded by those who highlight the role of institutions in the policy process. Here the focus is upon the way in which institutions can play a role in generating norms and routinizing values, creating 'standard operating procedures'. These institutional contexts are important, as norms become embedded and far more difficult to change than politicians and parties who change their role in office more regularly. In this sense, if we are to analyze policy we need to evaluate the institutional context and collective norms within that context which act as a guidance mechanisms for decision-makers (for further reading on this, see Johnson, 1975; Linder and Peters, 1990). The importance of institutions has been reasserted more widely in the theoretical literature (e.g., March and Olsen, 1984; Kato, 1996, and as discussed in the following chapter). More recently, March and Olsen (2006) have drawn attention to the interrelationship between institutions and agents, suggesting the opportunity to explore the dynamic interaction between institutions and political agents, rather than the linear stages process of the models suggested above. Our aim here has been to introduce the starting points of policy analysis and to get a fuller overview of how this debate has developed; this approach needs to be considered in conjunction with the debates around institutionalism in the following chapter.

IR approaches to policy-making: bureaucratic politics

Policy-making in IR largely refers to the field of foreign policy. Here the focus, as with the above account, is upon observable decision-making.

> ### Box 4.2   Climate change: behavioural systems approach to Copenhagen
>
> The stages approach and the systems model would highlight the number of states attending and the players in the process. Here attention would be drawn to the role of the Intergovernmental Panel on Climate Change (IPCC) in setting the agenda. It would focus upon the players in the process, mainly nation-states. It would then draw attention to the existence of the process of the talks, and the emergence of an outcome (the Accord). In effect, a systems model approach would describe who took part (world leaders), the two-week period of talks and the meetings held, and would note who attended those meetings (making the assumption that attendance could be equated with influence). This would highlight that while c. 180 countries attended, earlier sessions in the two-week period were where they had an opportunity to feed in to the policy process. They were part of the 'demand side'. Power would ultimately be seen to lie with those final 25 countries who drew up the Accord: the final agreement was worked out by the UK, US, China, India, Brazil, South Africa 'and about 20 other countries' (Samuelsohn, 2009). The systems approach would not explore, however, how the document was drawn up, nor what took place within that final meeting, but would focus upon the outcome – the creation of an Accord – as evidence of the success of the policy process. This analysis would, however, in contrast to those accounts which view policy as a process over time, as an event, a discrete period in its own right, largely be decontextualized beyond the actual decision-making activity.
>
> The systems approach describes the process; the actors involved and the policy outcome. It would not be interested in the motivations of the actors involved, nor the language used to define the document, nor would it draw attention to the interests which may shape the policy. These issues are explored within alternate perspectives and detailed below.

However, attention here is slightly different from the stages model outlined above. Based on Allison's (1971) *Essence of Decision* is the 'bureaucratic' politics model. This approach suggests that to analyze policy decisions we need to look at the conflicts between different bureaucratic offices of the state. The conflict and cooperation that takes place between them enables us to understand how policy is made. Allison argued that bureaucracies are not top-down hierarchical organizations; rather they compete for influence and resources across government (see also Dunleavy and Ward, 1991). As such, this approach suggests that, if we are to understand the policy process, we need to analyze the behaviour of bureaucracies and the way in which they compete for influence and resources. This tells us that policy is often a consequence of uncoordinated interaction across government departments. Allison's key point was to draw attention to the role of bureaucracies as key actors, rather than vested interests or politicians. As such, power is assumed to be observable and lie with bureaucracies. It is the bureaucracy as an organization which is the focus of analysis, rather than individuals within the organization. However, the bureaucracy as an organization is assumed to exhibit agency and we can identify this through observation of behaviour; in making these assumptions we can also recognize the approach as behavioural. The rationality assumption is also discussed explicitly in Allison's work, and the assumption has given rise to another model of policy analysis; that is the rational choice approach.

Rational choice

If we apply a rational choice model (for summary of assumptions, see Chapter 1) to institutions as individual units of analysis, we can start to analyze the political system as made up of unitary actors (e.g., Treasury, Executive). Rational choice accounts assume that individuals have preferences which shape their behaviour. As such, once we know what their preferences are (and we can establish this through observation of their behaviour) we can predict how they will act. So, once we have identified an individual's preferences we can identify the strategies they will pursue to maximize their own utility.

One of the tensions, of course, arises when we move from evaluating unitary actors as institutions, or organizations, and unitary actors as individuals. An individual may have preferences and interests which are ranked differently in order of importance. So they may be more important for that individual than they are for the institution. As such, an individual may pursue strategies which will maximize their own utility, yet at the same time this may produce an outcome that is collectively irrational (this is discussed in more detail in Chapter 9). Rational choice accounts focus upon observable phenomena. Power is also assumed to be located in

> **Box 4.3 Climate change: bureaucratic politics and rational choice**
>
> The bureaucratic policy model might suggest that the government has returned from Copenhagen with a desire to reduce climate emissions as outlined in the Accord. A series of policies will be proposed and, for example, there may be a policy to reduce carbon emissions from flying. However, pressure from the Department for Trade and Industry for 'business-friendly' policies (who may also be lobbied by the aviation industry), combined with pressure from the Treasury who do not wish to see a loss of revenue as a consequence of attempts to reduce carbon emissions, may mean that the original aims of policy proposed by the Secretary of State for Climate Change may be fundamentally altered by the time it is introduced (indeed, assuming that it is not dropped altogether, which may also happen).
>
> The rational actor model would make assumptions about the motivations of individuals, and through so doing account for the choices that they made. Obama, in this perspective, could be assumed to be a rational actor seeking to maximize his own self-interest. Here self-interest can be read in two ways: first, as the self-interest of the United States (as its leader and representative) and, second, as an electorally sensitive politician. Obama can be seen as seeking to preserve America's self-interest in the world (in terms of its economic prosperity and status in the global order). However, the rational actor model also suggests to us that Obama was seeking to maximize utility in the domestic arena in these negotiations. This was not the only policy decision he was making at that time, and he also needed to shore up support at home to get global warming legislation through the Senate, given the opposition of Conservative Republicans and more widely from longstanding lobbying industry opponents (Samuelsohn, 2009). In this way the rational choice accounts help us to understand the way in which policy-making is made through assumptions about the motivations of the individual actor (either organizations or the individual person). Once these assumptions have been made, we would then identify the preferences (e.g., get legislation through Senate in the face of significant opposition) and the choices which are made (i.e., an agreement which does not compel states to undertake any action) so that we can account for the outcome.

individuals who are observed. Individuals may take the form of political actors, or individual units such as bureaucracies operating as a cohesive unit. So, if we are analyzing the behaviour of bureaucracy, we are making the assumption that power is located within the bureaucracy.

Feminism

Feminist accounts provide for critique of the mainstream (or 'malestream'), and offer positions which can be located within positivist, realist and constructivist accounts. Indeed, within feminism there are debates as to its legitimate arena of analysis and feminism is usually referred to in the plural – feminisms – to reflect its differing approaches. The aim here is not to delve into those debates (not least as an eloquent overview is provided by Randall, 2010), but to show how feminism(s) can provide alternative means through which to evaluate public policy. Underpinning feminism is a concern with gender inequality, and feminisms provide differing accounts of the manner in which these inequalities become systemically embedded. As Hawkesworth observes, 'feminists have targeted public law and public policy as a site for political contestation for the past two centuries' (1994: 97). Gender itself is used as an analytic category. To understand the way in which society is organized to embed inequalities and injustices necessitates an understanding of the way in which gender is conceptualized as a system of power relations, rooted in a false dichotomy of difference between men and women.

Feminist policy analysis elsewhere notes the way in which policy is made 'in response to needs other than those expressed by women … Imperatives of economic growth, population replacement, and political stability have been the source of much of what we might construe as

Box 4.4   Climate change: the Copenhagen Accord and feminism

The ongoing inequalities as highlighted by feminism are arguably reinforced within the Copenhagen Accord. In a document published following the Copenhagen Accord, the Women's Environment and Development Organization (WEDO) (2009) highlight the increasing prominence that gender is playing in negotiations within this area. Their report details that a number of gender-sensitive texts were used as part of the negotiating documents, suggesting a breakthrough in the recognition of the need for an explicit recognition of the vulnerability of women but also the need for women's participation. However, what is also noticeable is that this gender-sensitive language and the issues raised in conjunction with this gendered sensitivity did not make it into the final document. The invisibility of women and gender in the final document means analysis needs to focus upon the unobservable and facilitates an account of underlying gendered relationships of power.

Indeed, this supports the wider mixed representation of women in the policy process. Buckingham observes that to some extent while policy and development rhetoric have acknowledged or included the role of gender, the situation 'masks a fundamental attachment to "business as usual" where social roles, pay differential, political representation and environmental degradation remain little changed' (2004: 146).

policy on women' (Lovenduski, 1986: 295). The argument is that the interests of the political and economic system are clearly privileged in the policy-making process, over the interests of women. The broad aim of feminist approaches according to Hawkesworth is to enable research that is neither gender-biased, nor gender-blind (1994: 98). Some feminist research around policy offers analysis, drawing attention to the significance of gender in specific policy areas (e.g., Cornell, 1991), whereas more radical feminists would emphasize relations of domination and subordination (e.g., Acker, 1988) which underpin gender-'neutral' legislation and policy (MacKinnon, 1993). Poststructural feminists, on the other hand, focus on diversity among women, and suggest it is difference which should be celebrated (see Butler, 1992). What all do, however, is draw attention to the role of women, in both private and public life, and the way in which this relationship between the two plays a role in reinforcing gender inequalities.

Foundational critical/scientific realist approaches

Marxism

As noted in earlier chapters, Marxist accounts focus attention upon the nature of socio-economic interest and their capacity to influence politics and the political system. For Marxist accounts it is usually assumed that it is socio-economic conditions which influence the nature of policy. Public policy is necessary to prevent economic collapse and to sustain the needs of the capitalist system. As such, the assumption is that power is systemic, it lies in the socio-economic system itself. Policy choices and options are inextricably linked to, and will be a reflection of, the economic basis and developments within society (Ham and Hill, 1984). This relationship is summarized by John, who argues that, for Marxist accounts, '[g]iven that the state provides a regulatory apparatus within which capital accumulation can take place, it follows that capitalism constrains policy-making' (1999: 93). In this way, he suggests, there are two main schools of Marxist thought in policy analysis.

The first derives from the regulationist school and highlights the importance of technology in structuring relations between the state and society. The state functions to regulate the technological basis of society, but it does so in order to support the accumulation of capital. For example, in the era of mass production, the techniques and technologies required bureaucracies to create standards for markets, and regulation of the economy which ensured consumer demand. It also required a healthy and trained workforce (supported through state-provided health and education systems). In turn the needs of mass production created large organizations and large bureaucracies. This kind of standardization became referred to as Fordism. Following changes in the markets and declining profits in the late 1960s, production techniques changed to become more specialized, more 'efficient' and became known as post-Fordism. To retain its legitimacy, the regulatory state had to respond to these changes in the means of production, requiring the state to design policies to reflect these new more flexible forms of production. For Jessop (1995) this has meant the emergence of the 'Schumpeterian workfare state', where policy is designed to enhance the markets and the flexibility of labour to advance the interests of capital, rather than policy designed to enhance the aim of extending citizenship.

The second set of Marxist theorizing has been concerned with the idea of globalization. Here the argument is that economies become increasingly interconnected through compression of time and space facilitated by new technologies. The deregulation of financial markets means that governments are unable to control finance and trade and this is combined with the rapid growth of multinational corporations. The policy implications are that states begin to compete internationally for capital and adjust their domestic policies to attract capital; to suit the needs and demands of multinational companies. This approach has been used to account for policy changes in terms of deregulation, privatization and reduction in welfare expenditure, and these have accounted for changes in policy at domestic level. More recently, this approach is able to explain policies of low tax rates for high earners, continued deregulation and failure to regulate the financial markets, with politicians afraid of the 'flight of capital'. This approach suggests an interconnectivity of markets and the interests of capital, which come prior to the boundaries and borders of the nation-state. This ordering leaves policy-makers somewhat constrained in the choices they can make. Indeed, the more structural version of this perspective would suggest that state managers have only one choice, and that is to protect the interests of capital (cf. Offe, 1984).

Power in these accounts is not the property of individuals; rather it is located within the socio-economic system – more specifically, within capitalism. In this sense, we cannot, as with earlier behavioural accounts, measure or observe it directly, but we can observe the effects of this type of power. The way we can do this is through reference to the way in which the interest of the capitalist classes are represented and protected through public policy.

Critical theory

Critical theorists also reject the overt behaviouralism of earlier approaches. Rather they argue, alongside Marxist accounts, if we are to understand

---

Box 4.5   Climate change: the Copenhagen Accord and Marxism

Marxist accounts would draw attention to the continued inequality of the West, and the owners of the means of industrial production exploiting the resources of the developing countries for their own advancement. Here accounts would reflect recognition of existing social and economic factors influencing policy decisions. For example, the significance of the structure of economic interests is highlighted as Vidal *et al.* (2009) report that 'Lumumba Di-Aping, [the] chief negotiator for the G77 group of 130 developing countries, said the deal had "the lowest level of ambition you can imagine. It's nothing short of climate change scepticism in action. It locks countries into a cycle of poverty for ever".' Here, then, Marxist accounts would highlight the way that the decision-making process simply reflected and reinforced existing social and economic inequalities.

In this perspective, if we are to understand why this has happened we need to begin by looking at the wider social and economic context within which this agreement was made. More widely, this approach highlights that sustainable policies may not be possible in a capitalist system which requires continual growth to maintain legitimacy. More specifically, within the Accord, is an implicit agreement that the interests of capital should be advanced. The globalization school also draws attention to the power of the multinational companies (MNCs) and the lobbying that they undertake with national governments (e.g., Shell) to ensure policy is made favourably, or at least not in a manner that is detrimental to business interests. This is not only achieved through proactive lobbying, but also more subtly through the threat of the 'flight of capital'. That companies will relocate their corporations in other countries and therefore the revenue accrued from that particular corporation (e.g., through taxes) will be lost.

---

what is taking place in the policy process we need to understand the nature of the system it is located within. For critical theorists this is about maintaining the legitimacy of the state. Whereas within Marxist analysis the analysis of capitalism comes prior to the state, within critical theory the state is the entry point of analysis. However, both accounts accept, or assert, interlinkage between the state and capitalism.

Critical theorists note the bureaucratization of society and suggest that this leads to a politics which is 'totally administered' and therefore 'one dimensional' (Marcuse, 1972). In this way it is the process of bureaucratization that creates a political reality that benefits the capitalist system. This highlights that bureaucracies have a function to play in the policy process, but the interests which are reflected are not those of the bureaucrats (as above), rather they reflect the interests of the capitalist system. Here, again, power is systemically located; however, it is manifest through its capacity to influence how an individual perceives reality. In this way, as Parsons notes, it is the 'rationality which expresses itself in the public policy agenda [which] is an instrument of domination and control' (2005: 147).

Critical theorists such as Habermas (1989) draw attention to the way in which public debate has become narrowed around areas of technical knowledge and expertise, thereby excluding many from opportunities to participate in public life, while at the same time functioning to reinforce the dominance of instrumental technical rationality. For Habermas, then, the way in which public policy problems are defined and agendas set are reflective of the underlying controls in operation in capitalist society, which operates to maintain the legitimacy of the state.

A key aspect of critical theory is to draw attention to exploitative relationships. Through awareness of this domination, through political literacy, lies the route to emancipation. More recently, theorists have expanded upon this and provide a normative template for the way in which policy should be pursued with the goals of achieving equality through public policy. This should be not only through the outcomes of public policy, but also through the formation and creation of public policy. Indeed, Forester encapsulates this normative notion of policy as an avenue for empowerment of citizens, and critical theory as a mechanism for achieving it, by arguing that a 'critical theory of public policy analysis ... is an empirical account of the contingent and variable reproduction – through policy development – of citizens' beliefs, consent, trust, and attention' (1993: 160). In this way, we are encouraged to consider the totalizing discourses that structure public policy debate and argue for a more deliberative dialogical approach, which transcends existing structural constraints.

Critical approaches to policy analysis draw attention to the importance of a commitment to social change and equality as a necessary condition for improving decision-making. This involves providing a more open, transparent process, whereby citizens are empowered and engaged, and provided with the opportunity to participate in the policy process. Dryzek suggests the 'argumentative turn' whereby opportunities are afforded which seek to improve communication between policy-makers and the public, to provide opportunities for reasoned discussion and debate, and through so doing increase opportunities for participation, in turn empowering discussion and public participation. The communicative model thus provides a site which is 'free from domination (the exercise of power), strategic behaviour by the actors involved [in contrast to rational choice accounts], and (self) deception'; all participants are assumed to be competent and as such 'there should be no restriction upon the[ir] participation'(Dryzek, 1993: 230). This ensures openness,

Box 4.6 Climate change: the Copenhagen Accord and critical theory

Critical theorists would draw attention to the way in which global warming and climate change are defined as a technical issue; debate around how global warming should be addressed and tackled are linked to the dominant scientific discourses. The Accord states 'that deep cuts in global emissions are required according to science' (UNFCC, 2009: 2 point 2). But while science and technical details define the issue, it is markets that are seen as the route to solution, and dominant scientific discourses are interlinked with dominant economic discourse. The view of the importance of markets as solutions is reinforced in the Copenhagen Accord: 'We decide to pursue various approaches [not specified], including opportunities to use markets, to enhance the cost-effectiveness of, and to promote mitigation actions' (UNFCC, 2009: 2 point 7). To frame climate change as a failure of markets highlights first the interlinkage of science with economic discourse, but, second, that if markets have failed in this case, the implication is, that there is a need to rectify the conditions for the market to operate in, and we will find a solution. That is, economic discourse proceeds and shapes not only the way in which we can understand the science, but also the parameters through which it is possible to create policy. In short, as economic discourse comes prior to scientific discourses the prospect of potential solutions is narrowed and fails to challenge the 'status quo'.

   Critical theorists also highlight the potential for deliberative solutions, and would draw attention to the importance of individuals engaging with political actors. Deliberative accounts would normatively draw attention to the possibility of citizen empowerment, not through engagement with the market (from whence neo-liberalism assumes empowerment flows) but through individual dialogue and engagement with political actors.

empowers participants and implies equality within that forum, as, for Dryzek, 'the only remaining authority is that of a good argument, which can be advanced on behalf of the veracity of empirical description, explanation, and understanding, and ... the validity of normative judgements' (1987: 434). In this way, and in contrast to the implied pluralism of the behavioural accounts, critical approaches to policy analysis are clear about their normative underpinnings.

Anti-foundational interpretivist approaches

Social constructivism

Social constructivist accounts of policy draw attention to the importance of understanding the ways in which particular understandings and interpretations of realities come to be constructed and legitimated. Social problems, they argue, are a product of their definition, rather than having an objective and independent existence (Blumer, 1971). As such, we can analyze the policy agenda as the sum of those interests which are able to mobilize sufficiently and collectively define an issue (Mauss, 1975). In this way, then, the establishment of an issue on the policy agenda, depends upon its definition, rather than its objective identification. This suggests, for example, that the existence of environmental concerns upon policy agendas have been as a result of their successful definition as a problem, rather than the discovery of their objective existence. While earlier social constructivist accounts draw attention to the importance of groups mobilizing to get their voice heard and influence the policy agenda, more recent work has drawn attention to the role of the media in presenting and framing policy issues. However, what is significant in all these approaches is the recognition of the way in which a policy problem is defined, framed, or not. The language and rhetoric are key to understanding how policy is constructed – as a response to a discursive reality, rather than any objective reality (as with earlier accounts).

A social constructivist account also highlights the importance of ideas and discourses. Parsons draws attention to the dominance of positivism in policy analysis, arguing that '[q]uantification – rather than deconstruction – still constitutes the operative ideology of policy making in the modern state' (Parsons, 2005: 105). He suggests, however, that there has been a shift in the personnel who define policy problems and offer potential solutions: whereas during the 1960s/1970s policy was the preserve of technicians, bureaucrats and experts, now the tendency is for policy to be a reaction to markets, managers, moralists and the media (Parsons, 2005: 105–6). For behaviouralists, then, it is sufficient to identify a shift in personnel. However, social constructivists would highlight the ways in which these actors define what counts as a policy issue, and so the change in personnel highlights not only the change in interests which are represented in public policy (as highlighted by behavioural accounts) but also the discourses used to define what is and is not seen as a policy issue. For example, research into the media construction of moral panics (Cohen, 1972), highlights the powerful role the media have been able to play in setting the policy agenda, through the way in which media coverage defines a policy issue/problem. In contrast, Edelman (1988) suggests that the media serve to obstruct or obscure an issue, and the ability of the media to set the agenda in preventing items reaching the policy agenda is also of significance. More recently debate has looked at the 'CNN effect' and the ability of the media to influence the policy agenda (which is discussed in more detail in Chapter 7).

There is a vast literature which has emerged to discuss the way in which policy issues and ideas come to prominence (grounded in three approaches: 1) 'policy streams', e.g., Kingdon, 1995; 2) 'punctuated equilibrium', e.g., Baumgartner and Jones, 1993; and 3) the 'Advocacy coalition framework', e.g., Sabatier and Jenkins-Smith, 1993). However, these literatures tend to be located in the behavioural traditions, and, while they recognize the importance of beliefs and ideas, they are taken as given and pre-existing, rather than socially constructed categories. For social constructivists, it is the narrative of the policy which is significant (McBeth *et al.*, 2007). For social constructivists engaged in policy analysis, what matters is how the policy is narrated, what is said and by whom, and in whose interests? Stone (2002) argues that the goal of defining policy problems is to do so that it appears that one's own personal solution coalesces with the public interest, but it is the framing which is important. Once we understand how a policy has been framed, then we can see whose interests are represented.

Poststructuralism

Similarly, poststructuralism draws our attention to the role of language, and the way in which language is used to name things. This approach suggests that there are not enough words in the world to name all the things that there are, and so instead we use categories. We use these categories to enable understanding; for example, we use categories such as race, sexual orientation or class or gender. But in order to understand these categories we also need to understand the essence of these categories: what do they contain? In this sense, then, poststructuralists draw attention to such issues as the way in which societies search for categories of identity (e.g., through race, class, sexual orientation, gender) that then become prior to any differences which may exist. Fixing these identities is a mechanism of domination and control. What is important here is the notion that the way to understand policy is to evaluate what is said – it is the language and rhetoric of policy which matters; these are constitutive of the ideas which shape and are shaped, what is possible and what is not. The way in which policy is framed is viewed as being crucial to its later success or failure, and indeed, prior to that, for its inclusion on the policy agenda. The way in which policy problems or potential solutions are defined enables us to understand what is there, what is possible and what is not. This type of approach is reliant upon a Foucauldian conception of power: that power is unobservable and located discursively; rooted systemically where discursive interactions serve to reinforce existing power relations.

These power relations can be challenged through the deconstruction of language (from ideas derived from Derrida, who suggests that meaning of a word is dependent on its social context). For Derrida it is the concept

Box 4.7   Climate change: the Copenhagen Accord, social constructivism and poststructuralism

For social constructivists, and poststructuralists, language plays a central role in analysis. The way in which global warming is framed as an issue or problem is crucial. To understand the outcomes of the Copenhagen event we need to understand the way in which the problems it sought to tackle were constructed. The inability to achieve earlier targets was, from this perspective, a consequence of their non-articulation. As was noted, 'all reference to 1.5C in past drafts were removed ... [and] the earlier 2050 goal of reducing global CO2 by 80 per cent was also dropped' (Goldenberg *et al.*, 2009). For social constructivists the construction of reality is contingent upon its articulation; therefore, put simply, if we don't discuss a target date, then one does not exist. In this sense analysis suggests that through the use of language political actors have re-created political reality so that the original aim is no longer signifi-cant, in short: remove the date, remove the existence of a problem. Moreover, the Accord 'recognizes' a case for keeping temperature rises to 2°C (UNFCC, 2009: 1) and, while stating that 'action should be taken' (2009:2), does not contain a clear commitment, or set of actions to take, to reduce emissions to achieve that goal, thereby rendering political action highly unlikely. In this way we see how language is crucial in shaping reality, in the form of shaping not only what we understand the issue to be, but also what possible outcomes are and are not available.

If we think about the wider discourse in which discussions about the envi-ronment are posed, then poststructuralism draws our attention to the way in which climate change is often posed in terms of a two-sided debate: sceptics or deniers v champions. Constructing the existence of others means that

→

of 'difference' which highlights how the meaning of language alters and is contingent upon its social context. As such meaning can always be disputed. In this way, then, we cannot understand meaning through the category that has been applied to it; rather we need to understand meaning through the practices and meaning that people give to them. The notion of deconstruction assumes, like social constructivism, that language plays a role in constructing the 'real world'. The purpose of deconstruction is to render this language, and by extension underlying power structures, visible.

For poststructuralists, understanding of phenomena entails under-standing the meaning that individuals attach to a particular phenom-enon. So, for example, for poststructural feminists, the category of female is a construct which serves to reinforce patriarchal societies, but the way in which we understand this is through analyzing the particular it becomes difficult to move forward and, for some, this dichotomy and the construction of binary opposites forms the very basis of the inability to construct and implement progressive climate policy legislation. Deconstructing the categories of difference (e.g., you believe in climate change or you don't) enables the debate to move beyond these categories in search of progressive policies to tackle this phenomenon.

Recognizing these underlying debates enables us to identity how policy-makers understand and attach meaning to policy debates, and it is the meaning that is attached which is significant in shaping responses. As such, if climate change is constructed as a market failure, and within that the categories for addressing the issue are either from climate deniers or champions, then there is little scope for progressive policies which integrate with the meaning attached to the issue by political actors themselves. This is revealed to us through deconstruction of the language that is used and the meaning affixed to the categories that are employed.

Consider Obama's statement following the event: 'we've accomplished a great deal over the last few days ... I want America to continue to lead on this journey, because if America leads in developing clean energy, we will lead in growing our economy and putting our people back to work, and leaving a stronger and more secure country to our children' (Samuelsohn, 2009). Here then Obama tells us, that America is a world leader, but that climate change is about America tackling climate change, which in turn will make America's economy stronger. But deconstructing this statement enables us to recognize the underlying assumption of categories of sceptics v champions. Indeed, it is the sceptics that Obama is appealing to here. Framing his speech in the language of markets is designed to appeal to businesses, who are more likely to be sceptical – given that policies posed to reduce carbon emissions tend to come with financial costs to business.

meaning that individual women attach to this, and the way in which they interpret and live that category. Emancipation then comes from the deconstruction of these categories and the rendering explicit of the structures generated through language. While little has been explicitly written on the notion of a poststructuralist's policy approach per se, what we are suggesting is that the tools provided by poststructuralism can equally be applied to the realm of public policy.

Comparison of theories and approaches

What we have sought to do in this chapter is present a variety of differing perspectives which come into play when analyzing public policy. While the dominant approach in the existing literature is that of positivism and behaviouralist accounts, challenges have emerged from those who admit the role of ideologies and discourses. We are not able to cover all approaches here; rather our aim has been to draw attention to some of the differing ways in which policy may be analyzed. For positivist accounts, emphasis is upon the observable and measurable. For behaviouralists, policy can be viewed as a system or a model, something which goes through discrete stages which are observable and identifiable. Other positivistic accounts, such as those provided by rational choice theory, draw attention to individual action, be that the action of an individual organization (behaving as a unitary actor) or an individual actor per se, such as a politician. In this way, analysis of policy is not necessarily viewed as a process, or a system; rather it is broken down into its constituent components, with the assumption being that to understand public policy we need to understand the motivations and behaviour of those engaged in the activity of policy-making.

In contrast, for critical realists we are also seeking to establish causal explanation; however, we need to look not only at what is on the surface, but also to focus upon unobservable features. Marxist accounts (broadly defined) suggest that to understand policy we need to step back from the political system and, in order to analyze policy, we need to take stock of the social and economic conditions within which policy is made. These contextual factors are viewed as the drivers of policy, and these features are not always observable (unlike the behaviouralist and rational choice accounts detailed above).

Interpretivists suggest that to understand policy we need to understand the way in which it has been constructed, and the norms, values, ideas and beliefs which inform that construction. In this way, constructivist accounts highlight how norms and values influence and shape our identities. From here, they facilitate understanding of how a policy problem is framed as an issue and how that provides for particular solutions, foreclosing others. For poststructuralists it is important to recognize the way in which language and discourses inform the creations of categories used to define policy issues. What is significant here is not only what is defined, but what is not defined, what is omitted and the way in which particular policy issues may not be discussed, or potential solutions are not explored. For poststructuralists this is one way in which the existing power structures are reinforced. Deconstruction of this language renders the power structures visible and open to the possibility of challenge, providing the opportunity to effect change.

Adjudicating between perspectives

As the comparison above suggests, if we assume that, to understand public policy, we must look at who makes public policy, and wish to empirically observe the process, then we are likely to adopt a systems account and behavioural approach. As we have noted, the systems model has been largely superseded by approaches which focus upon the role of institutions (see also Chapter 5). However, the focus remains largely behavioural, with submerged assumptions about power. If we think that the way we can understand public policy is though awareness of the assumptions that people make when they approach policy, then we are more likely to adopt a rational choice account. If we think that policy needs to be understood through reference to the wider socio-economic conditions which shape its emergence, then a Marxist approach is more likely. If we think that, actually, the way in which we analyze public policy is through recognition of the importance of the language which frames it as being key to understanding the way it takes shape, then social constructivist accounts, or postructuralist accounts are probably the most useful here. These are all ontological considerations, about what we assume we can discover, and these are intertwined with epistemological considerations – about how we think we might discover them.

Conclusion

The aim of this chapter has been to give an overview of just some of the differing ways in which we can analyze policy. Policy analysis matters as policy plays a significant role in the activities of the state. The state both generates policy and is bound by it, and while we may not directly be involved in its creation, it does have an impact on our everyday lives, defining the things we can and can't do.

As policy is a product of, or defined by, the state, the differences between IR and Political Science approaches are minimal. While analysis in Political Science tends to focus upon domestic policies, analysis in IR tends to focus on outward-facing policy, that defines the particular state on the world stage: foreign policy. What we have aimed to do with the case study is take a policy area which transcends the geographical, or socially constructed, boundaries of the nation-state, and seek to explore how both disciplines are able to provide insights into the analysis of public policy.

What we have also tried to show here is that policy analysis is complex and informed by a series of different assumptions and considerations. Before we begin policy analysis we need to decide what we are looking at. Are we looking at the process? A policy outcome? A policy document? Are we looking at the ideas that inform policy? Are we looking at the role of policy in reinforcing societal inequalities and seeking ways in which to rectify that? Are we looking at the domestic outcomes of policy or the international impact? Or are the domestic and international implications of policy inherently interlinked? These are questions we need to ask and the answers to those ontological questions inform the kind of approach we might adopt.

Reflection

Which perspective or approach does the best job of explaining or accounting for the Copenhagen Accord?

Why do you think this is the case?

Do we need to look at the observable behaviour of key actors such as the US and China to understand why the Copenhagen Accord appeared as it did?

Is further entrenchment of poverty (one of the negative effects of climate change) a consequence of capitalism's need for growth?

Do you think that to understand the events of Copenhagen we need to understand the dominant ideas and norms and the way in which they influenced action?

How can insights from Political Science and IR be combined to help us analyze the Copenhagen Accord? What are the reasons for your answer?

Seminar activities

Identify a public policy issue in the newspaper.

How is that policy reported?

Which theoretical model provides the most useful account of that particular policy or issue?

What assumptions about power are being made?

What assumptions are being made about what is possible and what we can know about the issue?

How have you come to this conclusion?

Download the Copenhagen Accord and/or look up proceedings from a policy debate in, for example, the UK Parliament (Hansard) or Congress (CQ News). Whose voices and interest are represented? Which theoretical framework fits best to analyze the Accord/proceedings and how have you made this judgement?

Chapter 5

Institutions

Introduction

Until the 1950s, the primary activity of Political Science, apart from political theory, was the description and comparative analysis across time and between countries of political structures and constitutions with a particular emphasis on the executive, legislature and judiciary. This institutional approach was largely uncontested and unexamined as 'common sense' assumptions restricted debate on the theoretical and methodological basis of institutionalism (John, 1999: 38). However, as the discipline progressed, behaviouralist, rational choice and structuralist theorists challenged these certainties and contended that political scientists needed to do more than simply examine parliamentary, presidential or totalitarian governance. The 1980s witnessed the revival of interest in institutions as a 'new institutionalism' emerged, broadening definitions of institutions and a new research agenda:

> The new institutionalists are concerned with the informal conventions of political life as well as with the formal constitutions and organizational structures. New attention is paid to the way in which institutions embody values and power relationships, and to the obstacles as well as the opportunities that confront institutional design. Crucially, new institutionalists concern themselves not just with the impact of institutions on individuals, but with the *interaction* between institutions and individuals. (Lowndes, 2010: 61)

Before exploring new institutionalisms, we first need to consider what it is that we mean by the term 'institutions'. From the narrow definition of institutions being components of a constitutional trinity of executive, legislature and judiciary a broader definition has emerged that incorporates organizations, bureaucracies, systems and networks. For Di Maggio and Powell institutions are a 'phenomenological process by which certain social relationships and actions are taken for granted ... conventions that take on a rule like status in social thought and action' (Di Maggio and Powell, 1991: 5). Peter Hall presents institutions as 'formal rules, compliance procedures and standard operating practices that structure relationships between individuals in various units of the polity and the economy' (Hall, 1986: 20).

Such definitions have the potential to make the institutional concept all embracing, covering everything, excluding nothing and thereby having little meaningful explanatory potential. New institutionalists, however, have sought to examine and theorize about institutions from an increasing number of different approaches or institutionalisms dependent on their epistemological and ontological position. Peter Hall and Rosemary Taylor, in a seminal essay in 1996, set out three new institutionalisms: historical institutionalism, rational choice institutionalism and sociological institutionalism (Hall and Taylor, 1996). A decade later, Colin Hay added his own variant of constructivist institutionalism to these while merging sociological with normative institutionalism (Hay, 2006a). Guy Peters (1999) went further in adding normative, empirical, institutions of interest representation and international institutionalism. In the most comprehensive coverage to date Lowndes produces nine institutionalisms: Hay's four, separating sociological and normative variants, Peter's empirical and international institutionalists, and network and feminist institutionalists (Lowndes, 2010). Many of these overlap and, indeed, Lowndes herself concentrates on just rational choice and normative variants.

Our objective in this chapter is to demonstrate how institutions are conceptualized; we explore: foundational/positivist approaches – which might ask: are institutions the sum of individuals' observable behaviour within them?; foundational realist approaches – which encourage us to consider whether institutions function to represent a particular set of interests?; and anti-foundationalist/interpretivist approaches – which ask: do we need to understand the norms, rules procedures and values of an institution to be able to account for them? We encourage the consideration of important questions such as how power operates within and between institutions, how institutions are formed and transformed and whether there are differences in how domestic and international institutions are conceptualized.

Power

The focus of institutionalists of every hue is an emphasis on institutions at the state and international level. The state comprises a 'set of institutions with superordinate power over a specific territory' (Hill, 2009: 19). International institutions, meanwhile, such as the United Nations, International Monetary Fund or the European Union act as superordinate states seeking to impose their will on member states. These institutions are expressions of power relations, which determine courses of action and in which actors are included or excluded from decision-making and policy-implementation processes (Lowndes, 2010: 70). For Finer, writing in the 1930s, the very essence of the state lies in its monopoly of legitimate coercive power. The state's political institutions embody power relationships between individuals within institutions and the different constituent parts that make up the state (Finer, 1932).

Officials within institutions and organizations are able to wield considerable power within the state and international apparatus as the technical superiority of bureaucracy over other forms of organization encourages society to play by institutional rules (Weber [1932], 1946: 214). Michels suggests that the structure of large-scale organizations inevitably leads to oligarchy with elites emerging to control those organizations. As organizations become increasingly complex with formal rules and functions, elites will exercise more power as other members of the organization become increasingly alienated (Michels [1911/1959],). Power resides with those politicians and bureaucrats who control the policy process. For Robert Goodin governance then becomes 'nothing more than the steering of society by officials in control of what are organizationally the "commanding heights" of society'. Those controlling or holding such positions are able to access power resources denied to others and therefore have a greater capacity to influence and implement the policies that affect all of us (Goodin, 1998: 13, 19).

Such views have resonance in the international realm as well. Realist IR scholars have always thought in terms of power relationships and the necessary duty of the state to maximize its own power in usually relative terms against those of competing states. International institutions are considered by realists such as John Mearsheimer to be no more than a reflection of the distribution of power within the world. The formation and continuance of institutions are based on the rational calculations of states determined to maximize their own power and influence. The institutions therefore become sets of rules that lay out how states should compete and cooperate with one another (Mearsheimer, 1995: 7–8). While Mearsheimer largely discounts the capacity of institutions to affect state behaviour, neo-liberal institutionalists (in the IR sense) consider that institutions can ameliorate the impulse of calculating self-interest, changing state behaviour in order to cooperate and achieve absolute rather than relative gains.

Box 5.1   Case study. The durability of the North Atlantic Treaty Organization (NATO)

The North Atlantic Treaty was signed on 4 April 1949 in Washington DC by 12 member states to bring into effect a military and security alliance in the face of suspicion and uncertainty about the intentions of the Soviet Union following World War II and the weakness of Western European states decimated by six years of warfare. The organization has now lasted over seven decades and expanded to a membership of 28 North American and European countries. The original objective of the alliance was to safeguard the freedom and security of its members by political and military means within Europe and the North Atlantic area. Members were in no doubt that any threat they might face came from the Soviet Union. Hastings Ismay, the first Secretary General of NATO, declared that the organization's purpose was 'to keep the Russians out, the Americans in, and the Germans down' (Robertson, 2003: 5). Over the course of just over 40 years of Cold War the organization developed complex institutional arrangements with an elaborate and integrated military planning and command structure, and a developed bureaucracy with 5,000 civilian staff (1,200 of them based in NATO headquarters in Brussels). The Secretary General heads an international staff and intergovernmental apparatus has been developed for consultation and decision-making. In addition, member countries send troops for deployment by NATO.

The unilateral withdrawal from the Cold War by Mikhail Gorbachev, the last leader of the Soviet Union, and subsequent East European revolutions and break-up of the Soviet Union ended the Cold War between 1989 and 1991. With the Soviet threat extinguished the reason for the

Foundational positivist approaches

Behaviouralism

Behaviouralism approaches institutions from the perspective of the need to study the observed behaviour of agents in order to understand the ways in which formal rules, standard operating procedures and organizational structures affect political behaviour (see Rhodes, 1995: 54–5). Behaviouralism seeks to both develop theory and improve methodology of understanding political processes and succeeded in dominating political science from the 1940s to early 1970s, introducing a theory that was 'positivist, ethically neutral and orientated to empirical science more than political practice' (Bevir, 2010: 442). Behaviouralism concentrates on individual agents, rather than structures and constitutions, to explain political decision-making. For behaviouralists, it is the observable interactions and transactions of all actors which make up the collective alliance also disappeared. Alliance theory, according to realist IR scholars, suggests that alliances emerge in order to balance the power and/or threat of other states or combinations of states. As long as the factors that caused the alliance to form in the first place remain, then the alliance will continue. If the threat subsides then the interest of member states in maintaining the alliance will dissipate. Stephen Walt (1997), John Mearsheimer (1990) and Kenneth Waltz (1993) all prophesied the weakening or demise of the alliance after the end of the Cold War, yet today it appears stronger than ever. NATO has almost doubled in size with an additional 12 Central and Eastern European states joining since 1999. NATO has since been involved in three combat operations – in Bosnia, Kosovo and Afghanistan – and developed a NATO Response Force to rapidly deploy to areas of conflict, provide disaster relief and humanitarian assistance. Out-of-area operations have been conducted in Iraq, Afghanistan, Pakistan and Darfur.

Celebrating the 60th anniversary of NATO, Secretary General Jaap de Hoop Scheffer wrote that 'Few of the people who were present at NATO's creation would have dared to hope that the Alliance would not only outlast the Cold War conditions that brought it into being, but indeed thrive in a radically different security environment.' Scheffer makes the grandiose claim that NATO 'turned from a temporary project to a permanent one' because 'the logic of transatlantic security cooperation is timeless' (Scheffer, 2009: 4). Alliance theory suggests that NATO should have disappeared with the fall of communism, yet it spectacularly did not do so. Rather than accept the Secretary General's taken-for-granted explanation of the organization's durability we will apply the theories considered throughout this chapter to see how they might explain continuation after the end of the Cold War.

behaviour. Behaviouralism's contribution is to examine not how institutions should operate but rather how they do operate. Although in the introduction we highlighted up to nine different types of institutionalism, they each start from the premise that institutions should be the starting point of political analysis. In this section, we consider the three most influential of the new institutionalisms: rational choice, historical and sociological institutionalism.

Rational choice institutionalism

Rational choice starts from the ontological and methodological assumptions that actors, voluntarism and rationalism are the defining features of analysis. Institutions consist of instrumental, rational, utility-maximizing actors producing outcomes that are interpreted as being the product of rational behaviour. Rational choices are limited to the knowledge available at the time decisions are taken and the impact of the institution on actors' strategic calculation, leading to a 'bounded rationality' (Simon, 1957). Individuals are able to achieve their personal goals through the actions of the institution and so allow their behaviour to be shaped by that institution.

Rational choice institutionalists focus their attention on the rational design of institutions and the functions they perform. Where it is possible they undertake theoretical or mathematical modelling to examine institutions, particularly legislatures and judiciaries where actors operate within clearly defined parameters. The rational choice approach is deductive, making assumptions about individual preferences and conceptualizing institutions as being the rules of the game (cf. Hay, 2006a; Lecours, 2005; Thelen and Steinmo, 1992). Rational choice institutionalists borrow heavily from economic game theories such as the prisoner's dilemma and some will emphasize structural rather than individual explanations of policy-making (see Tsebelis, 1990).

Historical institutionalists

Where rational choice institutionalists adopt a calculus approach to their theoretical assumptions historical institutionalists combine a cultural logic. Their analytical approach combines deduction and induction; although generalizations are made these are necessarily bound by time and space. Historical institutionalists seek to explore and explain difference over time and between countries using empirical research to explain difference in outcomes. This path-dependent approach conceptualizes institutions as formal rules, compliance procedures and standard operating procedures, which have to be considered over long periods (Hall, 1986: 19). They are concerned with initial formation of institutions and subsequent policies and how these lead to a path dependency that impacts on policy decisions such as resistance to downsizing the welfare state ingrained by the original policy ideas (Thelen and Steinmo, 1992; Leibfried and Pierson, 1995).

Historical institutionalists find the constraints imposed by rational choice institutionalists to be too limiting and reject notions of utility maximization. Instead, they posit that individuals follow societal-defined rules even when it is not in their interest to do so and, in institutions, serve as 'satisfiers', doing enough rather than being rational maximizers (Simon, 1985; Thelen and Steinmo, 1992). Institutions are able to shape political outcomes by first shaping actors' strategies and goals by mediating attitudes, norms and behaviour within an institutional context. Political agency and choices exist but within the constraints of the institution. Institutions are never the only cause of outcomes but they are an important factor. Organizations limit the extent of power that any one group of actors possess, while also shaping an individual actor's preference formation by their position, responsibilities and relationship to others within the organization. Historical institutionalists argue that these organizational factors can reveal both the ability of actors to influence policy and the likely shape that influence is likely to take (Hall, 1986: 19).

Sociological institutionalists

Sociological (and normative) institutionalism owes much to the writings of James March and Johan Olsen (1984, 1989, 1994) who criticized Political Science for being too contextual in emphasizing the social context of political behaviour to the detriment of interpreting the state as an independent cause. They accused mainstream political scientists of either being reductionist, in reducing politics to being the product of individual actions, or utilitarian, in explaining individual actions as being inspired by utility maximization (March and Olsen, 1984: 735–6). March and Olsen, drawing from psychology and organizational theory, argue that political institutions exercise a relatively autonomous role in shaping political outcomes. Institutions' standard operating procedures and organizational structures enable them to become 'political actors in their own right' (March and Olsen, 1984: 738). They argue that institutions are the ideal starting point for considerations of behaviour. Political scientists need to understand the organizational cultures and values of those engaged in governance. They posit that 'logics of appropriateness' define members' appropriate behaviour in institutional contexts. Members internalize this institutional-appropriate behaviour, which then influences their subsequent actions and thinking (March and Olsen, 1989, 1994).

Sociological institutionalism defines institutions in cultural and ideational terms of norms and values. The focus is cognitive rather than strategic or historical, and power relationships are understood in the context of the 'cognitive institutional web' (Lecours, 2005: 17). Once the values and processes of the institution are internalized by actors then the capacity to reproduce those institutions is present. In sociological institutionalism there is little place for rationalism or voluntarism; the individual's actions become an outworking of the institutional perspective absorbed and adopted by the actor.

IR approaches to Institutions

After the end of World War II IR scholars demonstrated great interest in the setting up of new institutions to rebuild economies devastated by the

Box 5.2　New institutionalist approaches to NATO durability

The three new institutionalisms considered in this section all have a slightly different approach to change within institutions. All approaches, however, consider that the bureaucracy will do all that is necessary to keep the organization alive. NATO needed to find new threats in order to ensure its survival in a post-Cold War world. Rational choice institutionalists adopt a calculus approach in which an actor's instrumental rationality is configured on a cost–benefit analysis of continuing the organization after the initial threat has disappeared. What are the positive functions that NATO performs? Can the benefits of the peace and stability achieved during the Cold War be achieved through other means at lower cost? From a US governmental perspective do the benefits of continuing the organization, such as maintaining US strategic involvement in Europe, justify the cost of maintaining that involvement? Rational bureaucrats will seek to justify their own position by emphasizing value for money and the importance and efficacy of what the organization achieves. They will also emphasize the

→

war and to maintain international peace. The Bretton Woods institutions comprising the World Bank and International Monetary Fund, the General Agreement on Tariffs and Trade and the United Nations were to be the cornerstones of a new international order designed primarily by the United States. The end of the Cold War dispelled notions of international peace but, combined with the perception of increasing globalization, there emerged a resurgence in IR academic interest in the ability of international institutions to increase interdependence while reducing threats.

Neo-liberal institutionalism

Neo-liberal institutionalists emphasize cooperation rather than confrontation in the international system, which they attribute to the perceived ability of international institutions to overcome the problem of cheating on international agreements. Cheating is overcome by institutional frameworks, which provide the prospect of future gains based on cooperation. States will only benefit if they acquire a reputation for trustworthiness and play by the rules of the game. Neo-liberal institutionalists argue that the risks of not cooperating and the prospects of punishing those states that cheat can persuade states to reconsider their capacity of the organization to develop new missions, which they have the infrastructure to deliver more effectively than any alternative resource.

For historical institutionalists, NATO longevity has its roots in the foundation of the organization – how the organization was initially constituted, the importance of founding documents (including the articles of the treaty) and tracing the pathway along which subsequent evolution has occurred. In such a reading NATO is not simply a security alliance but also brings member states around shared values and ideals. Prior changes such as the expansion of NATO to include Greece and Turkey in 1952 or Spain in 1982 point the way to further expansion from 1999 onwards. Sociological institutionalists also go back to the creation of the organization but place greater emphasis on the cultural and the institutionalization of appropriate behaviour. In this analysis, the continuation of NATO is attributable to shared norms between member nations. Although the immediate threat dissipated, existing security structures were premised on the role of NATO. The inevitability of NATO, the forum provided for cooperation and collective decision-making among member countries, became the only way to think about security and advancing shared values of democracy, markets, human rights and the rule of law.

utility-maximizing behaviour. Institutions make international cooperation more efficient and transparent, and hence more profitable, by increasing the information available. The existence and strengthening of these institutions, it is argued, leads states to reconsider their behaviour in order to achieve maximum gains (Ruggie, 1992; Mearsheimer, 1995).

Focusing on the observable behaviour of institutions, neo-liberal institutionalism, like realism, treats states as rational and utilitarian. As utility maximizers, they will only cooperate with other states when they have significant common interests. Keohane and Martin argue that 'institutions make a significant difference in conjunction with power realities' when they provide information and 'establish focal points for cooperation (Keohane and Martin, 1995: 42). Increased transparency, credibility and establishing international norms increase confidence and reduce the costs of transactions as they substantially remove large elements of risk. Institutions are formed by states in order to standardize and legitimate behaviour and the more they are seen to function in the interests of all states, removing the fear of unequal gains from cooperation, then the more predictable international relations becomes and, according to neo-liberal institutionalists, the more pacific and prosperous (Keohane, 1989b: 10; Keohane and Martin, 1995: 45–6).

Box 5.3   Neo-liberal institutionalism and NATO durability

For neo-liberal institutionalists the continuation of NATO after the end of the Cold War was uncontested. The failure of realism to predict the peaceful end of the Cold War and the economic and ideological victory of liberal democratic capitalism ushered in a new era of cooperation with the attraction of capitalism to the former Soviet bloc opening new possibilities for the expansion of Western values. NATO had embodied those values since its founding and therefore it made sense to expand its sphere of operations to advance the shared values of member states. A regional security area provides members with increased confidence in each other's reliability as partners and therefore the potential for trade is increased. Neo-liberal institutionalists posit a more peaceful and prosperous world based on the shared values of democratic governance and free trade. International institutions are essential to this process but the United Nations, many of whose member states do not support liberal democratic values, is unreliable in promoting these objectives. NATO, for members sharing liberal democratic capitalist values, is a more reliable vehicle, which has demonstrated its capability through military interventions in Bosnia and Kosovo. The continuation of NATO for neo-liberal institutionalists is explained by the security back-up necessary to undergird the promotion of liberal democracy and capitalism.

Neo-liberal institutionalism, although enjoying the support of British and America governments after the Cold War, is a heavily contested concept within IR, not least from offensive realists such as Mearsheimer, who consider that any form of security cooperation is constrained by the inevitability of security competition between states. The realist presumption of anarchy, offensive military capability, uncertainty about others' intentions, the imperative of state survival, rationality and the prospects for miscalculation generate fear, promotes self-help and causes states to maximize relative, rather than absolute, power (Mearsheimer, 1995: 9–11). Power maximizers, the most powerful states in the system, create and shape institutions in their own image and for their own advantage. Seen in this light, institutions are there to maintain existing power balances or even increase the advantage of the most powerful for as long as possible. For realists, states will continue to act selfishly and will cooperate over security in the form of alliances when it is in their interest to do so; but for Mearsheimer his 'central conclusion is that institutions have minimal influence on state behaviour, and thus hold little promise for promoting stability in the post-Cold War world' (Mearsheimer, 1995: 7).

Foundational critical/scientific realist approaches

Marxism and critical theory

Where institutionalists tend to contemplate institutions and organizations through a pluralist lens, Marxists have developed strong critiques of the role of organizations and institutions within capitalist society. Institutions and organizations are understood as vehicles to facilitate the smooth running of capitalism and relationships to the means of production. For Marxists the emphasis on socio-economic structures defines policy-making at the macro level. This means they tend to minimize the role of agency in determining political outcomes (Casey, 2002: 14; Thelen and Steinmo, 1992: 10). Marx and Engels' superstructure consists of 'legal, political, religious and other non-economic institutions' (Cohen, 2004: 45) and so institutions, particularly political institutions, serve to further class interests under capitalism. Marxists point to a 'qualitative asymmetry' between the ruling class and political institutions in shaping policies adopted by the state. The class structure determines the sorts of policies the state will consider and institutions operate within these given parameters, selecting only those outcomes that are in accord with this class interest (Wright *et al.*, 1992: 130).

Critical theorists have sought to build on these Marxist approaches and develop an emancipatory project based on self-reflection and critique that produces enlightenment. When examined by critical theorists, institutions are revealed as highly coercive bodies, which perpetuate capitalism by lulling workers into a false consciousness that these exist for their benefit. The acceptance and even production of social and political institutions by agents contributes to their continued subjection and exploitation. As Raymond Geuss explains:

> Social institutions are not natural phenomena; they don't just exist of and by themselves. The agents in a society impose coercive institutions on themselves by participating in them, accepting them without protest etc. ... In acting, the agents 'produce' their basic social institutions and it is the normal operations of these social institutions which maintains the world-picture. (Geuss, 1999: 60)

For Claus Offe, however, a leading proponent of the Frankfurt School, the state in capitalism is an institutionalized form of power seeking to 'implement and guarantee the *collective* interests of all members of a class society dominated by capital (Offe, 1984: 120). The liberal democratic capitalist state, and by implication its institutions, are excluded from organizing production, leaving investment decisions to capitalists

Box 5.4   Critical theory and the continuation of NATO

A critical theory perspective on the durability of NATO would seek to challenge taken-for-granted assumptions that such a continuance was inevitable to take account of the new security threats in the post-Cold War era. Rather than simply accept NATO as a regional security alliance, critical theorists will be eager to reveal the role of NATO in protecting and advancing the interests of global capitalism. They will be seeking to demonstrate that belief that NATO is protecting citizens in Europe and North America from terrorist attack at home is an indication of false consciousness. NATO's involvement in Afghanistan and Pakistan, far from protecting citizens of NATO member states, actually increases the threat from disaffected diasporic communities in those countries aggrieved by NATO's actions. Critical theoretical approaches towards NATO will examine NATO's role as protecting the existing capitalist order.

without direct state control. The state depends on tax revenue from capitalist production and in order to remain in power needs to provide conditions favourable to capital accumulation. In addition to these two factors, the liberal democratic state requires legitimation from the demos. State institutions enable the existing capitalist order to continue through their ability to deal with fiscal or economic crises and through resisting challenges to the existing social order (Dunleavy and O'Leary, 1987: 257). Here power is not directly observable. But it is located within the system. We can identify this through reference to its observable effects which take the form of exploitation and inequality.

Marxist international political economy

In the international arena, Marxists have become a powerful force within international political economy owing much to the influences of (neo) Marxists writing about domestic politics including Polanyi (1944), Gramsci (1971) and Poulantzas (1973a and b). Tracing its roots from seventeenth-century mercantilism and the classical economists of the eighteenth and nineteenth centuries (Ricardo, Smith and Marx) international political economy (IPE) has strong Marxist credentials. The rapid economic development and relative industrial success of real existing socialism in the Soviet Union led in the 1940s to debates surrounding the nature of international capitalism, differing modes of production and technological advance and the nature of imperialism. During the Cold War, Marxist IPE turned its attention to the relationship of the Third World to international capitalism with the emergence of dependency theory and world systems theory. More

Box 5.5 Marxist IPE and NATO durability

For Marxist IPE theorists the continuation of NATO beyond the Cold War is perfectly understandable. The institution, like all other institutions established by the United States following its victory in World War II, was created to further the interests of global capitalism and the United Sates as its leading proponent and beneficiary. NATO existed to protect capitalism against its communist rival. After the Cold War new challenges to US and capitalist hegemony emerged in the form of terrorism or non-compliant states such as Iraq and Afghanistan. The threat to capitalist interests through insecure or unreliable oil supplies and the potential to access those oil supplies in Iraq or secure natural resources and build oil pipelines across Afghanistan help explain NATO's continued existence more than any existential terrorist threat to the West. Article 2 of the North Atlantic Treaty describes how NATO members will 'seek to eliminate conflict in their international economic policies and will encourage economic collaboration between any or all of them', confirming, for Marxists, the institution's role as defender and promoter of capitalism.

recently, neo-Marxist scholars have continued to influence thinking in IPE through adapting Gramsci's notion of hegemony (see Cox, 1983).

Marxists contend that the modern state and economy are inseparable. Modern capitalist economies are embedded in society and culture and, rather than being at the disposal of Adam Smith's invisible hand, *laissez faire* economies have to be well managed (Polanyi, 1944; Jørgensen, 2010). Marxists are particularly interested in the institutionalization of power at home and abroad. Poulantzas argues that social classes entrench their democratic gains, normalizing and institutionalizing them so that they become accepted by all over time. The class-driven nature of society and the international system is obscured by this normalization. The state develops institutional structures to perpetuate, strengthen and deepen capitalist relationships while maintaining some degree of autonomy from these interests (Poulantzas, 1973a and b; Palin, 2000: 11–12). In this way, the ruling classes (those who own or control the commanding heights of the economy) are able to maintain their power, influence and control over the state and extend this through institutions in the international system such as the IMF, World Bank and WTO, without widespread resistance.

Anti-foundational interpretivist approaches

Constructivist institutionalism and poststructural feminism

Colin Hay has been at the forefront of developing new understandings of constructivist institutionalism. Although there are similarities with both sociological and historical institutionalism, it is the anti-foundationalist approach that provides social constructivist approaches with their distinctive ontological position. For constructivists, ideas are the crucial factor in understanding not only how institutions function but how they are formed, sustained and transformed. The constructivist institutionalist project is concerned to:

> identify, detail and interrogate the extent to which – through processes of normalisation and institutional embedding – established ideas become codified, serving as cognitive filters through which actors come to interpret environmental signals. (Hay, 2006a: 65)

For constructivists, institutions are vitally important because they are the subject and focus of political struggle between either political parties or competing interests. The institutions themselves are social constructs revealed and sustained by codified systems of ideas and perceptions. Constructivist institutionalists seek to discover how those ideas become codified over time and are then contested before being replaced. They seek to discover how actors shape those ideas and act strategically in order to achieve 'complex, contingent and constantly changing goals' (Hay, 2006a: 63). Actors can behave strategically and at the same time be socialized to pursue strategies and goals that are shaped by institutional norms, which have been internalized and acted upon by those actors. Actors' actions and motivations can be ascertained through process tracing and discourse analysis. The constructivist institutionalist uses both inductive and deductive analytical approach methods to explain institutional actions and those of individual actors.

Institutional change comes about through the contestation, challenge and replacement of existing ideas by actors. In order to trace this, social constructivists will examine the relationship between actors and the political or economic context they find themselves in. The position and influence exerted by actors within institutions is crucial in explaining institutional change, although a necessary component of institutional change is change in the political environment. Hay, and fellow constructivists, place special emphasis on the socially constructed nature of political opportunity structures. Theorists examine institutions when first formed and thereafter to discover what ideas have become institutionalized, codified and formalized. Rather than changing circumstances, constructivists posit that it is ideational change that inspires all institutional change. Crises may occur, which have the potential to change institutions, but they emphasize the need to examine the discursive construction of those crises to account for change occurring.

As we saw, for example, in Chapter 3, for some the global financial crisis of 2007–10 was caused by a liquidity crisis in the US banking system due to the overvaluation of assets and disastrous lending policies resulting in the closure of many financial institutions and large-scale government bailouts of others. International financial institutions such as the International Monetary Fund (IMF) initially came under severe criticism for their failure to persuade leading industrial nations, and major contributors to the fund, to regulate their financial sectors and reduce their propensity for risky speculation. However, the IMF were able to construct a discourse whereby rather than appearing to be a part of the problem they were able to transform their lending policies and present themselves as a solution to the problem. A revised lending framework and changes to conditionality was inspired by an ideational rationale that positioned the IMF at the centre of international efforts to undergird national initiatives undertaken by member states. In this way we understand behaviour through reference to dominant discourses which can influence and shape behaviour, and can also be appropriated by institutions to legitimate their own behaviour.

Poststructuralists are also passionately concerned with discourse whereby language consists not just of words, but also the construction of meaning and cultural practices that enable people to understand their world (Pringle, 1996: 254). For poststructuralists politics is all about power and power lies at the centre of discourse. The universal discourse, which seeks to present the political process as somehow inevitable and something other than about power, lies at the heart of poststructuralist agenda. Poststructuralism seeks to historicize and neutralize the significance of such discourse by exposing the nature of power and control within political systems through Derrida's 'cultural system of grafting' and Foucault's 'disciplinary power of the state' (Koch, 2007: 125). Culture and political power meet in those institutions, which then use cultural norms and values in order to discipline populations and establish their own legitimacy and continuation.

Radical feminists within the poststructuralist tradition consider that discourse provides a key role in understanding how institutions are organized and operate in the interests of men and to the detriment of women. Discourse is embodied within institutions as well in the words which are spoken and written. Rosemary Pringle claims that feminists have appropriated language, discourse, difference and deconstruction (Pringle, 1996: 254). This is strongest within the poststructuralist tradition where theories about 'language, subjectivity, social processes and institutions' are used to interpret existing power relationships and their capacity for change (Weedon, 2004: 40). Patriarchal power is located inside and outside institutions, but for feminists equal access to positions within institutions is insufficient to bring about change. The institutions themselves must be changed to account for women's experience (McLaren,

Box 5.6   Poststructural feminism and NATO durability

For poststructural feminists NATO longevity can be explained by the institution's ability to maintain a masculinist discourse that constructs security threats and the need for the institution to protect citizens. Feminists are concerned about the institution's ability to change its mission, extended out of area, and yet to remain the same patriarchal institution. Women are marginalized within the organization and used as subjects needing protection in the discursive conditioning of populations before and during conflicts where the abuse of women is used as a rationale to legitimate military intervention. To date, all 12 secretary generals have been men and at the time of writing each of the senior positions within the organization is held by a man. NATO survives because it employs a masculinist discourse of security threat in a patriarchal world. In doing so, existing power relationships within capitalism and between men and women are perpetuated.

1989: 8). Institutional change though can either serve hegemonic power interests and perpetuate inequality or overcome patriarchal power relationships. Linda Kauffman laments that 'one of the sobering discoveries I've made as a feminist is that institutions shape us more than we shape them' (Kauffman, 1993: 134; see also Kauffman, 1989).

Constructivist international relations

Constructivist IR emerged as an important voice within IR towards the end of the Cold War, when traditional positivist theories of IR seemed incapable of explaining the ending of the Cold War through the abdication and implosion of one of the main protagonists rather than decisive military victory. Social constructivism is regarded by many IR scholars, including Alexander Wendt (a leading constructivist in IR), as more of an approach than a coherent theory. However, this is probably doing a disservice to the numerous academics who, over the course of the past few decades, have propelled constructivism to be one of the most significant streams in IR today. Constructivist IR is far more developed and robust than its institutionalist counterpart. Hay describes the two disciplines as 'parallel if initially distinct developments' (Hay, 2006a: 64).

Constructivism may be viewed as approaches (in the plural rather than as a singular approach, or providing for a single theory). These range from Wendt's positivist epistemology and interpretivist ontology, content to supplement neo-realist or neo-liberal theories, to postmodernist and poststructuralist theories, which adopt anti-foundational epistemological and ontological positions and emphasize discursive practices. All constructivists agree, however, that taken-for-granted assumptions about knowledge and reality need challenging. The objects of our knowledge have already been subject to the intellectual filter of our interpretations. In turn, our interpretations – indeed, the way we see the world and ourselves – are the product of norms, rules, law and identities. For constructivists, the power of ideas and our interpretive understanding is far more important than material considerations. Rather than merely accepting traditional and mainstream understanding of identities and state interests, constructivism seeks to problematize these.

Constructivism rejects the notion of pure social scientific objectivity and instead seeks to discover, historically and empirically, the relationship of ideational factors and international structures. International society is work in progress in a world that does not have to be anarchic (Wendt, 1992, 1999). Ideational factors of rules, norms and law shape how the international system operates and how states and individuals consider their role within it. These influence both the identity and the interests of actors and produce behavioural expectations of self and others. The intersubjective interaction of people and states leads to the normalization of collective ideas that are agreed and worked out as norms, rules and laws through institutions, practices and identities (Viotti and Kauppi, 2010: 276–8). Norms and rules form value-based expectations of appropriate behaviour at all levels of domestic and international society.

For the constructivist, structure and agency are co-determinant and mutually constituent. How we define ourselves and develop relationships with others is shaped by the ideational structures we operate within. Nicholas Onuf expresses this interconnectivity as 'people make society and society makes people' (Onuf, 1998: 59). Institutional change is possible as agents interact with others and norm entrepreneurs such as Human Rights Watch, Médecins Sans Frontières or even Bob Geldof and Bono interact and construct new behavioural norms – on human rights, the environment, poverty alleviation – that are accepted by others and institutionalized in laws and operating procedures. The acceptance and normalization of shared ideas has far greater explanatory potential for constructivists than material forces, which in neo-realist IR would suggest that war, fear and mutual suspicion is the default position of international security. Constructivists in IR consider that international institutions are expressions of shared ideas, accepted and enacted by actors, thereby reinforcing those values and institutions. For them, institutional change occurs when human association produces new ideas and these then become institutionalized.

Box 5.7   Constructivist IR and NATO durability

Constructivist IR approaches the issue of NATO's continuation after the collapse of communism from the shared ideas, identity and interests of actors. From within the organization actors have internalized what NATO has said about itself over its 60-plus-year history. At the end of the Cold War norm entrepreneurs such as George H. Bush, Margaret Thatcher and Bill Clinton stressed a changed world full of opportunities to promote and advance capitalism and liberal democracy. The possibility of a revanchist Russia, the concerns that this posed to newly emerging democracies in Central and Eastern Europe, fears of nuclear, chemical and biological proliferation and the impact of Al Qaeda's attack on Washington and New York constructed a discourse of security threat. NATO was able to reinvent itself as the organization best able to deal with these new threats. Intervention to promote democracy, defend human rights, to ensure compliance with international norms and laws became part of the post-Cold War discourse and NATO's continuance, for constructivists, can be seen in this light. Whatever the threat constructed, NATO officials were able to construct a telling narrative for their continued role in meeting the new challenges. Consider, for example, NATO's use of the repression of Afghan women as a pretext or motivation for NATO intervention in Afghanistan, not simply in revenge for the 9/11 attacks but also to be seen as the protectors of repressed Afghan women.

Comparison of theories and approaches

The four new institutionalist approaches we have introduced in this chapter have been particularly influential in considering policy analysis and comparative politics. Rational choice institutionalism provides a useful and simple theory from which they argue it is straightforward to make predictions. Rational choice institutionalists deduce that actors are instrumentally rational and seek to maximize their utility. This calculus approach produces a view of society as governed by rules of the game, and individuals as operating in a bounded rational paradigm. This approach, however, is not particularly good at, or indeed interested in, explaining how institutions begin.

Historical institutionalists adopt both calculus and cultural approaches to examine institutions over time and place. The approach is path dependent assuming the path taken by institutions is determined by their historical origins. These theorists use both inductive and deductive analytical approaches and pay far more attention to norms and conventions than rational choice theorists. A weakness of the theory though lies in its lack of consideration of how institutions affect the behaviour of agents working within those institutions. This is an area sociological institutionalists have sought to overcome by adopting a cultural approach with deductive and inductive analyses to reveal how actors absorb and replicate institutional norms through appropriate behaviour. They attach importance to the genesis of institutional creation but assume prior institutions and borrowing from these.

Constructivist institutionalists consider that each of the preceding institutionalisms fail to adequately address the issue of institutional change. They tend to focus on how discourses of crises are constructed and how policy paradigms are normalized. The emphasis here is on the power of ideas, though norm entrepreneurs are a precondition for institutional change. Although Colin Hay points to parallel paths of constructivist institutionalism and constructivist IR, the similarities are abundant, albeit that constructivist IR has a longer history and stronger theoretical development. Both are concerned with the relationship between ideas and institutional origination, development and change.

Neo-liberal institutionalists, like rational choice institutionalists, operate in a positivist rational paradigm. Neo-liberal institutionalists assume rationality in states seeking to maximize their absolute, rather than relative, power through a cooperative world order. Institutions solve the problems of suspicions of cheating by other actors and posit a win–win international order where clearly understood rules, laws and norms facilitate interdependence based on mutual trust. Marxists tend to consider that socio-economic considerations are most important and that institutions perpetuate class inequalities and serve the interests of global capitalism. In international political economy, Marxists emphasize hegemony and the inseparability of the state and economies. False consciousness inculcated by and through institutions, is a main concern of critical theorists. They understand the state in terms of institutionalized forms of power. Poststructuralists are also concerned with power and combine Derridian cultural grafting with Foucauldian disciplinary power to explain how institutions establish legitimacy. In this chapter we discussed poststructural feminism with its emphasis on discourse. However, all feminisms focus on a patriarchal world order that excludes and suppresses women. Institutions reflect that world order and so feminists seek to expose these power relationships and inequality and how a masculinist discourse prevails within and through institutions.

Adjudicating between perspectives

When studying institutions we need to consider how they originated, how they function, and how they change over time. Depending on our ontological position we may also be concerned with which interests are served by institutions, how those interests are upheld and how power relationships are constituted. If we believe that the functions of institutions and the agents who work within them can be understood in terms of advancing their own best interests then we will adopt a rational choice approach as favoured by rational choice institutionalism; neoliberal institutionalism identifies cooperation as the way to maximize utility. If, however, we consider that they can better be understood by considering how they originate and change over time then historical institutionalism would be the favoured approach. If our concern is about institutional culture and why actors function the way they do, adhering to and advancing norms and conventions of appropriate behaviour, then sociological institutionalism would offer a clear theoretical perspective. These approaches do not necessarily explain a great deal about how ideas affect institutions, especially when they change policy and purpose. Constructivist institutionalism and its IR social constructivist equivalent, with its strong focus on discourse and norm entrepreneurship, hold out greater possibilities for understanding institutional change.

With the exception of constructivism, the new institutionalist theories seek to explain rather than challenge institutions; if our intention is to critique in order to radically change or reject existing institutions then we need to turn our attention to Marxist, critical theory, poststructural and feminist approaches. Just as theory is always for someone and for some purpose, so institutions are also for someone and for some purpose. If our concern is with institutionalized discrimination against women then feminist theories are able to expose patriarchal structures and the prevailing discourse to challenge taken for granted assumptions. Similarly, if we consider that socio-economic considerations are most important and want to understand how institutions uphold the existing order, then Marxist and critical theoretical approaches would appear to have most to offer. If, on the other hand, the most important issue is not so much the vested interests of class or gender but rather how existing power relationships emerge, are sustained and subsequently challenged, then poststructuralist emphasis on discourse, disciplinary power and cultural grafting represents a useful avenue of investigation.

Conclusion

Over the course of this chapter, we have sought to provide an overview of some of the main currents of thought surrounding institutions. In many ways, theoretical consideration of institutions cannot be separated from the policy analysis discussed in the preceding chapter. Rather than simply accepting institutions as a given, we have demonstrated that their purpose, function and potential is hotly contested. While most theoretical work on institutions has focused on policy analysis at the domestic level and in comparative analysis, through the example of NATO durability we have seen how new institutional analysis and other political science theories can be applied to an international institution. Similarly, constructivist institutionalism has emerged as a theoretical perspective within political science and this approach is learning and benefiting from constructivist thinking in IR.

We have seen how institutions both shape and are shaped by the world in which we live. If we want to understand how politics and international politics work, then it is not possible to neglect the study of institutions. What we have tried to do is to show how different assumptions about the role and function of institutions inform theoretical approaches to studying them. Political Science and IR approaches have a great deal of overlap and, indeed, institutions operate at national and international level and require similar methodologies to examine and analyze them. With all the approaches we have considered there are strong normative influences, whether these are acknowledged or not. Assumptions are made about how institutions behave and how they ought to behave, how they maintain existing power relationships and how these should be overturned. Before we start to examine institutions we have to consider carefully what we are trying to achieve or discover. Are we seeking to understand how institutions have developed over time? How they bring stability to the domestic and international polity? Do we want to discover the role of actors within institutions? How they influence policy? Perhaps we would like to discover in whose interest institutions operate, or the impact of ideas and culture. We need to think about what we are looking at. Is it the structures, the bureaucracy, the policies carried out, or maybe the agents? What can language, verbal and non-verbal, tells us about institutions? The approach we adopt and the questions we ask will be influenced by our ontological positions.

Reflection

Which perspective or approach does the best job of accounting for the continuation of NATO after the end of the Cold War?

Why do you think this is the case?

Can we understand the longevity of NATO through observation of the behaviour of bureaucrats and political elites? Or do we need to understand it in light of its historical development?

→

Is the continuity of NATO caused by the need to protect and advance the interests of global capitalism?

Do you think that NATO is a reflection or a result of the construction of masculinist discourses which emphasize a military security threat? Do you think it needs to be challenged and, if so, how might that be done?

How can insights from Political Science and IR help us analyze the continuation of NATO? What are your reasons for your answer?

Seminar activities

Download the 14 Articles of the North Atlantic Treaty and discuss which articles define NATO's mission in 1949. Consider how and why the organization was able to reinvent itself and expand its area of activities following the collapse of the Soviet Union. Consider the importance of the founding document to the subsequent development of NATO.

Consider what the world would need to look like for NATO to become obsolete.

Do international institutions exist primarily to serve the interests of global capitalism?

Which perspective does your answer fit most closely with and why do you think this is the case?

Chapter 6

Representation and Participation

Introduction

Representation and participation are the lifeblood of vibrant democracies and yet among Western democracies there has been much soul-searching about democratic deficits and crises of legitimation as voter turnout has become increasingly volatile over the past few decades. A veritable industry has grown up consisting of academics, political analysts, pollsters, media professionals, activists and politicians accepting the prevailing wisdom and proffering all manner of possible solutions to this seemingly intractable problem. Nothing less than the demise of democracy itself is forecast in a series of wonderfully titled books explaining why the West has become disengaged from the political process. *Why Americans Mistrust Government* (Nye *et al.*, 1997), *The Future of Freedom: Illiberal Democracy at Home and Abroad* (Zakaria, 2003), *Why We Hate Politics* (Hay, 2007) provide a small flavour of the genre. Gerry Stoker, in an antidote to gloom and despondency, warns of the dangers of cynicism and populism, urging active political participation in his *Why Politics Matter* (2006). Stephen Macedo and associates' report to the Brookings Institution, *Democracy at Risk*, presents a stark picture:

> American democracy is at risk. The risk comes not from some external threat but from disturbing internal trends: an erosion of the activities and capacities of citizenship. Americans have turned away from politics and the public sphere in large numbers, leaving our civic life impoverished. Citizens participate in public affairs less frequently, with less knowledge and enthusiasm, in fewer venues, and less equally than is healthy for a vibrant democratic polity. (Macedo *et al.*, 2005: 1)

Macedo and his team highlighted inequalities in participation based on material resources, the poor being disadvantaged and less likely to participate accordingly. After African-American participation in the civil rights struggles of the 1960s subsequent engagement has fallen. Immigration status affected levels of civic engagement and the phenomenal decline in membership of trade unions has also contributed to political disengagement. Macedo did discover a vibrant voluntary and non-profit sector, but notes that they are excluded from representing the interests of their poor, sick, aged or otherwise disadvantaged constituencies (Macedo *et al.*, 2005: 157). The report makes no fewer that 45 recommendations to encourage civic participation from voting reform, education, revitalized local politics, encouragements for philanthropic and charitable involvement, membership of churches and trade unions, to national service (Macedo *et al.*, 2005: 168–9).

Those prophesying political apathy and civic disengagement receive considerable support for their view from politicians, particularly in the UK and US, and numerous initiatives to reform voting practices have been instituted in Britain with the targeting of those sections of society traditionally least likely to vote. The pattern of voting decline in the 1980s and 1990s has, however, been reversed slightly in the 2000s. Russell Dalton's work highlights that, far from a democratic deficit, norms of citizenship are creating an increasingly engaged citizenry. Voter turnout in the 2000s was higher than the previous decade, and those taking part in campaigning, involvement with civic groups, signing petitions, protesting and community action are higher than in the previous three decades (Dalton, 2006: 9).

For Dalton, citizens are not disengaging from political processes, merely changing the way in which they participate politically. The increasing number of opportunities available to engaged citizens, when taken up, heightens the pressure on political elites. 'Citizen participation is becoming more closely linked to citizen influence. Rather than democracy being at risk, this represents an opportunity to expand and enrich democratic participation' (Dalton, 2006: 11). In this chapter, we look at the way the interests of citizens and other actors are represented at both the national and international level. Rather than concentrating on the electoral system and policy-makers, the chapter seeks to explore how organized groups are able to get their views represented and participate in the democratic process within states and internationally. We examine six different theoretical approaches to representation and participation. As with previous chapters, the theoretical positions are compared and we adjudicate between the competing theories. In our case study, we concentrate on the US Israel Lobby's support for Israel. In doing so we seek to emphasize that contemporary representation breaks down old barriers and now traditional IR concerns are very much part and parcel of domestic political realities. Political Science/IR distinctions evaporate in the face of international lobbying groups being able to influence government foreign policy and domestic priorities. This includes groups such as the Israel Lobby, but can also include foreign-based multinational corporations exercising influence over domestic government policy affecting their products or services.

Power

Participation and representation are principally about power, who has it, who can access it, and to what purpose. As we have seen in previous chapters, discovering who or which groups exercise power within democratic societies is a complex business with many competing theoretical claims and methodological approaches demanding our attention. In this chapter, we will concentrate on the citizen's ability to influence political processes individually and collectively through joining interest or pressure groups in a bid to influence decision-makers in favour of their preferred outcomes. We do not confine our attention to just domestic or comparative politics but also examine IR approaches to domestic sources of foreign policy and the role of transnational actors, multinational corporations and non-governmental organizations.

Interest groups, pressure groups and non-governmental actors, by definition, represent specific interests and seek to influence political authorities in favour of the causes they espouse. In pluralist societies, this has become an important and distinguishing feature of democracy, indicating a vibrant and engaged civil society. Jeremy Richardson describes a pressure group as 'any group which articulates demands that the political authorities in the political system or sub-system should make an authoritative allocation' (Richardson, 1993: 1). He emphasizes that such groups do not seek political authority themselves but rather to influence those who have the power to make and carry out decisions. By considering various theoretical approaches we explore how convinced, and convincing, theorists are about the ability of groups to affect policy decisions. In the process, we also examine the democratic deficit of the groups themselves, questioning how representative and democratic they are. How accountable are they and to whom? How convincing are NGOs' and other transnational actors' claims to be the representatives of global peoples? Are pressure groups reflective of existing class divisions and economic power structures? Do they reflect existing gendered power struggles? Does participation by women entail different characteristics than male participation?

Box 6.1   Case study. Representation, participation and support for Israel

In 2006, two prominent IR scholars John Mearsheimer and Stephen Walt (2006, 2007) wrote an article for the *Atlantic Monthly* which was to prove so controversial the journal refused to publish it; the authors therefore published it in the *London Review of Books*. The article was entitled 'The Israel Lobby' and presented compelling evidence of the existence of a well-organized, well-funded and politically efficient lobby group working in support of Israel. The Lobby is so successful, according to the authors, that they are able to exert influence at the highest echelons of US foreign policy and, in effect, make US foreign policy in the Middle East subservient to Israel's rather than the US's national interests. The Lobby is made up of supporters of Israel and comprises three main groupings – the Jewish lobby, represented principally by American-Israel Public Affairs Committee (AIPAC); the Christian Right, made up of Christian Zionist supporters of Israel; and neo-conservatives, who support Israel on ideological grounds as a democracy within the Middle East region. The subsequent book, published a year later, provided an enormous amount of detailed evidence of the power of this particular lobby.

The authors' main arguments are that the Lobby is so well organized and has such influence within the executive and legislature that US national interests are often jeopardized by supporting Israel against Palestinians. This comes at the expense of support for America in the Arab world and the targeting of the US by terrorist groups partly on the basis of support for Israel. It is not our intention here to comment on US support for Israel, rather to use this case study to serve as the basis for further consideration of the influence

Foundational positivist approaches

Pluralism and neo-pluralism

Robert Dahl's study of New Haven decision-making processes provides the basis for our understandings of pluralism and its neo-pluralist successor (as we also saw in Chapter 3). The study, which presents an effective rebuttal to elite theory and a reaction against institutionalism, presents an explanation of decision-making processes that recognizes numerous influences in a system of 'dispersed inequalities'. Dahl lists a set of six distinguishing characteristics:

1. Many different kinds of resources for influencing officials are available to different citizens.
2. With few exceptions, these resources are unequally distributed.

of interest groups within the domestic and international polity. Two of the leading actors within the Lobby are AIPAC and the Christian Zionist organization Christians United for Israel (CUFI), led by Pastor John Hagee. The two groups operate together and separately at different times, especially when they are appealing to different constituencies. AIPAC is one of the most successful interest groups in the United States and CUFI has largely copied its *modus operandi* to exert influence. The groups operate by cultivating good relationships with decision-makers they regard as friends of Israel. They keep scorecards of the votes of all legislators regarding issues of interest to Israel, including support for military campaigns in the West Bank 2002, Southern Lebanon 2006 and Gaza 2008/9. Constituents are informed of the voting records of their representatives and pro-Israel legislators receive campaign support while those considered not to be sympathetic towards Israel see support going to rival candidates. The Lobby has an instant rebuttal service designed to respond to any adverse criticism of Israel across the media immediately. Supporters are kept informed of their organization's activities and are part of a force that can be mobilized within hours to send emails, faxes and texts to legislators or the White House to condemn criticism of Israeli actions. Both organizations have annual conferences addressed by the prime minister of Israel, the Israeli ambassador and leading presidential campaigners. Appearance before AIPAC's annual conference is a right of passage for any aspiring president (see Marsden, 2008).

The organizations also provide moral and financial support for Jewish settlements in the West Bank and East Jerusalem and apply pressure to the White House and Department of State not to ask Israel to abandon its settlement-building programme. In terms of participation and representation, AIPAC, in particular, would appear to be the epitome of a successful interest group organization, listened to and achieving successes in its key objectives.

3. Individuals best off in their access to one kind of resource are often badly off with respect to many other resources.
4. No one influence resource dominates all the others in all or even most key decisions.
5. With some exceptions, an influence resource is effective in some issue-areas or in some specific decisions but not in all.
6. Virtually no one, and certainly no group of more than a few individuals, is entirely lacking in some influential resources. (Dahl, 1961: 228)

Here Dahl presents us with the possibility of myriad special interest groups with overlapping and competing interests being able to influence decision-making. Pluralists see these interest groups as having 'widely differing power bases and a multitude of techniques for exercising influence on decisions salient to them' (Polsby, 1970: 118). The empirical evidence collected by pluralists leads them to believe that power is fragmented and decentralized in Western democratic systems. Although not all interest groups will be successful, they are right to believe that they will get a hearing for their viewpoint. Pluralists contend that the dispersion of power is positive and that the only way to understand political practice is through observing the policy process. This adheres to the foundational and positivist roots whereby emphasis is upon observable measurable behaviour which defines the objective truth about political reality. Elections and parliamentary activity are thought to give a distorted view about where power is located. Political outcomes reflect different policy sectors, and policy-holders, the emphasis is upon individuals exhibiting agency (having the capacity to act). Pluralism also makes an assumption that it is the interaction of interests that provides a source of authority rather than the 'general will' (Jordan, 1993: 58).

In this perspective, the actions of government are thus attributable to the interplay of competing interest groups within and without political authorities. Interest groups, however, can only achieve their objectives through persuading government officials and elected politicians to accept their policy suggestions. Clearly, some groups will be more effective than others at the task of persuasion. Some will be far better resourced than others and be able to use propaganda, media resources, canvassers and political analysis. Well-funded pressure groups are able to use their resources to persuade officials and publics of the efficacy of their case. Efficient interest groups will be able to persuade members to sign petitions, write to elected representatives, organize demonstrations, ring in to talk radio shows and television programmes, subscribe to online blogs and newsletters, write to the press and even carry out acts of civil disobedience. Citizens can carry out such activities independently but are far more effective when they can unite with like-minded groups.

Charles Lindblom places some caveats to the assumptions of power-wielding interest groups. He points out that the motivations for joining an interest group might not be to influence policy decisions but rather be 'another device for delegation of the task of policy-making' (Lindblom, 1968: 50). Rather than seeing interest groups in antagonistic relationship with policy-makers, Lindblom describes how they cooperate with them. Interest group leaders build lasting good relationships, where possible, with policy-makers whom they attempt to win over to their policies by persuasion rather than force. Interest groups will develop expertise on partisan politics and seek favour with leading political parties and key decision-makers. He suggests that one of their main strengths is that they have become 'highly skilled practitioners of partisan analysis' something which is marketable to political opponents and decision-makers (Lindblom, 1968: 65).

There are weaknesses though which constrain their ability to achieve their objectives. Citizens may well be attached to more than one interest group and so their political energies dissipate. Conflicts occur between different interest groups, curbing the influence of all parties involved in the dispute. The emergence of new interest groups can detract from established groups and lead to members moving to the newer grouping. Further, much of the activity of interest groups tends to be internal briefings and clarifications removed from any attempt to influence policy-makers (Lindblom, 1968: 67–8).

Neo-pluralism presents a shift in pluralist thinking to accommodate the role of business interests in public policy-making. Business is now seen to be more significant than other social interests in influencing decision-makers. Corporations (now often multinational) will exploit their relationship with government to gain special treatment. With governments' dependence upon corporations to provide employment and pay taxes, corporations are able to manipulate them by promising to commit resources, investment and jobs to the country or alternatively to threaten withdrawal and the removal of jobs and tax revenue overseas. They are able to cooperate with or resist government policy-making.

> [Governments in liberal democracies] extensively anticipate corporate demands and preferences, building a concern for business profitability into policy-making at the most basic level, and consequently considerably reducing the need for corporations to engage in overt lobbying or observable political conflict. (Dunleavy and O'Leary, 1987: 294)

The success of multinational corporations (MNCs) in developing strategies of interdependence with national governments is seen by Dunleavy and O'Leary as constituting a unified 'planning system' in which MNCs set agendas and the 'parameters of public discussion' (Dunleavy and O'Leary, 1987: 295–6). What emerges is a dual-polity dominated by business influence, with governments representing the formal political equality of liberal democracies and business representing the inequality of capitalism (Dunleavy and O'Leary, 1987: 297–8). How such arrangements are formalized varies from country to country. Clearly, in such a polity, business, because of its proximity to government, exercises considerably more influence over government policy than other interest groups, although it doesn't dominate over the government's other objectives.

Liberalism

Liberalism in international relations, similarly takes a pluralist position and views the international system as state-centric but interdependent,

Box 6.2   Pluralism and support for Israel

Pluralism provides for a polity which is multifaceted, with the opportunity for interest groups to lobby and make their case before legislators and other decision-makers. AIPAC and CUFI are just two of many hundreds, if not thousands, of organizations whose main objective is to maintain and increase support for Israel. No matter how grandiose the claims of interest groups and other lobbying organizations, it is notoriously difficult to demonstrate policy influence. Given America's strategic alliance with Israel, shared market democracy and historic sympathies, has US support for Israel been as a result of lobbying, because of shared values, or strategic US national security interests? We can always pose the counterfactual question. What would have been the policy decisions on support for Israel at specific times if there had been no lobbying or no AIPAC? A research project of observing and interviewing the key policy-makers and their interaction with lobbying groups or examination of voting records on Israel-related issues would fit within a pluralist paradigm. Here the focus is upon observable behaviour of agents (acting either as individuals or in a cohesive unitary group).

with institutions serving to ameliorate the anarchical nature of the system. The theory is highly normative, taking a cosmopolitan view of the world and drawing on the writings of Kant, Adam Smith and Locke. Unlike realism, liberalism looks beneath the level of state borders to examine the domestic polity as a signifier of prospective international behaviour and character and to discover domestic sources of foreign policy. However, again the focus is upon the observable behaviour of political actors (either individuals or cohesive groups).

If we examine the making of US foreign policy, we discover a significant role for interest groups, business and individual citizens to seek to apply influence. There are a great many relevant agencies to attempt to influence, including the White House, State Department, Department of Defense, National Security Council, Central Intelligence Agency and Department of Homeland Security. Both Houses of Congress have foreign affairs committees and have budgetary responsibility for funding US foreign policy operations. The political nature of appointees in senior positions within the administration and elected representatives in Congress provide high levels of scrutiny and accountability, with the opportunity for public engagement.

Interest groups seek to gain a hearing within the executive and legislature in order to represent the interests of their members. Such groups include business, trade unions, churches and faith-based organizations, environmentalist activists, professional associations and trades. There are a significant number of diasporic communities that use their voting leverage and financial donations to win approval for policies supportive of their home country. In the United States, Cuban exiles based in Miami insist that the US government maintains pressure to undermine the Castro regime. Kosovar Albanians living in America were effective in persuading President Clinton to intervene in Kosovo (Hockenos, 2003). Exile groups, many of several generations standing, focus attention on their former or ancestral homelands. Irish Americans were very active in trying to bring an end to the Northern Ireland conflict and enjoy regular access to the White House (McGarry and O'Leary, 2004). Any interest group, to be effective in Washington, needs to be able to get access to the right people. When they have managed to get hold of the right person they need to present cogent arguments, and demonstrate knowledge of the subject in order to gain the confidence of the legislator, bureaucrat or member of the executive. Further, they require the ability to trade favours for successful outcomes (Goldstein and Pevehouse, 2010: 96).

Alongside interest groups, think tanks provide an informed analysis of foreign policy. Think tanks prepare reports on key foreign policy issues in an attempt to change policy choices or to endorse existing strategy. The military industrial complex, the collectivity of government agencies, corporations and research institutes, also discuss foreign policy issues. The vast sums of money spent on arms procurement, combat missions and development-related infrastructural support makes this intersection one of the most financially profitable, with vested interests in securing research and development contracts for corporations, research institutes (including universities) and arms manufacture in congressional districts (Pavelec, 2010). Public opinion also has some impact, although preference tends to be given to informed actors or the attentive public made up of a foreign policy elite of people in government and business, lobbyists, journalists, professors of political science (Holsti, 2004). As the CNN effect discussed in Chapter 7 highlights, the media themselves can also mobilize interests. The impact of the media can engage viewers and listeners with foreign policy issues leading to grass roots responses and demands to the executive and legislature members to act – for example, in response to environmental disasters or human rights abuses.

Those who espouse liberalism seek to reproduce liberal values abroad, believing that its values of liberal democracy, open markets, free trade and pluralism are universal values. In the Kantian tradition of democratic peace, liberals believe that democracies do not go to war with one another because they share the same values and if democracy spreads through programmes of democratization then the world will become more pacific and interdependent (Doyle, 1983a, b; Russett, 1994). Citizens, NGOs and transnational actors participate in the spread of democracy promotion initiatives largely through UN, EU and US initiatives seeking to promote the concept of market democracy with civil society around

Box 6.3   Liberalism and support for Israel

A liberal approach to support for Israel by lobbying groups would be to acknowledge the impact of lobbying on foreign policy processes. Liberalism is a theory of interconnectedness and interdependence and support for Israel by lobbying groups and government fits within this nexus. Liberal approaches will reflect on the importance of alliances, democracy promotion and support for a democracy within the context of democratic peace theory. Liberals will focus attention on diplomatic and economic consequences of support for Israel and the extent to which democracy can be promoted in the region. Liberal theorists could consider research projects on the development of civil society and the role of international institutions in bringing about an improvement in Palestinian conditions, peaceful co-existence, or the role of sub-state and transnational actors on the ground. In this perspective causal explanations are provided which are derived from observation of political behaviour.

the world. Liberal theorists do not challenge the legitimacy of unelected, unaccountable and even elitist transnational actors intervening in foreign polities. Here the focus is on observation and measurement, with the aim of generating explanations and predictions.

Foundational critical/scientific realist approaches

Neo-Marxism

Traditionally Marxist theory has focused on historical materialism; the idea that history is a linear progression marked by successive transformations from lower to higher levels of production and technology. The relationship to the means of production results in antagonistic relationships and class struggle between bourgeoisie and proletariat. This class struggle forms the organizational principle of liberal capitalist states. For Marxists the demise of the proletariat as we entered a post-industrial age has been problematic. The old certainties about class struggle have disappeared in the light of empirical evidence to the contrary. Neo-Marxists have begun repositioning themselves to reflect changed conditions on the ground.

Dunleavy and O'Leary (1987) identify five neo-Marxist approaches. Wright (1978) repositions the working class to incorporate those exploited not by hand, but by brain. All the wage earners carrying out other people's instructions, without supervising other wage earners or organizing work are workers (Wright, 1978). Przeworski (1977) identifies a two-tier struggle in which the working class needs to reconstitute itself as a class to overcome fragmentations. Thereafter revolutionary struggle can replace the bourgeoisie with socialism. Poulantzas (1973a and b; 1975) describes within-class conflicts in which classes can be divided in three ways, offering a far more nuanced account than Marx. Namely, where incompatible material interests separate political organization then fraction occurs. Second, those situations where temporary conflicts around economic interests do not produce separate political organization – for example, between skilled and semi-skilled workers. Finally, social classes with distinct corporate interests such as the army or state bureaucracy. Habermas (1976) and O'Connor (1973) identify differences of interests across class as lines of social division. This could be in situations where the interests of individuals cut across traditional class lines, such as the conflicting interests of small non-unionized firms and large unionized corporations, where the unionized workforce have more in common with their corporation than with unskilled workers. Finally, in Wallerstein's (1980) world system theory the locus of class is actually removed from industrialized counties to the periphery in the developing world (Dunleavy and O'Leary, 1987: 225–8).

Neo-Marxist theorists, far from seeing a pluralist world in which many different actors are able to get their interests on the political agenda, still see the world in terms of exploitation and alienation. Workers' interests are addressed ultimately in revolution as the ultimate expression of class consciousness. In the meantime, a trade union consciousness exists whereby conditions can be improved under capitalism. Most workers will identify with this form of consciousness, leaving a small vanguard of 'true believers' who seek to educate the masses about revolutionary class consciousness. Capitalism equips the ruling class and their associates with greater material resources, including control over workers' livelihoods. Capitalism's control of the state and the construction of liberal democracy as the only game in town is winning a battle of ideas. The final demise of revolutionary consciousness comes as the industrial proletariat becomes a small minority and is divided by raised living standards for Lenin's labour aristocracy. Przeworski (1980, 1985) could envisage workers actually choosing capitalism over socialism because of the costs of shifting to a socialist system. Power in these accounts is located within the system and, as such, emphasis is upon unobservable power structures and its observable effects which guide behaviour.

Critical theory

Since the 1980s, critical theory has become an important and growing stream of thought within international relations. We can trace its influence in IR through two main streams. First, the Frankfurt School of

Box 6.4   Neo-Marxism and the Israel–Palestinian conflict

Neo-Marxist approaches towards the Israel–Palestinian conflict are likely to see the issue in class terms rather than nationalist, religious or racial. Capitalism benefits the wealthy in both communities and obliges workers to compete against each other in order to maximize profit. Fractions across class lines remove class solidarity and mean that workers on both sides of the dispute share loyalty with their capitalist oppressors in their own community rather than with the fellow worker across the divide. In a world system theory account, then, Israel and Palestine would sit in different economic locations. Israel would reside in the semi-periphery or maybe core, while Palestine is firmly in the periphery. Palestinian suffering would not be theorized on national grounds but upon the economic grounds of needing to supply the capitalist core with raw materials and end-product manufactured goods. In this way the effects of the underlying power structures can be observed.

Horkheimer, Adorno, Marcuse and Habermas and, second, the Toronto School of Gramscian hegemony advanced most notably by Robert Cox. While the Gramscians have tended to play a significant role in the development of IPE (as discussed in Chapter 9), Habermasian critical theorists have become influential in the field of international society, ethics and security. Critical theorists within IR have largely abandoned economic Marxism and developed an ideological neo-Marxist approach that prioritizes the superstructure over the base. They are particularly interested in the interaction of culture, bureaucracy, the nature of authoritarianism, reason, rationality and knowledge (Hobden and Wyn Jones, 2008: 153). Critical theorists are concerned principally with emancipation for the disadvantaged but no longer see the proletariat exclusively as the embodiment of that emancipatory project:

> For critical international relations theorists, the good society is a just and democratic order that should be extended beyond the state to the international domain in the creation of a cosmopolitan community. (Viotti and Kauppi, 2010: 340)

Emancipation involves a social and political transformation in which relations of domination and repression end along with inequality and exploitation. The responsibility of the critical theorist is principally to expose class and elite interests and those theories that perpetuate domination and exploitation. For Habermas emancipation is closely connected with communication and the embrace of radical democracy which encourages the widest participation possible. Radical democracy

> ## Box 6.5   Critical theory and the Israel–Palestinian conflict
>
> Critical theory addresses the issue of participation and representation in the conflict with broad sympathy towards the Palestinian position. As part of an emancipatory agenda, then, Palestinians would receive theoretical support on the basis of being oppressed by the main ally of the global hegemon. Critical theorists would appeal to universalizing moral, political and legal principles to protest the blockade in Gaza, Operation Cast Lead in 2008/9 and the assault on the humanitarian aid shipping convoy to Gaza in 2010. Linklater's invitation to nurture emancipatory tendencies within the present system would suggest that critical theorists would turn their attention towards the EU and UN agencies to relieve the humanitarian suffering of both Palestinians and Israelis living under threat of rocket attacks.

spreads across, between and within borders embracing a cosmopolitan conception of rights and obligations. Citizens around the world are encouraged to gain knowledge with which to identify barriers to full participation and seek to overcome them.

Andrew Linklater (1998) understands emancipation as expanding the moral boundaries of political community internationally so that states no longer exert moral authority within their borders but rather are superseded by international solidarity which internationalizes duty and obligation to citizens in whichever country they are. In a practical way, Linklater urges critical theorists to identify and nurture tendencies within the present system, including the EU, which would point to the potential for emancipation (Hobden and Wyn Jones, 2008: 154). He believes that 'globalization and fragmentation pose new challenges to states and create new possibilities for transforming world politics' (Linklater, 1998, 2008: 554). The process can be helped by universalizing moral, political and legal principles, reducing material inequality and respecting ethnic, cultural and gender difference (Linklater, 1998). Here the focus is on underlying structures with an overtly normative emphasis designed to emancipate.

Anti-foundational interpretivist approaches

Postmodernist feminism

The issue of political representation and participation has engaged feminists from the many streams of feminism since the development of feminism as a theoretical approach. At first glance, what is at issue is the way in which women have been constructed as absent from mainstream political life throughout most of human history. It is less than 100 years since women were able to vote in the UK (1919 over 30 years old and 1928 over 21 years old) and the United States (1920). During this time, despite numerous initiatives to attempt to increase female representation in legislative assemblies, the percentage of elected women members of parliament in the UK stands at 21 per cent (its highest level since the introduction of universal suffrage). It is even lower in the United States at 17 per cent. Rwanda is the only country in the world to have over 50 per cent of its elected members of parliament women. Feminists divide among themselves about how to approach this situation. One strand of feminist thought seeks to encourage women's participation in formal institutional politics. This can be achieved through improving existing arrangements, advocating all-women short lists to overcome the weight of human history militating against women participating in mainstream political processes, encouraging women's participation and engagement.

Against this view are others, including postmodern feminists, who refuse to be bound by the masculinist construction of political activity and posit the personal as the political. These advocate rejecting formal representational politics altogether in favour of more informal and participatory forms of political engagement (Squires, 1999: 194). This extended definition of the political reveals and lauds women's extensive political participation that exists outside of mainstream political activity. In the second wave of feminism, women organized women's peace and ecological movements and campaigned against war, sexism and religious fundamentalism.

Out of this movement grew the postmodernist feminists influenced by Simone De Beauvoir, Michel Foucault, Jacques Lacan and Judith Butler. Postmodernist feminist writers emphasize difference and diversity and focus on language and power and the exposure of previously subjugated knowledge. Postmodern feminists are sceptical of the emancipatory agendas proffered by critical theorists and Marxists. They are accused of being a divisive voice within feminism for essentializing and emphasizing the difference not just of female to male but also class and racial differentiators between women with different lived experiences. Postmodernist feminist thought has been caricatured as andocentric (Marchand and Parpart, 1995: 128), a claim challenged by Eudine Barriteau, who considers that it 'allows women to redefine politics and political participation, and validates women's approach to the political process' (Barriteau, 1995: 149).

What postmodern approaches achieve for Barriteau is the distinction of women as the social construct of gender and their interaction with society rather than simply being regarded as non-male. Postmodern

> **Box 6.6 Postmodern feminism and the Israel–Palestinian conflict**
>
> Postmodern feminists would tackle the issue of the participation and representation in this conflict very differently from the previous case studies considered. Primarily the focus would be on the women and girls involved in the dispute. Women in the different communities should be considered separately on the basis of difference and unique perspective. Postmodern feminists would also be eager to consider the discursive aspects to the conflict, examining and analyzing texts, speeches and documents and uncovering meanings that would either prolong or shorten the conflict. Postmodern feminists would set little store on a satisfactory solution. Rather than consider the conflict in detail at governmental levels they would prefer to study examples of women's political activity outside the narrow confines of limited versions of participation and representation.

feminists seek to redefine political boundaries and act politically without being constricted to mainline participation in political processes:

> When women refuse to participate in politics which exclude their interests, mainstream scholars define this rebellion as non-participation. Yet women are in fact acting politically; they are rejecting politics that excludes their concerns. (Barriteau, 1995: 149)

Poststructuralist international relations

Poststructuralism's contribution to understanding participation and representation in IR is to deliberately challenge all our preconceptions convinced that there is no such thing as objective truth. Jacques Derrida's ontological position starts from needing to understand the world as whole and how different interpretations of that understanding not only represent, but also constitute, the world (Derrida, 1998). Like most poststructuralists, deconstructing texts is at the top of their research agenda and in doing so they are able to discover the knowledge/power nexus that maintains existing power relations. The workings of power can be revealed by undertaking a detailed historical analysis to discover how the practices and discourse about the social world are only 'true' within specific discourses (Smith and Owens, 2008: 185).

Traditional IR theories tend to be very prescriptive and poststructuralism questions why those boundaries exist and for whose benefit. Realism's omissions of sub-state actors, women, transnational actors and NGOs, among many others, are exposed to expand conceptions of political space. David Campbell, writing on security, explains

Box 6.7   Poststructuralist IR and the Israel–Palestinian conflict

From the outset, poststructuralists will tend to approach study of the conflict and representation and participation within it by examining the prevailing and historical discourse. How have we got to where we are? How was the discourse constructed and invested in to produce different identities for the protagonists in the conflict? Theorists will seek to uncover the unequal power relations between different parties, organizations and individuals. What investment has been made in prior discursive engagement? In the US context, it is necessary to deconstruct Zionist texts, particularly from a Christian Zionist point of view, that seek to legitimate support for Israel in terms of the fulfilment of God's promises and special covenants. Speeches and texts in Congress, presidential speeches to different audiences (especially presidential candidate addresses to AIPAC and to Arab audiences) can be analyzed. Texts of Israeli and Palestinian leaders can be analyzed in English, Hebrew and Arabic, discovering omissions, subtexts and insertions, changes of emphasis between audiences throwing new light on how the conflict has been and is being constructed.

poststructuralism's unique contribution to expanding political mindsets for those prepared to challenge the prevailing orthodoxy:

> For in a discursive economy, investments have been made in certain interpretations; dividends can be drawn by those parties that have made the investments; representations are taxed when they confront new and ambiguous circumstances; and participation in the discursive economy is through social relations that embody an unequal distribution of power. Most important, the effect of this understanding is to expand the domain of social and political enquiry. (Campbell, 2010: 367)

Campbell and other poststructuralists understand that the real world is dependent upon our interaction with it and that interaction is most pronounced at the level of discourse. In competition between competing 'truths' the dominant discourse wields power. Emancipatory potential is found in deconstructing dominant gendered discourses and power relations.

Comparison of theories and approaches

There are strong differences between behaviouralist accounts of representation and participation that believe that by observing the behaviour of political actors it is possible to understand the dynamics of power relationships and discover who influences political processes. Pluralist accounts present multiple actors with opportunities through citizen groups, interest and pressure groups to influence political decision-making. Neo-pluralist approaches recognize the influence that corporations can exercise over political processes, which is also shared by liberal IR theorists who acknowledge the role of the military industrial complex in influencing foreign policy. The to and fro of competing interests is believed to ensure that no one view prevails all the time. Liberalism suggests access to foreign policy decision-making by many interests, including individual citizens and organized groups. Pluralist systems provide opportunities to connect with decision-makers at a variety of levels.

Marxists are less convinced about open access to decision-makers confronting what pluralists and liberals only hint at – that there is differential access and influence for different actors. Money talks in pluralist and liberal IR circles, but in neo-Marxism it is set out explicitly as class division with an exploiter and exploited class. Workers are unable to access the levers of power accept through either declining reformist political parties or membership of a small revolutionary vanguard. The forces of capitalism are able to keep workers away from effective political participation that would change their material condition by fractures within classes and constructing representative democracy as meeting workers' participatory needs. Critical theorists offer a more optimistic note of political engagement through an emancipatory project of exposing elite interests and encouraging the development of cosmopolitan citizenship.

Postmodernist feminism approaches participation from the perspective of widening the masculinist discourse, which situates women as non-males who are not participating in mainstream political activity and reclaiming political activity and expanding its scope with women playing the central role. Poststructuralists in IR adopt a similar approach to postmodernist feminists, while broadening their focus to an examination of all discursive texts and narratives that enable us to uncover the history of discourses to see how they arrived and can be deconstructed to redress existing power relationships.

Adjudicating between perspectives

When considering which theory to adopt when embarking on research into participation and representation we should take into account how we approach the concept. If we believe that the system of representation and participation is fairly open and that, through observation, we are able to understand and analyze decision-making processes within existing political systems, then the behavioural approaches of pluralism or liberalism would be an ideal starting point. However, if we are more sceptical and believe that the underlying issues of class relationships and antagonisms, the economic impact and unequal distribution of resources are neglected in mainstream political theorizing then neo-Marxist approaches have something to offer. Maybe we reject the notion that Politics can be objective and quantifiable and believe that political analysts are actually engaged and involved in constructing the real world, through their engagement with it, rather than dispassion-ately commenting on it. In this way critical theory affords a normative approach to challenge existing understandings and advocate political change. However, the previous approaches may seem inadequate to understand where we are today. Postmodernism and poststructuralism offer an opportunity to unpick the prevailing discourses that normalize where we are today and provide a discursive framework to challenge often taken-for-granted assumptions. Why should we be restricted in our approaches to what constitutes participation and representation? A postmodern feminist approach offers a chance to break free from a masculinist political system and reflect on women's political capital.

Conclusion

In selecting a traditional international relations issue, US support for Israel and the Israel–Palestine conflict, as our case study, we have demonstrated that the divisions between IR and political science are minimal and that pluralist and liberal approaches, neo-Marxist and crit-ical theory, and postmodern feminist and poststructural IR approaches have significant degrees of overlap. Understandings of political partici-pation and representation are at centre stage when it comes to thinking about mainstream political science in democratic polities. As we have seen the subject is highly contested, with competition among theories over what should be examined, what has been overlooked and what has been disguised. As with the other topics we have studied, underneath our outline of each of the theoretical positions has been the notion of power relations. For foundational positivists power is observable and in the hands of political actors. For foundational critical/scientific realists power is located systemically; we can know this as we can see its effects. For anti-foundational interpretivists power is discursively constructed and constituted through social relationships, whereas postmodernists distrust any claims to truth about a better world or anything pertaining to a meta-narrative.

Reflection

Which perspective does the best job of explaining issues surrounding US support for Israel?

Why do you think this is the case?

Do you think the Israel Lobby is the cause of US support for Israel?

Do we need to understand the conflict between Israel and Palestine through reference to their positioning in the global capitalist system?

Is power located in an understanding of participation that is essentially male?

How can insights from Political Science and IR help us understand US support for Israel in the Israel–Palestine conflict?

What are your reasons for your answer?

Seminar activities

Look up the voting statistics for the last election in the United Kingdom or the United States and consider why more women are not MPs, senators or congressional representatives.

Should this be changed, and if so how?

Divide the seminar group into smaller groups; assign each group to be representatives of a continent and produce an emancipatory manifesto for your continent. Once each subgroup has discussed and written down a brief five-point manifesto, reconvene the seminar, with a spokesperson for each group presenting the manifesto. This should be followed by negotiating and bargaining between the groups to produce a five-point world manifesto.

Were the five points easy to arrive at?

Which theoretical perspective most influenced your five choices? Why do you think this was the case?

Chapter 7

The Media

Introduction

Most of the time, the way in which we find out about our politics is through the media. Whether it is via the TV, press, radio or the internet, these communications technologies play a central role in enabling politicians to communicate with us, and are the main way through which we find out about the political world. However, underneath these seemingly simple statements lies a complex series of relationships between media and politics. The media are not neutral actors, nor just passive conduits uncritically relaying information to us. The main aim of the media is to make money; they do this by attracting an audience, for without an audience there would be no purpose to the media. Thus, the media engage in tactics and strategies to attract us to them – for example, by using snappy headlines or striking images. Competition both between and within different media platforms, combined with a proliferation of technologies and outlets, means that an increasing number of media are competing for a smaller share of audiences. For some, this has led to a crisis in communication where we receive, and have access to, 'more and more information [which has] ... less and less meaning' (Baudrillard, 1983: 95). The impact of this has been debated (e.g., Brants, 1998); nonetheless there have clearly been interrelated changes in both media content and industry structure, brought about, in part through proliferating technologies and increasing media deregulation, and these changes need also to be situated within their wider social, political and economic context.

Within this complex media environment, political actors also have a set of goals. One of those is to communicate with the public: for some this is simply for the aim of gaining re-election; for others this may be a function of attempts to engage in democratic dialogue. Whatever the aim, the way in which politicians communicate with the electorate is largely via the media. Political actors increasingly use techniques and strategies to attract and manipulate media attention. For some this has had a damaging effect on the political process, reducing politics to a series of sound bites and denigrating political debate (cf. Franklin, 1994; Savigny, 2007), while for others this has been a positive phenomenon enabling politics to connect with the previously uninterested (cf. Temple, 2006). All of this suggests a very narrow definition of politics, which focuses attention upon the political system and political actors. A wider definition of politics enables us to reflect upon the way in which politics may be articulated through cultural forms and phenomena   that politics is not only what is on the news, but also takes place in cultural forms around the news; for example, in soap operas, or through film (see Street, 1997).

However, it is clear that the media are not neutral actors, but play a crucial role in the political process. While there is a complex relationship between the media and their publics (see Higgins, 2008) our focus here is upon the interaction between the media and the political system, which includes political elites. If we are to understand and analyze how politics works, we need to not only look at the behaviour of political actors, but also consider and reflect upon the roles that the media play, and analyze the interaction between the two. For some of the accounts we look at here, the direction of influence is from the media to politics, for others from politics upon the media. What we suggest is that the relationship between the two is most usefully conceptualized as a dialectical process, often with unintended outcomes. The aim of this chapter is to introduce some of the different ways in which we can analyze the relationship between the media and politics. This will be illustrated through reference to coverage of the Iraq war.

Power

There is a variety of ways in which power can be conceptualized when analyzing the media. One of the biggest assumptions that is implied is that the media have enormous levels of power, given that they are able exert some kind of effect on their audiences. There is an ongoing and wide-ranging debate about the effects of the media and the type of effects that the media may have. Some argue that the media 'inject us with message' (the hypodermic model derived from the Frankfurt School), although this was countered by the idea that audiences receive information 'selectively' (Klapper, 1960) and we need to consider how audiences 'decode' different messages (Hall, 1973). For some, the media simply reinforce our existing beliefs (Blumler and McQuail, 1968). Others, however suggest that while the media may not tell us what to think, they are stunningly successful in telling us what to think about. That is, power

Box 7.1   Case study. Media and the coverage the Iraq war

This case study will take examples primarily from the UK print media and explore the way in which different aspects of the war in Iraq were represented. The underlying assumption is that the media were not passive transmitters of neutral and objectively defined news; rather, each perspective draws our attention to differing motivations which influence the way in which news is presented.

In March 2003 Western forces, largely led by the US (and including three other countries: the UK, Australia and Poland) invaded Iraq. A further 36 countries became involved after 1 May 2003. The official justification was the eradication of weapons of mass destruction and to pursue the 'war on terror', despite the lack of discovery of such weapons. For some, and consistent with the realist paradigm, this was about power politics and viewed as retribution for the events of 11 September 2001. For others the war was about the need to protect access to oil supplies within the region. For example, Chomsky (2009) argues that the 'Middle East oil reserves are understood to be 'a stupendous source of strategic power' and 'one of the greatest material prizes in world

→

in this perspective conforms to Lukes' second dimension, as the ability to 'set the agenda' (McCombs and Shaw, 1972) or engage in 'framing' the debate or issues of the day (Entman, 1993). In effect, this suggests that the media can decide what it is we read about in the newspapers or see on TV, and what we don't see. For example, if we don't see an event happening, or don't read about it in the news, how will we know of its existence? How might we know of genocides, for example, unless we hear or see them in the media? This suggests that the media have an enormous capacity and potential to define what is real; to define our reality and to define political reality.

Indeed, the significance attached by politicians to the ability of the media to set the agenda is illustrated by the enormous energies and resources political actors exert in an attempt to find strategies to manage the media (as suggested above). This has become colloquially referred to as 'spin' (for excellent summaries of this and the wider relationship between media and politics see both Street, 2001, and Louw, 2010). But why is it that politicians seek to manipulate the media? Well, while there is a vast debate about the effects of the media upon voting intentions and behaviour (see, for example, Newton and Brynin, 2001), establishing the causal relationship between media influence and outcomes almost doesn't matter. It could be argued that the resources that politicians themselves devote to attempting to manage the media and present themselves and their message favourably suggests that they themselves history'; thus, the motivation for states to control that area (again, as suggested within the realist paradigm) is huge.

The aim here is not to discuss this legitimacy of legality of the war, but to offer a ways of analyzing how we knew about what was taking place. We did not witness events directly, but relied on different media forms to provide us with information about events as they took place in the fields of war, and the actions and responses of political elites. Journalists were embedded with troops, and for some this meant a compromise of their ability to be objective. That the media themselves were significant is highlighted by Hoskins, who states that the 'televising of the Iraq War, probably more than any other conflict in history, fundamentally disconnected the machinery of warfare from the bloody consequences of its use' (2004: 10). This reinforces the active and crucial role of the media, not only in providing information to us as citizens, but to and between political elites. The media also provide a site or arena where identities and discourses are structured and disseminated. The aim here is to explore the differing ways in which we can analyze the role the media played in shaping, influencing, or responding to the actions of those engaged in the activity of war.

perceive the media to be enormously powerful and so behave in a manner which reinforces this assumption and by extension reinforces or constructs media power. If this is so, does this perception or assumption ascribe power to the media where there may have been none before?

Foundational positivist approaches

Liberal theory

The liberal view of the media is by far the most prominent, and indeed is often thought to encapsulate not only the normative view of the way that the media should behave in the political process, but to encompass the media-held view that this is how they do behave. The theory is both normative and behavioural. Normative in that it contains assertions about how the media should behave. Behavioural in its focus upon how the media do behave. This is based upon analysis of observable and measurable behaviour, where power is assumed to be located.

Liberal theories are largely premised around the idea of a free press and, more widely, the principle of free speech (although this means free from government interference rather than from the pressure of advertising). This emphasizes the separation of the media from the state. In the UK, this separation of the media from the tripartite pillars of the State

(The Crown, Parliament and the Judiciary) means the press are referred to as a 'Fourth Estate', who are independent and above the fray, performing a watchdog function and acting as a check and balance on political power (for summaries, see Wheeler, 1997; Curran, 2002; Temple, 2008). Freedom of the press is achieved through light regulation and as a result of their funding structures: the press are financed independently by advertising revenues. This means the press exist in a 'free market' which is not only responsive to its audience, but also allows for a free exchange of ideas (available through the existence of competition).

Premised upon principles of representation and accountability, the press function to scrutinize elites and hold them to account in the name of the 'public interest'. The press also embody notions of representation and function to represent the interests and views of the public. Journalists themselves are assumed to subscribe to the view that they are there to 'serve the public' and, given the need to back up and verify their information (and sources), there will necessarily be a variety of viewpoints, as well as the aim of producing a 'truth'. The other key function that they are assumed to perform is to provide information: this is premised upon the Burkean notion of informed consent. However, it is the press that provide a mechanism through which the public are able to gain sufficient information to form a judgement about political elites. The press provide the basis from which individuals evaluate and judge those elites at election time and, through the act of voting, give informed consent to be governed. Citizens are assumed to be empowered through the professionalism of the journalists' quest for the truth, and the existence of rival viewpoints.

This pluralistic view assumes that power lies within the political system and that the media act as a check on power. In this way power also can be assumed to lie with the media themselves (rather than the markets in which they operate, as Marxist accounts might suggest). Power may also lie with individual journalists who play a role on holding those elites to account. For example, Woodward and Bernstein are perhaps the two most famous journalists who can be seen to have changed the face of politics with their uncovering of the Watergate scandal, which ultimately brought about the end of the Nixon presidency. Here then we see individual journalists upholding liberal values. And through observation of their actions we can see the exercise of power.

IR and the media: a behaviouralist account of the CNN effect

Normatively, in liberal theory, the media may claim to be representative of public opinion, but who is framing the political debate and defining its terms? We will discuss this later in the chapter. While we looked at

Box 7.2   Liberal theory, the war in Iraq and the *Sunday Times*

Liberal theory would draw attention to the coverage of the Iraq war and the willingness of the press to challenge elite authority, and to question the actions of the elites prior to the invasion. The UK allied itself with the US, so for journalists to challenge elite authority they would need to begin by challenging the decisions of US leaders. Notably, prior to the invasion, the British press was not united in support and many newspapers were openly critical.

This excerpt from the *Sunday Times* just prior to the invasion supports the ideas within liberal theory which provides information to its readers about the behaviour of political elites in the build-up to the war: 'America is stepping up the propaganda war in anticipation of an attack on Iraq. The battle for hearts and minds is being waged on two fronts: while the dovish State Department is taking charge of the cultural soft sell, the hawkish defense department is handling information warfare and black propaganda' (Baxter, 2003). The legitimacy of this action, however, was questioned by the journalist, and the article continues, 'The background noise is not encouraging, however. Surveys have shown considerable scepticism about American policies in Europe and to an even greater extent in the Muslim world – particularly among Washington's four principal allies: Egypt, Pakistan, Jordan and Turkey. A recent study showed that more than 78 per cent of people in all four countries thought the "spread of American ideas and customs a bad thing"' (Baxter, 2003). In this way, liberal theory would draw attention to the press as providing the public with detailed information from which they can evaluate the actions of political elites, but they also provide representation of dissent and the public interest. Journalists are assumed to be objective and neutral and challenge elite authority according to their liberal democratic function.

the way in which policy can be analyzed in Chapter 4, the articulation of issues through the media, for some, may mean that it is the media themselves who are driving the creation and formation of policy, through their role in setting the public agenda of the political debate. Here we begin to look explicitly at the role of the media and their capacity to influence the policy agenda, with specific reference to the foreign policy agenda.

The 'CNN effect' is a term which has become widely used (and debated among a variety of approaches, as we will see in this chapter) to suggest that the media have considerable influence over the creation and articulation of foreign policy. It claims that 'competing television images, such as images of a humanitarian crisis, cause US policy-makers to intervene in a situation when such an intervention might otherwise not be in the national interest' (Feist, 2001: 73). So, looking at this definition, why would policy-makers behave in a way that was counter to their definition of the 'national interest'? Well, the CNN effect encourages us to look at the relationship between the media agenda and the motivations of political actors and suggests it is the media that motivates such behaviour. The CNN effect literature was derived from empirical observation of the political responses to media representation of humanitarian crises. Notably, in Northern Iraq and Somalia, it was argued that US intervention was driven by emotive pictures of suffering, and US disengagement from Somalia was argued to be a response to the images of American soldiers being dragged through the streets of Mogadishu (Schorr, 1991; Livingston and Eachus, 1995). Shaw's (1996) detailed behavioural empirical analysis of the Northern Iraq–Kurdish crisis assumed that the media affect foreign policy through the impact upon public opinion. (The original thesis examined the impact of the CNN channel upon US foreign policy, but the assumptions and thesis arguably can be applied to the 24-hour news media and foreign policy-making in other Western states.)

In these behavioural accounts, the assumptions are made (almost in line with rational choice accounts) that politicians are responsive to public opinion; indeed, they are continually aware of electoral sensitivities. The observation is made that we are in a 24-hour media environment, where news is played out in 'real time'. Politicians and the public alike see this news simultaneously which is significant as politicians are increasingly reliant upon opinion polls and the impact of public opinion upon political behaviour has been widely documented (by academics and practitioners alike; see, for example, Morris, 1999). Because voters and politicians view the media and these images in 'real time', so politicians have one eye on the next election and are aware of the damage to their reputation that inaction could create. This in turn is assumed to motivate political actors to respond. The emphasis in these accounts is upon observable behaviour, and power is assumed to flow in one direction, from the media and exercised over politicians. This interaction assumes a causal link between news coverage and foreign policy outcomes. Power in this account is assumed to be observable, and flows in a unidirectional manner from the media to politicians (via the public).

This approach to the idea of a 'CNN effect' also embodies a series of liberal assumptions about the role of the media on the world stage. This thesis is underpinned by an assumption that journalists have the responsibility to place the public interest onto the political agenda, and in turn the media, specifically the news media, assume that they have the capacity to influence politicians and ensure that they pay attention to public opinion. This asserts power very firmly with the media, in their liberal 'watchdog' capacity. As Louw suggests, a core feature of CNN organizational culture is that CNN is a global actor (2010: 186) with a capacity

Box 7.3 The Iraq war and CNN; the CNN effect

The inquiry into the Iraq war heard how there had been talk of invasion long before 11 September. *The Daily Telegraph* reports how the Chilcott inquiry into the Iraq war heard that there had been discussion in the US up to two years prior to the events of September 2001. Indeed, while there was awareness of these discussions 'the inquiry heard that in 2001, the settled view of the UK government was that attacking Iraq would have been illegal under international law' and that political strategy in 2001 saw 'Britain and the US ... committed to a policy of containing Saddam, through economic sanctions, restricting his oil sales through the oil-for-food programme, and the imposition of no-fly zones in southern and northern Iraq' (Kirkup and Rayner, 2009). In this article, we see liberal theory at work, the press describing challenges to authority as evidenced through coverage of the inquiry. This policy dramatically changed, however, with the powerful imagery, shown live, and repeated, on CNN the day that two planes flew in to the World Trade Centre, reinforcing the impact of the visual medium which transmitted these events.

The powerful video imagery of the events of 9/11 provided elites with visual justification for invasion and the Bush/Blair foreign policy decisions that were taken. A key way through which the public were encouraged to support the war was through its continual coverage. As Hoskins (2004) suggests the demand for immediacy overrode the demand for accuracy or content. Technology enables audiences to witness events as they unfold. Bush's speeches initially referred to acts of terrorism, but within days referred to acts of war being waged upon America. Crucially, these speeches were linked with these evocative images with the aim of embedding the conflation of political objectives with the tragic events. In the initial aftermath the media reported shock at the loss of life, but arguably this mirrored the political agenda, which had responded to the imagery initially provided by CNN. While it may be too simplistic to suggest the media alone was responsible for the actions of political elites (indeed, Bush junior was also thought to have political motivations rooted in his familial past), nonetheless, the media agenda brought this issue to the front of the public agenda, which, in turn, the CNN effect thesis suggests, demanded a political response. From this perspective power lies with the media in directing political action, and we can study this linear relationship through observation of events portrayed in the media and the response of political elites. This, however, belies the complexity of the interactions between the two sets of actors, and highlights, perhaps, the difficulty of seeking to establish cause and effect relationships in social situations.

to hold others in the world to account, through its ability to influence (US) foreign policy.

There are criticisms of this behavioural approach. For example, Robinson (2002) contends that the CNN effect was asserted and not effectively demonstrated, arguing that it is power politics, *realpolitik*, which shapes intervention decisions rather than the media. Jakobsen has argued that governments have provided humanitarian intervention elsewhere where there had been no prior media coverage and that political elites used the media to mobilize public support, rather than the other way round (Jakobsen, 2000). Further critiques of this behaviouralist approach are expanded upon below.

Foundational critical/scientific realist approaches

Marxism and the manufacture of consent

There is a number of Marxist accounts of the media, but these are all underpinned by an account of the relationship between the mass media and capitalist relations of production within society. Marxism argued that the economic base of society – the structure – determined the ideological superstructure. The ability of the bourgeoisie to control the proletariat was a consequence of its control of the ideological superstructure. The structure/superstructure identification highlights an interconnection between the ownership of the material means of production and the simultaneous production and distribution of dominant ideas. Marxists further this and argue that capitalists not only own the means of production (the structure), but are also able to control the superstructure through ownership of the mass media. In this way, and as Wheeler suggests, 'ideas and systems of representation ... [may be viewed as] ideological weapons which allow societal elites to advance their interests' (1997: 19).

In this view, the media form an arena for ideological indoctrination and serve to reinforce class domination. Marxists view the media as agents of consensus in the interests of the capitalist classes. The media are seen as agents of control which have become tightly integrated and generally supportive of the political classes, providing a mechanism through which dominant economic forces can exercise control over the state, locating power systemically.

One account of this is provided by Herman and Chomsky (1988), who suggested that the primary function of the media was the 'manufacturing of consent'. They argue that while the media may periodically attack or expose political and economic wrongdoing, the watchdog function ascribed by liberal media is misguided. This is a consequence of the huge inequality of resources between elites and the public, who simply do not have access to the media in the way the political and economic elites do. As such the media function to reinforce the status quo, failing to fundamentally challenge dominant ideologies.

Herman and Chomsky make their argument through the construction of a 'Propaganda Model' (1988). They identify five stages, or 'filters', which shape the media output and by extension reinforce existing systems of inequality and domination. These filters (which interact with each other) are:

(a) The concentration of ownership – there are a large number of media organizations, owned by fewer and fewer individuals.
(b) Advertising is a primary source of income – therefore, copy will be produced which is attractive to advertisers in order to attract consumers for the advertisers' goods (rather than provide public information as suggested by liberal theory).
(c) An unhealthy reliance official news sources such as government or business.
(d) Flak – negative responses by vested interests which may prove costly for the medium producing them; so it may be in the interest of the newspaper, for example, not to print an exposé of corporate corruption for fear of expensive libel action.
(e) Anti-communism as a control mechanism and a form of 'national religion', although in contemporary Western society this term could be replaced with anti-Islam, or Islamophobia.

In this case, power is systemic. It is not immediately observable, but we can see its effects. As Herman and Chomsky argue, this form of critique enables us to see the influence of the capitalist class through the ways in which 'money and power are able to filter out the news fit to print, marginalize dissent, and allow the government and dominant private interests to get their messages across to the public' (1988: 2).

More recently the role of dominant business interests has been reaffirmed by Davies (2008), whose analysis of contemporary news agendas showed that little had changed. Indeed, he argues that this trend was continuing and had been reinforced, as contemporary media systems are characterized by a greater concentration of ownership, reduction of journalistic sources and ability to check those sources (as liberal theory assumes journalists do) and an over-reliance upon PR generated by business.

International relations, manufacturing consent and a critical theory approach to the CNN effect

While the manufacturing consent thesis above notes the convergence of the interests of political elites, the media and capital, extending this argument to the field of international affairs, highlights how consent can also be manufactured in relation to foreign policy decisions. Robinson provides a comprehensive review of the literature surrounding this debate (2001) and in this he draws attention to different versions of this thesis. The first he terms the 'executive' model, where research has highlighted the convergence between the media agenda and government officials (understood as members of the executive). So, for example, government spokespersons now provide press releases for the military; and embedded journalists repeat briefings from official government sources. Through not only observing the news that is presented, but also reflecting upon how it is produced, we can see a convergence between executive interests and the media agenda (Davies, 2008). From this approach, analysis of the underlying production processes enables us to reflect upon the convergence of elite-level interests. It is in the interests of government officials to present a positive perspective on military action, and it is in the interests of journalists embedded with troops who may well save their lives, not to question official accounts. The news media do not function to challenge elites and hold them to account (as with liberal theory); rather they speak in concert with the executive. However, what this also suggests, and contrary to the claims in the behavioural account of the CNN effects thesis above, is that the media do not influence policy, rather they simply reinforce it.

The elite version of the manufacturing consent thesis suggests that the media conform to the interests of political elites, irrespective of their political position (so they could be located outside of the executive, in the legislature, or any other politically powerful position in society). This opens up the notion that political influence is possible and significant outside of the executive. Crucially it allows for the existence of conflict between elites, which then provides the political conditions for media discussion of conflict (Hallin, 1986). Yet these political conditions are thought to precede the actions taken by the media (thus being a reversal of the assumption of media influence coming prior to politics as made within the CNN effect thesis). Bennett goes beyond this, suggesting that the coverage of conflict between elites reflects the professional role of the journalists in highlighting power struggles at elite level (Bennett, 1990: 110), conforming very much to the view of liberal theories assumptions about the function of journalists.

Critical theory: Habermas and the public sphere

The 'public sphere' is a phrase widely used to describe the space occupied by the media. The term is rooted in the work of Habermas (1962/2002), who provides an historical description of role of the media within a democracy and locates the public sphere as between, and separate from, the state and civil society. The normative assumption is that the public

Box 7.4   Manufacture of consent and the CNN effect

The manufacturing consent thesis draws attention to the production of news and the convergence of elite interest in this process. From this perspective it is possible to reflect upon the largely unchallenged acceptance by media organizations of the growth of PR and the strategic communications interventions of the military, largely uncritically accepted as necessary as reported in this excerpt from the *Sunday Times*: 'the joint chiefs of staff stressed the need for "strategic" deception and "influence operations" as tools of war. The army, navy and air force have been directed to devise plans for information warfare' (Baxter, 2003). The lack of critical discussion of this strategy suggests an acquiescence on the part of the media, that this was a necessary part of the war effort.

Not only were elite-level views dominant through the management of communications and PR in government and the military, but this was also reinforced through the changing role of journalists themselves. In the Iraq war over 600 US journalists were embedded with US-dominated forces (Hoskins, 2004: 57). This embedding not only shrank the physical distance journalists had from the war front, but also seemed to shrink their critical journalistic distance. This was reinforced by political elites speaking on TV about the success of media management of the war, with government officials on TV stating 'The American people won because they got to see how well-trained, how well-equipped and how well-led their US military is' (cited in Hoskins, 2004: 61). However, embedding meant that the military were able to tightly control what journalists covered, ensuring we saw an elite-level view of the war, representing the political and military interests of those involved, rather than, for example, wider representation of the damage and destruction and human costs of the war; human suffering was removed from war coverage.

Here, the manufacturing consent approach within the CNN effect literature enables reflection upon the way in which news is produced, the interests which are represented in the construction of the news agenda and its content. Power lies with the dominant interests able to inform and influence the news agenda, in elite, rather than the public, interest. Moreover, the elite interest becomes redefined and presented as the public interest, so that public interest is 'manufactured' through this process of news production to resemble elite interests.

sphere should represent the interests of civil society, but his historical account argues that the public sphere has been transformed to represent the interests of capitalism.

His account has been criticized for its 'golden age' assumptions (the idea that there were once halcyon days of a perfect relationship between media and democracy), but arguably this is to miss the point. His work is normative, directing attention to a series of assumptions and concepts necessary for a healthy relationship between the media and democracy. The public sphere, Habermas argued, was a place where rational, reasoned individuals would take part in debate and discussion. The public sphere was a place for reconciling and negotiating conflicting and competing interests and through this process arguments would survive or flounder on their own merit. While the public sphere in Habermas' account were the coffee shops of the mid-seventeenth century, the notion is that now these principles are/or should be embodied within today's media to provide the platform for a reasoned and rational discussion and exchange of ideas. In this sense, through public debate and articulation of interests, citizens are empowered to participate in public life. The public sphere is conceptually separate from the state and the economy, and provides for the articulation of civil society. A collective rational arena is a place where critical discussion could take place; debate among citizens was translated, through the public sphere, into collective opinion impacting upon the nature of the state.

However, Habermas' historical critique highlights how the growth of monopoly capitalism dominated by corporatism, advertising and ownership came to direct the public sphere. Rational public discussion became subsumed by public discussion between economic elites whereby major companies conducted debate with each other and the state, thereby excluding the public. (For an interesting account of the use of PR by business to negotiate market positions with each other via the media, see Davis, 2005). In this way society has been manipulated by the media which has redefined politics as a spectacle, the public have become consumers and public debate has been replaced with public relations. Feminist scholars draw attention to the way in which the public sphere is one in which the meaning of civil society is gendered. Historically, it was constructed to represent the interests of the male, educated, property-owning public, and characterized by a 'blindness to the actual material conditions which render its own existence possible' (Felski, 1989: 165). For feminists, the notion of a public sphere does not acknowledge that its construction reflects the interests of those who articulate it (the male bourgeoisie) rather than the interest of the society as a whole. This construction of interests is embedded in the notion of a public sphere, so while its form alters its assumptions remain – women (and the proletariat) continue to be excluded (Pateman, 1988).

Anti-foundational interpretivist approaches

Social constructivism and feminism

For social constructivist accounts, what becomes most important to consider when we look at the role of the media is the balance of power between the

Box 7.5   Critical theory, PR and privatized interests

Alongside the manufacturing consent approach detailed above, critical theory draws attention to the processes of producing news, and the interests which are represented. First, we see the importance attached to the management of the media agenda by the appointment of PR specialists into government departments. Advertising and PR consultants were also brought in to advise political elites and Charlotte Beers, one of the most powerful figures in the advertising industry, was brought in to lead the work of the State Department. In 2001 in the US the Pentagon's Office of Strategic Influence was formed (which latterly became the Office of Global Communication), with an explicit emphasis on 'information warfare', with government officials being dispatched to areas of 'media interest' to 'advise' journalists on government policy.

While PR officials in all aspects sought to manage the media agenda favourably, economic interests were also benefiting from lack of media critique. Unusually, *The Guardian* ran with a story which focused attention on the extent to which private security firms had become crucial for the coalition forces in securing their objectives; indeed, so integrated were they that they were 'the second biggest contributor to coalition forces in Iraq after the Pentagon' (Traynor, 2003). This observation and investigation provided for potential challenge to elite authority. However, any potential critique is negated by lack of quantity, and so reinforcement, of such critique. The emergence of information about private security companies was not seen as a particularly problematic issue for much of the mainstream media. Indeed, a study from the PEW Center for Journalism (2007) shows that in a four-year period (from 2003–7) in analysis of over 100,000 they found only 248 stories dealing in some way with the topic of private security companies. Moreover, where this was dealt with this tended to be within wider stories about events or issues in Iraq rather than as issues in their own right. Here, again, attention is drawn to news production which favours elite interests.

As political and economic interests coalesce, so critical theory draws our attention to the way in which these interests are reconciled through public relations rather than the public interest. This approach highlights the way in which the media operate as a site whereby if challenges to the status quo emerge they are marginalized and subsumed within wider discourses representing elite interests; indeed, the media function to prevent such challenges emerging in the first place. Power is located systemically, within the media's ability to suppress expression of interest other than those espoused by elites.

media and politicians. How is the agenda set for debate? Which issues make it into the news and which are excluded? What language is used? Whose voice is represented and in whose interests? The way in which we will do this here is through reference to some of the debates around feminism.

Feminist accounts highlight the role of actors in the construction of news, as well as the manner in which news is framed. Ross suggests women are 'most noticeable in the news media by their conspicuous absence or at least spectacular marginalisation' (2005: 287). This approach draws attention to the reinforcement of gender inequality within the production and framing of the news agenda. Not only does Ross draw attention to the lack of presence of women newsreaders, but also highlights the way in which news content is framed in the interest of men. Mulvey (1975) argued that media constructed the role of women to conform to the male gaze – that is, the ideal of what women should look like as defined by men, for men, and this is extended in feminists' accounts of news media production. Here the suggestion is that the masculine nature of news is constructed to appeal to a male audience, representing male interests, and the mainstream is characterized as the 'malestream'; news by men appealing to what interests men. For example, Ross (2005: 268) asks: where have been the women's voices in opposition to the reinstatement of the Taliban in Afghanistan? In this way, a social constructivist feminist account of the media can draw attention to the ways in which existing gendered relationships of inequality and power are reinforced through the processes of news production, both in the authoritative male personnel who present and report in the news and, as importantly, the

---

Box 7.6   Iraq, torture and feminism

In 2004 when photographs of atrocities of abuse at the Iraqi prison, Abu Ghraib, began to circulate, it was horror that a woman, Lyndie England, could be involved as much as the abuse itself which generated the story. As Ross notes (2005: 290), the news*men* asked 'How could a woman do such things?', rather than 'How could such things happen?'. In this way, then, feminist social constructivism draws attention to the way in which news is disseminated to us, predominantly by men, and the language that they use to reach their target audience, again, is male. In this way, socially constructed assumptions about the role of women in society are reinforced. The purpose of this critical feminist account, as with social constructivism (indeed, any critical account), is to question what we accept as knowledge; to challenge embedded assumptions about power, subordination and domination and the way in which these are articulated to reinforce inequalities. Power in these accounts is assumed to be located discursively, and brought into existence through its articulation. So, for example, it could be argued from within these social constructivist accounts that the way in which women are constructed in the contemporary news arena reflects and reinforces not intrinsic features of womanhood, but a wider system of gendered construction of the roles that men and women perform within society.

way in which the news is framed and constructed to exclude or marginalize women's interests.

When we look at media coverage of war we can see that discussion focuses around the notion of a public sphere; there is a clear assumption of a public–private divide. War is something which is conducted publicly, in the public sphere. We have discussions of bombing and loss of life and threats to the political authority of the state. What feminist theory draws our attention to is the 'private' costs of war, such as the effect upon women who have to respond to the devastation caused by armies and bombs. In war coverage, we see the way in which the news is constructed around the male agenda; for example, images of male soldiers and male bombers dominate. When women are presented in the context of war, this is largely as a shock at their performance of roles outside of those socially constructed as the 'norm' – for example, the use of the term 'female' suicide bomber, where the woman is presented as an aberrant woman rather than in terms of her religion or nationality, as with male suicide bombers (Naylor, 2001; Carter and Weaver, 2003). Such construction is encouraging us to view the aberration not as the actions of those engaged in war, but as aberrant in terms of the gender assumptions and stereotypes that we make.

The CNN effect: a poststructuralist approach

If we are to untangle the complex relationship between the media and the creation of foreign affairs news, for poststructuralist accounts we need to explore and deconstruct the categories of 'otherness' and we also need to reflect upon who is involved in the creation of such news.

As with feminist accounts, the background of those involved in the creation of the news is significant in informing the values and priorities that journalists bring to bear when constructing and creating the news. In the CNN effect literature, journalists have been identified as having a very narrow background – Westernized, middle class and part of professional discourses and practices which integrate them into the liberal capitalist system (Louw, 2010: 186). This means coverage reflects those Westernized values and belief systems (rather than challenging them) and so monitoring of and challenges to authority are not aimed at the system they are in, but at those outside of their own system. In turn, this ensures that coverage means that the media 'watch' governments and analyze them in terms of their fit within the Western liberal worldview. Not only are the media reinforcing dominant ideologies through their personnel, but, in the case of Western liberal capitalism, this also takes place through the construction of categories of 'us' and them'; 'us' being the West, the liberal capitalists, the others being those who behave 'undemocratically' (which generally means counter to the interests of

Box 7.7   Iraq wars and poststructuralism

During the first Gulf War, Baudrillard wrote a series of essays questioning the existence of the war (1991/2004). While none can deny the enormous loss of Iraqi life, or destruction of the physical infrastructures within Iraq, Baudrillard questions the 'reality' of that war: the way, for example, in which Hollywood scripts preceded the 'real'. We only need look back at CNN's reaction to the attack on the Twin Towers and the reporter who said 'Whoa, let's just see that again' in the way that one would respond to a Hollywood movie clip rather than a 'real' event. Hollywood precedes the 'real'; in this sense we have seen these images, this constructed event before. The simulation of the real is so pronounced that, for example, during the first Gulf War, CNN cameras crossed live to reporters, who were watching CNN to find out what was happening. Policy-makers and political elites found out about the 9/11 events from live media coverage. The first Gulf War saw increased media censorship by the military of what could be reported; the military had clearly learned from the damage done by unfavourable media coverage of Vietnam.

The integration of media with warfare has meant it is increasingly difficult to disentangle and establish the 'objective' role of the media. We are presented with sanitized images of smart bombs, rather than human casualties. Civilians who lost their lives were redefined by political elites as 'collateral damage' to lessen the emotional impact and potential loss of support of public opinion, the phrase repeated and reinforced by a

→

liberal capitalism). As Louw observes, we can see examples of this kind of reporting about Russia, Iran, Burma, Zimbabwe and North Korea (2010: 186).

Deconstructing the way in which news is presented to us also enables a reflection upon the processes involved, and particularly we need to explore the way in which elite-level actors actively seek to influence public opinion favourably to their own interests. Louw (2010: 192) suggests this takes place in four ways:

1. Policy elites use communication as a means to distract the public – which largely involves creating patriotic hype to focus attention on issues conducive to foreign policy.
2. Spin doctors and media management strategies are widely employed to prevent problematic issues from reaching the policy agenda.
3. Psy-ops and misinformation are used to confuse 'hostile populations'. This was evidenced in Iraq when 'leaflets to be aimed at Iraqi civilians were dropped by aircraft ... announcing five radio frequencies for broadcasts, transmitted from American planes, condemning Saddam's "lust for power" and explaining the role of the UN weapons

complicit media. While the death of each national soldier was initially reported, there is relative silence in the media about the number of Iraqi causalities. Here Iraqis are constructed as the 'other'; the bad guys, both as a state and through their invisibility as civilians. The power and 'rightness' of the West is reinforced through this clean, Hollywood-type, carefully choreographed simulation. In this way the media are performing to a script, constructing war in the way we have seen it in the movies and on TV, rather than showing us the reality of what is actually taking place.

Newly released photographs with unseen shots of the devastation caused on 9/11 prompted the *Daily Mail* to describe the photos in terms of their cinematic or Hollywood-like qualities 'All we see is the spectacular moment of collapse, what film directors call the wide shot, showing the towers in their urban setting, before, during and after their fall' (Delves Broughton, 2010). Even the events precipitating the war are described in Hollywood-like terms, suggesting a film-like quality to events, situating audiences as cinema-goers and removing them from the horrors of war. Once public opinion is removed and distanced from these events, it becomes easier for elites to pursue their interests unchallenged. As such the power to frame what we see and what we know facilitates a construction of what we assume of social world to be. In this way, the media then construct for us a reality of war, which is very different from the actuality. For poststructuralists a key issue is the questioning of the way in which this war is framed, in order to expose the way in which this embeds existing power structures.

inspectors' (Baxter, 2003) in an attempt to win the 'hearts and minds' battle as well as the physical war.

4. Campaigns will be used to stir the masses into appropriate support for 'belief systems', emphasizing the creation of good and bad guys, and much energy is devoted to the construction of scapegoats and bad guys to be blamed (for example, the use of terms such as the 'Axis of Evil').

What is highlighted here, first, is the significance of communication per se as a tool in warfare; and, second, the role of the media in acquiescing to the aims of policy elites. Rather than the media driving the policy process (as originally suggested by the CNN effect thesis) or holding elites to account (as suggested by liberal views), here the suggestion is that power is discursively located. Repetition of political categories and rhetoric serves to reinforce dominant ideological positions.

Louw's approach highlights the importance of deconstructing the processes by which news is generated; however, this largely assumes that it is policy or political elites driving the process. What we might also want to reflect upon is the role that the media play in this. The way in which the media 'frame' the news encourages us to accept a particular meaning or reading associated with it. Framing refers to the 'specific properties of ... narrative that encourage those perceiving and thinking about events to develop particular understandings of them' (Entman, 1993 7); that is, the way in which news is 'framed' encourages a particular reading. Thus, through deconstruction we are able to reveal the dominant interests which inform the news agenda. It is worth noting there is intense academic debate over the extent and nature of this 'effect' (for excellent summary, see Robinson, 2001). Nonetheless, with practitioners claiming the existence of such influence (Gilboa, 2005), and, indeed, as we suggested earlier, if politicians perceive the existence of an effect, there is potential that they will behave in a manner that renders the effect plausible. Therefore, it becomes the *idea* of a CNN effect which is significant in structuring responses and behaviour rather than the effect per se (a similar argument has been made by Hay 2002, in respect of globalization).

The argument that we would make in this section is that, to understand the relationship between the media and politics, it is not sufficient only to look at the strategies of political actors (politics) or the way in which the media frame the news agenda, or the particular role of journalists (media); nor does one precede the other. Rather there is a dialectical interaction between the two, with both seeking to influence and manipulate the other to achieve their own aims. In so doing, both the media and politicians act politically and strategically, reshaping the environment that they operate within. Power in this perspective is located discursively, in the language, assumptions, ideas and ideologies which dominate and shape media representations of the political world.

Comparison of theories and approaches

There is clearly a complex relationship between the media and politics. Behaviouralist accounts suggest we simply need to observe the behaviour of journalists and or the media, and the way in which they interact with, political elites. There are normative assumptions that the media act as defenders of democracy, and these normative assumptions, it is suggested, guide behaviour. Journalists are objective seekers of the truth, ready to challenge elites and hold them to account in the public interest. A clear manifestation of this is the production of news images which electorally sensitive politicians will assume that the public wish to see action taken on; in this way, the media are able to influence the nature of foreign policy. This affords enormous power and influence to the media, and also assumes that we can observe this exercise of power. These behavioural approaches largely situate the media prior to politics, making the linear causal assumption that the media shape and influence politics (informed by its positivist roots).

Conversely, Marxists and critical approaches highlight the way in which politics shapes the media; the media function to support and reinforce dominant political (and economic) interests. Politics is assumed to come prior to the media and while the media may engage in critique (as required by liberal theory) this is only to reflect elite-level disagreement, rather than a fundamental challenge to the actions of dominant interests. While the media may provide a site where discussion takes place, this discussion is around a narrow agenda which reflects the interests of elites and is increasingly characterized by public relations, rather than the public interest. A critical realist account thus enables us to make causal explanations while admitting unobservable features into the analysis and this is extended in the critical feminist accounts.

Dominant power relationships are also exposed through feminist accounts of the media which draw attention to the gendered nature of news production as a mechanism through which the status quo is preserved, both through the physical representation of women in the news environment and the construction of their roles in public life. Anti-foundational approaches also provide for a critique of the passive nature of the audience (assumed in foundational approaches) and this theme is continued in poststructuralist accounts that enable us, as audiences, to reflect upon the way in which news is constructed is an exercise of power. Unlike the foundational accounts there is not a linear assumption of causality; rather anti-foundational accounts draw attention to the dialectical interactive nature of the relationship between media and politics, reconstituting and reinforcing each others' positions in the social and political system.

Adjudicating between perspectives

If we are to understand the relationship between the media and politics we need to make a series of decisions about what to analyze and why we do so. If we think that the media shape the political agenda and determine the way in which political actors respond, or if we begin with the ontological assumption that what matters for analysis is observation of the media and observation of politicians' response to them, then we might want to adopt a behavioural approach. If we think that the media and politics is intertwined, both reinforcing each others' interests and neglecting those of the public, and that there is more 'going on' than we can see, that there are underlying economic interests structuring the media agenda, which we cannot directly observe, but are evident through their effects and representation within the media, then we might want to adopt a critical realist approach. If we think that really to understand the way in which media and politics interact we need to understand the language, the ideas and the context, the discourse in which this is played out, then we need to adopt a poststructuralist approach.

Conclusion

The media play a fundamentally important role in the world of politics. We, as audiences, and citizens, gain most of our knowledge about the 'world out there', about domestic and international politics, through the media. Significantly, the media are also one means through which social, economic and political elites communicate with each other and, in so doing, shape our political economic and social world. Yet the media are not passive conduits simply channelling information from elites to audiences or citizens. Rather, they have their own aims and objectives and so an understanding of the role that they play in the political process is essential for an analysis of the way in which politics is discussed, debated and is practised. Thus an understanding of the role the media play in politics is crucial. As the media transcend nation-state boundaries, in terms of their content and their reach with global companies broadcasting into homes across the world, the boundaries between domestic and international become blurred. Maybe, to understand the role contemporary media play in society, we need to consider both domestic and international aspects of their actions. Within this chapter we have sought to give an overview of just some of the approaches within Politics and IR that can help us start to understand and analyze this relationship and the implications of this relationship for the ways in which our politics takes place; for understanding what is real about the relationship between media and politics and how we can know that.

Reflection

Which perspective or approach does the best job of explaining or accounting for media coverage of the Iraq war?

Why do you think this is the case?

Do you think there is a causal relationship between media coverage of the events of 9/11 and the Iraq war?

Do you think that media coverage of the Iraq war reflected public relations rather than the public interest?

Did the way in which the women were constructed in the media during (and beyond) this war coverage reinforce dominant power relationships?

How can combining insights from Political Science and IR help us when analyzing media coverage of the Iraq war?

Seminar activities

Design a newspaper front page. What are the key motivations behind your design? You will need to consider the role of owners; advertisers; audiences; competitors. Where do you think power lies in what you are doing?

Analyze a TV news programme. What is the running order of the stories? What does this suggest is the most important issue of the day? How are the news stories 'framed'? What language is used to discuss the issue? Do you think the media are aiming to influence policy decisions? How do you establish this? Are they likely to be effective in this aim and why do you think this?

Analyze the front page of the newspaper. What function is being performed in the lead story coverage – are the press holding political elites to account? Or are they simply reinforcing the political and economic status quo? Where do women feature in this story? What role has been constructed for them?

Compare the coverage between Al Jazeera, the BBC, CNN and CCTV. What differences and similarities are there? How we can we explain this difference in content? Which perspective does the coverage fit most closely with and why?

Chapter 8

Security

Introduction

Security is among the most highly contested issues in Political Science and IR, complicated by the taken-for-granted assumptions about security that make up so much of the discourse of our daily lives, politicking and media coverage. In the study of Politics, a mainstream view might suggest that the issue of security is paramount to our understandings of how the world works and how people relate to one another. In this view, the topics we have discussed in previous chapters, such as the state, policy, institutions etc., while the subject of vigorous debate as to their constituent features, are premised on the idea of security as necessary to protect individuals from fellow citizens, the state, foreign citizens and foreign states. However, security is a highly contested concept. Not only that; for Edward Kolodziej (2005: 1) it has the added dimension that it is 'heavily laden with emotion and deeply held values'. Indeed, for James Der Derian 'no other concept in international relations packs the metaphysical punch, nor commands the disciplinary power of 'security'' (Der Derian, 1995: 24–5).

As such, we need to ask fundamental questions about what security actually is. As we have already discovered in previous chapters there are no clear-cut definitions that are uncontested by competing ontological and epistemological perspectives. A broad definition of security might be the alleviation of threats to deeply held values, beliefs, practices and way of life, which if unchallenged and resisted would result in their overthrow. Security, the absence of threats and fear, is then achieved by a willingness to resist and protect in order to maintain those values. Such a definition, however, would be too ambiguous for many theorists. Traditional IR perspectives in the realist tradition would be more comfortable with linking issues of security specifically to state survival and warfare. Ian Bellamy posits that security is 'a relative freedom from war, coupled with a relatively high expectation that defeat will not be a consequence of any war that should occur' (Bellamy, 1981: 102). Others may choose to focus on the individual rather than the state: 'If people, be they government ministers or private individuals, perceive an issue to threaten their lives in some way and respond politically to this, then that issue should be deemed to be a security issue' (Hough, 2004: 9).

When considering different approaches to the study of security we need to be clear which referent object we are seeking to examine as a subject of security. Are we interested in security at the level of the international system, the state, the individual or maybe even at the level of the eco system? We need to ask such core questions as: what is security? Who is it for? Who decides what constitutes a security issue? Which issues make, or do not make, it onto security agendas? How is security achieved? Do we conceptualize security as a commodity to acquire to make us secure by, for example, developing military resources, or do we believe that security should be more about human rights, justice and fairness – a freedom to achieve rather than just freedom from existential threats?

Security has become a sub-discipline, some would argue a separate discipline, within IR and has developed a robust theoretical tradition, whereas Political Science has tended to leave security issues to IR. We attempt to bridge this gap over the course of the remainder of the chapter. We argue such divisions are arbitrary and international security issues become domestic issues and vice versa, as in the case of international terrorism or civil unrest in one country destabilizing neighbouring countries and potentially inviting external intervention. In this chapter, we will examine foundational positivist liberal and neo-realist approaches on policing and civil–military relationships and traditional approaches to international security. We then consider foundational realist approaches of radical feminism and critical security and anti-foundational positions of critical/postmodern social constructivism and postmodern/poststructural approaches to security. Before doing so we now turn to the issue of power and security.

Power

Security and power are codetermining for many Political Science and IR theorists. Indeed, the dominant paradigm in IR since World War II has been realism and its structural variants with its overwhelming emphasis on power. Realists claim a long history from Thucydides, through Machiavelli and Hobbes, to E. H. Carr and Hans Morgenthau. What each of these theorists has in common is a belief that power determines international political outcomes. Based on a view of human nature that is essentially negative, one defined by aggression, selfishness, competition and destructiveness, realists agree with Hobbes that in a state of nature

Box 8.1   Case study. Nuclear weapons proliferation

Nuclear weapons have only been used by one country since being developed in 1945 and yet, thereafter, the awesome power of what were comparatively small devices has attracted and appalled states as they contemplate their own security requirements. The destruction of the Japanese cities of Hiroshima and Nagasaki by the United States in the final days of World War II introduced a new technological sophistication to warfare. This required theorists and political leaders to consider the security implications of acquiring or foregoing nuclear weapons and the consequences of other states making the same decision. Within 20 years of America developing nuclear weapons they had been joined by four other states: Soviet Union (1949), United Kingdom (1952), France (1960) and the People's Republic of China (1964). The UN General Assembly endorsed an Irish resolution in 1961 to limit the spread of nuclear weapons and in 1970 the Non Proliferation Treaty (NPT) came into force, which committed signatories to demonstrate good faith, where they were a nuclear weapon state (NWS), in pursuing their own nuclear disarmament and, for non-nuclear weapons states (NNWSs), to forego nuclear weapons. The NPT permitted NNWSs to develop civilian nuclear programmes for energy production.

The overwhelming majority of states have honoured the treaty and foregone the development of nuclear weapons, while many have developed civilian nuclear energy programmes. In the 1970s non-signatories to the NPT India and Israel developed nuclear weapons without sanctions, while in the 1980s and 1990s South Africa, Pakistan and the Democratic People's Republic of Korea developed nuclear weapons. Libya and Iraq were developing but not completing nuclear weapons programmes in the 1990s. At the time

humanity lives in 'continual fear and danger of violent death' (Hobbes, 1946: xiii). For realists this prospect is averted in domestic politics by the emergence of a settled political order (leviathan) with clear obligations and laws between rulers and those governed. In the international sphere, devoid of such order, anarchy persists and states must maximize their own power in order to survive. All states will need to act in the same way, although the less powerful are able to enhance their security and power by allying themselves with other states against perceived threats.

Realism considers that ultimately it is military power that is important as both an ends and means. Military power determines political outcomes and enables states projecting most power to demonstrate strength and achieve political objectives such as the reduction of external threats, the ability to acquire territory, trade and resources. Power-maximizing states enjoy greater international prestige and access to key international decision-making processes, through the UN Security Council and other international of writing Iran's nuclear programme is subject to intense speculation as their claims to be pursuing a legitimate civilian nuclear energy programme are disbelieved by the UN Security Council and sanctions have been instituted to force compliance with the inspections regime of the UN's International Atomic Energy Agency (IAEA). Nuclear arms races and the balance of power were major considerations during the Cold War. The lack of direct confrontation by the bipolar powers over 40 years suggested that the prospects of mutually assured destruction for both states made the world a more secure place, albeit with the fear of nuclear explosion also heightening security concerns. In the post-Cold War period attention has turned to the efficacy of such weapons of mass destruction. Presented with the opportunity to abandon nuclear weapons when the current British nuclear payload becomes obsolete in the mid-2020s successive governments chose to renew the programme and remain a nuclear power despite the opportunity to abide by commitments under the NPT. Other countries, including South Africa and former Soviet republics Kazakhstan, Ukraine and Belarus, decided to give up nuclear weapons in the early 1990s. Libya abandoned its nuclear programme in 2004 and Iran claims to not be interested in developing nuclear weapons. In Latin America, South East Asia, Africa and Central Asia there are nuclear-free zones.

So how can we account for such different perspectives? Why do some states seek nuclear weapons and others not? Should we be concerned by nuclear proliferation and does this make conflict more or less likely? Who gets to decide who has nuclear weapons and who is prevented from having them? Why is Iran rather than Israel targeted for sanctions over their nuclear programmes? We will consider the various theoretical positions and the direction research might take on the issue of nuclear proliferation.

and regional institutions. State power includes a strong military capacity but also wealth (measured in Gross Domestic Product [GDP] and natural resources), size of population, geographical position, the power of ideas, the ability to attract others and technological sophistication. Strong states will enjoy what Weber describes as a monopoly of legitimate violence within territorial borders (Weber, 1964: 154). State sovereignty that legitimates this domestic control and proscribes other states from interfering in the internal affairs of other countries is a central realist claim.

For the realist, states are unitary, sovereign and rational actors, which make strategic decisions within an international system made up of every state, all of whom will be attempting to maximize power. Realists make few claims as to the desirability of war but are assured of the inevitability of war as a demonstration of power:

> the ultimate ratio of power in International Relations is war. Every act of the state in its power aspect, is directed to war, not as a desirable

weapon, but as a weapon which it may require in the last resort to use. (Carr, 1946: 109)

Realist claims enjoy primacy in IR theory and are the starting point for critique and challenge from all other theoretical positions, including critical/scientific realism, feminism and poststructuralism, which dispute classical and structural realism's positivist claims to scientific objectivity. Realism in IR, and as we shall see its structural variants, are straightforward meta-narratives telling audiences how things really are; yet other theorists will want to know: how did they get that way? Why reify the state as the referent object? How sustainable are realist views of human nature? How can we explain periods of peace and the desire for peace? Where are women in realist accounts of history? Whose interests are being advanced and protected in the name of security?

As with realists, liberals focus upon the observable behaviour of individual actors as the site where power is located. Liberals would argue that the world is far more pacific than IR realists would have us believe, with military security subordinate to economic issues. Economic interdependence in a liberal capitalist world order tends towards mutual dependence rather than conflict; regional and international institutions and established norms of behaviour advance security. For critical/scientific realists, such as critical theorists and Marxists, security is more concerned with security for the individual or class than it is about security for the state. State-centric and systemic models of security are seen as aspects of domination and control by ruling classes whose authority is legitimated and reinforced by traditional approaches to security. Power is located structurally in the maintenance and securing of the class-based system. Individual security below the state level takes precedence and, according to world system theorists, the dominant security narrative exists for the core countries to exploit developing countries in the periphery.

For feminists security is more about the insecurity of women, both domestically and internationally. Traditional security approaches have virtually excluded women in ignoring the widespread abuse of women through domestic and military violence, and seeing it to be less important than state security. Liberal feminists press for the inclusion and equal representation in security structures, while radical feminists are more concerned with expanding security agendas to take into account the exploitation of women. Poststructuralists are interested in discovering and uncovering the discourse surrounding security issues, what counts for a security issue, how populations are conditioned to accept securitizing narratives and the implications this has for understanding security. Here power is located discursively in discourses which normalize male understandings of security (usually defined in realist military terms). The aim for this perspective is to challenge those understandings providing opportunities for emancipation.

Foundational positivist approaches

Behaviouralism in Political Science

Although questions of security have been dominated by security and strategic studies within international relations, many of these theories have been adapted and developed from the works of the leading political scientists including Machiavelli, Hobbes, Locke, Kant, Durkheim and Weber. Behaviouralist approaches to security at the domestic level seek to deal with questions about how security for populations and the government can be assured, and political control maintained, when reliant upon non-elected institutions to provide that security. The focus here is upon the observable and the empirically measurable. Liberal theory operates within a pluralist paradigm in which the role of the police and military are essential components of a democratic polity.

Liberal views towards policing within democracies see police officers as 'disinterested custodians of public order' (Brewer *et al.*, 1988: 214). Police forces should be independent of political control and enforce the laws of the land free from the individual officer's, or the institution's, opinion about the efficacy of such laws. Liberals, although they might be divided over whether policing should be administered under central government control or by local accountability, agree that policing should be by consent. Behaviouralists' focus of enquiry is to explain what is observed and explain political behaviour at the individual and aggregate level (Sanders, 1995: 10). Observation of policing leads liberals and other foundational positivists to ask questions about the nature of policing. Although policing in democracies is purported to be independent of political control, is it really the case? When ethnic minority groups are disproportionately stopped, searched, arrested and receive higher sentencing (as occurs in Britain and the United States), does that have either a political agenda or impact? What impact does this have on the security (freedom from threat) experienced by these minority groups? Who determines which citizens will be observed? Are these political or policing decisions?

In 2010 a UK media campaign led to plans to install 24-hour surveillance cameras, monitoring the movements of the mainly Muslim population in two areas of Birmingham; it was abandoned when it was discovered that it was to be funded by a counter-terrorism initiative (Lewis, 2010). At the time of writing, 10 per cent of the British prison population is Muslim and yet less than 3 per cent of the population are (Ford, 2007).

Numerous high-profile arrests of suspected terrorists, encouraged by the political expediency of securing quick convictions, have led to acquittal or detention without charge of British Muslims and, earlier, Irish men and women, bringing into question the independence of policing and whose security is being protected – the individual's or the state's? The use of the state to intervene in political/industrial disputes, whether breaking up picket lines in the coalminers' strikes in the 1980s or firing on demonstrators at Kent State University in the Vietnam protest in 1970, also blurs the lines, even in democracies, between safeguarding and impinging the security of citizens.

Liberal political scientists tend to be concerned with the relationship between the military and the state. A fundamental prescript for democracy is civilian control of the military. The military are entrusted with undertaking defence policy on behalf of elected representatives. Civilian politicians decide policy and the military decide how best to implement the strategy with the former retaining control and ultimate responsibility that can be tested at the next election (Hague *et al.*, 1993: 367–91). The government is responsible for the actions the military undertake on their behalf. For example, British troops were sent to Northern Ireland in 1969 to protect catholics against a sectarian police force, which was no longer able to maintain law and order following civil rights protests and sectarian violence. In the course of their duties over a 30-year period 150 civilians were killed by the army, including 14 murdered in Derry on 30 January 1972 (Sutton, 2001). The Saville Enquiry revealed that far from providing security, the army, acting as agents of the state, breached the security of civil rights protestors by shooting unarmed civilians; this was recognized by Prime Minister Cameron's public apology on behalf of the state (Saville *et al.*, 2010). Liberal theorists are particularly keen to understand the relationship between security forces, elected representatives and the people they represent as an aspect of democratic politics at the level of the state and below.

Structural realism

Structural or neo-realism has much in common with its realist forebear, including a pessimistic view of humanity; however, rather than attribute the course of human history to the basic depravity and frailty of humanity, structural realists point to a systemic cause for international insecurity. Kenneth Waltz's seminal work *Theory of International Politics,* published in 1979, set out Waltz's premise that systems are composed of structures and interacting units. Waltz developed his theory from examining states over time and noticing recurring patterns of behaviour with states and leaders seemingly unable to adopt different courses of action.

Box 8.2 Liberal theory and nuclear proliferation

Liberal theorists concerned with the civil–military relations will place considerable emphasis on civilian control of nuclear weapons. Although protected and deployed by the military, this is only possible in democratic societies with clearly specified rules of engagement approved by the executive and legislature. Nuclear weapons can only be used on the authority of the government accountable to the electorate. Liberals consider that authoritarian regimes are less stable and reliable and, without similar accountability mechanisms, present a greater risk of wilful or accidental nuclear weapons usage. While assumptions of rationality for democratic leaders are made this is not assumed where authoritarian rulers are concerned. Liberals, operating below the level of state as international actor, are concerned with the potential proliferation of nuclear weapons by non-state actors such as the Khan network, which included the proliferation of technological know-how to North Korea, Syria and Libya.

Research areas would include policing and anti-terrorist action and capability within democracies. Another line of enquiry might include the desirability of states attaining nuclear energy without nuclear weapons production. Dependable energy provision increases security and improves the prosperity of citizens while creating new markets for technological transfer and innovations and trade in nuclear materials. In an era of increased concern over global warming, nuclear energy provides a way of producing energy without contributing unduly to greenhouse emissions. On the other hand, environmental activists suggest that the current inability to destroy nuclear waste makes such energy production environmentally damaging. Liberal theorists are eager to engage in this debate.

Political structures comprise of three elements: an ordering principle such as hierarchy or anarchy; the characteristics of the units, either functioning differently or in the same way; and the distribution of capabilities. Waltz argued that the ordering principle is anarchic and therefore all states are obliged to operate in the same way on the basis of self-help. The only structural variable, therefore, is how capabilities are distributed, whether in a multipolar or bipolar system (Waltz, 1979: 88–99).

Structural realism departs from classical realism and liberalism by disregarding the internal make-up of states, the ideological character of the state, or the individual agency of leaders. States act in the way they do because they have no choice in an anarchical world with no overarching authority. Epistemologically they argue we can know this through observation of states' behaviour. Security, in this perspective, is seen purely in terms of the unitary state's own survival, states are unable to opt out despite their best intentions because they are in competition with other states whether they chose to be or not. States threaten the existence of other states and the only security is in the state's ability to protect and defend itself and its people. In a competitive international order each state will be uncertain and therefore suspicious of others' motives and intentions and will be wary of cooperation. The possibility of cheating or reneging on agreements makes every transaction potentially problematic. Structural realists believe that, because of this competitive international system, states will be wary of cooperating even when cooperation will result in absolute gains for all parties involved, preferring relative gains which will increase their own power. Power here is assumed to be measurable in terms of a states' position in the global order, defined primarily through its military power.

Waltz identifies a world order that is marked by a balance of power based on the imitation of best practice by other states seeking to compete and survive in the system (Waltz, 1979: 178). For structural realists, states are left with two options in order to acquire the power necessary for their survival. First, they can seek to balance threats by forming alliances and enjoy the protection and lower defence expenditure afforded by other states through mutual defence. Second, states could balance against threats by becoming more powerful themselves through increased military spending. A third alternative is for weaker states to bandwagon by forming an alliance with the stronger side such as a regional hegemon. Structural realists consider that security is attained through a balance of power. Waltz considers that a bipolar system, as in the Cold War, is the most stable international system, multipolarity is less predictable and unipolarity is unlikely because states will balance against a universal hegemon.

Offensive structural realists go further than Waltz and emphasize the importance of relative capability in an uncertain world. Survival is the primary goal of great powers, which tends to be their referent object, and because they are rational actors and realize that they can only rely on themselves do so by seeking to maximize relative power (Mearsheimer, 2001: 30–1). John Mearsheimer, the leading proponent of offensive realism, argues that relative power maximization should be the goal of each state. Clearly, the ideal position for a state, which is always going to encounter threats to its security, is to become the most powerful state or regional hegemon. The more powerful the state the more secure it is. Neo-realists caution against power maximization, arguing that if other states balance against an aspiring hegemon then it may not be the optimal course of action and could even be counterproductive. Mearsheimer rejects such caution, however, positing relative power-maximizing states as sophisticated actors which 'try to figure out when to raise and when to fold' (Mearsheimer, 2001: 40). Here, then, the emphasis is upon states

Box 8.3   Structural realist approaches to nuclear proliferation

Structural realists accept nuclear weapons proliferation as an inevitable consequence of an anarchic international system. However, rather than posit that every state should seek to acquire nuclear weapons to guarantee survival, Kenneth Waltz has argued that nuclear weapons have spread rather than proliferated because they have increased upwards as NWS have increased their own nuclear arsenals. When nuclear weapons have spread to other states this has only happened slowly, which is reassuring in an international system where surprises are unsettling. It is advantageous for nuclear weapons to spread gradually rather than not at all, or too quickly, because possession of nuclear weapons constrains action and produces responsible international actors, conscious of the dangers of using the weapons. The security environment improves by responsible nuclear weapons states as the defence and deterrent capabilities reduce the likelihood of war (Sagan and Waltz, 1995).

For structural realists, security is more readily attained if states possess nuclear weapons. Such a development is rational because no rational actor would risk destruction by attacking a NWS. Nuclear weapon states do not go to war with one another or if they do so it is likely to only be once. Power in this perspective is observable and very firmly assumed to be the property only of states. It should be noted, however, that if we assume power is the property of states, then this may pose a problem if we need to analyze the behaviour of those non-state actors or organizations who may have access to nuclear weapons.

as unitary actors and their observable and measurable behaviour; as with rational choice theory there is an assumption of individual rationality. It is assumed that states will behave rationally, which in turn brings a predictability to state behaviour.

Foundational critical/scientific realist approaches

Radical feminism

Radical feminism takes its starting point on security from its rejection of realist assumptions about international order, international relations and specifically security. Realist assumptions are comprehensively rejected as masculinist and as serving to perpetuate violence and both the invisibility and subjugation of women. Sandra Whitworth argues that 'security' is infused with 'gendered assumptions and representations' (Whitworth, 2009: 104) and challenges the presentation by positivist realists of security as gender-neutral. The realist reification of the state as the main referent object of security is also challenged because it fails to account for domestic politics and human security, particularly the security of women. A presentation of security that sets states apart as unitary, selfish actors bent on power maximization, fearful of the cheating behaviour and competition of other states becomes a self-fulfilling prophecy and carries heavy normative baggage. Radical feminism identifies this as a gendered presentation of security in which the privileging of state autonomy and sovereignty is indicative of a masculinist mindset that fails to account for alternative conceptions of security.

The realist prioritizing of war and military hard power to achieve security is rejected by radical feminists as evidence of a gendered approach to security that favours possession of the ability to harm others over 'celebrating and sustaining life' (Sheehan, 2005: 123). Such violence, for radical feminists, is on a continuum, which begins with gendered hierarchy with social subordination and domination, leading to domestic violence, as forms of structural violence that maintain women's insecurity at domestic and international levels (Tickner, 1995: 193). Real security needs to address these issues also, alongside issues of social justice, including the distribution of resources, which privileges warfare over welfare. They argue that an artificial division of the domestic and international equates states with inanimate billiard balls rather than bordered entities comprising the hopes and aspirations and lived experiences of real people. Their critique argues that the privileging of unitary state actors produces a mindset that sets state against state rather than considering peoples across and within borders linked by a common humanity.

Radical feminists seek to make women visible in discussions on security in their participation in security structures and combat, their experiences of conflict, as peace activists and as the vital component in bids to feminize institutions and conflict (Kennedy-Pipe, 2010: 111). Political Science tends to distinguish between policing and security and yet radical feminists would argue that issues of domestic law and order are even more important than military conflict for women most of the time. In economic systems with finite resources military expenditure draws resources away from welfare and social security provision, directly impinging on women's sense of security, and yet government's privilege international security issues. Cynthia Enloe has been at the forefront of demonstrating the importance of women in security, revealing women as being essential components of the military structure in their role as wives, mothers and daughters of male combatants, providers of domestic and sexual services, producers of armaments and an integral part of an industrialized workforce (Enloe, 1989, 1993). Both men and women are required to accept gender stereotyping in conflict, with men becoming 'men' through soldiering and women acquiescing in assumptions about 'mothering, marriage, and unskilled work' (Enloe, 1993: 253). Deviation from gendered roles is resisted within patriarchal societies and women are discouraged or disallowed to serve as front-line troops in combat situations, allowing men to acquire 'almost exclusive control over the means of destruction' (Sheehan, 2005: 124).

Power, for feminists in this perspective, is located in patriarchal structures. We can observe its effects, feminists would argue, as positivist realism's dominant position within international relations and security means that the different experiences of men and women in warfare is overlooked and marginalized. Women and children suffer disproportionately in war, despite international law's proscription against killing non-combatants. Women in combat situations are vulnerable to death, maiming, rape, displacement and economic hardship as infrastructure is destroyed. Rape, as an instrument and consequence of war, has been ignored by realist IR, which has paid little or no attention to the widespread use of rape as a weapon to subdue and humiliate women and to their male protectors for their inability to provide that protection. Rape is often used as a weapon of choice by invading armies such as the Red Army's march into Germany at the end of World War II, or the ethnic cleansing and systematic rape of Bosnian Muslims by Serbs in the 1990s. Radical feminists point out that women are also at risk from rape from their own soldiers, even when they are serving alongside male soldiers in a combat role, and even peacekeepers. The realist ontological

Box 8.4 Radical feminist approaches to nuclear proliferation

Radical feminists approach nuclear weapons as an extension of patriarchy and masculinist discourse. The primary status given to nuclear weapons diverts security attention and material resources to weapons of mass destruction while simultaneously downgrading or not recognizing other security considerations, in particular the individual and human security. When interstate security dominates security agendas, intrastate security issues become marginalized. Nuclear weapons are presented as an exclusively masculinist discourse of power projection and survival in traditional security studies and so radical feminists theorize and campaign against nuclear weapons. Radical feminists were particularly active in the 1970s and 1980s in anti-nuclear protests, including the protests at US nuclear missiles deployed at Greenham Common in the United Kingdom. Radical feminists are concerned with resistance to the dominant discourse and the reifying of security to exclude consideration of the domestic sphere, institutional and political discrimination and the disadvantaging/abuse of women.

assumption of the importance of the state rather than individuals fails to account for the state being a major source of insecurity to vulnerable people, including women within its own borders.

Critical security

Critical security and critical security studies are derived from a combination of Gramscian analysis and Frankfurt School critical theory. As with radical feminism, critical security is galvanized by its opposition to realist IR and takes issue with its problem-solving theoretical position. In contrast, it offers a critical theory that asks how a particular order came about. Once it is known how we arrived at where we are, we can make choices about where we would like to be. Critical security, as with critical theory, claims emancipatory potential by rejecting realism's exclusive focus on states and considering other referent objects. For Ken Booth, one of the founders of the Welsh School of Critical Security Studies: 'Security is what we make of it. It is an epiphenomenon intersubjectively created. Different worldviews and discourses about politics deliver different views and discourses about security' (Booth, 1997: 106).

For critical security theorists, that worldview challenges the prevailing order and emphasizes the state's role as a means rather than the ends of security policy. The real objective of security should be to emancipate rather than simply to preserve the state (Booth, 1991). The normative approach adopted by critical theorists considers that if social and political oppression is exposed, and people are equipped with the tools necessary to challenge the status quo, then they can be set free. Far from claiming dispassionate social scientific objectivity, critical security is intent on equipping readers to usurp the existing order and change priorities. Traditional theories of security have played their part in legitimizing international structures and creating a security environment where recourse to military action is the default position of the international system and the need to prioritize military expenditure over other claims on finite resources. Critical security theorists seek to change the entire way we consider security:

> Security means the absence of threats. Emancipation is the freeing of people (as individuals and groups) from those physical and human constraints which stop them carrying out what they would freely choose to do. War and the threat of war is one of those constraints, together with poverty, poor education, political oppression and so on. Security and emancipation are two sides of the same coin. Emancipation, not power or order, produces true security. (Booth, 1991: 319)

Rather than reifying the state as the enhancer of security, critical security posits the state as being the harbinger of insecurity. State-centricity,

Box 8.5 Critical security and the proliferation of nuclear weapons

Critical security theory approaches nuclear weapons proliferation from the critical standpoint of considering whom nuclear weapons are for, and what function they serve. Rather than being taken for granted as an outcome of the anarchic international system, the proliferation nuclear weapons relies on the construction of threats. Critical security will consider this construction and analyzes the construction of insider and outsider groups of NWS and NNWS and the tensions that are constructed between the two. Critical security theorists emphasize hegemony and the underpinning of hegemony by military force, in particular nuclear weapons. The United States' hegemonic position in the world rests on its possession of nuclear weapons alongside vast and technologically superior military forces. Critical security scholars will seek to shine light on the NWS's privileged position within the international system with permanent seats on the UN Security Council and in major international institutions. They will also emphasize the impact that nuclear weapons spending has on individuals and the potential, through deconstructing realist arguments, to empower people to resist nuclear weapons acquisition and abolition within NWSs.

claims of rationality and of national interest actually create identities that conceive a 'discourse of danger' around notions of insider and foreigner. The idea of nation-states reinforces the idea of separation and otherness, both within and outside borders, with such notions cutting across shared humanity and focusing on what separates rather than what unites enabling the ruling class within states to retain control (Sheehan, 2005: 163). Critical theory is highly normative and, in focusing on how unobservable power structures guide behaviour, they are able to focus on inequality in the world and proffer an emancipatory alternative view of security.

Anti-foundational interpretivist approaches

Postmodernism

Postmodernism rejects the foundationalist and positivist approaches completely and this is just as applicable when we consider security. At the core of postmodernism lies a rejection of the enlightenment project to which foundationalists ascribe. Postmodernism argues there is no single, objective reality but rather many experiences and perspectives. Jean-François Lyotard defined postmodernism as 'incredulity towards metanarratives' (Lyotard, 1984: xxiv). In a similar vein Derrida and Foucault consider postmodernism resistant to categorization. Indeed the purpose of postmodernism is to challenge all certainties through deconstructing texts and discourses, to uncover hidden meanings and omissions in the subtext. The leading postmodernists' writings are situated within Political Science rather than IR and yet the latter have appropriated their ideas to understand relations between countries and within international systems. In postmodernist deconstructions of realist IR texts, there is fruitful ground to uncover in the omission of individuals, women in particular, economic classes, multinational corporations, trade unions, transnational actors, religion and domestic politics altogether.

Postmodernism will deconstruct those assumptions taken for granted by realism, such as anarchy, the state, the international system and security. Postmodernists examine those assumptions from a position that there is 'no particular authority or set of values that in claiming absolute truth deserves unquestioned loyalty and obedience' (Sheehan, 2005: 136). Society makes choices about what is acceptable or unacceptable behaviour, those choices do not represent the truth but simply the construction that a particular society at a particular time declared to be true or acceptable behaviour. The concept of foreigner and citizen are constructs, as are friend and enemy, and these constructs are subject to change. For example, Iraq was constructed as a friendly regime to the West in 1988 but not in 1990. Dominant discourses defined Saddam Hussein's actions in invading Kuwait, a friendly regime and major oil supplier to the West, as responsible for changing the regime's status from one of amity to one of enmity. In order for Western populations to understand and endorse such a change in relations, then, a discourse had to be constructed positing Hussein as enemy and villain and, as such, we can see that power is located discursively.

Postmodernists are interested in unpacking such discourse to discover the intentions and motivations behind the construction in the first place. For postmodernists discourses are used not only to convey notions of what is or is not acceptable, but also to differentiate between the self and other, us and them. Using Foucault's power/knowledge nexus, postmodernists can explain how constructs of otherness are used to control those who are the same by constructing fear of the other. The demonization of the other in the Cold War led to mutual fear and suspicion between the US and Soviet bloc.

The discursive construct of the 'Red threat', from within and without, enabled the US government to increase military expenditure greatly and to construct a narrative of being un-American for opponents. The construction of external threats, real and imagined, persuades populations to cede rights and civil liberties to government in return for enhanced security. Postmodernists seek to determine how and for what purpose the pursuit

Box 8.6 Postmodernism and nuclear proliferation

Postmodernists are eager to deconstruct and challenge traditional security studies positions on nuclear weapons. Through analyzing texts and language, they are able to demonstrate how threats are constructed and the case made for nuclear weapons. Rather than seeing nuclear weapons' proliferation specifically as a security issue, postmodernists are anxious to discover how institutions and populations are conditioned in preparation for the acquisition of nuclear weapons or preventing other states from acquiring them. Postmodernist projects might include consideration of how discourse is utilized in order to legitimate some NWS and not others. The narrative of protection and security, the appeal to survival or power maximization are all subject to discursive analysis. Postmodernists might also be interested in the US–Indian nuclear cooperation agreement signed in 2005 in which the US provides India with materials and assistance on its civilian nuclear programme in return for IAEA inspectors having access to India's civilian nuclear power stations. A discursive analysis would shed light on justifications for this policy, which would appear to reward states which proliferate.

The acquisition of nuclear weapons is not simply a security issue but also entails tremendous prestige and a seat at the international top table. Postmodernists will be interested in deconstructing the discourse surrounding the status attached to nuclear weapons. Iran's pursuit of nuclear power and possibly nuclear weapons can be deconstructed by analysis of speech acts and texts that present Iran as becoming technologically proficient, desiring independent energy supplies, and facing security threats from Israel and the United States. Why is nuclear proliferation presented as a threat to international security rather than being praised as a demonstration of scientific expertise and technological progress? The process of discursive deconstruction is able to reveal strategic choices made by NWS to resist or acquiesce in nuclear proliferation.

of such strategies are successful. George W. Bush's global war on terror constructed an existential Islamist threat in perpetuity, enabling the forward projection of US military power into the Middle East, Indian subcontinent, Saudi peninsula and East Africa, while eroding civil rights in the US, under the auspices of Homeland Security (Dalby, 1992: 107; Jackson, 2005). Postmodernists argue that we can never be fully secure because, in order to construct our identity, it is also necessary to construct fear, threat and difference of the other.

Critical social constructivism

Social constructivism is a very broad church incorporating positivist and foundational approaches such as preferred by Wendt, Hopf and

Katzenstein at one extreme, to poststructuralist anti-foundationalism at the other. Increasingly, social constructivism in IR tends to be divided into two rival camps of conventional constructivists and critical constructivists. The designation of the more radical grouping as critical constructivists is somewhat problematic in that many scholars operating within this approach would not see themselves as critical theorists or foundational realists but adopt an anti-foundationalist position. The latter group is the focus of this section. Constructivists place considerable emphasis on cultural, historical and social factors and how these lead to the emergence, and perpetuation, of ideas, norms and identity. When dealing with security issues from a constructivist perspective then ideas are crucial to interpreting security practices and institutions.

Social constructivists dismiss the objectivity of the social scientist when s/he claims to be able to stand outside the world of security and not bring their bias to understanding the world. Some constructivists will pursue a normative agenda, seeking to influence and change policy by adopting an analytical approach that questions the use of language in constructing identity and security. For the critical constructivists working on security, then, the normative and ideational structures are of greater importance than material considerations. Ideas and identity shape security and any proper consideration of IR and the international system needs to reflect this. The action and interaction of actors requires an identity and interests, which change over time in accordance with changed circumstances. The power of narrative, including language and texts, has the capacity to shape the construction of security. Narratives frame security issues as threatening or benign and determine consequently, what action needs to be taken. Over time narratives become accepted and internalized and provide sets of values and norms of appropriate behaviour.

Appropriate behaviour in international security may include not using nuclear weapons, warring according to the principles of just war, honouring agreements and state sovereignty, but these norms have to be socially constructed and as such are subject to change. How referent objects see themselves is of considerable importance in how they deal with others, at the individual, state or system level. According to Christine Agius: 'Culture can have an impact on how states see security, but it is also crucial in terms of constructing the values and rules that inform identity' (Agius, 2010: 56). States that share similar cultures are more likely to enter into security arrangements with one another in alliances or regional security communities. The shared values, identity and meaning of similar nations, or rather nations which see themselves as similar, can lead to deepening security ties, trust and a sense of togetherness with like-minded states (see Adler and Barnett, 1988).

The power of ideas leads critical constructivists to spend much of their time working on discursive analysis and deconstructing those speech acts Nicholas Onuf describes as being assertions, directives or commitments (Onuf, 1998). For Onuf it is 'by speaking that we make the world what it is' (Onuf, 2002: 12–17). In security terms, the language used to define or describe security situations has the power to bring those into being.

Box 8.7 Critical constructivists and nuclear proliferation

Critical constructivist approaches to nuclear proliferation adopt a critical perspective towards neo-realist orthodoxy. Rather than accepting policy on nuclear proliferation as a given, critical constructivists will seek to unpack the organizational, institutional and bureaucratic interests involved. Scott Sagan suggests that military organizations are inflexible, parochial and institutionalize organizational behaviour in a way that makes deterrence failure and accidental warfare a possibility. He also contends that the character of states seeking to acquire nuclear weapons has the potential to lead to the use of nuclear weapons, as authoritarian governments lack the checks and balances to constrain action (Sagan and Waltz, 1995).

A less pessimistic view is adopted by Adler, Price and Tannenwald, who suggest that epistemic communities, norms of responsible and appropriate behaviour and taboos against the use of nuclear weapons makes proliferation less threatening (Adler, 1992: Price and Tannenwald, 1996; Tannenwald, 1999). Social constructivists are concerned with the role that identity and culture plays in constructing an environment in which non-proliferation is the norm, and why most states choose not to become nuclear weapons states, or even abandon nuclear weapons altogether (Krause and Williams, 1997; Campbell *et al.*, 2004).

Nick Ritchie, in discussing the UK decision to renew its Trident nuclear submarine programme, emphasizes the importance of actor-networks and collective identities, social constructions of ourselves and others that become seen as normal. These networks and identities institutionalize understandings of how states are perceived and how individual actors perceive their role and the national interest. British identity, Ritchie argues, is coterminous with an identity as a global power, a responsible, interventionist state. Britain's reluctance to abandon nuclear weapons is reflected in the construction of its special relationship with the United States and co-warrior. The status the UK enjoys because of its nuclear status precludes consideration of abandoning nuclear weapons and leaving France, as the sole EU nuclear power. The justification to citizens is presented as a discursive narrative of perceived threat from a revanchist Russia or threats from rogue states or international terrorism (Ritchie, 2010).

The United Kingdom sets great value in its special relationship with the United States and the discursive power of continually referring to the special relationship and the counter-affirmation from the US that the relationship is indeed special. The prevailing relational narrative predisposes UK governments to think and act favourably to the United States and support foreign policy adventures, including Iraq and Afghanistan, in order to stand shoulder to shoulder with its special friend, whether it is in the national interest or not. The United States has many special relationships, not least with Israel and Canada, that are equally important and only pursues polices in its national interests; yet it engages in the special relationship narrative to construct a security relationship with the UK. Social constructivists, rather than taking the special relationship for granted, will want to deconstruct the concept asking in whose interest the discourse operates, the extent to which it is true, investigate examples of evidence to the contrary and ask what the impact of the construction of such a relationship is. In a similar vein, critical constructivists challenge the taken-for-granted assumptions not just of realists but all other theoretical approaches as well.

Comparison of theories and approaches

We have considered six different approaches reflecting different aspects of security, which are either neglected or under-emphasized by competing and complementary theories. Behaviouralists in liberal theory tend to focus on domestic security and in particular the relationship that exists between military and civilian political leadership and policing within pluralist systems. The emphasis is on making democracy and its citizens secure from threats without and how to deal with the danger of threat from within by an unanswerable or unaccountable police or military force. Structural realists consider that it is not worthwhile considering domestic politics when thinking about security. They argue that there are fundamental differences between the order and contractual relationship between ruler and governed at the domestic level and an anarchical world system without an overarching authority. In such a world, only the most powerful survive and those who are not powerful need to arrange with others to balance the power of mightier states. In a system where the raison d'être for states is survival, then realists argue that states need to be self-reliant. Other states are not to be trusted and so suspicion and the fear of cheating on agreements leads to an international system, which is perpetually insecure. War is only prevented by states either balancing against more powerful combinations of states or bandwagoning with the most powerful state. Offensive realists believe that rather than simply surviving, states want and need to maximize power and if possible become a regional hegemon to ensure their own security.

Structural realism is the main antagonist of all the other theories and approaches considered. The rationalist and positivist approach adopted by structural realists has dominated and has also served to legitimate realist approaches to US foreign policy. It is also the theory most readily critiqued for what it overlooks. From a critical perspective, then, radical feminism considers that realists, in setting foreign policy agendas and positing an anarchic world order of unitary power-maximizing states, distort the security agenda by privileging a masculinist discourse and the state over other referent objects, principally individuals. Radical feminists expose the gendered assumptions of realism and the invisibility of women in traditional security studies. They argue that security should not begin at states' borders but should acknowledge the continuum of violence that begins with domestic violence and ends with international conflict.

Those working in the field of critical theory are broadly sympathetic with radical feminist perspectives but also seek to project a normative and emancipatory agenda. Although critical theorists consider the state as a referent object they also look to the individual and classes as well. The construction of threats leads critical theorists to consider the insider/outsider divide and how this breaks down solidarity and constructs security threats. Postmodernists adopt a similar approach to critical theorists, although they reject an enlightenment paradigm of progress and are less impressed by the prospect for emancipation than critical theorists. Instead, they challenge realists for their meta-theoretical position and challenge the notion of objective reality. Through deconstructing language and texts, they reveal a world in which the prospect for security will remain elusive. Identity construction requires the insecurity to separate insiders from outsiders. Postmodernists are also interested in how external threats provide the state with opportunities to control its own citizenry. Critical constructivists are very close to postmodernists but differentiate themselves by a focus on culture, ideas and identity as the main frames for security. They draw our attention to norms and appropriate behaviour, which shape how security is perceived, structured and conducted.

Adjudicating between perspectives

If we are more interested in how democracies control security within their borders then a behaviouralist approach offered by liberal theory would be useful in understanding civil–military relations and policing.

On the other hand, if we consider that security is primarily about power on the international stage, and how states pursue and exercise power, then a structural realist approach would be more appropriate. Structural realism, for all its claims to the contrary, is a normative approach that believes that international security and international relations should only operate at the state level and that individuals are of little importance in maintaining and projecting power. The normative approach is that citizens are kept secure by a strong and powerful state that other states do not wish to fight. If, however, we consider that security should be about 'security to' rather than 'security from', about emancipation rather than violence and intimidation, then critical theories of critical studies or radical feminism would offer fertile ground. Security which places the individual first and considers issues of the role and fate of women in warfare, child soldiers and non-combatants more generally than critical theories challenges traditional concerns of security itself.

Foundational critical approaches hold out the prospect of a better world order and emancipation based on a belief in the enlightenment and the progress of modernity. Equally critical and yet far less optimistic theories of postmodernism or critical constructivism offer opportunities to deconstruct narratives and discourses that construct identities which pit insider against outsider and enable the state to control its own citizens or condition them to appropriate behavioural norms. Clearly, no one approach is effective in considering every aspect of security. When researching in this area we need to be conscious of what we are hoping to discover. Positivists claim that this can be done dispassionately and objectively, while interpretivists require us to recognize our bias based on our lived experience and reject positivist claims to the contrary.

Conclusion

For successive post-war generations realism dominated discussion; indeed, it dominated real foreign policy decision-making for much of the post-World War II period. In the period following the end of the Cold War new avenues of enquiry have opened up, several of which we have highlighted in this chapter. Although realism still occupies a significant place in the foreign policy of the major powers, the challenge from critical, feminist, constructivist and postmodern theorists has challenged this paradigm. Within this chapter, we have challenged the traditional division of labour between Political Science and IR in understanding security. Understanding of security beyond state borders has traditionally been left to IR theorists, while political scientists have tended to reflect on policing issues within states or regions. The issue of violence, whether domestic, terrorism or nuclear energy and nuclear weapons, are issues that should be of concern whether one is a political or IR theorist. Increasingly there is concern within academia, governments and populations about individual security. The widespread use of rape as a weapon of war and domestic violence, the abduction of children to serve as sex slaves or soldiers in intrastate conflict has begun to receive far greater academic attention. Discursive approaches have examined how language and texts shape our perceptions of security issues and what is included or excluded as a legitimate item for security discussion.

Over the course of this chapter we have sought to encourage examining security from multiple perspectives to consider which referent object is of most concern. We have presented realism as the traditional perspective that all other perspectives are obliged to challenge and usurp to widen a security agenda which realism has made prescriptive. We have sought to raise the question: is security about power or about people or, indeed, is it about both or neither? Interpretivist approaches require us to question every taken-for-granted assumption we may have possessed, while critical approaches seek to encourage a normative response that would seek to emancipate those who are able to see beyond traditional security perspectives and overturn the status quo, which privileges the militarily powerful states.

Reflection

Which approach does the best job of explaining nuclear proliferation?

Why do you think this is the case?

Does the possession of nuclear weapons by states ensure their own security and in turn cause stability in the international arena?

Does the focus on nuclear weapons as a source of security undermine the security of women within states?

Which perspective may be most useful in helping us understand the threat posed by non-state actors with access to nuclear weapons?

Why do you think that nuclear proliferation is presented and discussed as a threat to international security rather than as an example of scientific progress?

How can insights from Political Science and IR help us when analyzing nuclear proliferation? What are the reasons for your answer?

Seminar activities

Why have realists been the dominant force in international security since World War II?

What should be the relationship between civilians and the military in a democracy? Do we need to expand traditional conceptions of security?

How far is it possible to expand the concept of security without it becoming so all embracing it becomes impossible to theorize about it?

How useful is it to deconstruct language and texts?

Is the environment a security issue, if so why?

Why was the response to 9/11 seen as a military and not a police action?

Why attack a state in response to the criminal activities of individuals?

What does this tell us about the relationship between politics and international relations?

Which perspective does your answer fit most closely and why do you think this is the case?

Chapter 9

International/Political Economy

Introduction

Why is business so powerful? How is it that decisions taken in the City or financial markets can affect our everyday lives? Can we challenge our position in the existing global or domestic economy? Do states regulate markets in the interest of businesses or the public? What role is there for the public interest in political analysis of markets? How and why do ideas about economics become embedded in our social and political systems? In short, can we understand politics through reference to economics? The differing approaches within this chapter all assume a linkage between politics and economics, as disciplines, or as practice. The purpose of this chapter is to outline theories which discuss the relationship between politics and economics and explore the ways in which the two have been linked, in terms of their content and approach.

The way in which we study politics and economics has tended to be as though they are separate topics (although, as we will see below, historically this was not always the case). This contemporary disciplinary separation of politics from economics has been accompanied by a reshaping of how the term 'political economy' is understood. What is also interesting to note is that contemporary academic literature is characterized by a division of definition and therefore approach. This division has meant that there are two key ways in which political economy has been defined: either in terms of its subject matter (the relationship between states and markets) or by the methods and assumptions it adopts (the application of economic models, techniques and assumptions to the study of politics). The latter perspective has been highly influential, particularly in the practice of domestic politics (as in Chapter 3, for example, the influence of public and rational choice theories in shaping new right theories of the state). The former perspective is more wide ranging. The term 'political economy' has also long been associated with the works of Marx, and for Marxism, political economy is about the production of commodities and

197

accumulation of wealth. At the international level, Political Economy (or International or Global Political Economy – IPE/GPE) has also become a sub-discipline of study in IR (for a comprehensive discussion of this influence, see Watson, 2005), with a focus upon the relationship between states and markets. Within IPE there are further definitional divisions between those who view states and markets as actors with clearly defined interests and goals, and those who view states and markets as arenas for political action where interests are negotiated and constructed.

One the one hand then, political economy is a topic; in the 'states and markets' approach, attention is drawn to the way in which states may seek to shape markets in the interest of the domestic economy, or in the interests of the international order and, for many, political economy is taken to mean the management of the economic affairs of the state (Caporaso and Levine, 1992: 1). There is a second layer of division within the states and markets approach where we see ontological and epistemological differences which in turn influence the nature of that which is theorized and studied.

On the other hand, political economy is a method: it has been developed through formal theory and applies economic methodologies to the analysis of political phenomena. Formal theory does not share the meta-theoretical divisions of the 'states and markets' IPE approach, and is very firmly located in the positivist tradition. We offer an overview of these positions below.

Political economy as topic: states and markets

For those concerned with the economic affairs of the state, analysis focuses around the relationship between states, markets and actors (such as businesses) within those markets. In the 'states and markets' approaches, both tend to be viewed as actors in their own right, rather than as sites or arenas of political action. For Adam Smith, often seen as the founder of the discipline of neo-classical economics, 'political economy' was the science of managing the nation's resources in order to generate wealth, so study is based around markets and the actors within them. Politics and economics are seen as interrelated because political actors set the conditions and frameworks through which markets can operate.

Historically, the question was: how does politics affect economic outcomes? The term 'political economy' reflected the view held by philosophers such as Adam Smith and J. S. Mill that politics and economics are inseparable; political factors are crucial in determining economic outcomes and politics precedes and is a necessary condition for economics. (For neo-classical economists such as Smith and Ricardo, the state should play as small a role as possible; indeed, the normative prescription was that markets should be free from government intervention – markets were assumed to work best when unconstrained by the state.)

At the international level, rejecting the state-centrism of traditional IR approaches, IPE focuses upon the interconnectedness of politics and economics, and the interaction between states and markets. Analysis may focus, for example, upon the operation of financial markets, or the manner in which globalization has been thought to facilitate an interconnectivity of markets (commercial, cultural and financial). But, as with domestic accounts, analysis focuses upon the extent to which political systems and actors can, and should, regulate economic activity. The focus is also upon the objective social and material conditions which influence domestic and international economic relations. For Marx these material conditions were crucial, and his political economy was concerned with the way in which ownership of the means of production influenced and shaped historical processes in order that wealth was accumulated. This material relationship, he argued, was sustainable through the generation of a supportive ideological climate; here the focus becomes the role of ideology in providing the conditions for the material base to continue in existence. It is this ideological aspect of IPE that we will map out below. For others, however, neither states and markets as actors, nor the operation of the economy per se are the focus, rather the aim is to problematize and understand economic relations. In this sense, the emphasis is upon the way in which knowledge is constructed and the way in which knowledge becomes imbued with meaning, so we need to unpack the way in which economic relations are structured.

Political economy as method

Another way in which neo-classical economics has been influential is through the appropriation of methods from economics to analyze politics. Indeed, for Weingast and Wittman (2006: 3) 'political economy is the methodology of economics applied to the analysis of political behaviour and institutions'. This type of approach is also known as formal theory (reflecting its mathematical base). This is fundamentally different from the focus upon topic or subject matter (noted above). Political economy as method is not necessarily concerned with states and markets as above; rather its priority is to explain political behaviour, situations and action, through tools derived from economics. Its starting assumptions are those derived from economic models which in turn are used to model (often statistically) many areas of political life. In this way formal theory has been applied to analyze a variety of topics, such as legislatures, voting behaviour, party competition, bureaucracy and coalition governments (to name but a few). Its emphasis is upon the possibility of predictions and measurement of observable behaviour places formal theory clearly in the positivist school of thought.

This chapter continues by noting the influence of the discipline of economics in public political life, and notes the interrelationship between political practice and economic theory. It then moves to outline some of the other ways in which states and markets have been analyzed within both disciplines. As with previous chapters a case study of the oil industry as it operates within Nigeria is offered to illustrate the differing ways in which we might understand the relationship between politics and economics.

Power

In this field some argue that politics shapes economics; others that the direction of causality flows from economics to influence politics; and a third position is that politics and economics interact and influence each other. Those accounts which highlight the methods of economics influencing politics conform to the notion that power is located with individual actors. Once we have identified these actors, and their preferences, we can make assumptions about their motivations and undertake analysis. Moreover, these positivist accounts suggest that power is observable; to analyze power is to analyze behaviour of individuals. For others in the behavioural tradition power is the observable property of individual states. What we need to understand from this perspective is that it is the states' position in the system which enables us to analyze how states react and interact with economies and economics. For critical realist accounts, power is located systemically, in the system of ideas which privileges the economy prior to society and states operate to support the pursuit of the aims of actors within those markets. We cannot observe power directly in these accounts, but through analysis of the consequences of its exercise we can establish its existence and effects, which for these accounts serve to reinforce and embed inequalities. This is supported by a system of ideas, which lead us to unquestioningly accept the existence of capitalism – is it possible to conceive of an alternative? For interpretivists, where the discipline, methods and ideas from economics have influenced the discipline and practice of politics, it could be argued that power then lies, as Foucault suggested, within knowledge, and lies with those who produce the knowledge. However, the accounts themselves don't contain this critical reflection upon power, which might be provided by a poststructuralist account which draws attention to the structuring of power relations through language, discourses and the construction of knowledge.

Box 9.1   Case study. The oil industry in Nigeria

The Niger Delta supplies 40 per cent of all crude US imports (Vidal, 2010). The Nigerian economy is rooted in oil production, oil sales providing around 95 per cent of export earnings, and 25 per cent of GDP (Okonta and Douglas, 2003: 53). Oil production has resulted in the region of the Niger Delta and the country of Nigeria being ravaged of its resources, resulting in serious damage to its people and ecosystems. The history of oil production in Nigeria stems back to 1956 when Shell first drilled in the Niger Delta region (although earlier exploitation of Nigeria's natural resources and its peoples dates back to 1444, see Okonta and Douglas, 2003: 6). The formal political context in which the oil industry operates sees Nigeria's history as one of British colonialism, violence, instability of political regimes, characterized by corruption and exploitation.

Shell is the largest operating company in Nigeria, accounting for 50 per cent of oil production in the country, and, as Okonta and Douglas observe, the profits from the production of oil remain firmly shared between the Nigerian government, Shell and other oil companies (2003: 2). At the same time local communities are reaping the costs of elite-level wealth. For example, on 1 May 2010 a ruptured Exxon Mobil pipeline spilled more than a million gallons in seven days, in Ibeno, Nigeria (Vidal, 2010). Oil spillage is common, and the World Bank estimates that oil companies spill around 9,000 cubic feet of oil in 300 major accidents every year (cited in Okonta and Douglas, 2003: 66). The environmental and harm costs are evident; for example, where uncontrolled oil spills have often led to the total extermination of local fish and crops (Jimoh and Aghalino, 2000).

A political economy account of this industry enables us to explore the wider relationships between states, business and the markets in which they operate. It focuses our attention on the interaction between the oil companies and states; or it encourages us to look at the underlying systems of exploitation which characterize this industry, and can encourage us to consider the way in which Nigeria's position in relation to oil companies has been constructed to benefit the interests of capital, or we might explore the discourses which reflect and embed power relationships.

Foundational positivist approaches

Formal theory and economic methods and ideas in public life

A clear alternative to the 'states and markets' approach of political economy is reflected in *The Oxford Handbook of Political Economy*, which defines political economy, entirely in terms of the application of methods from economics to the analysis of political phenomena. The discipline of economics has had an enormous influence in both the study and practice of politics, and the primary way in which this has happened has been through the influence of the methods (and the ideas which underpin them) of the discipline. Economic methodologies have been influential in politics in a twofold way. First, in the study and analysis of politics and, second, in that their influence has reached beyond academia, into the practice of politics.

The formal approach has been enormously influential both in the 'real world' of politics, heavily influencing the governments of the Thatcher and Reagan years, and informing and underpinning the legacy bequeathed to subsequent governments, which has largely taken the form of neo-liberalism and a commitment to the role of markets in public life. The dominance of economics as a method, informing the practice of government, is further evident in the UK Conservative/Liberal Democratic government coalition document which, in setting out its agenda for consumer protection, notes the way in which it will aim to achieve its goals is through insights from behavioural economics (HM Government, 2010: 12). Behavioural economics, derived in part from psychology, is also method. It proceeds by observing behaviour, but differs (from RCT) in the relaxation of the rationality assumption, and the modification of theory in response to observed behaviour. Here then the role that economics plays is evident in influencing politics as practised in public life. Whether economics as a method is influencing 'real world' politics and political analysts respond to these observations (as with behavioural economics and with work just starting to emerge, see John *et al.*, 2009), or as with new public management, we see economic ideas informing political action; both accounts suggest that economics precedes and influences politics.

Formal theory is located within and informed by neo-classical economics. The notion of formalization is derived from the use of mathematical models to represent theoretical arguments (although that is not to say all rational choice accounts are informed by mathematical modelling, as some highly influential work in this field is not mathematical to any extent [for excellent summary, see Snidal, 2002]). The unit of analysis is the individual (be that state or person), assumed to have clearly identified preferences which are expressed, and acting to maximize this self-interest. Human agency is reduced to individual utility-maximizing behaviour, but this focus means that the wider social implications of action are negated and the idea of a society is missing from these accounts. In this kind of political economy approach, the focus is purely upon decisions taken by individuals in a formal relationship between state and the market.

One of the most significant and influential applications of this has been through the development of game theory. The rationalist assumptions which inform this approach have also formed the basis of rational choice and public choice theory and have also become integrated into economic and political discourse (as noted above and discussed in Chapters 1 and 3). Game theory has been widely applied to analyze political behaviour, most prominently during the Cold War. Economists such as Thomas Schelling were highly influential in influencing the thinking of political actors and strategists (such as Kissinger) during the Cold War. Here we see political actors adopt strategies which reflect the predictions of economic models. One of the most prominent during the Cold War was the prisoner's dilemma (a comprehensive overview is provided by Hargreaves Heap and Varoufakis, 1995). Here the assumption is that individual actors (either a person or cohesive state) will act in their own self-interest and this overrides the possibility of cooperation. In this way, then nuclear weapons during the Cold War worked as a deterrent. It was in the self-interest of both sides to maintain the balance of power. Neither side knew how the other was going to behave and so both acted in their own self-interest, which was to aim to make themselves the most militarily powerful. As we know, this resulted in an arms race, with both sides seeking to become more militarily powerful than the other. As O'Brien and Williams show (2010: 32–3), the prisoner's dilemma can also be used to enable us to understand why a country may pursue protectionist polices. Free markets and free trade internationally may mean that all countries would benefit from the ability to trade with each other. However, once one country introduces a trade barrier, they become better off than other countries as they are still able to export, but protect their own domestic trade. Thus all countries become incentivized to create trade barriers and pursue protectionist polices in the self-interest of their own country. As such, there is little incentive for any individual country to reduce trade barriers, even if collectively they would all be better off if they did. This problem has become known as the 'collective action' problem (see, for example, Olson, 1965).

One of the issues that game and rational choice theory draws attention to is the way in which individually rational strategies generate collectively irrational outcomes. Hardin's (1968) seminal article is instructive here. He took the example of farmers allowing their animals to graze on the village common. He argued that if one farmer decided to pursue his own self-interest by allowing his cattle to graze on the common, others, also in pursuit of their own self-interest, would follow. The outcome of this individual rational behaviour would be collective irrationality, as eventually there would be no common available to the villagers – ultimately it would be destroyed. This argument has been used to draw attention both to the degradation of the environment and in providing critique of rationalist accounts by demonstrating how individually rational action leads to collectively irrational outcomes (as we also noted in Chapter 4).

There is a series of widely discussed criticisms and weaknesses with this approach (for example, there is no discussion of how preferences are formed or how we know that observable behaviour reveals someone's true interests. What role does altruism play?). (For a detailed critique, see Waylen, 1997; Hay, 2002). Moreover, there is also a need for greater methodological reflection. Here then we need to think about the way in which we use models from economics. Do we use them to abstract from reality and to make predictions about things that might happen under certain conditions? Or do we use these assumptions to describe how people should behave? For example, the assumptions behind the formal political theory approach was intertwined with thinking from theorists such as Von Hayek (1991) and went on to inform wholesale changes in political programmes under the term 'new public management' and more widely, as part of the neo-liberal political programme (discussed in more depth in Chapter 3). The problem of conflating prescription where economic models have been used as templates for action has been problematized elsewhere (see for example, Savigny, 2007) and we come back to this issue in Chapter 12.

The focus in this approach is upon observable behaviour and, crucially, to explain that rationalist economic models have been proposed which explain the behaviour of individuals through reference to assumptions about their motivations. Power is assumed to rest with the individual, who is free from constraint and with fully formed expressed preferences. As noted above, what this account does not provide is a discussion about where these preferences come from (as noted above), nor does it account for the wider social, political and economic context within which political action takes place (although for a critique of the embedded structuralism of rational choice theory, see Hay, 2004).

Realism and hegemonic stability

Still within the behavioural frame, but with a slightly different modus operandi, realist IPE draws attention to the balance of power between states, and notes, normatively, the need for an economic hegemony to maintain system stability. So while we maintain focus upon the observable, the emphasis here is upon the relationship between states and markets. The focus is trained on the observable behaviour of economies within states, their political regulation, but, more importantly, the way in which they play a role in enabling states to achieve their political aims. In this way, the political, of the political economy approach, is that which is doing

Box 9.2   Formal theory and oil

In the analysis of the oil industry and its behaviour in Nigeria, formal theory explores the role of the political actors involved in the process and an analysis of their motivations. It has been used to show how interested groups seeking to maximize their own profits at the expense of society, can become involved in 'violent and other regime-destabilizing activities' (Mbaku, 2004: 43). One of the features which characterizes African development more widely, Mbaku observes, is that it is the state, rather than private interests, which is the largest economic unit in each country (2004: 46). Therefore control of the state, means control of economic resources. As such, there has been often violent struggle for opportunities to capture the state (and so in turn have the opportunity to control the economic infrastructure). Assuming rationality on the part of individuals then enables us to understand why conflict may occur over resources.

Public choice theory has also been widely used to account for development in African states (for an excellent review, see Mbaku, 2004). It has also been used more narrowly to account for the poverty that has resulted from the existence of the natural resources in Nigeria. Despite the wealth attached to Nigeria's oil supply, ultimately the existence of this resource has produced 'poverty, underdevelopment, and conflicts since its commercial exploitation began' (Olarinmoye, 2008: 22). The post-war discourse articulated that oil production was a 'good thing' as it would bring benefits, should bring revenues and jobs, investment in economic infrastructure, providing the basis for an economic 'bonanza' (Rosser, 2006, cited in Olarinmoye, 2008). Yet, the reason that this didn't happen, for some public choice accounts, is 'poor' decision-making or domestic institutional design by politicians (for a review, see Olarinmoye, 2008). For Olson (1996), in the public choice approach, good institutional design, leads to good policy outcomes. Therefore, we would analyze the successful construction of political institutions in the West, where MNCs were located, who were able to regulate firms successfully to the benefit of the host state and its economy. We would also have to look at the poorly constructed political institutions in oil-rich states such as Nigeria, which enabled oil companies to operate in this way. Implied in this theoretical frame, however, is the suggestion that there is a normative, correct way. This reinforces the idea that the 'correct' way to structure institutions is one which, by extension, serves to benefit those at the top of the existing 'global order' (see hegemonic stability theory below).

the explaining. To understand political economy, then, we need to understand political action and motivation. In this approach, the rationality assumption is thought to guide behaviour. This suggests that under conditions of anarchy in the international system it is rational to act self-interestedly. States act to preserve their own security under conditions of anarchy and one way to strengthen the capacity and influence of the state is through a successful economy. This, for some, paves the way for mercantilist strategies to be adopted. Mercantilists argue that there is only so much wealth in the world and, therefore, states must secure their own interests, and block the interests of other states. The economy and the state are interlinked, wealth creation is a means through which to achieve the desired end (increase the power of the state). This may lead to protectionist strategies (which run counter to the liberal notion of a 'free market'), which are justified by states from the perspective of a need to protect economic sovereignty. The management of a successful and dynamic economy is one way in which states can increase their power. A successful economy, combined with strong military power, puts states on the road to hegemonic status.

For this perspective the normative assumption is that the existence of a hegemon leads to stability in the international arena. In this way hegemonic status is presented as necessary and thereby, in turn, also legitimates the existence of the hegemon. As Gilpin notes, this perspective argues that 'there would be economic instability if there were no leading power in the world economy' (2005: 368). As such, a hegemon is viewed as necessary and a precondition of a stable and functioning world economy, the implication here being that the pursuit of self-interest by the hegemonic states has unintended benefits for the rest of the states in the international system: economic stability. (Interestingly, this extension of logic runs counter to the logic of the prisoners' dilemma in game theory and its collective detrimental outcomes.)

Following the Cold War, the US has been generally regarded as the world hegemon. But there has been wide debate about the role and nature of this hegemony and its impact (or not) upon the functioning and stability of the system (for example, Keohane, 1984; Strange, 1987). More recently, some suggest that the EU has provided a counter to US hegemony (Jørgensen, 2010: 142), and it could also be argued that with its increasing economic growth and success it is now China who is providing this challenge.

Here, again, power is assumed to be observable and located within individual states as actors, consistent with behavioural schools of thought. Politics comes prior to markets and, while economies play a role in providing the basis for states to claim and declare that power, it follows that analysis in this view begins with the state as the location of power. What is noticeable, however, is that those who point to the importance and need for a hegemon have been those involved in its definition. As we will see from accounts below, those in less developed countries, for example, could highlight the role that this definition plays in continuing systems of inequality, which are negated and subsumed by a Western desire for hegemonic stability.

Box 9.3   Realism, hegemonic stability and oil

One way in which the hegemonic system may also be maintained is through the existence of economic bodies such as the IMF and World Bank, which, while international organizations, are dominated by Western economic interests. For example, in 1985, 44 per cent of Nigeria's export earnings were going to service debts. Western creditors wanted the Nigerian government to accept further IMF loans, with conditions attached beneficial to Western interests, which would further impoverish the people. The upshot of the refusal of the leader Bhuhari, to comply with Western financial interest, ultimately led to his removal from power, and the replacement with Babangida, supported by a coalition of Western oil and banking interests (Okonta and Douglas, 2003: 31). This suggests that the support of Western governments for Western corporations and their business interests are reinforced and embedded in international institutions, which serve to maintain the existing structure of the international system.

Accepting the rationalist assumptions of formal theory, that states operate to pursue their own self-interest and ultimately power, in a hegemonic analysis, we might also explore the notion of democracy promotion. This has been an explicit aim of the US, in particular to oil-rich countries (Collier, 2008: 42). In this account, one of the reasons for democracy promotion to oil economies is to enable the US to free itself from reliance upon the Middle East; a hegemon would not want to be over-reliant upon one (volatile) region for its oil supplies. For promoters of democracy the route to achieving democracy is through economic development (Collier, 2008: 51), which ties in other states and institutions (such as the World Bank and IMF). This is seen, in this view, as necessary for the maintenance of stability in the international order, although, as we shall see below, critics might suggest this is an attempt to legitimate exploitative behaviour of natural and social resources; the hegemon then seeks to reinforce its legitimacy and positioning in the world order through presenting its approach as the right approach, which are two clearly different things.

Foundational critical/scientific realist approaches

Marxism, Gramsci and hegemony

As we have already seen, class is the main explanatory feature within Marxist schools of thought. Within political economy as an approach, it is the way in which class becomes embedded and defines our position in the system ideologically (as well as materially) that is central to those concerned with the notion of hegemony.

Class is defined in terms of an individual's position in relation to the means of production, either as an owner (and so member of the capitalist class) or worker (and so selling labour power to the owners). This relationship is the basis for exploitation of the workers by the owners of the means of production and this is supported through the apparatus of the state. Marx's political economy highlights the way in which the capitalist order is built upon systems of exploitation and inequality, as well as how the creation of wealth in a capitalist economy reflects the subordination of, rather than freedom for, individuals. Capitalists who own the means of production are thus able to create wealth by harnessing the labour power of others. The firm is a crucial actor and in a global economic arena, we can see how multinational corporations play a key role in the continued exploitation and oppression of the working classes. The visible concentration of capital in these companies is a form of imperialism in the global economy. The state, in these accounts, functions to protect and represent class interests.

That the workers could become complicit in their own exploitation represents a successful integration of the interests of the owners of the means of production and states structures, which become ideologically embedded within society. It is here that Gramsci's work on hegemony has been extremely significant in the development of IPE. Here hegemony plays a different role from that outlined in the foundational positivist realist account outlined earlier in this chapter. While hegemony is still taken to describe the dominant position, and both are rooted in the material world, in Gramsci's account hegemony is a concept which is used to analyze the relations of and between forces in society. Consent, rather than coercion, characterized the relations between state and civil society in a hegemonic order. As Cox argues 'hegemony is a form in which dominance is obscured by achieving an appearance of acquiescence ... as if it were the natural order of things' (1994: 366). While for positivist realists the hegemon is observable and measurable in terms of a state and its economically supported position in the world order, for critical/scientific realists hegemony is unobservable, but we can see its effects – for example, in the suppression of conflict.

Informed by Marxist thought, Gramscian IPE highlights how dominant ideologies are rooted in systems of exploitation and supported by the state. Here the state apparatus is employed to support and advance the interests of the capitalist system. Market ideology is crucial to generate the consent needed to maintain the status quo and system stability. A critical theory of hegemony draws attention to the ideological processes and interaction between processes of production and exploitative social relations. The foremost theorist in the field, Robert Cox, argues that production is not only about the material, but also includes the 'production and reproduction of knowledge and of the social relations, morals and institutions that are prerequisites to the production of physical goods' (1987: 39). It is the economy and the market which provide the material basis for an individual to establish and understand both their identity and their role within society. This understanding and positioning is reinforced by the creation of political institutions to support and embed the role of markets, and integrate the individual into society, to the extent that an alternative to the market system is inconceivable. The notion of a capitalist economy becomes increasingly difficult to challenge; indeed, it becomes the 'common sense' view of society. Can we conceive of an alternative to capitalism? That we don't have an answer to this question, or indeed that as a society we don't ask that question in the first instance, would highlight, from this perspective, the enormous success of the market ideology which constrains possibilities of an alternative, providing stability and support for the status quo.

In this way the production processes maintain and reinforce existing exploitative social relations, not only through existing physical or material practices but also through the integration of this practice with ideas which serve to bind individuals to the prevailing social order. IPE also draws attention to the notion that this is something which does not only take place at the level of the state; as Morton observes 'world hegemony can be attained when international institutions and mechanisms support a dominant mode of production and disseminate universal norms and ideas ... in a move to transform various state structures' (2003: 161).

The interlinkage of states, capital and markets is highlighted by Gill and Law who argue that '*capital as social relations depends on the power of the state to define, shape and participate in a regime of accumulation*' (original emphasis, 1989: 479). In this way power is both systemically rooted and located within political and economic structures. There is a suggestion of agency, implying the state's capacity to act; however, on closer reflection we can see that the state's capacity to act is within the structures which foster wealth accumulation and benefit the interests of capital. For example, at a global level, the power of MNCs is evident through differing states having differing regulations. Corporations then seek to find conditions operating regimes, so corporations can play states off against each other, finding the conditions which suit their quest for capital accumulation the best. In this way capital plays off one state against each other, increasing its relative bargaining power, tying states into capitalist structures. And so business confidence in governments and their capacity to provide supportive legislative structures become significant in the relations of power played out between states and capitalists at international and domestic levels. Ideas such as 'sound finance' and 'fighting inflation' may constrain governments (Gill and Law, 1989: 485).

Box 9.4   Marxism, hegemony and the oil industry

The Nigerian state is heavily dependent upon oil rents, taxes and royalties paid by the oil companies (Omeje, 2005: 321). The integration of the state and oil industry is evident further not only through reference to the economy, but also through legislation and the 'revolving door' of integrating of personnel, between the oil industry to government and vice versa (Omeje, 2005). The relationship between the state and the oil companies is one that, for some, characterises the only political stability in Nigerian history (Holzer, 2007) and oil companies have been widely involved in the creation of domestic legislation throughout Nigeria's history (Okonta and Douglas, 2003).

However, the domestic integration of the state and business interests is also evident in policy instruments at the level of the international arena. International-level polices have arguably reflected the economic and political interests of those involved in their creation. The Nigerian state, from this perspective, is compelled to protect and advance the interests not only of oil investments, but also against a wider set of neo-liberal political and economic reforms and conditionalities under the 'Washington Consensus' (comprising the IMF, World Bank and the White House) (Omeje, 2005 321–2). These conditionalities are not simply institutional but generate operating conditions which reinforce dominant ideologies. Critics of the World Bank and IMF have argued that their main goal has been to 'integrate countries into the capitalist world economy' (Danaher, 1995: 2). For example, structural adjustment programmes (SAPs), which provide lending programmes to developing states, have been designed in Washington and implemented by the World Bank and IMF, with conditions favourable to the interests of the lenders. This secures economic and (by extension) hegemonic dominance in the world order, and many now argue that these institutions have become the mechanisms through which distribution of wealth occurs from the poor to the rich countries (Mbaku, 2004: 148).

Attention is drawn to the suggestion of inevitability of responses to economic crises and events, which support the long-term interests of capital. At international level the relative mobility of capital is juxtaposed against the relative immobility of labour, reinforcing the inequalities of production at a global as well as at domestic level.

Feminism

Feminist accounts focus upon exploitation, but instead of the axis being class, they argue it is gender. Here attention is drawn to the way in which a woman's role in the economy is defined by their reproductive capacity. In this way the economy is integrated and constituted by broader

Box 9.5 Feminism and the oil industry

Development studies have shown it is women who disproportionately bear the costs of, for example, restructuring programmes (see Peterson, 2002) and in the wider context of globalization (Perejra, 2002). Access for women in the South/developing world to productive mechanisms such as farmland and capital is often reliant on their husbands; thus, women are subordinated to their husbands in the private decision-making process. Their status is further reinforced at the level of the 'public' through the actions of corporations and states. For example, in Nigeria the state was prepared to support the state sponsorship of repression against protesting oil communities, whose military tactics included the rape and injuring of women and young girls (Ukeje, 2004: 508). Both public and private spheres are intimately linked in positioning women and their role in society, as well as the interrelationship between the domestic and international levels.

Women in the Niger Delta region have reacted vociferously to their positioning and research has shown the ways in which they have started to mobilize and respond, seeking to effect social and ecological transformation through non-violent means of opposition (Turner and Brownhill, 2004). As Ukeje observes conflict and violence have characterized the region and elite response to social protests at the exploitation of resources and peoples, 'usually at the instigation of multinational oil companies, [meant that] successive regimes retaliated with military subjugation, harassment, intimidation, incarceration, and sometimes, extra judicial murder ... as was the case of Ken Saro-Wiwa and eight other Ogoni minority rights activists in November 1995' (Ukeje, 2004: 605). Major protests were mobilized by women involving, for example, the occupation of major oil platforms owned by Chevron Texaco, and protests in front of Shell HQ. Research suggests that women have had some degree of success in protests; however, in order to understand the emergence of these sites of resistance, what attention is drawn to is the structural conditions which create the source and site for struggle. As Turner and Oshare observe, 'in Nigeria not only did capitalism break up women's social order but it also created and strengthened the conditions for resistance' (1994: 126).

social trends. The state functions to normalize these economic relations, which feminists argue are gendered. Here feminists provide for an account which looks beyond the observable interaction between states and markets, and draws attention to the gendered foundations upon which this arena is premised. Analysis takes place at the site whereby states and markets interact and it is this space where feminists highlight the possibility of contestation and negotiation. As Marxist accounts draw attention to the way in which exploitative production relations are rendered 'normal' in this arena, so feminists argue that the relationship between states and markets is one where exploitation continues because of relations characterized by reproduction. Feminist political economy introduces the concept of social reproduction, which refers to biological reproduction as well as the ongoing production of labour power (Bakker and Gill, 17–18). So, the biological reproductive capacity of women is integrated into the economic system as a mechanism through which exploitative power relations are reproduced. This also highlights the way in which this is a process, the relation between states and markets being negotiated and contested, yet, as with Gramscian accounts, this also highlights the existence of the interaction of states and markets as a site where consensus reflecting dominant interests is reproduced.

At a global level where discussion has focused upon the changing nature of markets, government and technological responses, less attention has been paid to the role of gender (Waylen, 1997). Feminists' analyses of restructuring and structural adjustment programmes have drawn attention to the inherent gender blindness of such programmes which do not account for the reproductive economy, nor women's unpaid labour upon which such policies rely (i.e., that women are providing childcare for free, enabling men to engage in production) and so while men are associated with production (and its subsequent exploitative processes) women engage in the reproductive economy and, in this way, their exploitation is viewed as gendered.

Anti-foundational interpretivist approaches

Constructivism

As we have noted earlier, constructivists argue that beliefs and values are important when we are seeking to establish our social and/or political ontology. In contrast to behavioural accounts that we have outlined, constructivists suggest that norms and values go beyond shaping an actor's interest, but they themselves constitute interests. O'Brien and Williams suggest that, from this perspective, IPE is 'a set of material conditions and practices, a set of normative statements ... and an academic discipline (2010: 36). And as such it is the interaction between the three which comprises constructivist IPE. Constructivists ask questions about preferences identities, interest and ideas and ask how they have come about. How have they been shaped? How might they change? Why do some ideas become dominant over others? To understand how the economy works we need not to look at the institutions which guide or operate it, but at the underlying values, norms and belief systems which shape, underpin and guide behaviour within it.

John Ruggie, a key constructivist theorist in IPE, argues that the rules of the international system are constructed in a manner which reflects the interests of the actors who construct those rules. When reflecting upon trade arrangements, his argument states that they have been constructed to benefit the normative preferences of the domestic state. For example, the US and UK both pursued full-employment strategies and so created international regulation and legislation which would support their domestic strategies (Ruggie, 1992). He also suggested that to understand a state's behaviour and the nature of that state we need to understand its identity. For example, a British hegemony would look very different from a Polish or French hegemony. But how do we understand the characteristics of this difference? We may look at political systems and institutions, for sure, but what is also needed is analysis of political actors' understandings of those institutions and the norms and values which guide behaviour are crucial. In this way power is located in the norms, values and beliefs systems which shape political identities. We cannot necessarily observe the existence or the exercise of power,

---

Box 9.6   Constructivism and oil protests

Holzer (2007) provides a constructivist account of the interconnection of Shell and public response to its actions. His account focuses specifically upon (Brent Spar and) the execution of Ken Saro-Wiwa and his fellow protestors. The protestors had sought to reclaim the oil reserves, which, they argued, were exploited and profited from by oil companies and the federal government, leaving damage and poverty in its wake. Shell was irrevocably linked with the executions of the protestors in 1995, which John Major termed 'judicial murder' (*Daily Telegraph*, 1995). Holzer's analysis highlights that, although Shell sought to manage their PR by highlighting their positive contribution to the Nigerian economy, consumer political activism already had been able to successfully influence the discourse, to one of moral outrage, which in turn impacted to a degree upon political and public reaction to these events. For him, the capacity of protest groups to frame Shell as a moral actor was significant. Having been able to do this, Shell was then constructed as being responsible for human rights issues, making it more difficult, Holzer argues, for the corporation to deny their liability and responsibilities.

   Here, then, social constructivism draws attention to the existence of norms in explaining or accounting for political behaviour. The norms and values in this example were moral outrage and demands for action; what social constructivism highlights is the way in which these norms came to be constructed and expressed. From this perspective, to understand behaviour means an analysis of how norms and values come to be constructed and publicly articulated.

but we can see its manifestation through an analysis and understanding of political identity and the way in which this reflects a particular set of interests.

Poststructuralist IPE

Poststructuralist IPE draws attention to the way in which the notion of interaction of states and markets suggests they are autonomous, until the point at which they interact. It is this point of interaction which is important and analysis focuses reflection upon economic relations rather than economies or states per se. To do this we need to understand the constituent features of the categories of politics and economics. We further need to understand how identities are constructed through the normalization of economic ideologies (like with neo-Gramscian accounts of ideologies), but for poststructuralism (and unlike Marxism) these are not rooted in the material world. Rather these are based in dominant discourses and ideas and ideologies. From this perspective IPE enables analysis and understanding of the discourses and ideas which come to characterize state strategies, and how these reflect certain economic interests and ideologies. This occurs as a result of the interaction of individuals with discourses, and the economy represents and signifies this as a 'production of linguistic and institutional forms through which human beings define their relationships' (Hutton, 1988: 127, citing Foucault, 1979: 88–92, 158–65). Power is systemically located. Within these discourses and their institutional manifestation are meaning systems which normalize and routinize identities and culture. This process enables us to map our identities in relation to social practices and processes, and, in this case, in relation to the economy.

Language is important for poststructuralists and in IPE the application of poststructuralism to financial arrangements highlights their intensive politicization (de Goede, 2003). In this way language and discourses are crucial when seeking to analyze economic and political relations and reality; what is not discussed is significant in the way in which an issue is framed, and is as significant as what is discussed. For example, the construction of particular financial instruments, such as conditions of IMF loans, may be seemingly neutral. However, what may be missing is an account of the impact that procedures have upon the environment, and the damaging impacts of economic activity, that may be highlighted from an ecological perspective; or an account of the impact that such conditions may have on the women within the state, which a feminist account may add. What poststructuralism does then is draw attention to the language used to construct a particular version of reality, but it also situates this within wider discourses and ideas. So, for example, the leading financial institutions are dominated by Western states and so discourses are also likely to reflect the neo-liberal free market beliefs of those states.

Poststructuralism unpacks this seemingly 'neutral' language and assumptions and situate the language which is used to construct reality within its wider discourse. Discourses are negotiated and constructed through the interplay of language, ideas and action. Gibson-Graham (1996) combines postructuralism into Marxist accounts and argues that the most useful way to understand capitalist hegemony is as discourse rather than structure (1996: xi). In this way we are able to establish the way in which states and markets are arenas for negotiating competing interests, but the capitalist ones succeed in rendering only capitalist concepts and ideas visible, and making non-capitalist concepts invisible. Thus, capitalism is normalized and legitimized discursively. For post-structuralists, then, questions would revolve around what the dominant discourse is here. What language is being used and what does it reveal about the relationship between states and markets? What does this tell us more broadly about power relationships, the way they operate and become embedded and the interests which they reflect?

Box 9.7 Poststructuralism and the oil industry

The IMF and World Bank's discourse of 'good governance' is one which has been used to support neo-liberal political and economic reforms in Africa. Africa's problems have been characterized as a 'crisis' of governance, and this discursive construction of the problems which Africa faces has been used as a mechanism to pave the way for to promote a Western neo-liberal agenda, democracy promotion (as noted in Box 9.3) and the private market as key to social and economic development (Perejra, 2002). In this way the language and discourses of neo-liberalism become normalized and routinized. The way in which legislation favourable to the oil industry has been integrated into the Nigerian system is perhaps evident through a discursive approach which highlights how, according to Nigerian commentators, 'Nigeria is a mere geographical expression created by multinational companies and continues to be governed by multinational companies ... These companies (Shell, Chevron, Mobil, Elf etc.) actually dictate the direction in which the country should go' (cited in Omeje, 2005: 325). The Western discourse of economic growth and development, then, has been so significant, as promoted through domestic and international agreements (as noted above), that for some the physical attributes of Nigeria are understandable through reference to its discursive construction as a site of resources for Western companies' profit.

Comparison of theories and approaches

In the foundational positivist accounts, all share an adherence to the notion of causal explanation and are concerned with engaging in a scientific enquiry. In behavioural accounts the focus is upon observation, but there is a difference of method, with formal theory focusing upon the rational behaviour of individuals and providing an economic basis to modelling of politics. The 'Economic' is the driver here. For realists, however, it is the 'International' part of IPE which is operative. It is the structure of the international system which leads states to behave the way in which they do and, again, we can know this through our observation of their behaviour.

In critical realist accounts, causal explanation is a goal, but this rests on the recognition of unobservable features which need to be included into analysis. For Marxist and feminist accounts, it is underlying structures which are unseen but have causal capacity. For Marxist and critical theory accounts, it is also the 'Economic' in IPE which is the dominant feature; however, this operates somewhat differently from the positivistic accounts above. Along with feminists it is the interaction of states and markets, the arena of negotiation and contestation which generates consensus and in turn hegemonic dominance, which is of interest and the way in which states and markets negotiate and construct, dominant exploitative power relationships.

For interpretivists, understanding of meaning is sought for. The aim for poststructuralist accounts of IPE is to understand the ways in which state strategies come to reflect economic ideologies. It is the interaction of the 'Political' with the 'Economic' which provides the site where explanation can take place in this perspective. Whereas for neo-Gramscian accounts this has a material base (in the ownership of the means of production and the exploitation which flows from there), in poststructuralist accounts, this understanding is through reflection upon discourses and ideas, and as these conditions have no necessary material basis they cannot be said to exist prior to their construction. So, while critical realist approaches recognize the role of ideology, it is interlinked with its material basis. In contrast, interpretivist accounts highlight the independent role that ideas may play in the political process. For behavioural and rationalist accounts power is assumed to be observable and to be located with the individual. For Marxists accounts power is assumed to lie in the structures, whereas for poststructuralism power is situated discursively.

Adjudicating between perspectives

To analyze political economy, we need to begin with a reflection upon what we think is at stake here. If we think political economy – and indeed the way to analyze political phenomena is through the appropriation of economic methods and the assumptions that inform them, as this enables us to simplify the world, understand the motivations of individual actors, abstract from reality and so make predictions – then we might adopt a formal or positive theory approach. In a similar vein, if we accept that the unit of analysis is the individual (actor, either politician or state), then we may also adopt a behavioural approach; however, we may think that rather than using the methods of economics we need to reverse our analysis and reflect upon how politics informs and regulates the economy. If we think that the economy informs the way in which politics is conducted and the state behaves and if we consider there is a relationship between material features of reality and unobservable ideas, then we may adopt a critical realist approach. If we accept that ideas are important, and the role that they apply in producing norms and values which construct our identities and our political realities, or if we argue that ideas matter, and the way in which we can challenge dominant ideas is through deconstruction of language and dominant discourse, then we might adopt an interpretivist approach.

Conclusion

Economics and the economy are intimately bound up with political life and political economy as an approach enables us to unpack and explore some of these complex relationships and their consequences. For some the study of political economy is focused upon actors and individuals, for others the focus is upon ideology, while for interpretivists the focus is upon the constitution of the political and the economic in the first place. But this division of approaches is also characterized by focus upon individuals and systems, the role of economics as a discipline in informing political analysis and the way in which the subject matter is constructed. This breadth of analysis can be very roughly distinguished between the content or area of study, and where political economy is viewed as a formal method.

As such our questions revolve around the relationship between states and markets. How do states regulate markets? Whose interests are reflected? Are markets the 'natural order' of things or could we conceive of an alternative way to structure society? How is it that dominant ideas about the economy become embedded? More widely we might want to consider whether the analysis of economies and markets is something which belongs in the realm of the domestic or the international?

Reflection

Which perspective or approach does the best job of explaining the oil industry in Nigeria?

Why do you think this is the case?

Is it the existence of oil in Nigeria that has caused problems for this state, or the pursuit of profit by Western companies?

Can you imagine a Nigeria without oil; do you think there would be less exploitation and abuse?

To what extent do you think that states and oil industries share common interests? How are these articulated and reconciled?

What happens if the interests of a state and oil industry conflict?

Do you think that the discourse of neo-liberalism has been significant in the exploitation of Nigerian oil resources?

How can combining insights from Political Science and IR help us analyze the oil industry in Nigeria?

What are the reasons for your answers?

Seminar activities

Find newspaper coverage of an oil spill in the West and an oil spill in an African or Middle Eastern state.

Which theoretical approach is most suitable for analysis here?

Are the same approaches applicable to both cases?

What assumptions underpin this coverage?

What does the coverage tell us about the relationship between states and markets? What political discourse(s) inform this coverage?

Role play. An oil company wishes to drill for oil, develop and construct and oil refinery in a country in the global South. A public inquiry is being launched. Divide into groups to represent and put forward cases for the following (and be prepared to be quizzed by the adjudicator):

The indigenous community

The central government

The oil company

An environmental interest group

→

The host nation of the oil company

The World Bank/ IMF from whom the country has loans

What decision does the adjudicator reach and why?

What evidence has been provided?

Whose interests are served?

Where has power been located in this exercise?

Chapter 10

The Environment

Introduction

The environment poses and contains some of the most pressing problems and challenges of our age. But how do we respond to it? Is it something which requires a scientific solution? Do we need to generate more knowledge about the natural world, and develop technologies which enable us to respond to changes in the earth's climate? Or is it something which requires a social, economic or political response, such as that provided through the markets or through the actions of states? How important are governments and regulation in tackling this phenomenon? What role does that leave us as citizens as we go about our everyday lives? To what extent are we connected to the global natural system as well as the social systems (such as the economic and political ones)? How can we live within what the natural resources of the earth can provide? What happens when we start to live beyond our natural means? What might this mean not only for our generation, but also for future generations? In a way like no other topic, analyzing the environment can represent an explicit integration across disciplines, of both natural and social science. It can be conceived of as an economic issue; a political issue; a technological or scientific issue. It can require solutions from all of these approaches, singularly or as an integrated response.

When we analyze the environment, one of many issues that arises is that of global warming. The scientific explanation is that it has been caused, in part, by the build-up of greenhouse gases. One political explanation might be that there is insufficient regulation to prevent this from happening. Another political account might suggest that the way in which earth's resources have been exploited mirror the social systems of exploitation across the planet. In this chapter, we accept the scientific consensus that anthropogenic climate change is happening (Anderegg *et al.*, 2010). However, in order to understand why this has happened, we argue that scientific accounts need to be supplemented with political

220

questions. What are the social, economic and political causes of climate change? What kind of political responses are necessary? In this chapter we give an overview of some of these political concerns and forms of analysis.

There is a clear Western-centricity in the approaches and perspectives that are offered below; however, we accept Carter's assertion that as it is the industrialized West that has been largely responsible for creating the problems associated with global warming, it is essential that the West takes a lead in solving them (2008: 3). We also recognize the importance of integrating the insights from critical perspectives. This reminds us of the importance not only of reflecting upon the way in which we might 'solve' this particular problem but how the emergence and existence of this problem can reflect exploitative relationships. By using critical perspectives to analyze the tackling of climate change, we may also be able to address the exploitative relationships upon which environmental damage thus far has been predicated. For some, this may be an issue through which we recognize the existence of a plurality of identities, and that the search for one 'solution' to the 'problem' is too narrow. For some the way in which climate change is defined as a problem highlights difficulties of finding a singular solution; rather we should look at the variety of available ways in which we respond to and therefore may be able to tackle the issue (cf. Hulme, 2009).

Power

Behaviouralists may ask: what are the political causes of climate change? This question lies very much within the positivist school of thought and encourages us to reflect upon the 'real world' interaction between states that, according to realist thought, are operating in an international arena. Power in this view is assumed to lie with states and the way in which they address the issue is a combination of pressures and incentives from both domestic and international levels. This also implies that solutions are available through legislative measures and that regulation is the necessary response. For this approach, states and politicians are holders of power and have the capacity to provide a solution to the consequences of manmade global environmental degradation. More widely, we might want to reflect upon why the environmental issue has reached the political agenda. How has it got there in the first place? Is this because of powerful scientists who interact with government? Or because of environmental lobbyists? Is it a reaction to 'real world' events? Is it a response to public opinion and public demands that governments should tackle this issue?

Box 10.1   Case study. Climate change and global warming

As Levy and Egan observe 'Climate change is a global environmental problem of potentially devastating proportions' (1998: 337). While climate change has become a handy byword to encompass all environmental problems, it is also an issue in its own right. 'Climate change', in common usage, is a term which refers to the warming of the earth's temperature. The terms 'global warming' and 'climate change' are often used interchangeably. The former is a subset of the latter; global warming is one example of climate change. It is generally agreed that the causes of global warming are a combination of natural and manmade (or anthropogenic) activities. Its complexity of definition and causes, as well as the identification of possible solutions, is vast. Scientists, business, governments and society globally need to tackle this issue. What is of interest in this chapter is the politics behind the way in which climate change, global warming and the environment are addressed.

As noted in Chapter 4, the aim of the Copenhagen summit was to find a solution to keep the global mean surface temperature rise to no more than 2°C by 2050. This may not sound like a significant increase; however, that temperature rise is not like a bit of extra warmth in the summer when we go on holiday and the temperature goes up a few degrees. Rather it is like a 2°C increase in our whole body temperature. Keeping temperature rise to below 2°C means avoiding the very worst of the problems, which will include ice

→

Within the critical realist perspective, the question of political causality is still important; however, the answer here requires a reflection upon the global structures of capitalism which prioritize economic growth over environmental sustainability. Here power is systemically located; we can observe its effects, which, starkly put, have resulted in environmental degradation. In this sense, we might suggest that power also operates to obscure our real interests. Our real interests may lie in providing a sustainable lifestyle and providing for future generations, but the capitalist imperative obscures this, structuring our interests so that the capitalist logic is sustained prior to the environment. The aim in this perspective then becomes to draw attention to the tensions between current demands (of capitalism) and the demands of the natural system, which requires us to readjust our expectations in order that the earth's resources can continue to provide for us and for future generations.

Interpretivists draw attention to the ways in which environmental concerns are framed. For example, analysis may focus around the way in which political actors perceive environmental problems, and the norms and values which inform those understandings and subsequent responses. Interpretivists highlight the importance of reflecting upon the caps melting, changes in ocean and wind currents. We will see changes in crop growth, changes in the ecosystem, which in turn can have an enormous array of impacts such as flooding, food shortages, increased spread of disease and ultimately increased potential for conflict over scarcer and scarcer resources (such as food and water). Yet what should be noted is that 2°C is not an absolute threshold below which these events will not happen. These events and issues are beginning to happen, and a rise of over 1.5°C, the Association of Small Island States (including states such as the Maldives) argue, would mean that sea level rise would be sufficient that those islands would no longer exist.

Global warming clearly is a serious issue which needs to be urgently addressed; and in order to tackle this we need to understand it. It also provides a lens through which we can most clearly see the complexity of the world 'out there' as efforts to address climate change arise from within science and technology, business and economics, society and politics at both a domestic and international level. Arguably, the study of climate change also enables a reflection not only on the role of the state, or the role of scientists but the wider systems of exploitation upon which our society is premised. Climate change is a consequence of exploitation of natural resources, facilitated through existing systems of social, economic and political domination, so efforts to address this issue, for political analysts, arguably need to begin with consideration of not only what physically is happening, but also what political reasons are at its roots. Once we understand these reasons, then we can begin to look for solutions.

way in which the language and discourses surrounding the topic are crucial in influencing responses and as such it is not only the framing of the issue which is important. The politicization of the environment, from this perspective, is not then about the mechanisms of governance (as with positivist accounts) but about the way in which our ideas and views about climate change are negotiated and constructed through dominant discourses, ideologies and language. Rendering these explicit has a twofold function: 1) as a means through which dominant power relations can be contested; and 2) as a way in which we can reconcile competing ways to tackle environmental degradation.

Foundational positivist approaches

Behaviouralism in Political Science

There is a vast literature around environmental politics and the politics of the environment. In one of the leading textbooks on the topic, Carter (2008) suggests that there are three main areas that we need to consider: normative theory; the role of parties and pressure groups; and policy-making. These three areas reflect the more traditional concerns of political science. Normative theory has been concerned to address the bigger issues and ideas which are intimately bound up with this topic, such as those surrounding the nature of citizenship, how we position ourselves as citizens of the environment (as well as, or in contrast to, citizens of a nation-state) (see, for example, Dobson, 2003; Dobson and Bell, 2006). Normative theory has also been concerned to discuss justice (a key concern of political science), and the way in which we reflect upon the justness of our actions and their impact upon future generations (see, for example, Dobson, 1998; Page, 1999, 2007). (For a wider discussion of green political theory see Dobson, 2000; Paterson *et al.*, 2006.) The role of social movements, with a particular focus upon environmental movement(s), has been widely discussed (see, for example, Doherty, 2002) and their influence on the policy process has probably been more significant than in any other policy area.

Our aim in this section is to focus upon behavioural analyses of environmental politics. Consistent with other behavioural pluralistic analyses attention is drawn to the observable and measurable behaviour of actors within government and the state. In this way, we might chart the emergence, existence and behaviour of green parties in legislatures across Europe and within the European Parliament itself. These parties do not operate in isolation, from their institutional context, and at a domestic level, what has been observed is that while most governments are formally committed to addressing environmental degradation, Carter agues, electoral politics is still dominated by materialist concerns, such as taxation and the state of the economy, rather than an a priori commitment to sustainable development. As a consequence of this, priority is almost always given to economic growth, rather than environmental protection (Carter, 2008: 2) (as also illustrated in Chapter 4).

The tension between the imperative for economic growth and environmental protection was highlighted in the Brundtland report which generated the concept of 'sustainable development' defined as 'development that meets the need of the present without compromising the ability of future generations to meet their own needs' (1987: 43). A vast literature has emerged which discusses this concept (for review and summaries of debate, see Williams and Millington, 2004; Jordan, 2008) and specifically in relation to climate change (see Grist, 2008).

One of the aims of this report, and of the concept of sustainable development, is to try to find ways to address the twin, and implicitly united, issues of the North's environmental agenda with the developmental agenda of the South. These tensions have been reinforced as not only theoretical but also geopolitical issues. For example, at the Johannesburg conference (2002) the West (or North) was seen as concerned to focus upon economic development as the basis from which environmental protection can be achieved, whereas the developing world (or South) advocated environmental improvement as the basis for economic development (Wapner, 2003: 5–6). This tension between the demand for environmental protection and economic growth is not only a global issue, but also one that states face domestically too. The twin issues of economic growth and environmental protection are at the heart of the concept of sustainable development, but tensions exist as sustainability provides limits to growth; a sustainable society can only survive if it does not exceed the ecological carrying capacities of the planet. Yet, economic growth has involved exploiting and creating further demand which relies on the exploitation of earth's resources, which has led to resource depletion, destructive production and pollution (Carter, 2008: 48).

There have been efforts, both in theory and practice, to integrate the idea of sustainable development into contemporary governance processes. The aim of sustainable governance, then, is to negotiate and manage these tensions (economic growth and environmental protection). Crucially, in the West, in this perspective, the idea of markets as the basis of solutions is not challenged (and markets and the system they represent as a source of the problem are detailed below). Here the focus is upon states, both as actors internationally and domestically, and their response to other states and non-state actors (such as NGOs and MNCs). More recently, states, through international agreements and within domestic policy, have pledged a commitment to sustainable development alongside traditional non-state actors such as the World Bank, businesses, trade unions, universities and consumer groups.

Given these pledges and commitment, as Jordan notes, one of the questions that a political scientist may ask is 'How will sustainable development be implemented?' (2008: 19). One way in which this can be analyzed is through theories of governance which suggest (alongside some other policy-making positions, see Chapter 4) that governance is enacted in a densely structured context. Governance is not the same as government, however. While the latter is primarily concerned with political actors and institutions of the state, the former, like the liberalism of IR, incorporates both state and non-state actors (e.g., businesses and NGOs) into analysis. The environmental policy literature reflects this and discussions of governance identify three main forms of governing: hierarchies, markets and networks (Jordan, 2008).

In this perspective, what environmental politics encourages us to do is to explore the extent to which the concept of sustainable development, however defined, informs governance strategies. Governance is assumed to be an empirical phenomenon and the focus is upon observation of behaviour. Power is assumed to lie with political actors and with those who inform, advise and interact with governments in the process of governance. The implied assumptions about behaviour are pluralistic. All actors are normatively assumed to be operating in the public interest, and in this is the specific collective pursuit of an agenda of sustainable development. Public policy tools provide a way to examine the role of environmental discourse and issues in public life. What is not explained in these accounts, however, is how the beliefs, values and norms which inform these discourses come to be formed in the first instance. The ontological supposition within these accounts is that to undertake analysis we need to observe the behaviour political actors. From this we can

Box 10.2   Behaviouralism and global warming

A special issue of *Global Environmental Politics* (Bulkeley and Moser, 2007) details a variety of domestic policy areas where state and non-state actors interact in a complex process of governance. They draw attention to the interrelationship between differing levels of governance, as well as a wide range of actors involved in creating and enacting policy. For example, at the international level policy-makers may agree to targets for emission reduction mechanisms; this is then implemented at the national level through, for example, carbon governance schemes (2007: 5). The complexity of the interaction between domestic and international levels, between the supranational, sub-national regions and communities as small as cities (see Bulkeley and Betsill, 2005) is teased out through analytic separation. The point implied, although not explicitly discussed, however, is that these regions and actors are not ontologically separate from the other; rather they are interdependent, in the process of governance.

The empirical observations suggest that tackling global warming is no longer simply about international agreements or negotiators. Traditional accounts of environmental policy-making had focused upon non-state actors and the state, in so far as there is an impact upon policy-making (Auer, 2000). However, more recent accounts suggest that policy-making combating climate change is an interactive process, involving differing levels of society, both within and beyond the policy arena. Integration between levels of government and between businesses and government form processes of governance, where hierarchies of governance integrate with businesses in markets and networks of actors, including those outside the state, such as interest groups and NGOs. In this approach, analysis is through observation of behaviour of these actors, the processes they engage in and outcomes, such as policy instruments and multilateral agreements. Power in this sense is implicitly assumed to be dispersed and pluralistic.

read off their motivations and preferences and, given their institutional setting, we are able to describe what is taking place (unlike accounts below which explore the underlying systems of exploitation upon which analysis of global warming is premised).

Behavioural IR

The concept of governance becomes a key tool in analyzing the environment both within Political Science and IR and as suggested above there are overlaps between the two disciplines, not least as it is a global issue. Governance at the international level is evident through the wealth of interstate agreements, multinational institutions and organizations, and new forms of public/private and private/private cooperation (Levy and Newell, 2004). But while the concept of governance is derived from Political Science, and reflects its traditional concerns, the IR literature also tends to revert to the traditional paradigms of the discipline. O'Neill (2009) provides a comprehensive behaviouralist account of the analysis of the environment as a political issue. From this perspective, to analyze global warming, we need to consider the political causes and consequences (as above). Accepting a traditional definition of politics as being about the institutional arrangements of the state, she argues that we need to analyze global governance (as opposed to the idea of domestic governance detailed above). Consistent with developments in the policy-making literature which admit the role of norms into analysis, she argues that we need to consider not only what global environmental governance is but what accounts for its shape, its emergence and the institutional norms and values which account for its institutional arrangements (see also Chapter 5). While admitting norms and values into analysis this account remains behavioural as there is no reflection on how these norms and values came into existence in the first instance, rather they are taken as a given and as variables to be included in the observation of behaviour.

In this behavioural IR approach to the environment the focus is largely around policy-making (for detailed literature review, see Mitchell, 2008). There is an acceptance of the state theories (realism, liberalism, as outlined in Chapters 2 and 3) as explanators of behaviour and in this way the major difference is the substantive topic. States are assumed to exist in an anarchic system, and for realists the aim is to protect their own interests; this holds true across the policy spectrum, including in relation to the environment. While science details the changes taking place in the environment, state theories such as realism and liberalism enable us as analysts to evaluate policy responses to environmental problems. In this way, a realist paradigm enables us to describe why states may focus upon and prioritize security rather than environmental issues (Conca, 1994). For states the consequence of global warming is an increase in scarcity of resources, which in turn may lead to conflict. States must act to protect their own interest and, as other states face those scarce resources, conflict and war is likely to ensue. In this way, we see that realists frame problems around the environment, as security issues for states. These security concerns, and the profit motive of multinational corporations, mean that both will ignore environmental issues unless forced to address them by NGOs or environmental movements (Lipschutz and Conca, 1993).

But the empirical actions of states can contradict realist theory. States do sometimes act to address environmental concerns. So, our next question becomes: why is it that some issues reach the agenda and some don't? IR scholars have highlighted the role of 'shocks': environmental 'accidents' such as Chernobyl; or scientific breakthroughs which can put environmental issues on the agenda (Keohane, 1996). The media also play an important role in placing environmental issues upon the international agenda, as do environmental groups. But, as Mitchell observes, and in line with state-centric IR theories, positioning in the international system is important: 'environmental problems in developing countries tend to garner attention only when people in agenda setting states become concerned, and even then, those issues may languish or fail to lead to adequate solutions' (Mitchell, 2008: 502). This reinforces, then, the realist account of states as the units of analysis and action; ultimately states are the protectors primarily of their own self-interest. And it is through the realist paradigm that we can understand why environmental concerns have little chance of reaching the policy agenda: the 'low' politics of environmental issues are outside the realist agenda and have little impact upon states' survival, therefore states can afford to pursue absolute gains and downplay environmental concerns (Mitchell, 2008: 504). Indeed, the lack of a hegemon willing to create or maintain environmental cooperation is a significant problem within the realist paradigm.

Two significant trends, however, have shifted the analysis of the environment from within these behavioural perspectives. First of all, 'real world' events, such as the 1972 Stockholm conference, precipitated a growth of international treaties concerned with the environment (e.g., on ocean dumping; climate change; hazardous waste trading; biodiversity) coordinated by the United Nations Environment Programme (UNEP). This also marked the beginning of the debate around the relationship between environmental protection and economic development. Second, there was a shift in IR theory towards international cooperation as a mechanism through which to address collective problems (Keohane, 1984; Krasner, 1983).

More recently there have been high-profile attempts at cooperation and diplomacy, such as Kyoto and Copenhagen, and it is these multilateral environmental agreements, as a type of regulatory regime, which comprise, for liberal institutionalists, the dominant form of contemporary environmental governance. The liberal institutionalist concern to highlight the role of non-state actors would suggest that actors such as Greenpeace, or the Third World Network, or international organizations such as the UN or World Bank, and multinational corporations such as Chevron, Texaco, or Shell, become as significant in influencing the outcomes of negotiations as states themselves. Non-state actors are also assumed to play a key role in raising awareness and crucially also mitigate the costs of cooperation, monitoring and enforcing agreements (Haas *et al.*, 1993). Because environmental change does not respect national borders, liberal institutionalists highlight the importance of cooperative arrangements, which are necessary across states if environmental degradation is to be tackled successfully. Indeed, they argue not only is cooperation in environmental matters highly desirable, but, further, it is necessary to address the collective action problems generated through realism.

Within this approach, sustainability, or sustainable development is something which is located within the context of a global economy. The existence of a global economy is taken as a given. As Williams details (1996: 53) the market is assumed to provide the most efficient way to resolve problems, and the market comes prior to environmental protection. The market is a route through which environmental protection is pursued. Sustainable development policies can be pursued through the creation of economic incentives. Notably, the idea of economic growth per se is not challenged. In this approach there is a tension between managing the environment and tackling poverty. Economic growth is seen as significant for poverty reduction. But poverty is assumed to lead to environmental damage. The reconciliation of these differences comes through the efficient use of resources as allocated via the market. It is the role of states and non-state actors to coordinate their regulation. This highlights the underlying (and implicitly unquestioned) acceptance of the neo-liberal belief in the market as providing the solution to societal and, in this case, environmental problems.

Power is still assumed to lie with individual actors, primarily states, although in liberal institutionalist accounts this power is dispersed among pressure groups and those involved in the cooperative process. What these accounts don't provide for, however, is the way in which interests are shaped, whose agenda this serves and how these institutions are shaped in the first place, and these issues are teased out more explicitly in the more critical accounts provided below.

Box 10.3 Global warming: liberal institutionalism and realism

It is only in the last few decades that states have come together to begin to tackle the problems of environmental degradation and more specifically climate change. International awareness of environmental damage began to be addressed through a series of international conferences and agreements which began with the Stockholm conference of 1972, followed by later UN 'mega-conferences' in Rio (1992) and Johannesburg, (2002) which were aimed at raising international awareness, setting environmental norms, goals and principles and establish the procedures for meeting these goals (Seyfang, 2003). The primary actors here are countries whose aim is to establish legal and political frameworks to achieve environmental goals.

So how did this reach the international agenda? Liberal institutionalists draw attention to the beginnings of increased levels of action in the 1980s where states increasingly began to respond to empirical events and pressure from non-state actors. Initial willingness to generate cooperative agreements was attributed to four interrelated features: first, strong representation of a scientific consensus that demonstrated that manmade climate change was taking place; second, an increasing awareness of other environmental issues on the political agenda, such as ozone depletion and deforestation; third, an economic boom in the West (which overrode the usual economic objections to environmental action); and fourth, freak weather conditions and that the 1980s had provided the hottest six years on record (Paterson, 1996: 60). Liberal institutionalists highlight that cooperation between states and other actors meant a key outcome was the establishment of the Intergovernmental Panel on Climate Change (IPCC). The IPCC is supposed to be a forum which provides a scientific basis of reports for policy-makers. It was also used as a basis from which targets to reduce carbon emissions were produced. The significant international agreements which also emerged were the UN Framework Convention on Climate Change (1992) and the Kyoto Protocol (1997) and, more recently, the less binding Copenhagen Accord (2010).

What both realist and liberal institutionalist accounts provide, however, is political analyses which focuses upon the state, and while liberal institutionalists emphasize cooperation rather than the conflict of realism, they also admit non-state actors into analysis. For realists, global warming is a security issue; however, they concur with liberal institutionalists that the market provides the mechanism through which it can be tackled, the implied assumption being that effective solutions can be discovered through ensuring that markets work efficiently. This prevents a discussion about the contribution of markets per se to environmental damage and climate change, and also downplays the way in which climate change issues are constructed in the first instance. These issues are discussed below.

Foundational critical/scientific realist approaches

Radical accounts

For foundational critical realists, Marxism informs the first approach which we outline here. Historically, Marxism has been diametrically opposed to environmentalism, the latter traditionally associated with postmaterialism and therefore assumed to be of interest mainly to those who had achieved a particular level of wcalth and standard of living. Environmentalism then became seen as a lifestyle issue, the preserve of the wealthy. (For a detailed account of the history and reconciliation, see Guha and Martinez-Alier, 1997: 22–37.) However, more recently, as economic accounts increasingly inform the way in which we understand the environment, so Marxism has developed a critique (for wider historical overview of the relationship between Marxism and ecological modernization theory, see Mol and Spaargaren, 2000). These, for IR, have taken the form of radical accounts, and this approach to environmental analysis provides for a critique of the realist and neo-liberal perspectives detailed above (see also Chapters 2 and 3).

Radical accounts draw attention to capitalist development as the root cause of environmental degradation. While the above approaches advocate market solutions, radical approaches suggest that environmental degradation is not an accidental outcome of industrial development; rather it is a direct result of the processes of accumulation, production and reproduction central to the capitalist process. In this way, the focus of analysis is not upon the institutions (which liberals assume regulate and cooperate) nor is the market seen as the solution; rather the market is one embodiment of a set of wider underlying structural conditions. Multilateral agreements simply reinforce existing power structures. These underlying structures generate the conditions through which natural resources are exploited and as such analysis needs to focus upon these structures as generative of environmental damage (Williams, 1996: 51).

The historical materialism of Marxism also characterizes this approach (that systems of exploitation are materially and historically situated), and within radical accounts exploitation of natural resources is a consequence of the wider systems of exploitation embodied within the capitalist system. Sustainable development from this perspective is not possible within existing capitalist structures which obscure and heighten the tension between economies and environmental protection. Here the argument is that the contemporary emphasis 'on "growth" has served to obscure the fact that resource depletion and unsustainable development are a direct consequence of growth itself' (Redclift, 1987: 56). This draws attention to the irreconcilable tensions between the capitalist demand for economic development and the need for environmental protection.

In these accounts, which Schnaiberg (1980) labels the 'treadmill of production', the economy and the environment are intimately interlinked, and the phrase refers to the need to continually pursue 'growth' and generate a profit through the creation of consumer demand, irrespective of the impact upon the expanding ecosystem. In turn this means that states respond to support the accumulation of capital, pursuing policies which encourage expansion. In this way, policies are pursued not to reduce consumption, but to open up new areas to exploitation. Where states do intervene with environmentally protectionist measures, this is to a limited extent, with the aim of preventing resources from being entirely depleted, and a bid to retain public legitimacy. In this way states are engaged in a process of 'environmental managerialism' (Redclift, 1986), whereby states legislate a small degree of protection, sufficient to appease public opinion, or deflect criticism, but without preventing the continuation of (economic) 'growth'. This manifests itself through an interrelationship between businesses and state managers which 'transcends any one class

---

Box 10.4   Radical accounts and global warming

As policy-makers view cheap energy as crucial to economic growth and prosperity, we see the tensions emerge between economic objectives and the need for environmental protection. Radical or Marxist accounts draw attention to the way in which the power of capital becomes structurally embedded. Levy and Egan give an example from within the oil industry, one of the biggest sources of greenhouse gas emissions. Here the relations between state and business managers are evident, with the oil industry heavily contributing to campaign funding (e.g., in 1995–6 the oil industry provided funding of $15.5 billion, 80 per cent of which went to the Republicans [targeted often to those able to influence climate policy]). Personal connections also exist at the senior level, so government and industry and the interrelationships between business and government elites serve to reinforce the structural power of capital (Levy and Egan, 1998: 343). For example, the oil and automobile industries have been particularly successful in the domestic political arena. As Levy and Egan observe, a fuel tax proposed by Clinton was dropped and the automobile sector has been able to exert an effective veto preventing a gas tax (1998: 344). What they highlight is the structural embedding of the relations between state managers and business interests and the importance of the interlinkage of state managers and business interests.

$\longrightarrow$

and is bound together through common identities and interests by material and ideological structures' (Levy and Egan, 1998: 338). This coalition then means that 'capital's international hegemony is not uncontested in the international sphere; rather it secures legitimacy and consent through a process of compromise and accommodation that reflects specific historic conditions' (Levy and Egan, 1998: 339).

With a particular focus upon the environment we see the environment and the economic system as intimately linked and interrelated; however, it is through reform of the underlying economic structures that we are able to address the environmental damage to which capitalism itself has contributed. Power is located systemically. It is contested and negotiated both at state and international level. This would suggest that to address and provide for environmental protection requires a fundamental rethink of the structures which underpin our social, economic and political systems.

As noted above, liberal theorists embrace free trade and see this as one mechanism through which environmental benefits will flow. In contrast, radicals point to free trade as a fundamental contributory factor to environmental damage and degradation. Free trade, it is agued, contributes to inequality and in turn contributes to environmental damage – for

While the power of capital is embedded at national level, this takes place at international level too. For example, analysis of the Rio climate change discussions detailed how a group representing 48 of the world's largest MNCs were represented and it has been argued that the conference provided a structure and privileged business in a way that was simply not available to NGOs (Finger, 1994). Radical accounts also highlight the role of PR as a mechanism through which to attempts to favourably influence public and elite opinion. For example, Levy and Egan (1998: 349–53) provide a detailed account of the different PR strategies adopted by fossil fuel industries to keep us consuming, convince us and policy-makers that climate change is riven with scientific uncertainties, and hence promote the strategies which protect wealth and capital accumulation. From this perspective we can see the way in which state strategies are pursued to support the accumulation of wealth, and the prioritization of capital accumulation. Radical accounts draw attention to the way in which existing geopolitical inequalities are reinforced, with MNCs transferring pollutant industrial bases to states with more lax environmental frameworks, in need of economic investment and development. This global inequality and exploitation of resources of the developing world, both economic and natural, means that while global change is a global phenomenon, 'there are potentially catastrophic effects on the economically and politically marginalized in many areas of the world' (Adger, 2001: 921).

example, the production of raw materials for export, rather than food for internal consumption serves to reinforce existing inequalities in countries (Ropke, 1994). At the same time, liberal trade agreements encourage companies to move pollution-intensive industries from the developed world to the developing world where regulations are relatively lax, thereby increasing pollution, reinforcing the exploitation of those countries in the developing world, both through the depletion of their resources and exacerbating the damage to the environment (Williams, 1996). Our attention is focused by these accounts upon the problems of overconsumption, particularly in the West. As the West continues to exploit the developing world for natural resources, this simply reinforces the system of economic exploitation, so existing and growing global inequalities between the rich and poor are seen in this perspective as a root cause of environmental degradation. The focus of analysis here remains the interaction between states and the firm and their interaction in the pursuit of capital accumulation. This is assumed to come prior to the desire to protect the environment. Power, again, is rooted systemically, and it is through changes to the system that environmental damage can ultimately be addressed.

Ecofeminism

Like other accounts detailed here Ecofeminism seeks to provide an account of the relationship between the social and the biophysical, or ecosystem, and takes the social as the starting point of analysis, it has grown as both a theory and an activist movement (Lahar, 1991; Buckingham, 2004). Its twin concerns and common features are: ending the domination of women and nature, and the pursuit of ecological survival and human and ecological justice. However, along with other feminisms, ecofeminism is characterized by competing perspectives. Some of the behavioural accounts look at the position of women in public life in relation to their capacity to influence policy and influence the policy agenda on climate change, or detail the way in which women's issues are spoken to in public policy both internationally (Bretherton, 1996; Wamukonya and Skutsch, 2001) and domestically (Buckingham, 2004). Some accounts highlight the interconnectivity of female exploitation with the power structures of capitalist society (e.g., Salleh, 1997), showing the way in which the exploitation of the earth's natural resources is akin to the exploitation of women in society. The earth system has been linked to the wisdom of Gaia, an historical goddess, but named with Greek words of feminine gender (Gaia has more recently been used as a scientific term to refer to the interconnectivity of the natural system in Lovelock's [1979/2000] Gaia theory). Ecofeminism argues that, to understand the mechanisms of exploitation of women and nature, the connections between the two need to be understood (Adams, 1993). Women have been historically constructed as closer to nature, culturally through science and religion (Merchant, 1980) and biologically because of their involvement in the reproductive process (Williams and Millington, 2004: 103). This link between imaging the earth and nature as female and the exploitation of the ecosystem and natural resources and the exploitation of women is highlighted through this approach.

Here the argument is made that the issue is not *anthro*pocentrism – human-centredness, but *andro*centrism – male-centredness. In this view, it is patriarchal society which sets the normative background for domination of both women and nature. The term 'anthrocentrism' masks this system of exploitation, so ecofeminism uncovers this relationship and provides a basis for cultural transformation, which in turn leads to ecological transformation (Spretnak, 1987). Ecofeminism seeks to reverse the system of exploitation by arguing that social transformation is possible by learning the lessons of nature; here they argue that 'nature teaches non-dualistic and non-hierarchical systems of relations that are modes of social transformation of values' and in turn 'human and cultural diversity are values in social transformation' (Howell, 1997: 231). Through critique of the existing order, ecofeminism not only renders existing power relations explicit, but also provides an alternative account of how we can view our social world, modelled on the natural world (in contrast to the existing order which models relations with the natural world based upon expositing assumptions of exploitation in the social world).

Ecofeminists advance an argument which rejects the existing relationship between human beings and the ecosystem, rejecting the relationships of domination, control and exploitation imposed by men upon women and nature. Emancipation, survival and justice lie in the challenge of existing power relations and their social transformation. This process needs to reassess equality and diversity, and one way through which this can be embodied is by the creation of non-hierarchical, fully participatory associations (Birkeland, 1993). (This combination of theory and practice is known as praxis.) Ecofeminism argues that intellectual transformation is also necessary; we must reconfigure the way in which we construct and articulate the world, and transcend existing dualisms such as that of 'public-male/private-female', 'culture/nature', 'human/animal' and 'individuality/interconnection' (Birkeland, 1993; King, 1989). This is because dualist thinking engenders hierarchies, which justifies and reinforces domination. The basis of ecofeminist thought is the opposition to the dualisms which negatively present women and nature, and

Box 10.5   Ecofeminism and climate change

Ecofeminists draw attention to the way in which women are disproportionately affected by, and more vulnerable to, the effects of climate change. This
is further reinforced by geopolitical positioning, having greater impact upon
women in the South, who are generally poorer than men and seen as more
dependent upon the primary resources most threatened by climate change,
such as agriculture and fisheries (Denton, 2000). Once observed, these issues
may be addressed on one level through international policy and governance
(see Buckingham, 2004). However, as has been noted, there is often considerable difference between normative aim and outcome. Indeed, while these
conventions and agreements may recognize or acknowledge gender, the state
structures which implement polices are still rooted in structures of inequality and, as such, these conventions and agreements make little more than
superficial changes (Rai, 2008), making the process business and politics 'as
usual' (Birkeland, 1993).

The observation of women's position in society and the consequential
disproportionate effects are visible evidence in these accounts for a wider
set of trends and processes which underpin the social system. These visible
effects are a consequence of a broader set of social relations that are embedded into our global and domestic political and social systems, which in turn
are integrated into our natural environment. Transformation of these social
systems requires rethinking and redefining our social relationships. Once we
reject social relationships based on dominance and exploitation, then female
emancipation and environmental protection and justice are possible. We can
witness evidence of the success of ordering relations in this way through
observation of, and reference to, nature.

some ecofeminists argue that the struggles of nature are the struggles of
women (King, 1989: 19).

Power here is assumed to lie in the patriarchal structures which underpin and shape society, and, again, while we cannot see these structures,
our awareness of their existence is evidenced through their effects, in
society and upon the natural world; for these to be challenged they need
to be made explicit, through which the twin aims of social transformation and environmental protection can be achieved.

Anti-foundational interpretivist approaches

Social constructivism

Social constructivists draw our attention to the way in which environmental issues are 'framed' and presented to us; it encourages us to think

about the social and political processes which inform the way in which we and political elites respond to issues surrounding the environment. Social constructivism includes in its analysis the norms and values which inform political behaviour, but it goes beyond the positivist accounts which include these simply as variables. Rather it encourages us to reflect upon how these norms, values and belief systems are shaped in the first instance. As noted elsewhere, the creation of these norms is viewed as a process, which in itself is political. Environmental constructivists note the significance of these social and political processes in generating action and responses. It is assumed that political elites are more likely to act on those issues which make the public agenda (as noted, for example, by the CNN effect, see Chapter 7). Thus, environmental constructivists note that an issue is more likely to reach the agenda, not necessarily because 'the reality of the problem is most well documented or where the real impacts are greatest, but ... where the agents that propel issues into the public consciousness have worked the most effectively' (Yearley, 2002: 276). Constructivists may want to reflect upon questions such as why is so much focus upon consumers, when the biggest impact is made by industrial producers? Constructivists thus draw our attention to the significance of the way in which issues are 'framed' and, as importantly, to the actions of those who do the 'framing'. In this way for social constructivists 'environmental problems and solutions are end products of a dynamic social process of definition, negotiation and legitimation (Hannigan, 1995: 24). A social constructivist account therefore enables us to seek to understand the social and political processes which define some problems and solutions onto the public agenda and some outside the agenda (see Chapter 2). However, where the 'mobilization of bias' thesis assumes that power resides with those who set the agenda, what social constructivists draw our attention to is the way in which power lies with the social and political processes which frame and construct issues which agents articulate.

For social constructivists, debates around the environment are characterized by ontological and epistemological uncertainty. The notion of climate change, then, is not one monolithic certain whole; rather it is a series of contradictory certainties. It is characterized by 'divergent and mutually irreconcilable sets of convictions both about the difficulties we face and available solutions' (Hannigan, 2006: 29). Poststructuralism builds on this and what this draws attention to is the notion that there are competing and complementary 'solutions' to the issue of climate change. That, rather than searching for a single unitary solution to the 'problem', the way in which we tackle climate change is a consequence of the way in which we define and understand it leads us to a particular outcome.

Box 10.6　Social constructivism: climate change and the Stern report

The Stern Review was commissioned by the UK government to explore the impact of climate change and its economic costs (Stern Review, 2006: vi); the executive summary details the stark conclusion that 'the benefits of strong and early action far outweigh the economic costs of not acting' (Stern Review, 2006: vi) – but this impact is upon the economy. The report overtly linked science, economics and policy. If we look more closely at some of the policy pronouncements which have emerged to tackle the climate change agenda we can see, as with the IR approach above, that policy agendas retain and embed the link between economics and the environment. Indeed, the interlinkage of science and markets are seen as so significant, that the existence of environmental problems were attributed to the failure of markets. Stern began an article two years later stating: 'Greenhouse gas (GHG) emissions are externalities and represent the biggest market failure the world has seen' (Stern, 2008: 1). In this way the implication, and indeed the overt suggestion, was: make the market work effectively and we can address the problem of climate change. Climate change is a problem in this perspective because the markets aren't working properly. The role of the state then becomes to regulate the markets to work effectively and efficiently.

Poststructuralism

Poststructural accounts highlight the way in which issues around the environment are the product of a discursive negotiation and contestation. That is not to deny the existence of climate change or environmental degradation, rather to draw attention to the way the discourse and underlying social relations through which the existence of environmental issues are constructed (and in turn acted upon or not). Poststructuralist accounts have drawn attention to the environment as a site of discursive struggles within North–South relations. In this approach analysis focuses upon the term 'South' and the way in which it is used not only to refer to a geographical region (such as Asia or Africa), but also to reflect the experience of those living within the countries and to recognize that it is a consequence of their historical social and economics positioning within the global system (Anand, 2004: 1).

This perspective draws attention to the interlinkage of discourses and their biophysical environment and the way in which they interact with each other; the way in which dominant discourses shape our response to our physical environment. This interaction of social, political and

However, the starting point is that the market is the way through which environmental protection can be achieved. While it linked science and markets, and the environment and the economy, markets were still seen as the solution to the problem. Regulate the market effectively, ensure the market operates efficiently and the environment will be protected is the underlying assumption. And this assumption is embodied in the actions of both state actors and global capitalists, who embrace this assumption and pursue actions which imply the climate change can be tackled through capitalist investment and entrepreneurial innovation – one of the very paradoxes at the heart of the concept of sustainable development (for an insightful and thought provoking account of Richard Branson's approach to tackling climate change, see Prudham, 2009).

What we see here, then, is the embedding of the norm of the market in environmental policy and manifest through behaviour within the market. The report received international attention and response from states and, notably, from business. The Prince of Wales Corporate Leaders Group on Climate Change, made up of 14 executives from leading UK businesses, argued for a closer working of government and business, in light of the report, to 'ensure that we have first mover advantage in these massive new global markets' (Muspratt and Seawright, 2006). While other approaches might account for the existence of norms in analysis, social constructivism encourages us to uncover the way in which these norms are constructed and explore the way in which they inform political action.

economic systems and process with the biophysical environment has, for some, meant that the aim of discourse such as sustainable development has been to 'capitalize nature' (Escobar, 1996). In this way, we can understand how the natural environment has been exploited for social, political and economic means, and thus we need to look at societal structures if we are to address environmental problems. Goldman and Schurman (2000) have shown how discourse analysis can be employed to understand discourse around nature, the natural environment and environmental degradation, and how this clashes with the dominant discourses of the interests of the North and, more narrowly, the state and transnational corporations. They also argue it is useful for exposing underlying power relationships in national and global conservation agendas.

Poststructural accounts have highlighted the way in which climate change, rather than a naturally located problem, is a social product of discursive struggles (Oels, 2005: 185). From this perspective, the way in which climate change is constructed contributes to the way in which it is tackled. Drawing upon Foucault's notion of governmentality, Oels argues that the way in which climate change is discursively constructed reflects a governmentality which renders climate change governable (2005). In this way climate change become something which is manageable by policy and political elites. Analysis then needs to consider not only

Box 10.7 Postructuralism: climate change and water stress

One of the issues associated with climate change is changing patterns of food production and supplies. There is general agreement upon the problem of access to drinking water. This is known as 'water stress' and refers to the way in which demand outstrips supply. There are two main contributory reasons for the water supply problem: the inadequacy of existing water infrastructure and storage systems and, second, geographical locations competing for the same supplies. As Hannigan notes, about a third of the world's population lives in countries experiencing water stress, and this is likely to rise to two-thirds by 2025. Within this context polluted water is also said to contribute to the death of around 15 million children per year under the age of five (Hannigan, 2006: 58). Here then we see the way in which the management of water has been addressed as largely structured through a neo-liberal agenda. The 'rolling back of the state' has meant that the state has become a 'strategic enabler' rather than a provider. This has paved the way for MNCs and businesses to become providers of community services. The way in which this has become possible in the utilities industry is where the state has been 'discursively constructed as a site of crises' (Haughton, 2002: 792). This in turn paves the way for solutions to be provided by private companies (predominantly from the North). This is estimated to be a $200 billion business, with the potential to be worth $1 trillion by 2021 (Luoma, 2004: 53). MNCs have targeted the West and cities in Latin America and Asia, where the infrastructure is in place and the risk of investment is low (Haughton, 2002). In the South some of the biggest drives for privatization come from the World Bank and the IMF, couched in the rhetoric of neo-liberal reforms, which promote the privatization of water supplies, and justify this in the language of 'freeing the state to address other social priorities' (Hannigan, 2006: 59). Yet this has negative consequences socially – for example, in Ghana, where the government accepted a privatization deal to receive an IMF loan, resulting in the doubling of water rates (Luoma, 2004).

In this way, discursive accounts draw attention to the embedding of neo-liberalism in the social, economic and political relationships between the interests of the North, and the way in which those interests are embedded in institutions such as the World Bank and IMF, prioritizing those interests rather than those of the people who inhabit the countries enduring water stress. Here exploration of the dominant discourse enables attention to focus upon a continuation of existing relations of domination and exploitation.

what is visible, but also what is obscured and the ways in which this takes place. In this perspective, this is done through the construction of identities and discourses.

Here power is embedded in language and systems of meaning, and is also discursively embedded in social relationships and, as such, a fundamental aspect of everyday life and daily relationships. Power relationships can often give rise to domination where power relationships are asymmetrical. Power relationships are manifest through discourse which reduces resistance and encourages the internalizing of consent by individuals. Discourse therefore provides a powerful mechanism to incorporate individuals into relations of domination. As Davidson and Frickel note, control over the production of discourses can, for example, mean the capacity to 'delimit both the actors that can legitimately engage in politics and the issues that are subject to debate' (2004: 478): Control over discourse defines how debate is conducted, and on what terms.

Comparison of theories and approaches

Foundational positivist accounts have focused our attention upon the behaviour of political actors within the political system. At both national and international levels we can analyze observable behaviour which takes place within political institutions and as such we can explain outcomes, in this instance in terms of policy. However, what these observations miss is the way in which beliefs preferences, norms and values about the environment come to be shaped. They also fail to explore the way in which discussion about the environment is premised upon existing systems of exploitation either in terms of the capitalist system, workers and producers, or developed and developing countries, as highlighted by foundational critical/scientific realist accounts. Within this perspective feminists also draw attention to the way in which the construction of the environment as an issue has been premised upon accounts of gender which reinforce these systems of exploitation, and through this exposé and recognition we can find ways to change and transform social structures and create a more just environment (both social and natural) for contemporary and future generations. Here attention is focused upon structures, which downplays the capacity of individuals to have too much of an ability to act autonomously within them. And this feature is characteristic of the anti-foundationalist interpretivist position in which poststructural accounts make reference to embedded systems, reinforced through practice, which shape our social world. In this account, however, in contrast to critical realist accounts, the basis is not rooted in the material world, rather it is rooted in systems of ideas and discourses which serve to construct and create our environment.

Adjudicating between perspectives

As with other topics, this adjudication is rooted in our starting ontological and epistemological assumptions. To understand the environment as a political issue, do we need to observe the behaviour of governments, states and the processes of governance in generating agreements and policy instruments? Do we need to establish how the social and economic world is regulated in political attempts to mitigate the environmental damages being wrought on our planet and the effects this will have on its inhabitants? If this is so, we are more likely to adopt a positivist approach. Or do we explore the ways in which existing social and economic structures are built on exploitation, or labour, and through gender, and, therefore, the way in which environmental resources are exploited can be conceived of in the same way? Through this conceptualization we are able to provide routes for transformation; if we are keen to analyze the effects of underlying structures or seek out the causes of exploitation then we may adopt a critical realist approach. If we believe that environmental degradation is in part a product of social struggles and that these are discursively embedded through social relationships, reinforced through daily practice and more narrowly through the language that we use to define what an environmental issue is (often defined favourably so that it can be managed), then we might adopt an interpretivist account.

Conclusion

In his thought-provoking account of climate change, Hulme (2009) argues that climate change is not a 'problem' awaiting a 'solution'. Rather it is a set of environmental, cultural and political phenomena which are fundamentally reshaping our physical and social world. As such, an overarching narrative or discourse is unhelpful, as it masks the difference in approaches to climate change and as such denies the possibility of a progressive set of strategies to tackle climate change, as opposed to the seeking of one overarching solution.

While not explicitly poststructural in his approach, Hulme does draw attention to the problems of seeking to adopt an overarching narrative, choosing to highlight the importance of understanding difference as a means through which differing schools of thought may approach the issue. He suggests that, rather than seek a unitary solution, competing approaches can make their own contribution and so the whole may become greater than the sum of its parts. He also highlights the way in which we can situate our social selves in relation to the environment as noted also within some of the accounts above. What this suggests, more broadly, is that an integrated understanding of our ecosystems and our social systems is necessary if we are to effect transformation and justice in either or both. Indeed, for many the issue of global warming is not only about the impact that human-induced climate change has upon the physical nature within our planet, but the costs and impacts of climate change in human terms (see, for example, Caney, 2008).

The accounts detailed above provide just some of the alternative ways through which we can understand attempts to address the urgent issues around environmental degradation, and while some focus upon governance, others on social or discursive structures, all are concerned to address the issue of climate change. While the routes differ, we argue here that, given their underlying assumptions, all are informed in different ways by conceptions of power, they are all inherently political, whether their focus is upon the actions which take place within the nation-state or activities of the state at the international level. For us the distinction between Politics and IR dissolves as the issue is not one which can be categorized into disciplinary or 'real world' geographical boundaries.

Reflection

Which perspective or approach does the best job of explaining or accounting responses to global warming?

Why do you think this is the case?

Are inadequate structures of governance the cause of failure to fully address the issue of global warming?

How might a rational choice approach explain the Stern Review?

Do you think that the need to pursue economic growth means that sustainable development is not possible?

Do you think that women are likely to be disproportionately affected by global warming?

Do you agree with the argument that global warming has been discursively constructed in such a way as to make it governable and is this problematic?

How can combining insights from Political Science and IR help us analyze global warming?

Can the boundaries between Politics and IR remain when analyzing global warming? What are the reasons for your answer?

Seminar activities

In seminar groups use a range of current newspapers and offer some analysis of the following:

How many articles within the whole paper address the environment/the issue of climate change or discuss sustainable development?

Does the number of articles tell us anything:

a)   about the importance society attaches to the environment?
b)   about the ability of particular groups to get their issues onto the agenda?
c)   about the political context within which the environment is or isn't discussed in the news?

Where articles do explicitly discuss the environment, what assumptions are made (whether implicitly or explicitly) about:

a)   the way in which climate change should be tackled?
b)   the way in which society is ordered?
c)   alternate ways in which climate change can be addressed?

For discussion: what is the dominant discourse of the article and what norms and values does it embody? Which theoretical framework detailed above provides the most useful account of the political reality represented in the article?

Policy documents have been produced by the Climate Action network website http://climatenetwork.org. How far have their aims and ambitions been translated into policy agendas? What might prevent their goals being achieved? What discourses do they engage in?

Activity: Take an issue such as water stress. In groups, develop positions for key actors, such as: central government; local government; the water industry; scientists; householders; the local community. Who is most likely to achieve their preferred outcomes and why? Where is power located? Whose interests are represented? Which position does this conform to?

Chapter 11

Globalization

Introduction

The concept of globalization has become a taken for granted assumption by policy-makers and shapers since the end of the Cold War, with academics such as Anthony Giddens, in his 1999 Reith Lectures, and leading politicians proclaiming an 'era of globalization'. The assumption is widespread that we live in a globalized world; indeed, one of the best-selling introductory IR textbooks is Baylis, Smith and Owens' *The Globalization of World Politics* (Baylis *et al.*, 2008). However, as with the other chapters, there are keenly contested empirical and theoretical debates. In this topic this debate takes place around the extent to which we are in era of globalization and what the implications of this might be. Before beginning to consider the theoretical and empirical arguments surrounding this concept we first need to consider what we actually mean by globalization.

The Penguin Dictionary of International Relations defines globalization as: 'The process whereby state-centric agencies and terms of reference are dissolved in favour of a structure of relations between different actors operating in a context which is truly global rather than merely international' (Evans and Newnham, 1998: 201). However, such a definition is somewhat vague and ambiguous. What is the difference, for example, between the global and the international? If state-centric agencies do not dissolve, does this mean that we are not operating in a globalized world? David Held and colleagues, while emphasizing that the modern world is characterized by 'the widening, deepening and speeding up of worldwide interconnectedness in all aspects of contemporary social life' (Held *et al.*, 1999: 2), define globalization as: 'a process (or set of processes) that embodies a transformation in the spatial organization of social relations and transactions, generating transcontinental or inter-regional flows and networks of activity, interaction and power' (Held *et al.*, 1999: 2).

Colin Hay, while reaching different conclusions to Held, as we shall see later, broadly supports this definition, with the added proviso that 'to count as evidence of globalization, the process under consideration must be genuinely *globalizing* (increasingly inter-regional and/or inter-continental in character)' (Hay, 2006b: 3).

Unlike other topics we have covered, theorizing about globalization does not neatly conform to the usual theoretical positioning but rather has been dominated by new theoretical positions based on attitudes towards the ways in which we understand and define the existence of globalization. Held (2004) identifies four different theoretical perspectives consisting of positive and negative globalism, internationalism and transformationalism. Martell (2010) focuses on hyper-globalization, scepticism, transformationalism and postmodernism/post structuralism and constructivism. We do not consider transformationalism, a hybrid approach between globalism and scepticism, in this chapter due to space limitations (although this approach has a growing following [see Goldstein and Pevehouse, 2010; Kelly and Prokhovnik, 2004; McGrew, 2004; Sinclair *et al.*, 1996]).

In this chapter, we maintain our divisions of foundational positivism, foundational critical realism and anti-foundational interpretivism to examine the cultural, economic and political aspects of a contested globalization, examining the respective theoretical positions of globalists and neo-liberal institutionalists who embrace the concept that we are living in an era of globalization. We then consider the sceptical theoretical perspectives of critical theorists and internationalists, who consider that contemporary global circumstances are not without precedent and that globalists claims are overstated. We next turn our attention to poststructuralists and postmodern feminists, whose discursive approach to globalization opens possibilities for emancipatory potential. We will compare and adjudicate between the different theories. Before we do so, let us first consider the implications for power in a globalized or globalizing era.

Power

We live in a world which appears to becoming much smaller as the internet provides instant communication across borders, opening up new social networks and empowering people with unprecedented amounts of information. The financial markets that dominate our economies, travel, news, goods and even jobs are becoming increasingly global. All countries experience the impact of global warming, environmental pollution, ozone depletion, sex trafficking and drug-related crime, which have become global phenomena. Anthony Giddens, in his first Reith

Lecture, summed up a sense of apprehension about the approach of globalization: 'For better or worse we are being propelled into a global order that no one fully understands, but which is making its effects felt upon all of us' (Giddens, 1999).

The perspective we adopt on globalization will reflect our ontological and epistemological approaches. These will be reflected in the sorts of questions we ask about globalization. Does it really represent a radical departure from what has gone before? How can we tell? Are states still important in this new age? Is globalization a good or a bad thing? Are all states affected in the same way? Who wins and loses in an era of globalization? How does globalization affect the lives of ordinary people across the world?

Advocates of globalization theories argue that the end of the Cold War saw the dominant position of the nation-state challenged. Increased interdependency and interaction between states has brought with it a necessity to surrender, or forgo, aspects of sovereignty in order to reap the benefits of globalization with its promise of greater prosperity for all. The Treaty of Westphalia (1648) established the principle of sovereignty within territorially defined borders, providing rulers with the opportunity to determine what takes place in their own country and excluding outside interference in the internal affairs of the state. Economic development and technological progress led to greater interdependence, formalized in treaties and alliances, which involve the ceding of some aspects of national sovereignty as experienced by member states of the European Union. The question about how much authority the state still possesses and its ability to act independently of global trends lies at the heart of the debate on globalization. Political scientists including Anthony Giddens, Colin Hay and David Held have been at the forefront of this debate, while IR theorists in the realist tradition have been reluctant to engage in a debate which challenges their core beliefs on state sovereignty, anarchic world order and military competition rather than economic cooperation.

What is uncontested is that rapid changes are taking place in the cultural, economic and political realms today. Anthony McGrew, a self-declared transformationalist, suggests that there has been a significant institutionalization of political networks, including intergovernmental and transnational organizations such as Greenpeace, the United Nations and organized crime. New centres of authority 'above, below and alongside the state' have grown, like the WTO, regional assemblies and foreign MNCs. An evolving global polity and transnational civil society is emerging in which global and transnational rules are implemented and advocacy networks established. New forms of multinational, transnational and global politics are emerging (McGrew, 2004: 140). These changes have implications for existing power relations.

Box 11.1 Case study. Human rights and globalization

Human rights are not a new phenomenon but can be traced back to ancient religious texts of all the world religions. The American Declaration of Independence proclaims that: 'We hold these truths to be self-evident, that all men are created equal, that they are endowed by their Creator with certain unalienable Rights, that among these are Life, Liberty and the pursuit of Happiness'. Political and legal philosophers including Thomas Paine and Mary Wollstonecraft have sought to proclaim the rights of man and woman. Following the holocaust in the middle of the twentieth century greater attention has been paid to the issue of human rights at an institutional level. In an era of globalization, with greater access to and awareness of other countries, with instant news reportage throughout the world available to all with access to the internet, satellite television, mobile phone or radio, the focus on human rights has significantly increased since the end of the Cold War. A series of international treaties underlines an assumption of the universality of human rights.

1948 Universal Declaration of Human Rights
1969 International Convention on the Elimination of all Forms of Racial Discrimination
1970 International Covenant on Civil and Political Rights
1970 International Covenant on Economic, Social and Cultural Rights
1981 The Convention on the Elimination of all forms of Discrimination Against Women
1987 The Convention Against Torture
1990 The Convention on the Rights of the Child
2003 International Convention on the Protection of the Rights of All Migrant Workers

→

The authority of the nation-state is challenged if citizens and businesses are able to bypass national governments to enter into relationships and arrangements with others. The loyalty of citizens can no longer be taken for granted once transnational networks of advocacy, business and religion become more meaningful to organizations and their members. The emergence of suprastate bodies such as the WTO, UN, EU and G8 or G20 of industrialized nations impose codes of conduct, rules and appropriate behaviour on states that shift the power balance away from the state. Sub-state actors, such as California or Northern Ireland, are able to enter into political and economic arrangements with other countries and regions without recourse to national government, again diminishing the power of the state.

Human rights, like globalization, are heavily contested. Fierce debates rage between those who advocate the universal applicability of human rights and those who adopt a relativist position, arguing that rights are culturally specific. At issue is the remit of an international order determined to promote universal rights and the right of sovereign nations to determine their own approach to human rights within their territorially defined borders. The erosion of those borders through processes of globalization leads to increased tensions between these polarized positions. At issue also is which rights constitute human rights. Do civil and political rights take precedence over economic and social rights or are both equally important? Are the right to freedom of speech and assembly, to protest, vote or religious freedom universal rights? Are equal protections under the law, freedom from arbitrary arrest or maybe the right to a good standard of living, a good education, and health and welfare provision, universal human rights?

Cosmopolitans argue in favour of universal rights and that the international community should promote and defend those rights. The principle of humanitarian intervention when governments abuse their own citizens has become established in international law with the Responsibility to Protect (2005) requiring governments worldwide to act to save civilians from genocide and crimes against humanity. Humanitarian intervention, however, appears arbitrary, with rich states choosing to intervene based on national interest. Communitarians argue that attempts to promote universal rights replace heterogeneity with homogeneity and seek to impose Western, rather than universal, values. Meanwhile, human rights activists detect considerable hubris among political elites from cosmopolitan and communitarian camps operating at the level of national interests rather than a concern for individual or group rights. US politicians regularly criticize Chinese officials for their civil/political human rights record, while China castigates the US for its economic/social record of poverty and inequality.

The exercise of power is crucial to discussions of globalization. We need to know if states are willingly cooperating with the processes of globalization as passive participants, or recipients of globalization, or if they are active agents engaged with the process. In the structure–agency debate, are structures changing, with agency either unable or unwilling to resist or shape such change? Have some states become powerless in the face of modernization, interdependence and globalization, or do they still have important roles to play? If states no longer enjoy, if they ever did, a monopoly of power, who has benefited from that power transfer? Advocates for globalization suggest that citizens are empowered by the diminution of the relative power of the state. Whereas some opponents consider that states are still the most important actors within the international system, others argue that globalization favours hegemonic states or an international capitalist class. Maybe MNCs or transnational corporations (TNCs), or the bureaucracies running international institutions are the new power holders and brokers. In the theoretical sections below we will explore these competing claims.

Foundational positivist approaches

Behaviouralism and globalism

Globalists are in no doubt that globalization is a fact of contemporary life, dominating culture, the economy and politics. They examine a real world out there, which has an independent existence, suggesting that a singular truth about this world is available to be discovered. For globalists globalization is empirically testable, and explanations can be generated leading to predictions and general laws. Globalization, to globalists, is a fact of life, and observation of the way states, individuals and businesses behave and interact provides the supporting evidence. States have experienced huge economic and political change in a comparatively short period. Meanwhile the concept of nation-state has become increasingly redundant, as the power of state leaders has gradually eroded. Giddens' suggests that states are 'too small to solve the big problems but also too large to solve the small ones' (Giddens, 1999). In such a world, overarching authorities in the form of international institutions such as the WTO, to regulate global trade, the IMF and World Bank, to regulate global finance and the UN and its agencies, to provide basic infrastructure in a globalized world, are better equipped to deal with the larger problems (Cochrane and Pain, 2004: 16).

For globalists, social, economic and political processes operate overwhelmingly at the global rather than national or sub-national level. Everyone feels the impact of globalization across a world that is increasingly interconnected. Global networks break down local and national differences and weaken state autonomy and sovereignty. In place of cultural and economic differences homogeneity breaks out as the culture and economic practices of the hegemonic power dominates global fora, introducing new global structures with enforceable rules of conduct. Kelly and Prokhovnik (2004: 90–1) identify five interrelated drivers of change in the world economy:

1. growing international trade as a result of lower tariffs and greater competition;
2. foreign direct investment and lower technology transfers;
3. increased communications through the internet and other media;

4. technological advances;
5. increased labour mobility.

We are presented with an embryonic global economy where the impact of decisions taken in one part of the world has a significant impact on other parts of the world. The 1997/8 financial crisis caused by currency speculation in East Asia resulted in bankruptcies and the collapse of economies in Thailand, Malaysia and South Korea, spread to Russia, Japan and Latin America before being resolved by a devaluation of US interest rates and an enormous structural adjustment package underwritten by the United States. Western banks were obliged to act to prevent the economic problems in a specific region of the world affecting economies across the globe.

In similar fashion, the 2008 financial crisis, caused by the failure of the US subprime mortgage market, had implications not simply for those economies exposed to US subprime mortgages but to all economies with large budget deficits. Governments in the US, UK and Ireland sunk billions of taxpayers' money into bailing out banks in order to prevent a collapse of the global banking system and confidence in the international system. Bad lending decisions in Washington and New York led to huge deficit reduction measures being introduced throughout the EU due to the immediate and adverse affect on global confidence.

For globalists the quantitative evidence revealing enormous increases in trade and interdependency, including foreign direct investment (FDI), financial flows, travel and tourism, telephone calls and internet communication, are all indications of globalization. Information and communication technology has transformed over the past two decades so that physical presence is no longer required in order to conduct business. Rather than the individual proclivities of nation-states determining patterns and conduct of transactions and monetary policy, increasingly these are being transferred to international financial institutions which introduce codes of conduct and rules of behaviour that acquire international legitimacy.

Economic factors determine the cultural and political and it is this economic evidence that is the most significant factor in a globalized world (Kelly and Prokhovnik, 2004: 101). In this perspective, economic liberalism opens the way for free markets and increased efficiency, passed on in lower prices to consumers. Integrated global markets reduce the role of national governments and thereby reduce regulation and the potential for corruption. Poorer countries benefit from a trickledown effect and technology transfers from advanced countries affording the opportunity to develop, industrialize and climb out of relative poverty. Alongside economic interdependence, political structures are realigned to facilitate

Box 11.2 Globalism and human rights

Globalists approach human rights as an outworking of globalization. Liberal economic systems, free trade and liberal democratic political systems have led to greater prosperity for market capitalist nations and, as this extends to a global system, then those principles of freedom extend to the social and political sphere. Human rights are seen as universal because liberal capitalism is universal and the benefits accrue to all. Globalism removes the tyranny of the narrow and parochial and replaces it with the universal, where individual freedom, within the capitalist order, is prized. The globalization of human rights frees women from religious and cultural controls and prohibitions to be who they want to be. Growing trade will provide greater prosperity for all, reducing poverty, and lead to greater accountability and transparency; states will benefit to the extent to which they conform to the requirements of the global economy and adopt behavioural norms, which include universal human rights. Globalists will place greater emphasis on civil/political rights rather than socio/economic rights which must remain subordinate to the requirements of global capitalism. Globalists, from a foundational perspective, will avoid normative positions, emphasizing instead the empirical evidence pointing to the benefits of liberal economic models and associated human rights agenda.

this interdependence. The role of politicians and government is globalized, with increasing numbers of international fora and the emergence of G7, G8 and, most recently, G20 largest industrialized nations. National governments must work to a global agenda and their role is increasingly to facilitate the processes of global capitalism to benefit their citizens.

New media technologies have provided hitherto unknown opportunities to have access to unregulated information and to enter the public sphere without having to depend on elites in government, academia or public service broadcasting to filter and disseminate knowledge. Globalists observe the increased interaction through online communication, tourism and cultural transfer and the sharing of cultural and understandings which has the potential to improve the quality of life of all and help tackle problems of the global commons such as pollution, global warming and piracy (see Mulgan, 1998: 19).

Neo-liberal institutionalism

Globalization offers the advance of capitalism and liberalism, freedom and democracy that neo-liberals advocate in domestic and international contexts. Neo-liberal institutionalists operate within a behaviouralist paradigm and, like IR realists, consider the state a key actor. They also acknowledge an anarchic world order but one in which institutions serve to increase knowledge, understanding and norms of acceptable behaviour that create predictability and stability within the international order. Rather than international institutions bypassing states, they need to cooperate with and enjoy the support of states for legitimacy and efficiency.

Robert Keohane, probably the world's leading neo-liberal institutional theorist (1984, 1989a,b, 2002), sees a rapidly changing world, but one where states and institutions working together remain predominant rather than surrendering to an irresistible tide of global economic forces. No one state, even one as powerful as the United States, has the capacity to deal with most global issues, so formal, intergovernmental and cross-national international institutions, often with NGO representation, international regimes, norms, practices and conventions, are seen as effective managers of the global commons and trade (Viotti and Kauppi, 2010: 136–7). For Keohane, greater institutionalization is the key to increased trade, financial flows, security and the environment. Effective institutional design, without replacing the role of states, is crucial in creating a fairer world but this does contain risks, as Keohane acknowledges, 'if we bungle the job, the results could be disastrous' (Keohane, 2002: 246).

Neo-liberal institutionalists describe a 'partially globalized world' with 'thick networks of interdependence in which boundaries and states nevertheless matter a great deal' (Keohane, 2002: 258). Keohane invites us to consider the impact of the relatively open Canadian–US border, which still has strong impact on economic activity between the two countries. Even their proximity has not brought about a convergence in welfare policies, for example, any more than it has within the EU (Hay, 2006b). Therefore, states are not quite submerged in a global system but they do operate under conditions of complex interdependence with increasing linkages, interactions and interconnections among states and non-state actors. In this interconnected world there is little distinction between high and low politics, a recognition that there are multiple channels of communication across national boundaries and awareness that military power is no longer the most useful form of statecraft (Lamy, 2008: 132).

As neo-liberal institutionalists focus their attention on institutions and governance there is, however, increasingly a tacit acceptance of globalization as an empirical reality. Neo-liberal institutionalists are entering theoretical territory occupied by globalists in seeking to shape those international institutions according to neo-liberal cultural, economic and political principles. They are still wary of downgrading the relative importance of the state, envisaging a world shaped in their image that

Box 11.3   Neo-liberal institutionalism and globalized human rights

For neo-liberal institutionalists, human rights are such a large international issue that international institutions must address them. Hegemonic states such as the United States have taken the lead in establishing appropriate standards of conduct in respect to human rights. American political scientists and politicians should therefore lead the way in designing new institutions which reflect a globalizing world. The global reach of liberal economics and the success of liberal democracies encourage neo-liberal institutionalists like Tony Blair and Bill Clinton to believe that such values can and should be universalized. In order to uphold the principle of universal human rights they advocate humanitarian intervention in defence of human rights. This principle has now become enshrined in the Responsibility to Protect imperative for states to intervene on behalf of civilians subject to genocide and crimes against humanity.

will continue America's hegemonic role and privileged position within the global system. In doing so, they are in danger of confirming the position of sceptics and internationalists that the globalization project operates in the interest of rich and powerful nations like the US and/or a transnational global capitalism. Suspicions which Robert Keohane's challenge to fellow political scientists does little to allay: 'the challenge for American political science resembles that of the founders of the United States: how to design institutions for a polity of unprecedented size and diversity' (Keohane, 2002: 245).

Foundational critical realist approaches

Critical theory and globalization scepticism

Critics of the globalization thesis are far more sanguine than globalists and neo-liberal institutionalists about the impact of globalization. For them globalization is all about the inevitability of a world that is more homogeneous and less diverse. The emphasis is upon underlying unobservable systems which structure and shape the form which globalization takes. A world dominated by the global North, which operates in its own interests and further disempowers the weak in the North and South. Critical theorists, inspired by Adorno and Horkheimer for the Frankfurt School, see a world becoming not just homogenized but, more especially, Americanized. Globalization is seen as cultural, economic and political imperialism dominated by global corporations such as McDonald's, Disney and Microsoft. In this way culture becomes no more than a commodity to be bought and sold. Far from globalization providing more opportunities and more choice, critical theorists contend that it offers less, for example as media conglomerates such as News International buy up competitors. The use of the English language as the language of business, knowledge and communication privileges the West and elites to the disadvantage of the poor and non-English-speaking countries whose cultural traditions are downgraded (Schiller, 1991; Dorfmann and Mattelart, 1975).

Whereas globalists present a world liberated by free trade and open borders, sceptics counter that these inevitably lead to greater inequalities within and between countries. The weakening of state sovereignty leads to greater control by unelected international institutions that set the rules of the game, such as the IMF imposing structural adjustment measures in return for loans. National governments become unable to control their own economies and taxation levels because of international pressure and global economic forces. Critical theorists see a world in which states increasingly lose the capacity to pursue progressive social policies because of the demands of the global economy. Workers in industrialized countries are disadvantaged when the ease of transferring jobs to cheaper production areas leads to a loss of jobs, or reduced wages and benefits under the threat of moving jobs overseas. The interconnectedness of the global economy means that profligacy and/or poor financial decision-making in part of the world now affects the entire world.

Globalization, for the sceptics, emphasizes the downside of greater international mobility, physically and virtually, whereby enhanced communications provides benefits for organized crime and terrorism, with people trafficking, drug cartels and unofficial arms deals. Environmental concerns of ozone depletion, global warming, deforestation, desertification, pollution, pandemics and contaminated foodstuffs all increase in a globalized world. As decision-making leaks from national governments to senior politicians, finance ministers, central bankers, bureaucrats, business leaders and multilateral institutions, what is described by McGrew as a 'cosmocracy' emerges and a democratic deficit grows as this elite manage global capitalism (McGrew, 2004: 153).

Internationalism

Internationalists dispute the very concept of globalization believing that globalists have greatly overstated their case. They argue that there are considerable continuities between the past and present and what is being experienced today is the continued outworking of processes that emerged with industrialization and the development of capitalism in

Box 11.4   Critical theory and human rights

Critical theorists see the cosmopolitan advocacy of universal human rights as simply another device by global capitalism to dominate the world. Global capital requires flexible and compliant workforces and structures to facilitate increased trade and hence profit. Communitarian impulses, which resist globalizing trends, have the potential to disrupt the onward march of capitalism and must be thwarted. The promotion of human rights is considered to be a tactic rather than a commitment. This tactic is used to undermine the international credibility of economic rivals, as in the case of the US, China and Russia, and to challenge communitarian values that confine women, for example, to the private sphere and release them into the globalized workplace, providing cheap sources of unprotected labour. Human rights are thereby used as an excuse to justify the invasion of other countries such as Iraq or the former Yugoslavian republics in the pursuit of the national interests of powerful nations. Human rights abuses within economic trading partners and allies are continually ignored, or downplayed, by the most powerful nations in the interests of global capitalism. Globalization becomes seen as a reflection of the self-interest of rich states at the expense of the poor; the human rights discourse should be considered only within this context. Human rights, for critical theorists, will also include those things necessary for survival, including food, shelter, clothes and jobs, all of which are ignored by neo-liberal promotion of free markets. Critical theorists will rail against the violation of human rights but ultimately consider that progress will be based on the need of international capital rather than the individual.

Western Europe and the United States. From this perspective, most cultural, economic and political activity takes place regionally rather than globally. For example, in his first major speech as UK Foreign Secretary in July 2010, William Hague revealed that the United Kingdom exports more to its near neighbour Ireland than it does to China, India and Russia put together. In this view, nation-states remain significant international actors despite the globalist forecast of their demise. Internationalists seek to provide scientific accounts and causal explanation to explain the emergence of internationalism rather than globalization. They also admit unobservable layers of reality into analysis, acknowledging the value-laden nature of analysis. For example, for internationalists the failure of states to defend welfare or determine a progressive economic policy can be 'covered up' by shifting the blame to the nebulous forces of global markets.

While information technology and communications developments in the last few decades have been remarkable, are they any more remarkable than the development of the telegraph linking London to Paris in 1852 or the 1858 transatlantic cable link? These earlier developments just as significantly revolutionized their time and led to increased information flows and transnational crime as surely as the internet. For internationalists Tom Standage summed up this earlier technological age: 'If any generation has the right to claim that it bore the full bewildering, world-shrinking brunt of such a revolution, it is not us – it is our nineteenth-century forebears' (Standage, 1998: 199–200). Internationalists believe that continuities rather than changes are more significant in understanding the present economic order. This is evident in the privileged position enjoyed by the hegemonic power, which determines the pattern of global governance:

> The world in which we are now living, the modern world-system, had its origins in the sixteenth century [located in Europe and North America] ... It expanded over time to cover the whole globe. It is and has always been a *world-economy*. It is and has always been a *capitalist* world economy. (Wallerstein, 2010: 225)

In the nineteenth century, the British Empire dominated the world economy and was able to shape the structures of global governance. In the twentieth century, the US superseded Britain and was able to introduce global systems of its own design after World War II, including the UN and the Bretton Woods institutions. The dominant power(s), although unable to control global structures, are nonetheless able to exercise considerable power and influence by their veto rights in international institutions and their ability to bypass international bodies (McGrew, 2004: 152). Other states remain important as they continue to perform indispensable functions of taxation, laws and defence. The forces of nationalism, national identification and the emergence of new states following the dismantling of the USSR, Yugoslavia and Czechoslovakia confirm the continued importance attached to statehood. Earlier versions of non-state actors are found in the early trade unions and religious organizations, NGOs in the movement to abolish slavery and multinational corporations (MNCs) in the Dutch East India Company trading throughout Asia from the seventeenth century.

If we truly lived in an era of globalization then Paul Hirst (2001) argues that we should be experiencing rapidly escalating trade to GDP ratios. There should be a shift in output and trade to new locations, as transnational corporations (TNCs) seek competitive advantage by relocating to newly emerging economies. Although there is some transfer, most processes remain in one country (Scholte, 2001: 535). National capital markets should dissolve as locally sourced investment is replaced by global flows of FDI. Short-term financial flows beyond the control of national central banks or international regulatory institutions should become globalized, while true TNCs, without a distinct national base and with supranational management, should organize production and trade. However, very few TNCs actually exist; rather they should be seen as MNCs with a clear national base manufacturing parts of the end-product overseas (Thompson, 2000: 103–6). If Hirst's five indicators of a globalized economy are accepted then so must his conclusions be, that we are not quite able to describe the present era as one of globalization (Hirst, 2001: 115).

Paul Hirst and Grahame Thompson seek to differentiate between an international economy and a universal global economy. They suggest that, rather than globalization, which would imply the development of a new economic structure, we are experiencing greater international trade and investment within 'an existing set of economic relations' (Hirst and Thompson, 1999: 7). For internationalists there is a distinct difference between interdependence, which they accept, and integration, which they do not recognize. Instead of a globalized world, the present era is one in which the term 'globalization' is used to justify the

Box 11.5   Internationalists and the globalization of human rights

Internationalists still see a key role for states in an interdependent age and, as such, are concerned that states protect the human rights of citizens. They emphasize historical continuity and see human rights in the context of local and transnational demands for human rights. In historical context the movement for the abolition of slavery, the ending of capital punishment, extension of the franchise and religious toleration each herald an international trend in human rights. As in previous periods, attitudes towards human rights are reflected in the approach adopted by hegemonic and dominant powers. In the present age, with the US as the hegemonic power, attempts to universalize human rights will reflect not universal but American rights. Economic and social rights will be subordinate to civil and political rights. There will be little pressure to see capital punishment as a human rights issue. As the dominant power, the United States, will try to force weaker states to comply and pressure stronger ones to comply with its understanding of human rights. Meanwhile, the US will not be subject to those same standards and refuses to be bound by the International Criminal Court. The US is willing to circumvent international institutions in order to take military action when and where it deems necessary and to violate human rights through programmes of extreme rendition, waterboarding and, until recently, detention without trial of enemy combatants.

continued domination of the international sphere by the powerful states of the global North. These are now 'able to exercise their power by pleading powerlessness in the face of the supposed globalizing market forces' (Brah *et al.*, 1999: 8). As such, their focus is upon unobservable entrenched systems of power, and the aim is to expose and challenge these relations.

Anti-foundational interpretivist approaches

Poststructuralism and globalization

Poststructuralism is concerned with subjectivity, identity and power, and rejects theoretical approaches that would seek to explain globalization. With discursive analysis, poststructuralists seek to challenge prior assumptions about globalization and subject it to the 'problematic of subjectivity' (Campbell, 2007: 226). Whereas other approaches are content to argue the case for whether or not globalization exists or contest epochs of globalization or internationalization, poststructuralism argues that there is no reality other than that constructed through discourse, so, effectively, globalization is what we imagine and say it is. The ideational takes precedence over the material and 'what we *think* about globalization is more important than globalization itself' (Martell, 2010: 36).

Poststructuralists place greater emphasis on the signifier than what is signified. Foucault's studies of medical and psychiatric discourses, for example, posits that the gay or mad are such only by having been labelled as such; without the label the concept would not exist (Foucault, 1979). In similar vein, globalization exists not so much because of any material realities but because it is said to exist. Consciousness of globalization affects the way governments, businesses and individuals behave in the world. When neo-liberal discourses are ascendant then governments and businesses will act in a way consistent with the prevalent view of globalization, that of economic interdependency and international capital, multinational corporations and job flows. Martell suggests that it is 'constructions of globality [which] determine how we make sense of the world' (Martell, 2010: 37). Argument around the existence or otherwise of globalization in a world dominated by a globalization discourse that permeates every level of society in the television programmes we watch, newspapers we read, political speeches we listen to and the football teams we support.

The construction of a dominant discourse affords great power to those able to create the new truth. A dominant globalization discourse gains acceptance and credibility from those elites and masses who internalize it, creating a globalization paradigm that subordinates individual state actions to the demands of global capital in a 'globalized world'. Poststructuralists seek to reveal the nature of discourse in order to deconstruct those taken-for-granted assumptions about the nature of globalization or internationalization. In elevating discourse above material consideration, poststructuralists force us to reconsider and re-evaluate the familiar through interpreting how the prevalent view was constructed and for whose benefit.

Poststructuralists place a great deal of emphasis on the importance of 'ideas, agency, communication, contingency and normative change' (Held and McGrew, 2007: 6). Individual and collective agency is an essential component of creating discourse; poststructuralists identify how prevailing discourses have been constructed and adopt a normative approach about the sort of world that should exist rather than the one constructed using the prevailing globalization narrative. They reject a positivist epistemology that claims that a science of Politics is possible and desirable with an emphasis upon empirical observation and measurement. They reject the idea that facts and values can be separated;

Box 11.6   Poststructuralism, human rights and globalization

Poststructuralists approach human rights seeking to interpret the prevailing discourses on human rights rather than having a predetermined normative agenda. A cosmopolitan discourse on human rights and globalization would appeal to the universality of human rights and yet poststructuralists would look to contest the idea of universality. Poststructuralists would seek to discover the source of the prevailing narrative, examining the texts and subtexts which make up the globalization and human rights discourse. The discourse that claims that liberal economics and values are, or should be, universal would be contested, suggesting that economic liberalism uses human rights as a justification for Western expansionism. The universalist rhetoric that claims that free trade and open markets are indeed free and open, rather than unequal and operating in the interest of the rich and powerful, is open to contestation (Martell, 2010: 39). Poststructuralists would argue that Western governments advocate individual freedoms and rights as a precursor to freedom to exploit and dominate. Western values, presented as universal values, devalue collective rights and obligations in favour of an individualistic approach that resonates in the West but not necessarily in other parts of the world. In exposing the prevailing discourse poststructuralists hope to challenge approaches to human rights that favour individual over collective rights, although they do not offer their own narrative and alternative viewpoint on human rights and globalization.

indeed, there are no facts. They also reject a foundationalist ontology – that there is a real world out there; the only world out there is the one constructed in our consciousness through discourse. The powerful determine which discourse prevails and it is left to critique as a means to resist and contest the dominant paradigm.

Postmodern feminism and globalization

Some feminists see transformative potential in the process of globalization, with opportunities opening up for a transnational level of networks and solidarity movements linking feminists throughout the world and within states. Postmodern feminists, however, also see the problematic side of globalization, which can be seen as a masculinist discourse and construct that transposes patriarchal structures within the domestic polity into the international realm. In the same way that IR has been male-dominated and women made invisible, so – in considering globalization – feminists are eager to deconstruct the concept and examine its impact on women. World politics, dominated by realism, is constructed on masculine behaviour and experiences, essentializing how women see the world. This provides a very particular viewpoint, which when universalized through globalization contributes further to women's subjugation (Tickner, 1988).

Postmodern feminism, through its use of Derrida and Foucault's work on power and knowledge, recognizes that those who construct meaning and create knowledge gain power (Derrida, 1998; Foucault, 2002). In a worldwide social hierarchy, which privileges masculinist characteristics over female, gendered structures signify the unequal power relationship between male and female. The global economy, at the heart of globalization, for postmodern feminists, represents a gendered hierarchy that has its origins in seventeenth-century Europe when the needs of emergent capitalism produced a gendered division of labour. The construction of a private and public sphere suited the needs of capitalism and relegated women to the private sphere as 'housewives and mothers', while men were regarded as 'wage earners'. The gendered division of society mapped out different socially acceptable activities for men and women that continue today. Women and girls were regarded as naturally dexterous and nimble-fingered and therefore craft and needlework were not regarded as skilled work and wages were kept low. This marks the beginnings of the double burden of low paid employment and unpaid housework (Smith and Owens, 2008: 271).

In a globalized world, this gendered division of labour is perpetuated and encouraged. Among the key concepts of the global economy is the desirability or necessity of flexible labour forces and home working. For feminists, such terms are heavily laden with the implication for

Box 11.7   Postmodern feminism, human rights and globalization

Postmodern feminists approach human rights from the perspective of how much there is still to achieve and protect. While welcoming human rights conventions they have also pointed out that until comparatively recently human rights was a masculinist discourse. Declarations have tended to assume traditional gender roles and favour civil/political rights with an emphasis on activities within the public sphere. The private sphere, where many women are located, has been largely neglected, which often leaves women at the mercy of cultural and religious systems that would seek to curtail rights other women in the world might take for granted. Postmodern feminists critique both cosmopolitanism and communitarianism for different reasons. Cosmopolitanism, with its universalization of human rights, is seen as using human rights, and the rights of women in particular, as a continuation of a masculinist discourse that regards men as protectors and women as in need of safeguarding. Cosmopolitans use the issue of women's rights as a justification or legitimation for intervention in countries such as Iraq and Afghanistan. When it serves cosmopolitan's national interests to reach an accommodation with biddable political leaders in these countries concern for women's rights are soon forgotten.

Postmodern feminists also reveal the double standard of cosmopolitan concern for women's rights in hostile countries while enjoying close relationships with countries such as Saudi Arabia and Egypt with poor human rights records, especially regarding women. Communitarians are criticized by postmodernists who point out that women can suffer exclusion at the hands of local communities and are obliged to comply with gendered expectations (Linklater, 2008: 549). Postmodern feminists consider that the issue of women's human rights receives less attention than it deserves because of neo-realism's focus on the state and security and neo-liberalism's focus on international institutions and economics. For postmodern feminists, the transnational linkages between women's groups afforded by globalization do nonetheless represent a positive opportunity to offer support, encouragement and advice to advance women's rights from the grass roots.

women and girls of low wages, no benefits or job security, and terms and conditions that exclusively benefit the employer. When international relations specialists or economic theorists concentrate on the 'impersonal structures of states and markets, it is not possible to see how women's activities have been demoted to the "private" sphere'. Unpaid work is disregarded and not treated as economically significant and so women are further disregarded (Steans, 1998: 132–3). Women are at the bottom of socio-economic indicators in all societies, are disproportionately affected in times of recession and rewarded less than their male counterparts in times of relative prosperity. The 2006 UN Development Report revealed that 60 per cent of the world's poorest 1 billion people are female (UNDP, 2006: 20).

Nonetheless, globalization does provide opportunities of work for women that might not have been previously available. From this perspective any income is better than no income and can provide financial independence and raise status within patriarchal communities. While concentrating on inequalities and disadvantages to women in an era of globalization, feminists acknowledge these positive benefits. The tremendous growth in feminist NGOs and social movements facilitated by accessible travel and communications has led to the emergence of growing local, national and international women's movements and organizations across the world. Moves towards gender equality originate and are sustained by these organizations, forcing women's issues onto global agendas, including the UN and international financial institutions. Foreign assistance by leading industrialized countries targets resources specifically at issues highlighted by feminists and women's organizations.

Comparison of competing theories

Globalization is a concept that arouses strong feelings and very different approaches from denial, through scepticism to inevitability, acceptance and wholehearted embrace. The pace of change over the past two decades has been phenomenal. Whether it has been as revolutionary as the nineteenth century is a matter of dispute among the various theories we have considered. Those most enthusiastically embracing globalization are globalists who laud the virtues of the global village, the benefits of globalization such as free trade, global capital flows, instant communication and global connectedness. Old prejudices and loyalties can be replaced by new identities as global citizens with shared culture and understandings. For globalists the evidence is incontrovertible – the impact of globalization is felt everywhere in the world and it brings with it the capacity to improve the quality of all our lives. Neo-liberal institutionalists are making the shift towards a more globalist position but still insist on the importance of the state in a partially globalized world. They recognize thick networks of interdependence but affirm that states negotiate these. Neo-liberal institutionalists are increasingly concerned to improve governance and accountability among international institutions developed and sustained by the hegemonic state.

Critical theorists are highly critical of globalization; they identify a world that is becoming ever more homogeneous. A world in which Americanization and the dominance of the global North is destroying difference and diversity. An era where national states and sovereignty have lost currency and the global economy operates to the advantage of the rich while further weakening and alienating the poor, the majority of whom are women. In this scenario, little can be done to challenge the inexorable drive towards a neo-liberal international order serving the needs of global capitalism. Internationalists are also highly sceptical and consider that globalization is exaggerated, a social construct rather than an empirical reality. Indeed, they dispute the empirical evidence offered by globalists as simply misleading. The empirical evidence they prefer suggests that most activity is regional. The national state remains a key international actor and its willingness to acquiesce to global economic conformity is a political rather than an economic choice by those states. Internationalists point out that the nineteenth century was equally revolutionary in terms of liberal economics, transnational linkages and free trade, under a different hegemonic state, and that the 'globalization' era is but a continuation of the development of capitalism.

Poststructuralists are more concerned about the signifiers of globalization than any material reality of globalization itself. Once the globalization discourse has been assimilated then it becomes a reality as governments and business act as though globalization existed, thereby ensuring that globalization comes about. The idea of globalization has been constructed through a globalization narrative that few are unaffected by. Material factors such as economic expansion and the increase in multinational corporations all serve to reinforce the globalization discourse so that it becomes a self-fulfilling prophecy. Postmodern feminists are ambiguous about the benefits of globalization; while accepting the concept, they point out continuities with previous eras. In particular, the continuance of patriarchy and gendered inequality, and the invisibility of women is an ongoing challenge. In an increasingly interdependent global economy, those disproportionately adversely affected will be women. On the other hand globalization affords new opportunities for building women's movements across regions and globally. There exist new possibilities for non-state actors, NGOs and social movements to obtain an effective voice within international institutions highlighting gender issues.

Adjudicating between the different theories

When beginning to contemplate an analysis of globalization, we first need to reflect on the crucial issue of whether the concept is valid or not. If we are convinced by internationalist arguments that what is known as globalization is a continuation from earlier periods in the ongoing development of capitalism, then we will approach our research from this perspective, seeking out those continuities and reflecting on the extent of any changes. If, on the other hand, we consider that the evidence of globalization is all around us, then we might approach research in this area on the benefits and disadvantages of living in a globalized world. Globalist and neo-liberal institutional perspectives would provide us with the theoretical tools to do this. If we are convinced that globalization is a material reality but that it operates against the best interests of working people and the developing world then critical theory offers the potential to critically examine the benefits and disadvantages of glo balization. We might consider that the prevalence of the globalization narrative requires investigation and contestation as such poststructural approaches offer the potential to challenge the acceptance of the prevailing narrative and challenge claims of universal benefit. Postmodernist feminist approaches, on the other hand, will inspire us to re-examine the knowledge/power nexus and research the affects of globalization on women, redressing the balance of masculinist discourse.

Conclusion

Whether globalization is an empirical reality, a social construct, or a discourse, it remains a subject of vital importance to understanding our world, how we live, relate to others and are governed. The term 'globalization' is in common currency and widely used, even if it remains contested. As researchers, the theoretical approach we adopt towards globalization has great significance. The six theoretical positions discussed in this chapter are all strongly normative, despite foundational positivists' claims to the contrary, and tell different stories about the world we live in. Globalists accept the inexorable march towards global governance, capitalism and a weakening of the state and difference as a good thing, which will benefit all. Neo-liberal institutionalists are convinced of the ascendancy of the liberal democratic capitalist model in a globalized world.

Critical theorists accept globalization but see this as a disadvantageous to the poor and dispossessed. Internationalists accept the principles of hegemonic domination of the international system as a continuation of capitalism but are not prepared to write off the role of the state and other actors just yet. Poststructuralists and feminist postmodernists prefer to consider how dominant discourses became dominant and how they increase or perpetuate inequalities. All six theoretical approaches have resonance within politics and international relations. Poststructuralism, for example, is equally effective in understanding domestic and international perspectives on globalization. It is interesting to see that many of the academics involved in globalization are from traditional

Political Science and IR backgrounds and yet, rather than bring traditional perspectives to discussion of globalization, develop new perspectives breaking down the artificial barriers of two separate disciplines. As researchers, we can position ourselves within one of these streams or even seek to accommodate different perspectives. We also decide whether we want to report things as (we think the evidence suggests) they are, or whether we seek to use our research to shape how things should or could be.

Reflection

Which approach does the best job of explaining globalization and human rights?

Why do you think this is the case?

Do you think that human rights are universal?

What is your view of the claim that the universalization of human rights is a ruse to impose Western values in the developing world in order to advance capitalism?

Do dominant discourses shape understandings of human rights in such a way as to disadvantage women?

How can combining insights from Political Science and IR help us when analyzing globalization and human rights? What are the reasons for your answer?

Seminar activities

Look through a national newspaper and identify all the stories that represent aspects of globalization. Then discuss whether these represent significant changes from stories which could have been told in nineteenth-century Western Europe or the United States.

Debate whether international terrorism is a product of globalization and, if it is, what are the implications for individual states?

Divide the seminar group in two or more groups, depending on the size of the seminar. Hold a debate on the universality of human rights – groups should present a cosmopolitan or communitarian perspective. Further groups could represent a human rights group, a religious tradition or Asian values.

Which theoretical perspectives were represented in the debate and which were most convincing? Why do you think this was the case?

Chapter 12

Doing Your Own Political Science and International Relations

Introduction

Our aim in this book has been to illustrate that, whatever the political issue or problem, there are competing ways in which we can do our analysis. These are informed by assumptions that we make both prior to (as we outlined in Chapter 1) and during our analysis. The aim of this final chapter is to reflect upon this latter point and discuss some of these wider issues and concerns that we bring to our studies, both implicitly and explicitly, and irrespective of the framework we use, the approach we adopt, or the political questions we ask.

We begin the chapter by discussing the kind of questions that we might ask as political analysts. We then continue with an overview of some of the broader theoretical issues that we need to have a critical awareness of when undertaking our work. We suggest this critical aware-ness is a process, one which occurs both prior to and throughout the analysis that we undertake. We concur with Jørgensen (2010) that to use theory is to be active; theorizing is a verb, which requires engage-ment to be successful (Jørgensen, 2010: 207). This also can be extended to suggest that within the activity of theorizing we need to interact critically with a series of issues. We argue that, alongside the theories that we adopt (whether pre-existing, or our own, as Jørgensen [2010] demonstrates how to construct), we also need to consider a set of issues that are pertinent to the way in which we use the theories that we do.

The issues outlined below, we argue, are significant and of relevance whichever perspective or approach we adopt. As such, this chapter is set up differently from the previous chapters. Rather than highlight the division between the three 'worldviews' (as in the substantive chapters) the following issues, we argue, are of relevance every time we apply theory in our political analysis. One of our critiques of positivism is that it is less likely to overtly reflect upon the underlying assumptions which inform its theories. For us and the argument we put forward in this

267

book, every time we use theory in Political Science and IR, irrespective of its ontology and epistemology, we need to engage in some form of critical reflection. As such, the aim of this chapter is to reflect on some of the wider issues which are at stake when we apply our theories. These issues both inform and are informed by the questions that we ask and so it is to those questions that we first turn.

The questions we ask

We have argued throughout that the doing of Politics, political analysis, is the act of asking theoretically informed questions about what is, how we can know that and what could and/or should be. We can begin by dividing these questions into two types. The first type are positive questions, concerned to establish the nature of political reality, and ask 'what is' questions about political issues, events and processes (however widely defined). So we might ask: what does government look like? How does the shape of government influence policy? Why does social and economic inequality exist, both globally and domestically? What can we do to protect the environment? Why do we have the political processes that we do? Why do states go to war? How can we achieve a more equal society? Is it possible to change the existing social order? Underpinning these positive questions is a concern with power: who has power or where is it located? How is it exercised? In whose interests does it operate? What are its effects? How can we effect its transformation?

The other kinds of questions are normative, and concerned with what *should* be. What should a good society look like? How should we achieve a just society and what form should that just society take? How should we distribute scare resources? What is the proper role of the state and government? What should an equal society look like? For example, is it just to distribute scarce resources by lottery (Goodwin, 2005)? How do we establish the limits and boundaries to our personal responsibility and that of the state (Brown, 2009)? How can we tackle the problems posed by the environment to ensure just outcomes for current and future generations (Page, 1999; 2007)? Can principles of distributive justice be applied to all human beings in the world irrespective of nation-state borders (for review see Caney, 2001) or physical ability (see Handley, 2003)? Normative political theory provides a vast array of philosophical discussion around a wide range of moral, ethical and political issues. It also 'aims to explain, justify or criticize the disposition of power in society' (Goodwin, 2007: 4). Normative theory enables us to reflect on some of the underlying ideas which inform society. It is critical as it enables us to discuss competing arguments and responses to particular ideas or arguments. It enables us to assess the merit of a particular idea and is also used, like other critical approaches, to enable us to think about how the world could be and 'rests on the ability to escape from the existent' (Goodwin, 2007:4). In short, it enables us to reflect upon what is a good and/or right way to live, and within that reflection is an assumption that change is possible.

The theories that we have used in this book initially seem to be driven by the first set of positive questions outlined above. We argue that before we ask those questions we are making a series of assumptions about how we might go about answering them, and our aim here has been to show how the differing assumptions that we make can lead to differing outcomes and forms of analysis. We would argue, however, that all our theoretical positions have a normative edge. Some are explicit about their normative aims such as the critical approaches to policy, security and media that we have seen in earlier chapters. Others make implicit normative assumptions, such as the equality which is assumed to flow from markets implied within liberal accounts. Even foundational positivists adopt normative positions, although they may be less willing to acknowledge them as such. The IR realist, for example, in reifying the state, takes a normative position that the interests of states are more important and implicitly reinforce the view that they are of more value than those of the individual. The positivist's normative position, albeit hidden, is often an endorsement of the status quo rather than a dispassionate empirical observation of what the positivist considers significant. We also need to be aware of some of those normative suppositions which inform our work. This integration forms the basis of this chapter.

We now turn to reflect on some of the theoretical issues which inform our analysis and briefly discuss the role of: ideology and theory; history; natural and social science; structure and agency; the material and ideational; and dualisms. We then proceed with a very brief overview of some of the key concerns from normative theory: equality and justice. Our argument is that when we do political analysis we begin with a series of normative and positive assumptions, not only about what is real, and how we can know about it, but what that reality should look like. The theories that we use reflect our assumptions, and our aim in this final chapter is to highlight that we need to be aware of the assumptions that we make, and the questions that we need to reflect critically upon when we 'do' Political Science and IR.

Theoretical concerns

Ideology and theory

The theory that we use is not neutral, and represents ideological positions and beliefs (which are sometimes implicit). It is useful to be conscious of these, so that we can maintain a critical awareness of the interests that are represented in the approaches that we adopt. As we noted in Chapter 2, one of the key insights Robert Cox provided was that '[t]heory is always *for* someone and *for* some purpose' (1981: 128, emphasis added). What this statement illustrates is that theory itself is not value-free, and that each theoretical framework also contains ideological assumptions (as well as epistemological and ontological assumptions). So, when we adopt a particular theory, we also need to think about the underlying ideological agenda and suppositions which inform it. For example, rational choice theory/public choice largely embodies neo-conservative/neo-liberal/new right political values. One way in which these are evident is through its making implicit assumptions about the appropriate role of the market in relation to politics and society (which fits with the neo-liberal/new right/neo-conservative 'free market' agenda).

Not only does theory contain ideological assumptions, but it also has differing applications. For some, theory is about problem solving, and the idea of theory as a method of solving problems adheres arguably to the empiricist and, as we have used it, positivist view of the world. Theory from this perspective looks at the world as 'it is' (making onto-logical assumptions that there is a world out there awaiting discovery, and available to observation). It concentrates on how problems can be solved and issues addressed within the existing system. Within this approach (which is usually associated with positivism), not only is there an acceptance of the status quo, but also this is reinforced both through the act of the usage of the theory and the uncritical acceptance of its assumptions and aims.

Positivism lays claim to being able to stand outside a situation, to set aside personal opinion and values, and dispassionately and fairly allow the evidence to speak for itself. It identifies facts rather than opinions and is concerned to discover knowable truth. Positivism has dominated both Politics and IR for much of its shared history because it offers a straightforward approach to the discipline that is easily understood by practitioners, students and the man or woman in the street. It makes expansive claims to problem solving and, in identifying how the present system works, enables politicians and policy advisors to use their evidence to make policy decisions. Quantitative evidence enables policy-makers and citizens to make comparisons over time and statistical evidence appears far more impressive than ideological contestation to politicians and other policy-makers who have to be seen to be effective.

In contrast, for critical theorists, theory is a mechanism through which challenges to the status quo can bring about social change; therefore theory plays a potentially transformative role. Critical approaches take a step back, and ask how the status quo came into existence, and what could be done to change it and make it better? For example, Cox's (2002) work was underpinned by questions such as: how can a global system function in a hegemonic way? How can we create a system of humane governance? His work is supported by the concern of how we might make the international order more egalitarian and sustainable; in short, how to change it. Critical perspectives claim emancipatory potential through rendering explicit the dominant power mechanisms, through which we are afforded the opportunity to both challenge and change them.

Within critical accounts we also have the capacity to problematize. Through problematizing an issue we can see alternative positions, outcomes, solutions and possibilities for change (rather than the singular outcome suggested by problem-solving approaches). It should be noted that neither positivist nor critical accounts as discussed here are able to tell us how successful a particular theory has been in achieving its aim. However, there is a stark contrast between the way in which each approach uses theory and, as O'Brien and Williams astutely observe, 'Problem-solving theory is about managing the system and critical theory is about changing the system' (2010: 43).

The way in which we might reflect upon our use of theory or approach could be encapsulated in the following questions. What are the underlying assumptions or the approach/theory? Whose interests are represented? Does the theory/approach that we use reinforce the status quo or provide us with opportunities to challenge it? Do we choose the worldview on the basis of normative implications, or vice versa?

History

A behavioural defence of the role of history as a method of analysis is provided by Gaddis, who argues against the scientific turn and in defence of the role of history in IR (1996). He, like many others of this view, suggests that the methods of science are simply inappropriate for the study of human behaviour. Reflecting this wider debate of the appropriateness of scientific method (see Chapter 1), he argues that our analysis is of human behaviour, the essential features of which are contingency and subjectivity. As such, this is incompatible with the methods of the natural sciences which emphasize measurement, modelling and objectivity. Within this school of thought, history then provides for rich description of behaviour over a period of time. However, as is noted below, this description and approach is imbued with an acceptance of the status quo, it is often conservative – serving to describe and reinforce, rather than challenge and offer possibilities for emancipation.

For critical theorists, social (and political) phenomena must always be understood in their historical context. For Alvesson and Sköldberg, this means that 'realized patterns must be understood in terms of negation, on a basis of their own opposite and of the possibility of social conditions of a qualitatively different kind' (2000: 110). That is to say, the emancipatory potential of critical approaches lies in their ability to contest the basis of the existing order and reflect upon the possibility of alternatives. For critical theories history is at the centre of explanation and where meaning is located. We can only understand an event or phenomenon through reference to its historical context and situation. For Marxists this historicism is located in material conditions (hence historical materialism). It is through recourse to history that we can understand particular phenomena, so, for example, explanation of the exploitation of the South/developing world, would need to account for the historical imperialism of the North/West. It should be noted that historical and empirical approaches are inherently conservative in the absence of theory.

History also matters in the sense that it detracts from the possibility of universalizing assumptions which hold true across space, time and cultures. Norton (2010) provides a compelling account of the role of history in political analysis. She suggests that traditional understandings of history are linear, unidirectional and unidimensional. For her history is none of these things; she argues history is both multidirectional and multidimensional. Rather than being linear it is an interactive process, history is constructed and reconstructed through its articulation. In order to understand the present we need to understand how the past was constructed and this particular construction influences not only the present but also the future. Indeed, her approach suggests that all knowledge is contingent and that we cannot draw easy lessons from history. She argues in favour of cyclic views of history which 'recognize that a given historical moment is close in time to those moments that precede and follow it, but it is also close to those times whose attributes mirror its own' (Norton, 2010: 346). In this way temporal proximity is less significant than the event or the understanding of the event and its relevance to contemporary and future events.

Norton also draws attention to the inherently political nature of the construction of history. She argues that the conventional method of understanding history through the imposition of temporal boundaries (rather than cyclically) not only limits what we can know, but also serves to reinforce existing political orders and orthodoxies (Norton, 2010: 348). In this perspective, the critical reflection upon history and the way in which we use history in our analysis has the capacity to be emancipatory, rather than simply descriptive of the prevailing order.

When we are considering the role that history plays in our analysis, we might reflect upon the following questions. How are we using history?

Are we describing historical events, rather than scientifically measuring phenomena? Do we need to use history in order to explain why particular events occurred? Does the existence of a particular history lead to a path-dependent outcome? Is only one reading of history available to us? Do we accept a singular reading of history? Or does this singular reading simply reinforce the status quo and existing power relationships?

Natural and social science

The discussion about the relationship between natural and social science, and the appropriateness of methods and assumptions, is one which has characterized debates within the social sciences for generations. Here we argue that it is not a debate that demands a unifying solution. Rather, for us, the existence of this debate is healthy; it enables us to problematize and reflect upon the theories and approaches that we adopt, and the claims that we can make as a consequence. As we detailed in Chapter 1, debate around what constitutes knowledge is often organized through reference to the natural sciences. How far are the methods and assumptions of natural sciences appropriate to political analysis? This question underpins our thinking about how we can access and gain knowledge about political life. The discussion of the appropriateness of science in social science is widely debated and contested and it is not our aim here to engage more widely in that discussion (not least as it has been so comprehensively done elsewhere; for example, an eloquent discussion is provided by Moses and Knutsen [2007]). However, this debate does inform and shed light on the way in which we might approach our analysis, and this is structured around metaphysical discussions about ontology and epistemology.

The kind of ontological questions we might ask centre around: what does political reality and political life look like? What is its character? Is it characterized by complexity and choice? Or is it consistent? Does political life contain the traits of nature? Our answers to these both influence and are influenced by our assumptions about how we can find out about the character of political reality, and what we can know about it. Our reflections on how we can know about political reality, as we discussed in Chapter 1, are epistemological and take the form of what kind of knowledge then might be possible? Is political knowledge always quantifiable, through the use of statistics, for example? Can we establish regularities and make causal claims about behaviour in the political world? Is our knowledge contingent on a series of ideological, historically situated and culturally specific interactions and meanings? However, when we address these issues our work is also informed by a series of normative questions. What purpose does our research serve, who will it benefit? Who should benefit? What values should guide our work? Underpinning our work, then, are three key questions, as Kasza succinctly puts it: 'what is out there, what can we know about it and why should we want to?' (2006: 223).

Structure/agency

In Chapter 1 we discussed the importance of the relationship between structures and agents in the theoretical analysis that we use, and here we reflect briefly on the kind of issues this debate problematizes for us. We notice that, in the accounts we use, one or the other tends to be privileged. So, for example, if we are using a critical account, we might draw attention to the historical structures which shape outcomes. This suggests a certain path dependency: given those particular structures was any other course of action available? How then do we account for individuals and their capacity to exhibit agency and effect change within those structures? Marx suggested, 'Men make their own history, but they do not make it as they please; they do not make it under self-selected circumstance, but under circumstances existing already, given and transmitted from the past' (1852/2008: 15). Marx acknowledges the role of individuals, although they have limited autonomy, constrained as they are by the historically developed structures in which they find themselves in the present. Althusser later extended this notion of structuralism, arguing that individuals were merely bearers of structural roles: *trager*. In contrast, some of the accounts we have explored highlight the autonomy of agents (either individual people or individual states). Rational choice accounts, for example, assume that agents are unconstrained by their environment; indeed, in rational/public choice accounts they are completely divorced from their context. Behaviouralist accounts will observe the behaviour of agents and how they interact with and influence structure.

What we see, then, are accounts which privilege structures as driving the behaviour of agents, or agents privileged over structures. What we need to reflect upon when we do our own analysis is: how far do we accept these deterministic assumptions? How far do we think individuals have little opportunity to act beyond the structures that they find themselves in? Are structures self-referential and self-reinforcing? Is it possible for individuals to change structures? Does this mean that to effect change we have to change structures before individuals? Should we simply consider the actions of the individual? How far do we think that individuals can be separated, analytically or ontologically, from their context? Should we explore the way that actions have the potential to reinforce and reconstitute structures?

Material and ideational

A further aspect that we need to reflect upon is the role that ideas play in our analysis. For some behavioural accounts ideas simply do not matter, the material environment is all that we need to observe and describe. As we have seen, however, other behavioural accounts, and some rational choice approaches, admit the role of ideas into the analysis. In this way culture and/or norms become 'variables'. These are aspects of political life that can be described and measured, with little consideration of where these beliefs and values come from. In rationalist accounts, individualist ontologies mean that theorists can only see ideas as tools to enable rational actors to achieve their goals. 'Ideas were produced *by* individuals, therefore ideas could not be seen as constitutive *of* individuals without making the theory incoherent' (Blyth, 2002: 309, original emphasis). Here then ideas are functional devices and pre-existing rather than constructed and created. Individuals exist prior to ideas, and ideas are something which individuals can choose or discard as befits their aims. In this way, rationalist and behavioural accounts may admit ideas exist, but not be concerned with how they came to be created or their content.

In contrast, and as has been noted throughout, constructivist accounts highlight the importance of understanding how norms and values are shaped; indeed, ideas can play an independent role in analysis. For behaviouralists, where ideas are part of analysis they are treated as measurable variables. For constructivists, however, ideas can structure and shape outcomes (Finnemore and Sikkink, 1998). How are ideas framed and how do they become embedded? How do they form part of our identities? Can ideas exert independent and causal influence (see Hay, 2002: 194–215)? For Marxists, ideas take the form of ideology which is located within and generated by material conditions. In contrast to individualist accounts above, ideas in Marxist accounts come prior to individuals and can influence and shape an individual's preferences. Therefore, when dominant ideas change, preferences will change. These dominant ideas, however, are rooted in a material base. Therefore, for Marxists accounts, change in the material base will change ideas and ideology, and in turn this will change the preferences of an individual.

One of the issues that we need to reflect upon is the role of ideas. Just how important are they in our analysis? Are they predetermined in terms of which actors can pick and choose at will? Are they something which can be measured as an influential variable? Or do they inform preferences and shape the way in which we behave? Do we need to understand the content of ideas and how this content came to be in order to make sense of the political world? Can ideas play an independent causal role in analysis?

Dualisms and the use of theoretical models

We have presented above a series of dualisms about the way in which we tend to think about and categorize issues which are pertinent to our theoretical reflection and application. The Enlightenment produced the notion of Cartesian dualisms, and they tend to inform our thinking today. The idea behind the Cartesian mind/body distinction has continued to structure the way in which we view the world when we consider, for example, subjectivity/objectivity; structures/agents; male/female; facts/values; nature/society.

However, do we need to accept that the world is structured in this dualistic way? Is it possible to transcend these dualisms and, in turn, alter the way in which we see the world? We argue that the existence of these theoretical dualisms performs a particular function for theory. That is, they perform a modelling function; a way in which we can simplify and understand the world. However, once we have simplified it, in order to understand it, we can then use these dualisms as a starting point from which to problematize the world. So, rather than accept these categories as definitive descriptions of reality, we need to be aware that what they are actually doing is providing a simplification of reality, rather than an accurate representation. It is important, then, to be critically aware of how we use these dualisms and definitions; they are not empty categories or signifiers (cf. Laclau and Mouffe, 1987). If we engage more critically with these dualisms we highlight the ability of theory to problematize. Problematization then provides us not only the opportunity for solutions, but also invites us to consider and reflect upon what we know. Is it possible to do things differently? Would they be better as a result?

This discussion leads on to a secondary concern about the way in which we conduct our analysis and we can reflect on this through asking the question: is it possible to separate these issue – analytically, ontologically and normatively? If we separate issues analytically, this provides us with a means to simplify and abstract from reality. However, this does not necessarily mean that an issue can be ontologically separated. For example, we may be able to analytically separate the role of world leaders in discussions about poverty. We may be able to focus simply upon them, their actions and their discussion and our analysis may draw attention simply to the discussion that they have. Yet in 'reality' these leaders come with different political baggage and issues and concerns which will shape their response to the issue. Therefore, while some theoretical frames may enable us to extract the leaders from their context, analyze their behaviour and make predictions about what they are likely to do, it is important not to mistake this analytically simplified view of the world for reality. Analytical simplifications are used to break down political phenomena into manageable units of analysis. Theoretical frameworks function as Weberian 'ideal types', to abstract from and simplify reality. In this way analytic variables are separable from their ontological basis. This separation of analytical variables from ontological ones is possible for the purposes of simplification, generalization and possibilities to explore alternative forms of action.

As we discuss below, our approach to political analysis is premised upon the assumption that we need to be aware of normative issues when reflecting upon the implications of our theoretical approach. We argue that, while analytic separation is possible, it is not possible to separate normative beliefs and values from that which we study. Some of those normative beliefs are centred around the role that theory plays in our analysis: as a means to describe or change the world. Other normative beliefs can be focused around a more overt political agenda and can be framed in terms of 'left' or 'right' – assigning us a place upon the political spectrum. Irrespective of where we are located on that spectrum, all political analysis is underpinned, be that explicitly or implicitly, with concerns about the roles of equality and justice in society, and it is to these two concepts that we now briefly turn.

Equality

The issue of equality is one of the most central in political thought. While early accounts assumed a natural order or a hierarchy within societies, modern political thought recognizes that all human beings have equal moral worth. This assumption has been reflected, for example, in international legislation such as the Universal Declaration of Human Rights (1948), but what exactly is meant by equality? Across the political spectrum those on the left and the right have accepted the need to address the issue of equality; indeed, it would be highly unlikely that we would hear a politician publicly and explicitly renounce equality. However, actions of politicians are reflective of a wider debate about what equality is. Equality has very different meanings to the left and the right, so in turn we see very different political objectives and outcomes all in the name of equality.

The distinction between opportunity and outcome is one aspect of the equality debate, but how do we achieve this equality? For those on the left, the state has a key role to play in society, and one of the aims of the state is to ensure the level playing field through, for example, the provision of a universal education. For those on the right, the market is the mechanism through which equality is achieved. According to theorists on the right, all are equal at the point of entry into the market; equality here would mean equality of access to the market. What these neglect, however, is that not all have access to markets in the first instance, nor are all equal once they enter the market (i.e., some can afford to pay more than others).

For example, the introduction of markets into education means that, for those on the right, all 'consumers' in this market (i.e., students) are empowered through the provision of choice. Students can choose which schools they go to, either those which are privately funded or those provided by the state. In this view the market can and should provide. The role of the state is to regulate the market. Equality, for the right, is assumed because the supposition is made that all are equal within the marketplace. This equality, however, is reliant upon the capacity of an individual to gain entry to the marketplace in the first instance. Yet, as Irvin observes 'the notion of equal opportunity cannot be reduced to merely legislating against unequal access, unequal treatment before the law ... and so on. If equal opportunity is desired, then ... the means of access must be provided' (2008: 200). Private education is available not to all, but to those who have sufficient levels of income. And so it is only those who can afford to pay fees who are able to enter the market; equality of opportunity to access the market is premised upon a particular pre-existing level of income. For critics on the left the idea of markets in education has served to reinforce existing societal divisions. This has also led to inequalities of outcome, whereby students from privately funded schools ultimately have better life opportunities than those from state-funded schools (cf. Barry, 2005).

Another way in which we might reflect upon equality is through the notion of equal rights. This is a kind of formal equality; equality enshrined in legislation and protected by law. This has its roots in contract theories such as those of John Locke, who argued that all men (sic) were born equal and vested with a set of natural rights (1689/1965). Yet in this statement what role is there for women's rights? The discussion of rights in terms of men, rather than human rights, served to construct gender and reinforce gender divisions within society. These were first challenged by Wollstonecraft (1792/1993) who claimed equal rights for women on the basis of 'personhood' rather than sex. The continuing struggle for equal rights across humanity is not bound only to gender. It extends to race and class. While legislation may exist prohibiting race and gender discrimination, this does not necessarily counter learned cultural behaviour, nor does it address the consequences of economic and social disadvantages which racial minority groups and women may suffer. It is also worth noting that the exploitation of classes remains also unaddressed in domestic legislation and is constructed as largely the remit of trades unions, not the state.

The approaches we have identified in this book make assumptions about equality, which we can categorize very broadly in two ways. First, rationalist accounts tend largely to neglect explicit discussion about the issue of equality. Either it is a variable in analysis, or it is assumed to be implicitly achieved through the market (as above). For critical accounts, the issue of equality is crucial and often explicitly informs analysis. Achievement of equality takes the form not only of the legislation of equality, but also equality in all areas of life, both public and private; domestic and international. For critical accounts, revision of existing structures provides the route to emancipation and subsequent equality.

The issue of equality then is one which underpins much of the work that we do, whether that is implicitly or explicitly. Liberal accounts tend to assume that equality can be achieved via the use of market mechanisms, and we have seen this belief in the supremacy of the market as a mechanism for providing social solutions in the rationalist, realist and liberal institutionalist accounts that we have used. In contrast, critical accounts will draw attention to the role of markets as a cause of inequality, not a solution to it. This snapshot of the debate around equality, then, serves as a reminder that assumptions that are made more widely about the role of states and markets in society are embedded with assumptions about equality, what it is and how it may be achieved or hindered. Thus, we need to reflect upon the assumptions we are making: what does the approach we are using assume about equality? How does it aim to achieve equality?

Justice

The other key issue which underpins political analysis is a concern with justice. What does a just society look like? How can we establish what is just or unjust? Is justice the property of individuals? Is it a feature of situations? Is it located in rules, regulations and social norms which bring about particular outcomes? While justice may be enshrined in constitutions and legislation, it also features in social norms; we might say something is unfair or unjust, not because we know the legislation which prohibits this action or situation, but because we have a sense of justice and equality in the norms and values which influence and guide our behaviour. In society, we would need to think about the principles which underpin how justice is distributed, which can be either equally or unequally.

Egalitarian theories of justice would suggest that each individual in society deserves to be treated equally and rest on principles of equality. In contrast, merit-based approaches to justice suggest that justice should be linked to either an individual's talents or their contribution to society. This notion of justice based on contribution is a fundamental feature of liberal theory, and based upon notions of equality of opportunity.

A third way in which justice is conceived of is on the basis of need. Marx's famous dictum 'from each according to his (sic) ability, to each according to his needs' suggests that all have a set of needs that should be met, irrespective of merit. This can be linked to the idea of equality of outcome as noted above. There are tensions both between and within these ways of conceiving of justice, as needs based; based on merit; or equality (an excellent overview is provided in Goodwin, 2007: 397–424).

An example may illustrate the point. Income differentials between those at the top and those at the bottom of society have dramatically increased over the last 20 years. In the US the top 20 per cent of earners, received more than half the national income, with the top 1 per cent receiving 14 per cent. At the same time, the bottom fifth received only 5 per cent (Irvin, 2008: 16–17). Those who offer a merit-based account might argue that those at the top have illustrated their worth through the contribution that they make to society – for example, through the provision of jobs and through income into the economy. Financial gains in this view are therefore justly received. What is interesting to note, when reflecting upon the merit-based accounts highlighted above, is the way in which contemporary society has seen merit as located within the generation of wealth (which implies economic determinism). Societal contribution is defined primarily through an individual's financial position. We can see this because of the rewards that are given: top rates of income tax have massively decreased across the world; for example, in 1980 the top income tax rates in Australia, the UK and the US were 63 per cent, 83 per cent and 70 per cent respectively. In 2004, these top rates had been reduced to 47 per cent, 40 per cent and 35 per cent (again, respectively) (Irvin, 2008: 21, 26–7).

This also illustrates the way in which, in Western liberal capitalism, wealth creation is prized as a societal contribution. The benefits to society from greater levels of taxation on the super-rich may come in the form of collective goods such as health and education. However, the reduction in tax rates for those on top incomes sends the message that individual wealth creation is more important than the social goods that may flow from higher rates of taxation. The increasing under-investment in public services, and the high level of public service provision now needed, means that, for Barry, 'countries such as Britain and the United States might be unable to afford social justice' (2005: 217) in their present situation. As the wealthy increasingly use private services, instead of contributing to public goods, the 'trickledown' effect of economic growth simply does not materialize. In the neo-liberal political agenda, informed by merit-based conceptions of justice, growth and redistribution are treated as incompatible, whereas for egalitarian conceptions of justice they are complementary.

Critics of merit-based justice, might also argue that those at the top have not got to their position simply through their own merit and talent, but have relied upon the labour of his or her employees and as such some of the benefits of the accrued wealth should be redistributed back to them and, as society has provided the conditions in which this wealth accumulation can take place (for example, the educational infrastructure and healthcare provision), then it would be just, according to egalitarian views of justice, that benefits were redistributed to society.

Historically, the idea of merit played a progressive role, challenging the assumption that people were entitled to their place in society, whether rich or poor. However, more recently, merit has become interpreted as contribution, and so the conception of justice rests, in this view, on the idea that those who contribute more deserve more (Goodwin, 2007: 400). Young (1958/1973) satirized this in the term 'meritocracy', which was meant as a critique of this conception of justice, reliant as it was upon unequal access to resources and inequalities of opportunities. Yet in contemporary society, and certainly in the UK, paradoxically, it has become an ideal to aspire to. 'New' Labour espoused the desire to achieve a meritocracy, but this was based very narrowly on wealth creation, not rooted in ideals of equality of opportunity. A significant outcome of this merit-based approach has been an increase in the differentials between the very rich and the very poor and a decline in social mobility (Barry, 2005; Irvin, 2008: 62–82).

Issues of justice are not only the preserve of the internal mechanisms of states. Justice and issues related to the structural inequalities of wealth, and the just mechanisms of its redistribution, are also clearly significant in the international arena. To reflect upon justice as only identifiable through economic measurements such as GDP and wealth indicators is only one part of the story. Staggering levels of economic inequality have other impacts and affect populations' or communities' health; welfare; ability to use their own natural resources and resist exploitation (among other things). Forty per cent of the world's population live on less than $2 a day, accounting for 5 per cent of global income, while the richest 20 per cent account for 75 per cent of global income. Millions of children live without adequate food or shelter, and in 2006 over 26,000 children died every day. The majority of these deaths occur in 60 countries in the developing world (all figures from Smits, 2009: 189).

More recent political thought has also drawn attention to the issue of intergenerational justice and the way in which we need to balance the demands of present generations around the needs of future generations. This underpins particularly the work in relation to the environment. It is interrelated to the concept of sustainability, which argues that we should look for ways to live sustainably, not only in order to meet our own needs, but to recognize and meet those of future generations. In this way not only does the notion of justice transcend nation-state boundaries, the site where justice is traditionally assumed to be enacted (see Caney, 2001, for an excellent review), but it also transcends temporal boundaries. That is, we need to consider future generations and the impact of our behaviour upon them. Thus we need to consider future histories. As Norton (2010) suggests, if the future affects the present, and the relationship is cyclical rather than linear, this then enables us to reflect upon an awareness of the needs of future generations, which in turn impacts upon what we conceive of as just today.

Considerations of justice underpin all of the theories that we have looked at within this book, whether implicitly or explicitly. Rationalist accounts, for example, assume that markets provide for the most equal distribution of goods and, as such, provide a just way in which society can be achieved. Critical accounts emphasize the distributive aspect of justice, arguing in favour of a redistribution of wealth. In this perspective markets are not the solution for the provision of all social goods. Rather markets can be seen as emblematic of the structural inequalities which underpin the existing system. For critical accounts, these fundamental structural inequalities need to be addressed in order that a more just society can be achieved.

The integration of normative theory and positive approaches

Our contention here is that normative theory and positive theoretical positions are intimately interlinked. The assumptions that we make about what a just society should look like, what an equal society should look like invariably inform the theories that we choose when we do our analysis. For some, theory should be separate from the real world of politics, and is used to explore 'what if' questions, rather than to provide directives to policy-makers. Nardin, in a discussion of what it means to be a theorist of justice, argues that 'the aim of the theorist of international justice ... is not to prescribe policy; it is to clarify and make coherent the meaning of international justice in an international context' (2006: 449). That is, theory, in this view, is separate from the 'real world' that it analyzes and, rather than pursue a normative agenda, it should simply shed light on that which it defines as a political issue.

For critical theories, however, the function of theorizing is integrated with a political agenda of social change. For example, as we saw in Chapter 10, ecofeminism is both positive and normative. Ecofeminists shed light on the political sites of exploitation, but also provide the opportunities to reflect on the possibility of social change. This particular perspective suggests that the integration of positive and normative theory is emancipatory for those who adopt it.

Our argument is that all theory has a normative aspect to it – in terms of the way in which theory is used and the political values it espouses. This may be explicitly stated (as with some critical theories) or implicit (as we have seen with some empirical theories, such as pluralism, for example). As our discussion above suggests, those who advocate a problem-solving role to theory normatively are suggesting that the system as it functions is working, needs no real change. Moreover, this also implies that the way in which issues of equality and justice are dealt with within the system are also adequate. In contrast, critical accounts are normative in their advocacy of systemic change and the emancipatory potential of their theories as routes to achieve justice and equality.

Some of the theoretical approaches we have explored within the book account for the role of ideas, norms and values in analysis. Constructivist accounts have explored how those norms, values and belief systems emerge and what ideas they contain and how they become embedded. What normative political theory enables us to do is to reflect upon the rightness, or justness of those ideas. As Weale elegantly argues, 'we need to consider the *merits* of political principles and arguments in politics as well as the *influence* of traditions of political thought and culture' (2010: 268, original emphasis). Integrating and recognizing the role of normative theory and the kind of questions normative theorists might ask enables us to reflect more explicitly upon what the theory we are using is seeking to achieve. What are its underlying goals and aims? Are they ends or objectives that are 'good', or just? Do they lead to greater equality?

Conclusion

Our primary objective in this book has been to argue in favour of critical reflection upon the way in which we carry out political analysis. One of the tools that we use to do this is theory, but theory is not neutral. Our theories, approaches and analysis are all informed by a series of assumptions and ideological suppositions, which we need to critically appraise when we engage in the study of politics. Theory, whether of a Political Science or IR background, can be used to provide universalizing generalizations, or in opposition to challenge and deconstruct grand overarching narratives. It can be used to reinforce or to oppose the status quo. It can be used to reaffirm stability, or it can be a mechanism for social change. As we have emphasized throughout, we accept that there is more than one way to 'do' Politics. We have suggested that the divisions between Political Science and IR have been constructed around substantive topics, around content, and that these can be somewhat limiting. We have also suggested that each substantive topic can be analyzed in different ways, and these differences are, for us, methodological, not disciplinary. We have sought to reflect our concern with these twin issues through our presentation of competing theoretical positions within each of the substantive topics we have discussed. For some, the way in which we 'do' our political analysis revolves around the empirical methods that we adopt (such as discourse analysis, or surveys) (for comprehensive treatment, see Burnham *et al.*, 2004; Bryman, 2008). However, we argue that preceding these empirical methods must be a consideration of how we theorize and understand our topic and the kind of questions we might ask when we undertake our study.

We argue that using theory is not simply about mapping a framework onto a topic of analysis. We need to reflect upon a number of issues. Why are we using the theory that we are? What are its underlying assumptions? What does it assume about reality and all we can know about it? What ideological assumptions are embedded in the theory? Will the analysis lead to better (e.g., more socially just or equal) outcomes? Can we use the theory to effect or consider the possibility of change? Or do we wish to assume objectivity and use empirical data to record our observations, allowing others to put our research to use? So it is that when we come to begin our analysis we make a series of theoretical assumptions about what issue, event or question is a legitimate area of study, and about how we might go about our analysis. While these are big questions, and ones which we may not be able to provide a definitive answer to, they are still issues that we need to reflect upon. We also make a series of normative and theoretical assumptions and it is these assumptions that we make both prior to and throughout the analysis that we do, which we discuss within this chapter. A critical awareness of these underlying issues means that we should be able to turn our attention to any theoretical framework and appraise its suitability for the political analysis that we seek to do.

Our aim in this book has been to highlight some of the different ways in which we might use theory and the different issues we need to consider when we do political analysis. We have sought to discuss not only the theories themselves but also the way in which we use them. We recognize there are complexities within each of the theories and approaches that we have presented here, all of which are subject to internal and external critique, but we have aimed simply to provide a starting point. We have also sought to illustrate some of the broader analytical issues which underpin the theories and approaches that we use, and to high-light the different ways in which we can use theory. For some, the aim is to describe, measure and quantify the political world, so that we can make predictions, produce universalizing narratives and laws, and make generalizable claims about politics. For others, theory is used to high-light the contingent nature of political reality and provides a mechanism to critique the status quo and reflect upon possibilities to effect social change. We have aimed to illustrate that we make a series of choices and assumptions when we 'do' political analysis. It is those choices and assumptions which we hope to encourage a critical reflection upon when you do your own Political Science and International Relations.

Bibliography

Acker, J. (1988) 'Class, Gender and the Relations of Distribution', *Journal of Women in Culture and Society*, 13(3), 473–97.

Adams, C. J. (ed.) (1993) *Ecofeminism and the Sacred*. New York, NY: Continuum.

Adcock, R. and Bevir, M. (2005) 'The History of Political Science', *Political Studies Review*, 3, 1–16.

Adger, N. (2001) 'Scales of Governance and Environmental Justice for Adaptation and Mitigation of Climate Change', *Journal of International Development*, 13, 921–31.

Adler, E. (1992) 'The Emergence of Cooperation: National Epistemic Communities and the International Evolution of the Idea of Nuclear Arms Control', *International Organization*, 46 (Winter), 101–45.

Adler, E. and Barnett, M. (1988) 'Security Communities in Theoretical Perspective', in E. Adler and M. Barnett (eds), *Security Communities*. Cambridge: Cambridge University Press.

Agger, B. (1991) 'Critical Theory, Poststructuralism, Postmodernism: Their Sociological Relevance', *Annual Review of Sociology*, 17, 105–31.

Agius, C. (2010) 'Social Constructivism', in A. Collins (ed.), *Contemporary Security Studies*. Oxford: Oxford University Press.

Allison, G. (1971) *The Essence of Decision: Explaining the Cuban Missile Crisis*. Boston: Little, Brown.

Almond, G. (1988) 'Separate Tables: Schools and Sects in Political Science', *Political Science and Politics*, 21(4), 828–42.

Althusser, L. (1967) *For Marx*, trans. Ben Brewster. Harmondsworth: Penguin.

—— (1969) *Essays in Self Criticism*, trans. G. Locke. London: New Left.

Alvesson, M. and Sköldberg, K. (2000) *Reflexive Methodology: New Vistas for Qualitative Research*. London: Sage.

Anand, R. (2004) *Environmental Justice: A North–South Dimension*. Aldershot: Ashgate.

Anderegg, W., Prall, J., Harold, J. and Schneider, S. (2010) 'Expert Credibility in Climate Change', *Proceedings of the National Academy of Sciences*, June online early edition. http://www.pnas.org/content/early/2010/06/04/1003187107

Ashley, R. (1984) 'The Poverty of Neorealism', *International Organization*, 38 (Spring) 225–86.

Auer, M. (2000) 'Who Participates in Global Environmental Governance? Partial Answers from International Relations Theory', *Policy Sciences*, 33(2), 155–80.

Bachrach, P. and Baratz, M. (1962) 'The Two Faces of Power', *American Political Science Review*, 56, 947–52.

—— (1970) *Power and Poverty: Theory and Practice*. New York, NY: Oxford University Press.

Bakker, I. and Gill, S. (2003) 'Ontology, Method and Hypotheses', in I. Bakker and S. Gill (eds), *Power, Production and Social Reproduction*. Basingstoke: Palgrave Macmillan.

Barrett, M. and Durrell, R. (2005) 'Power in International Politics', *International Organization*, 59, 39–75.

286

Barriteau, E. (1995) 'Postmodernist Feminist Theorizing and Development Policy and Practice in the Anglophone Caribbean: The Barbados Case', in M. Marchand and J. Parpart (eds), *Feminism/Postmodernism/Development*. London and New York: Routledge.

Barry, B. (2005) *Why Social Justice Matters*. Cambridge: Polity.

Bates, S. and Jenkins, L. (2007) 'Teaching and Learning Ontology and Epistemology in Political Science' *Politics* 27 (1) pp 55–63

Baudrillard J. (1983) *In the Shadow of Silent Majorities*. Cambridge, MA: MIT Press.

—— (1991/2004) *The Gulf War Did Not Take Place*. Sydney: University of Sydney, Power.

Baumgartner, F. and Jones, B. (1993) *Agendas and Instability in American Politics*. Chicago, IL: University of Chicago Press.

Baxter, S. (2003) 'Adwoman Leads the Global Battle for Hearts and Minds', *Sunday Times*, 5 January, 21, http://www.timesonline.co.uk/tol/news/world/article808659.ece (accessed 18 May 2010).

Baylis, J. and Smith, S. (eds) (2004) *The Globalization of World Politics: An Introduction to International Relations*. Oxford: Oxford University Press.

Baylis, J., Smith, S. and Owens, P. (eds) (2008) *The Globalization of World Politics: An Introduction to International Relations*. Oxford: Oxford University Press.

BBC News (2008) 'Who Voted for Obama?', *BBC News*, http://news.bbc.co.uk/1/hi/world/america/us_elections_2008/7709852.stm (accessed 10 December 2009).

Bellamy, I. (1981) 'Towards a Theory of International Security', *Political Studies*, 29(1), 100–5.

Bennett, L. W. (1990) 'Toward a Theory of Press–State Relations in the United States', *Journal of Communication*, 40(2), 103–25.

Bevir, M. (2006) 'Political Studies as Narrative and Science, 1880–2000', *Political Studies*, 54, 583–606.

—— (2010) 'Interpreting Territory and Power', *Government and Opposition*, 45(3), 436–56.

Birkeland, J. (1993) 'Ecofeminism: Linking Theory and Practice', in G. Gaard (ed.), *Ecofeminism: Women, Animals and Nature*. Philadelphia, PA: Temple University Press, 13–60.

Blumer, H. (1971) 'Social Problems as Collective Behaviour', *Social Problems*, 18, 298–306.

Blumler, J. and McQuail, D. (1968) *Television in Politics: Its Uses and Influences*. London: Faber.

Blyth, M. (2002) 'Institutions and Ideas', in D. Marsh and G. Stoker (eds), *Theory and Methods in Political Science*. (Basingstoke: Palgrave Macmillan, 292–310).

Booth, K. (1991) 'Security and Emancipation', *Review of International Studies*, 17(4), 313–26.

—— (1997) 'Security and Self: Reflections of a Fallen Realist', in K. Krause and M. Williams (eds), *Critical Security Studies: Concepts and Cases*. London: UCL Press, 83–119.

Brah, A., Hickman, M. and Mairtin Mac an Ghail (1999) (eds) *Global Futures: Migrations, Environment and Globalization* London: Macmillan.

Brants, K. (1998) 'Who's Afraid of Infotainment', *European Journal of Communication*, 13(3), 149–64.

Bretherton, C. (1996) 'Gender and Environmental Change: Are Women the Key to Safeguarding the Planet?', in J. Vogler and M. Imber (eds), *The Environment and International Relations*. London: Routledge, 99–119.

Brewer, J., Guelke, A., Hume, I., Moxon-Browne, E. and Wilford, R. (1988) *The Police, Public Order and the State*. London: Macmillan.

Brown, A. (2009) *Personal Responsibility: Why it Matters*. London: Continuum.

Brundtland, G. (ed.) (1987) (The Brundtland report) 'World Commission on Environment and Development', *Our Common Future*. Oxford: Oxford University Press.

Bryman, A. (2008) *Social Research Methods*. Oxford: Oxford University Press.

Buchanen, J. and Tullock, G. (1962) *The Calculus of Consent: Logical Foundations of Constitutional Democracy*. Michigan, MI: Ann Arbor.

Buckingham, S. (2004) 'Ecofeminism in the Twenty-first Century', *The Geographical Journal*, 170(2), 146–54.

Bulkeley, H. and Betsill, H. (2005) 'Rethinking Sustainable Cities: Multilevel Governance and the "Urban" Politics of Climate Change', *Environmental Politics*, 14(1), 42–63.

Bulkeley, H. and Moser, S. (2007) 'Introduction. Responding to Climate Change: Governance and Action Beyond Kyoto', *Global Environmental Politics*, 7(2), 1–10.

Burnham, P. (2010) 'Class, Capital and Crisis: A Return to Fundamentals', *Political Studies Review*, 8(1), 27–40.

Burnham, P., Gilland, K. and Grant, W. (2004) *Research Methods in Politics*. Basingstoke: Palgrave Macmillan.

Butler, J. (1992) 'Contingent Foundations: Feminism and the Question of Postmodernism', in J. Butler and J. Scott (eds), *Feminists Theorize the Political*. New York, NY: Routledge.

Campbell, D. (1998) *Writing Security: United States Foreign Policy and the Politics of Identity*. Minneapolis, MN: University of Minnesota Press.

—— (2007) 'Poststructuralism', in T. Dunne, M. Kurki and S. Smith (eds), *International Relations Theories: Description and Diversity*. Oxford: Oxford University Press.

—— (2010) 'Writing Security', in P. Viotti and M. Kauppi (eds), *International Relations Theory*. New York, NY: Longman.

Campbell, K., Einhorn R. and Reiss, M. (2004) *The Nuclear Tipping Point: Why States Reconsider Their Nuclear Choices*. Washington, DC: Brookings InstitutionLittle, Brown.

Caney, S. (2001) 'International Distributive Justice', *Political Studies*, 49, 974–97.

—— (2008) 'Human Rights, Climate Change, and Discounting', *Environmental Politics*, 17(4), 536–55.

Caporaso, J. and Levine, D. (1992) *Theories of Political Economy*. Cambridge: Cambridge University Press.

Carr, E. H. (1946) *The Twenty Years' Crisis*. London: Macmillan.

Carter, C. and Weaver, C. (2003) *Violence and the Media*. Maidenhead: Open University Press.

Carter, N. (2008) *The Politics of the Environment*. Cambridge: Cambridge University Press.

Casey, C. (2002) *Critical Analysis of Organizations: Theory, Practice, Revitalization*. London: Sage.

Childs, S. (2008) *Women and British Party Politics*. London: Routledge.

Chomsky, N. (2009) 'Imminent Crises: Threats and Opportunities', http://www.monthlyreview.org/0607nc.htm.

CNN (2003) 'Bush, Blair: Time Running Out for Saddam', *CNN.Com*, 31 January.

Coates, D. (2010) 'Separating Sense from Nonsense in the US Debate on the Financial Markets', *Political Studies*, 8(1), 15–26.

Cochrane, A., and Pain, K. (2004) 'A Globalizing Society', in D. Held (ed.), *A Globalizing World? Culture, Economics, Politics*. London: Routledge.

Cohen, G. (2004) *Karl Marx's Theory of History: A Defence*. New York, NY: Oxford University Press.

Cohen, S. (1972) *Folk Devils and Moral Panics*. London: Paladin.

Collier, P. (2008) *The Bottom Billion: Why the Poorest Countries are Failing and What Can be Done About It*. Oxford: Oxford University Press.

Conca, K. (1994) 'Rethinking the Ecology-Sovereignty Debate', *Millennium*, 23(3), 1–11.

Cornell, D. (1991) *Beyond Accommodation: Ethical Feminism, Deconstruction and the Law*. New York, NY: Routledge.

Cox, R. (1981) 'Social Forces, States and World Orders: Beyond International Relations Theory', *Millennium: Journal of International Studies*, 10(2), 126–55.

—— (1983) 'Gramsci, Hegemony and International Relations An Essay on Method' *Millennium: Journal of International Studies* 12 pp 162–75.

—— (1986) 'Social Forces, States and World Orders: Beyond International Relations Theory', in R. Keohane (ed.), *Neorealism and its Critics*. New York, NY: Columbia Press, 204–54.

—— (1987) *Production, Power, and World Order: Social Forces in the Making of History*. New York, NY: Colombia University Press.

—— (1994) 'The Forum: Hegemony and Social Change', *Mershon International Studies Review*, 38(2), 366–7.

—— (2002) 'Reflections and Transitions', in R. Cox (with M. Schecter) (ed.), *The Political Economy of a Plural World: Critical Reflections on Power, Morals and Civilization*. London: Routledge.

—— (2010) 'Gramsci, Hegemony and International Relations', in P. Viotti and M. Kauppi (eds), *International Relations Theory*. New York, NY: Longman.

Curran, J. (2002) *Media and Power*. London: Routledge.

Dahl, R. (1956) *A Preface to Democratic Theory*. Chicago, IL: University of Chicago Press.

—— (1957) 'The Concept of Power', *Behavioural Science*, 2, 201–5.

—— (1958) 'A Critique of the Ruling Elite Model', *American Political Science Review*, 52, 463–9.

—— (1961) *Who Governs? Democracy and Power in an American City*. New Haven, CT: Yale University Press.

—— (1982) *Dilemmas of a Pluralist Democracy: Autonomy versus Control*. New Haven, CT: Yale University Press.

—— (1985) *A Preface to an Economic Theory of Democracy*. London: Polity.

Daily Telegraph (1995) 'Outrage at Nigeria Executions', 11 November.

Dalby, S. (1992) 'Security Modernity, Ecology: The Dilemmas of Post Cold War Security Discourse', *Alternatives*, 17, 95–134.

Dalton, R. (2006) 'Citizenship Norms and Political Participation in America: The Good News Is ... the Bad News Is Wrong', *Occasional Paper, Center for Democracy and Civil Society*. Washington, DC; Georgetown University.

Danaher, K (1995) *50 Years is Enough: Case Against the World Bank and the International Monetary Fund*. Cambridge, MA: Southend Press.

Davidson, D. and Frickel, S. (2004) 'Understanding Environmental Governance: A Critical Review', *Organization and Environment*, 17(4), 471–92.

Davies, N. (2008) *Flat Earth News*. London: Chatto & Windus.

Davis, A. (2005) 'Media Effects and the Active Elite Audience: A Study of Media in Financial Markets', *European Journal of Communications*, 20(3), 303–26.

de Goede, M (2003) 'Beyond Economism in International Political Economy', *Review of International Studies*, 29(1), 79–97.

Delves Broughton, P. (2010) 'Dramatic Images of World Trade Centre Collapse on 9/11 Released for the First Time', *Daily Mail*, 12 February.

Denton, F. (2000) 'Gender Impact of Climate Change: A Human Security Dimension', *Energia News*, 3(3), 13–14.

Denver, D. (1994/2003) *Elections and Voting Behaviour in Britain*. Hemel Hempstead: Prentice Hall/Harvester Wheatsheaf.

Der Derian, J. (1995) 'The Value of Security: Hobbes, Marx, Nietzsche and Baudrillard', in R. Lipschutz (ed.), *On Security*. New York, NY: Columbia University Press.

Derrida, J. (1988/1998) *Limited Inc*. Evanston, IL: Northwester University Press.

de Tocqueville, A. (1956) *Democracy in America*. New York, NY: Mentor.

Di Maggio, P. and Powell, W. (1991) *The New Institutionalism in Organizational Analysis*. Chicago, IL: University of Chicago Press.

Dionne, E. (1991) *Why Americans Hate Politics*. New York, NY: Simon & Schuster.

Dobson, A. (1998) *Justice and the Environment*. Oxford: Oxford University Press.

—— (2000) *Green Political Thought*. London: Routledge.

—— (2003) *Citizenship and the Environment*. Oxford: Oxford University Press.

Dobson, A. and Bell, D. (eds) (2006) *Environmental Citizenship*. Cambridge, MA: MIT Press.

Doherty, B. (2002) *Ideas and Actions in the Green Movement*. London: Routledge.

Dorfmann, A. and Mattelart, A. (1975) *How to Read Donald Duck: Imperialist Ideology in the Disney Comic*. New York, NY: International General.

Dowding, K. (1996) *Power*. Buckingham: Open University Press.

Doyle, M. (1983a), 'Kant, Liberal Legacies and Foreign Affairs I', *Philosophy and Public Affairs*, 12 (Summer), 205–35.

Doyle, M. (1983b), 'Kant, Liberal Legacies and Foreign Affairs I', *Philosophy and Public Affairs*, 12 (Fall), 323–53.

Dryzek, J. (1987) 'Complexity and Rationality in Public Life', *Political Studies*, 35, 424–42.

—— (1993) 'Policy Analysis and Planning: From Science to Argument', in F. Fischer and J. Forester (eds), *The Argumentative Turn in Policy Analysis and Planning*. London: UCL Press.

—— (2006) 'Revolutions Without Enemies: Key Transformations in Political Science' *American Political Science Review* 100 (4) pp 487–92.

Dunleavy, P. (1991) *Democracy, Bureaucracy and Public Choice*. London: Harvester Wheatsheaf.

Dunleavy, P. and O'Leary, B. (1987) *Theories of the State: The Politics of Liberal Democracy*. London: Macmillan.

Dunleavy, P. and Ward, H. (1991) 'The Bureau Shaping Model', in P. Dunleavy *Democracy, Bureaucracy and Public Choice*. Hemel Hempstead: Harvester Wheatsheaf.

Dunne, T. (2008) 'Liberalism', in J. Baylis, S. Smith and P. Owens (eds), *The Globalization of World Politics: An Introduction to International Relations*. Oxford: Oxford University Press.

Easton, D. (1953) *The Political System: An Inquiry into the State of Political Science*. New York, NY: Knopf.

Edelman, M. (1988) *Constructing the Political Spectacle*. Chicago, IL: Chicago University Press.

Edkins, J. (1999) *Poststructuralism and International Relations: Bringing the Political Back In*. Boulder, CO: Lynne Rienner.

Elster, J. (1986) *Rational Choice*. New York, NY: New York University Press.

Enloe, C. (1989) *Bananas, Beaches, and Bases: Making Feminist Sense of International Politics*. London: Pinter.

—— (1993) *The Morning After: Sexual Politics at the End of the Cold War*. Berkeley, CA: University of California Press.

Entman, R. (1993) 'Framing: Towards Clarification of a Fractured Paradigm', *Journal of Communication*, 43(4), 51–8.

Escobar, A. (1996) 'Constructing Nature: Elements for a Post-structural Political Ecology', in R. Peet and M. Watts (eds), *Liberation Ecology*. London: Routledge.

Evans, G. and Newnham, J. (1998) *The Penguin Dictionary of International Relations*. Harmondsworth: Penguin.

Evans, M. (2006) 'Elitism', in C. Hay, M. Lister and D. Marsh (eds), *The State. Theories and Issues*. Basingstoke: Palgrave Macmillan.

Feist, S. (2001) 'Facing Down the Global Village: The Media Impact', in R. Kugler and E. Frost (eds), *The Global Century*. Washington, DC: National Defense University Press.

Felski, R. (1989) *Beyond Feminist Aesthetics: Feminist Literature and Social Change*. Cambridge, MA: Harvard University Press.

Finer, H. (1932) *The Theory and Practice of Modern Government, 2 Volumes*. London: Methuen.

Finger, M. (1994) 'NGOs and Transformation: Beyond Social Movement Theory', in T. Princen and M. Finger (eds), *Environmental NGOs in World Politics*. New York, NY: Routledge.

Finlayson, A. and Martin, J. (2006) *Poststructuralism*, in C. Hay, M. Lister and D. Marsh (eds), *The State: Theories and Issues*. Basingstoke: Palgrave Macmillan.

Finnemore, M. and Sikkink, K. (1998) 'International Dynamics and Political Change', *International Organisation*, 52(4), 887–917.

Fischer, F. (2003) *Reframing Public Policy: Discursive Politics and Deliberative practices*. Oxford: Oxford University Press.

Ford, R. (2007) 'Jail Imams Vetted by Security Services and Muslim Books Screened for Code', *The Times*, 26 February.

Forester, J. (1993) *Critical Theory, Public Policy, and Planning Practice: Toward a Critical Pragmatism*. Albany, NY: State University of New York Press.

Foucault, M. (1979) *Discipline and Punish*. Harmondsworth: Penguin.

—— (2002) *Power: Essential Work of Foucault 1954–1984 Vol. 3*. Harmondsworth: Penguin.

Franklin, B. (1994) *Packaging Politics*. London: Edward Arnold.

Gaddis, J. (1996) 'History, Science, and the Study of International Relations', in N. Woods (ed.), *Explaining International Relations Since 1945*. Oxford: Oxford University Press,

Gamble, A. (2009) *The Spectre at the Feast: Capitalist Crisis and the Politics of Recession*. Basingstoke: Palgrave Macmillan.

Garand, J. and Giles, M. (2003) 'Journals in the Discipline: A Report on a New Survey of American Political Scientists', *Political Science and Politics*, 36 (April), 293–308.

Geuss, R. (1999) *The Idea of a Critical Theory: Habermas and the Frankfurt School*. Cambridge: Cambridge University Press.

Gibson-Graham, J. K. (1996) *The End of Capitalism (as we knew it) : A Feminist Critique of Political Economy* Cambridge, MA: Blackwell

Giddens, A. (1984) *The Constitution of Society: Outline of the Theory of Structuration*. Cambridge: Polity.

—— (1999) 'Runaway World: The BBC Reith Lectures', London: BBC Radio 4 BBC Education.

Gilboa, E. (2005) 'The CNN Effect: The Search for a Communication Theory of International Relations', *Political Communication*, 22, 27–44.

Gill, S and Law, D. (1989) 'Global Hegemony and the Structural Power of Capital', *International Studies Quarterly*, 33, 475–99.

Gilpin, R. (2005) '"Conversations in International Relations" Interview with Robert Gilpin', *International Relations*, 19, 361–72.

Goldenberg. S, Vidal, J. and Stratton, A. (2009) 'Copenhagen Heading for Meltdown as Stalemate Continues over Emission Cuts', *The Guardian*, 18 December.

Goldman, M. and Schurman, R. (2000) 'Closing the "Great Divide": New Social Theory on Society and Nature', *Annual Review of Sociology*, 26, 563–84.

Goldstein, J. and Pevehouse, J. (2010) *International Relations*. New York, NY: Longman Pearson.

Goodin, R. (1998) 'Institutions and their Design', in R. Goodin (ed.), *The Theory of Institutional Design*. Cambridge: Cambridge University Press.

Goodin, R. and Klingemann D. (1995) *A New Handbook of Political Science*. Oxford: Oxford University Press.

Goodwin, B. (2005) *Justice by Lottery*. Thorverton: Imprint Academic.

—— (2007) *Using Political Ideas*. Chichester: John Wiley & Sons.

Gramsci, A. (1971) *Selections from the Prison Notebooks*, ed. and trans. Q. Hoare and G. Nowell Smith. London: Lawrence & Wishart.

Griffiths, M. (1999) *Fifty Key Thinkers in International Relations*. Abingdon: Routledge.

Grist, N. (2008) 'Positioning Climate Change in Sustainable Development Discourse', *Journal of International Development*, 20, 783–803.

Guha, R. and Martinez-Alier, J. (1997) *Varieties of Environmentalism*. London: Earthscan.

Gunnell, J. (1995) 'The Real Revolution in Political Science', *Political Science and Politics*, 37, 47–50.

Haas, P., Keohane, R. and Levy, M. (eds) (1993) *Institutions for the Earth: Sources of Effective International Environmental Protection*. Cambridge, MA: MIT Press.

Habermas, J. (1976) *Legitimation Crisis*. London: Heinemann.

—— (1989) *The Structural Transformation of the Public Sphere: An Inquiry into a Categorisation of Bourgeois Society*. London: Polity Press.

—— (1962/2002) *The Structural Transformation of the Public Sphere*. Cambridge: Polity.

Hague, R., Harrop, M., and Breslin, S. (1993) *Comparative Government and Politics: An Introduction*. London: Macmillan.

Hajer, M. and Wagenaar, H. (eds) (2003) *Deliberative Policy Analysis: Understanding Governance in the Network Society*. Cambridge: Cambridge University Press.

Hall, P. (1986) *Governing the Economy.* Cambridge: Polity Press.

Hall, P. and Taylor, R. (1996) 'Political Science and the Three New Institutionalisms', *Political Studies*, 47(5), 936–57.

Hall, S. (1973) 'Encoding and Decoding in the Television Discourse', in S. Hall, D. Hobson, A. Lowe and P. Willis (eds), *Culture, Media, Language: Working Papers in Cultural Studies 1972–79.* London: Hutchinson.

Hallin, D. (1986) *The Uncensored War.* Berkeley, CA: University of California Press.

Ham, C. and Hill, M. (1984) *The Policy Process in the Modern Capitalist State.* Brighton: Harvester Wheatsheaf.

Handley, P. (2003) 'Theorising Disability: Beyond "Common Sense"', *Politics*, 23(2), 109–18.

Hannigan, J. (1995) *Environmental Sociology: A Social Constructionist Perspective.* London: Routledge.

—— (2006) *Environmental Sociology.* London: Routledge.

Hardin, G. (1968) 'The Tragedy of the Commons', *Science*, 162, 1243–8.

Hargreaves Heap, S. and Varoufakis, Y. (1995) *Game Theory. A Critical Introduction.* London: Routledge.

Haughton, G. (2002) 'Market Making: Internationalization and Global Water Markets', *Environment and Planning A*, 34(5), 791–807.

Hawkesworth, M. (1994) 'Policy Studies Within a Feminist Frame', *Policy Sciences*, 27, 97–118.

Hawkins, V. (2002) 'The Other Side of the CNN Factor: the Media and Conflict', *Journalism Studies*, 3(2), 225–40.

Hay, C. (2002) *Political Analysis.* Basingstoke: Palgrave Macmillan.

—— (2004) 'Theory, Stylised Heuristic or Self-fulfilling Prophecy? The Status of Rational Choice Theory in Public Administration', *Public Administration*, 82, 2–33.

—— (2006a) 'Constructivist Institutionalism', in R. Rhodes, S. Binder and B. Bowman (eds), *The Oxford Handbook of Political Institutions.* Oxford: Oxford University Press.

—— (2006b) 'What's Globalization Got to Do With It? Economic Interdependence and the Future of European Welfare States', *Government and Opposition*, 41(1), 1–22.

—— (2006c) '(What's Marxist About) Marxist State Theory?', in C. Hay, M. Lister and D. Marsh (eds), *The State: Theories and Issues.* Basingstoke: Palgrave Macmillan.

—— (2007) *Why We Hate Politics.* Cambridge: Polity Press.

Hay, C., Lister, M. and Marsh, D. (eds) (2006) *The State: Theories and Issues.* Basingstoke: Palgrave Macmillan.

Held, D. (2004) 'Introduction', in D. Held (ed.), *A Globalizing World? Culture, Economics, Politics.* London: Routledge.

Held, D. and McGrew, A. (eds) (2000) *Polity Global Transformations Reader.* Cambridge: Cambridge University Press.

—— (2007) *Globalization Theory: Approaches and Controversies.* Cambridge: Polity.

Held, D., McGrew, A., Goldblatt, D. and Peraton, J. (1999) *Global Transformations: Politics, Economics and Culture.* Cambridge: Cambridge University Press.

Herman, E. and Chomsky, N. (1988) *Manufacturing Consent: The Political Economy of the Mass Media.* New York, NY: Pantheon.

Higgins, M. (2008) *Media and Their Publics*. Maidenhead: Open University Press.

Hill, M. (ed.) (2009) *The Public Policy Process*. Harlow: Pinter.

Hirst, P. (2001) *War and Power in the 21st Century*. Cambridge: Polity.

Hirst, P. and Thompson, G. (1999) *Globalization in Question: The International Economy and the Possibilities of Governance*. Cambridge: Polity.

HM Government (2010) *The Coalition: Our Programme for Government*, http://www.cabinetoffice.gov.uk/media/409088/pfg_coalition.pdf.

Hobbes, T. (1946) *Leviathan*. Oxford: Blackwell.

Hobden, S. and Wyn Jones, R. (2008) 'Marxism', in J. Baylis, S. Smith and P. Owens (eds), *The Globalization of World Politics: An Introduction to International Relations*. Oxford: Oxford University Press.

Hockenos, P. (2003) *Homeland Calling: Exile Patriotism and the Balkan Wars*. Ithaca, NY: Cornell University Press.

Hogwood, B. and Gunn, L. (1984) *Policy Analysis for the Real World*. London: Oxford University Press.

Hollis, M and Smith, S (1990) *Explaining and Understanding in International Relations*. Oxford: Clarendon.

Holsti, O. (2004) *Public Opinion and American Foreign Policy*. Michigan, MI: Michigan University Press.

Holzer, B. (2007) 'Framing the Corporation: Royal Dutch/Shell and Human Rights Woes in Nigeria', *Journal of Consumer Policy*, 30, 281–301.

Hooper, C. (2001) *Manly States: Masculinities, International Relations and Gender Politics*. New York, NY: Columbia University Press.

Hoskins, A. (2004) *Televising War. From Vietnam to Iraq* London: Continuum.

Hough, P. (2004) *Understanding Global Security*. Abingdon: Routledge.

Howell, N. (1997) 'Ecofeminism: What One Needs to Know', *Zygon*, 32(2), 231–41.

Hulme, M. (2009) *Why We Disagree About Climate Change*. Cambridge: Cambridge University Press.

Hunter, F. (1953). *Community Power Structure: A Study of Decision Makers*. Chapel Hill, NC: University of North Carolina Press.

Hutton, P. (1988) 'Foucault, Freud, and the Technologies of the Self', in L. Martin, H. Gutman, and P. Hutton (eds), *Technologies of the Self*. Amherst, MA: University of Massachusetts Press.

Ingram, H., Schneider, A. and de Leon, P. (2007) 'Social Construction and Policy Design', in P. Sabatier (ed.), *Theories of the Policy Process*. Colorado, CO: Westview Press.

Irvin, G. (2008) *SuperRich: The Rise of Inequality in Britain and the United States*. Cambridge: Polity.

Jackson, R. (2005) *Writing the War on Terrorism: Language, Politics and Counterterrorism*. Manchester: Manchester University Press.

Jakobsen, P. (2000) 'Focus Upon the CNN Effect Misses the Point: The Real Media Impact on Conflict Management is Invisible and Indirect', *Journal of Peace Research*, 37(5), 547–62.

Jessop, B. (1995) 'Towards a Schumpeterian Workfare Regime in Britain: Reflections in Regulation, Governance and Welfare State', *Environment and Planning A*, 10, 1613–26.

—— (2004) 'Critical Semiotic Analysis and Cultural Political Economy', *Critical Discourse Studies*, 1(2), 159–74.

Jimoh, H. and Aghalino, S. (2000) 'Petroleum Exploitation and Environmental Degradation in Nigeria', in H. Jimoh and I. Ifabiyi (eds), *Contemporary Issues in Environmental Studies*. Ilorin, Nigeria: Haytee.

John, P. (1999) *Analysing Public Policy*. London: Pinter.

John, P., Smith, G. and Stoker G. (2009) 'Nudge Nudge, Think Think: Two Strategies for Changing Civic Behaviour', *The Political Quarterly*, 80(3), 361–69.

Johnson, N. (1975) 'The Place of Institutions in the Study of Politics', *Political Studies*, 23, 271–83.

Jordan, A. (1990) 'Sub-government, Policy Communities and Networks: Refilling Old Bottles', *Journal of Theoretical Politics*, 2(2), 319–38.

Jordan, G. (1993) 'The Pluralism of Pluralism: An Anti-Theory?', in J. Richardson (ed.), *Pressure Groups*. Oxford: Oxford University Press.

—— (2008) 'The Governance of Sustainable Development: Taking Stock and Looking Forwards', *Environment and Planning C: Government and Policy*, 26, 17–33.

Jørgensen, K. (2010) *International Relations Theory: A New Introduction*. Basingstoke: Palgrave Macmillan.

Joseph, S. (1988) *Political Theory and Power*. Leiden: Brill.

Kant, I. (1795) *Perpetual Peace: A Philosophical Essay*, http://www.mtholyoke.edu/acad/intrel/kant/kant1.htm (accessed 19 May 2010).

Kasza, G. (2006) 'Unearthing the Roots of Hard Science: A Program for Graduate Students', in S. Schram and B. Caterino (eds), *Making Political Science Matter: Debating Knowledge, Research and Method*. New York, NY: New York University Press.

Kato, J. (1996) 'Review Article: Institutions and Rationality in Politics: Three Varieties of Neo-institutionalists', *British Journal of Political Science*, 26, 553–82.

Kauffman, L. (ed.) (1989) *Feminism and Institutions: Dialogues on Feminist Theory*. New York, NY: Basil Blackwell.

—— (1993) 'The Long Goodbye', in G. Greene and C. Kahn (eds), *Changing Subjects: The Making of Feminist Literary Criticism*. London: Routledge.

Kelly, B. and Prokhovnik, R. (2004) 'Economic Globalization?', in D. Held (ed.), *A Globalizing World? Culture, Economics, Politics*, 2nd edn. London: Routledge.

Kennedy-Pipe, C. (2010) 'Gender and Security', in P. Williams (ed.), *Security Studies: An Introduction*. Abingdon: Routledge.

Kenny, M. (2004) 'The Case for Disciplinary History: Political Studies in the 1950s and 1960s', *British Journal of Politics and International Relations*, 6, 565–83.

Keohane, R. (1984) *After Hegemony: Cooperation and Discord in the World Political Economy*. Princeton, NJ: Princeton University Press.

—— (1989a) *International Institutions and State Power*. Boulder, CO: Westview.

—— (1989b) 'Neoliberal Institutionalism: A Perspective on World Politics', in R. Keohane (ed.), *International Institutions and State Power: Essays in International Relationsm* Boulder, CO: Westview Press,

—— (1996) 'Analyzing the Effectiveness of International Environmental Institutions', in R. Keohane and M. Levy (eds), *Institutions for Environmental Aid: Pitfalls and Promise*, Cambridge, MA: MIT Press,

—— (2002) *Power and Governance in a Partially Globalized World*, New York and London: Routledge,

—— (2010) 'From Interdependence and Institutions to Globalization and Governance', in P. Viotti and M. Kauppi (eds), *International Relations Theory*. New York, NY: Longman Pearson.

Keohane, R. and Martin, L. (1995) 'The Promise of Institutionalist Theory', *International Security*, 20, 39–51.

Keohane, R. and Nye, J. (eds) (1972) *Transnational Relations and World Politics*. Cambridge, MA: Harvard University Press.

—— (1977) *Power and Interdependence: World Politics in Transition*. Boston, MA: Little, Brown.

King, Y. (1989) 'The Ecology of Feminism and the Feminism of Ecology', in J. Plant (ed.), *Healing the Wounds: The Promise of Ecofeminism*. Philadelphia, PA and Santa Cruz, CA: New Society.

Kingdon, J. (1995) *Agendas, Alternatives and Public Policies*. New York, NY: Longman.

Kirkup, J. and Rayner, G. (2009) 'Iraq Inquiry: British Officials Heard "Drum Beats" of War from US before 9/11', *Daily Telegraph*, 24 November, http://www. telegraph.co.uk/news/newstopics/politics/6643302/Iraq-inquiry-British-officials-heard-drum-beats-of-war-from-US-before-911.html (accessed 18 May 2010).

Klapper, J. (1960) *The Effects of Mass Communication*, Glencoe, IL: Free Press.

Koch, A. (2007) *Poststructuralism and the Politics of Method*. Plymouth, MA: Lexington.

Kolodziej, E. (2005) *Security and International Relations*. Cambridge: Cambridge University Press.

Krasner, S. (ed.) (1983) *International Regimes*. Ithaca, NY: Cornell University Press.

Krause, K. and Williams, M (eds) (1997) *Critical Security Studies: Concepts and Cases*. London: University College London Press.

Laclau, E. and Mouffe, E. (1987) 'Post-Marxism without Apologies', *New Left Review*, 79–106.

Lahar, S. (1991) 'Ecofeminist Theory and Grassroots Politics', *Hypatia*, 6(1), 28–45.

Lamy, S. (2008) 'Contemporary Mainstream Approaches: Neo-realism and Neo-liberalism', in J. Baylis, S. Smith and P. Owens (eds), *The Globalization of World Politics: An Introduction to International Relations*. Oxford: Oxford University Press.

Lasswell, H. (1936) *Politics: Who Gets What, When, How*. New York, NY: McGraw-Hill.

LaVaque-Manty, M. (2006) 'Bentley, Truman, and the Study of Groups' *Annual Review of Political Science*, 91–18.

Lecours, A. (2005) 'New Institutionalism: Issues and Questions', in A. Lecours (ed.), *New Institutionalism: Theory and Analysis*. Toronto: University of Toronto Press.

Leftwich, A. (2004) *What is Politics?* Cambridge: Polity.

Leibfried, S. and Pierson, P. (1995) *European Social Policy Between Fragmentation and Integration*. Washington, DC: Brookings Institution.

Levy, D. and Egan, D. (1998) 'Capital Contests: National and Transnational Channels of Corporate Influence on the Climate Change Negotiations', *Politics and Society*, 26, 337–61.

Levy, D and Newell, P (eds) (2004) *The Business of Global Environmental Governance*. Cambridge, MA: MIT Press.

Lewis, J. (2008) 'The Role of the Media in Boosting Military Spending', *Media, War and Conflict*, 1(1), 108–17.

Lewis, P. (2010) 'Legal Fight Over Spy Cameras in Muslim Suburbs', *The Guardian*, 11 June.

Lindblom, C. (1968) *The Policy-Making Process*. Englewood, NJ: Prentice-Hall.

—— (1977) *Politics and Markets*. New York, NY: Basic Books.

Linder, S and Peters, B. (1990) 'An Institutional Approach to the Theory of Policy Making: The Role of Guidance Mechanisms in Policy Formulation', *Journal of Theoretical Politics*, 2, 59–83.

Linklater, A. (1998) *The Transformation of Political Community Ethical Foundations of the Post-Westphalian Era*. Cambridge: Polity.

—— (2008) 'Globalization and the Transformation of Political Community', in J. Baylis, S. Smith and P. Owens (eds), *The Globalization of World Politics: An Introduction to International Relations*. Oxford: Oxford University Press.

Lipschutz, R. and Conca, K. (eds) (1993) *The State and Social Power in Global Environmental Politics*. New York, NY: Columbia University Press.

Lipsky, M. (1971) 'Street Level Bureaucracy and the Analysis of Urban Reform', *Urban Affairs Quarterly*, 6, 391–409.

Livingston, S. and Eachus, T. (1995) 'Humanitarian Crises and US Foreign Policy: Somalia and the CNN Effect Reconsidered', *Political Communication*, 12, 413–29.

Locke, J. (1690/1965) *Two Treatises of Government*. New York, NY: New American Library.

Louw, E. (2010) *The Media and Political Process*. London: Sage.

Lovelock, J. (1979/2000) *Gaia: A New Look at Life on Earth*. Oxford: Oxford University Press.

Lovenduski, J. (1986) *Women and European Politics: Contemporary Feminism and Public Policy*. Amherst, MA: University of Massachusetts Press.

—— (2005) *Feminizing Politics*. Cambridge: Polity.

Lowndes, V. (2010) 'The Institutional Approach', in D. Marsh and G. Stoker (eds), *Theory and Methods in Political Science*. Basingstoke: Palgrave Macmillan.

Lukes, S. (1974) *Power: A Radical View*. London: Macmillan.

Luoma, J. (2004) 'The Water Thieves', *The Ecologist*, 34(2), 52–7.

Lyotard, J.-F. (1984) *The Post Modern Condition: A Report on Knowledge*. Manchester: Manchester University Press.

Macedo, S. *et al.* (2005) *Democracy at Risk: How Political Choices Undermine Citizen Participation, and What We Can Do About It*. Washington, DC: Brookings Institution Press.

MacKinnon, C. (1993) *Only Words*. Cambridge, MA: Harvard University Press.

Marcuse, H. (1972) *One-Dimensional Man*. London: Abacus.

March, J. and Olsen, J. (1984) 'The New Institutionalism: Organizational Factors in Political Life', *American Political Science Review*, 78(3), 734–49.

—— (1989) *Rediscovering Institutions: The Organizational Basis of Politics*. New York, NY: Free Press.

—— (1994) *Democratic Governance*. New York, NY: Free Press.

—— (2006) 'Elaborating the "New Institutionalism"', in R. Rhodes, S. Binder and B. Rockman (eds), *The Oxford Handbook of Political Institutions*. Oxford: Oxford University Press.

Marchand, M. and Parpart, J (1995) 'The Relevance of Postmodern Feminism for Gender and Development', in M. Marchand and J. Parpart (eds), *Feminism Postmodernism Development*. Abingdon: Routledge.

Marsden, L. (2008) *For God's Sake: The Christian Right and US Foreign Policy*. London: Zed.

Marsh, D. (ed.) (1998) *Comparing Policy Networks*. Buckingham: Open University Press.
—— (2002) 'Marxism', in D. Marsh and G. Stoker (eds), *Theory and Methods in Political Science*. Basingstoke: Palgrave Macmillan.
—— (2010) 'Meta-Theoretical Issues' in D. Marsh and G. Stoker (eds) *Theory and Methods in Political Science*, 3rd edn. Basingstoke: Palgrave Macmillan. pp 212–31.
Marsh, D. and Furlong, P. (2002) 'A Skin Not a Sweater: Ontology and Epistemology in Political Science', in D. Marsh and G. Stoker (eds), *Theory and Methods in Political Science.* 2nd edn. Basingstoke: Palgrave Macmillan.
Marsh, D. and Savigny, H. (2004) 'Political Science as a Broad Church: The Search for a Pluralist Discipline', *Politics*, 24(3), 155–68.
Marsh, D. and Smith, M. (2002) 'There is More Than One Way to do Political Science: On Different Ways to Study Policy Networks', *Political Studies*, 49(3), 528–41.
Martell, L. (2010) *The Sociology of Globalization*. Cambridge: Polity.
Marx, K (1845/1969) *Theses on Feuerbach*. Moscow: Progress Publishers; also available at http://www.marxists.org/archive/marx/works/1845/theses/theses.pdf.
Marx, K. (1852/2008) *The Eighteenth Brumaire of Louis Bonaparte*. Rockville, MD: Wildside Press. Also available via www.marxists.org/archive/marx/works/1852/18th-brumaire/ch01.htm.
Mauss, A. (1975) *Social Problems as Social Movements*. Philadelphia, PA: Lippincott.
Mbaku, J. (2004) *Institutions and Development in Africa*. Asmara, Eritrea: Africa World Press.
McAnulla, S. (2002) 'Structure and Agency', in D. Marsh and G. Stoker (eds), *Theory and Methods in Political Science*. Basingstoke: Palgrave Macmillan.
McBeth, M., Shanahan, E., Arnell, R. and Hathaway, P. (2007) 'The Intersection of Narrative Policy Analysis and Policy Change Theory', *The Policy Studies Journal*, 35(1), 87–108.
McCombs, M. and Shaw, D. (1972) 'The Agenda Setting Function of Mass Media', *Public Opinion Quarterly*, 36(2), 176–87.
McGarry, J. and O'Leary, B. (2004) *The Northern Ireland Conflict: Consociational Engagement*. Oxford: Oxford University Press.
McGrew, A. (2004) 'Power Shift from National Government to Global Governance', in D. Held (ed.), *A Globalizing World? Culture, Economics, Politics*. London: Routledge.
McLaren, M. (2002) *Feminism, Foucault, and Embodied Subjectivity*. Albany, NY: University of New York Press.
McLaren, P. (1989). *Life in Schools: An Introduction to Critical Pedagogy in the Foundations of Education*. New York: Longman.
Mearsheimer, J. (1990) 'Back to the Future: Instability in Europe After the Cold War', *International Security*, 15(1), 5–56.
—— (1995) 'The False Promise of International Institutions', *International Security*, 19, 5–49.
—— (2001) *Tragedy of Great Power Politics*. New York, NY: W. W. Norton.
Mearsheimer, J. and Walt, S. (2006) 'The Israel Lobby', *London Review of Books*, 28(6), 23 March.
—— (2007) *The Israel Lobby and US Foreign Policy*. London: Allen Lane.

Media Watch (1995) *Global Media Monitoring Project: Women's Participation in the News*. Ontario: Media Watch.

Merchant, C. (1980) *The Death of Nature: Women, Ecology and the Scientific Revolution*. San Francisco, CA: Harper & Row.

Michels, R. (1911/1959) *Political Parties: A Sociological Study of the Oligarchical Tendencies of Modern Democracy*. New York, NY: Dover.

Miliband, R. (1969) *The State in Capitalist Society: An Analysis of the Western System of Power*. London: Weidenfeld & Nicolson.

Mill, J. S. (1848/1994) *Principles of Political Economy*. Oxford: Oxford University Press.

Minford, P. (2010) 'The Banking Crisis: A Rational Interpretation', *Political Studies*, 8(1), 40–54.

Mitchell, R. (2008) 'International Environment', in W. Carlsnaes, T. Risse and B. Simmons, *Handbook of International Relations*. London: Sage.

Mol, A. and Spaargaren, G. (2000) 'Ecological Modernisation Theory in Debate: A Review', *Environmental Politics*, 9, 1–17.

Morgenthau, H. (1948/1955) *Politics Among Nations: The Struggle for Power and Peace*. New York, NY: Knopf.

Morris, D. (1999) *Behind The Oval Office: Getting Reelected Against All Odds*. Los Angeles, CA: Renaissance.

Morton, A. (2003) 'Social Forces in the Struggle over Hegemony: Neo-Gramscian Perspectives in International Political Economy', *Rethinking Marxism*, 15(2), 153–79.

Moses, J. and Knutsen, T. (2007) *Ways of Knowing: Competing Methodologies in Social and Political Research*. Basingstoke: Palgrave Macmillan.

Mulgan, G. (1998) *Connexity: Responsibility, Freedom, Business and Power in the New Century*. London: Vintage.

Mulvey, L. (1975) 'Visual Pleasure and Narrative Cinema', *Screen*, 16(3), 6–18.

Muspratt, C. and Seawright, S. (2006) 'Amber Alert over Green Taxes', *Daily Telegraph*, www.telegraph.co.uk/finance/2949852/Amber-alert-over-green-taxes. html (accessed 16 June 2010).

Nardin, T (2006) 'International Political Theory and the Question of Justice' *International Affairs*, 82(3) 449–65.

Naylor, B. (2001) 'Reporting Violence in the British Print Media: Gendered Stories', *Howard Journal of Criminal Justice*, 40(2), 180–94.

Newton, K. and Brynin, M. (2001) 'The National Press and Party Voting in the UK', *Political Studies*, 49, 265–85.

Niskanen, W. (1971) *Bureaucracy and Representative Government*. Chicago, IL: Aldine, Atherton.

Norris, P. (1997) 'Towards a More Cosmopolitan Political Science', *European Journal of Political Research*, 30(1),17–34.

Norton, A. (2010) 'Politics Against History: Temporal Distortions in the Study of Politics', *Political Studies*, 58(2), 340–53.

Nye, J. (1988) 'Neo-realism and Neo-liberalism', *World Politics*, 40(2), 235–51.

—— (2004) *Soft Power: The Means to Success in World Politics*. New York, NY: Public Affairs.

Nye, J., Zelikow, P. and King, D. (eds) (1997) *Why Americans Mistrust Government*. Cambridge, MA: Harvard University Press.

O'Brien, R. and Williams, M. (2010) *Global Political Economy*. Basingstoke: Palgrave Macmillan.

O'Connor, J. (1973) *The Fiscal Crisis of the State*. New York, NY: St Martin's Press.

O'Neill, K. (2009) *The Environment and International Relations*. Cambridge: Cambridge: University Press.

Oels, A. (2005) 'Rendering Climate Change Governable: From Biopower to Advanced Liberal Government', *Journal of Environmental Policy and Planning*, 7(3), 185–207.

Offe, C. (1984) *The Contradictions of the Welfare State*. London: Hutchinson University Library.

Olarinmoye, O. (2008) 'Politics Does Matter: The Nigerian State and Oil (Resource) Curse', *Africa Development*, 23(3), 21–34.

Okonta, I. and Douglas, O. (2003) *Where Vultures Feast: Shell, Human Rights and Oil*. London: Verso.

Olson, M. (1965) *The Logic of Collective Action*. Cambridge, MA: Harvard University Press.

—— (1996) 'Big Bills Left on the Sidewalk: Why Some Nations are Rich, and Others are Poor', *Journal of Economic Perspectives*, 10(2), 3–24.

Omeje, K. (2005) 'Oil Conflict in Nigeria: Contending Issues and Perspectives of the Local Niger Delta People', *New Political Economy*, 10(3), 321–34.

Onuf, N. (1998) 'Constructivism: A User's Manual', in V. Kubalkova, N. Greenwood, N. Onuf and P. Kowert (eds), *International Relations in a Constructed World*. Armonk, NY: M. E. Sharpe, 58–78.

—— (2002) 'Worlds of our Making: The Strange Career of Constructivism in International Relations', in D. Puchala (ed.), *Visions of International Relations: Assessing an Academic Field*. Columbia, SC: University of South Carolina Press.

Page, E. (1999) 'Intergenerational Justice and Climate Change', *Political Studies*, 47(1), 53–66.

—— (2007) 'Fairness on the Day After Tomorrow: Reciprocity, Justice and Global Climate Change', *Political Studies*, 55(1), 225–42.

Palin, K. (2000) *Global Political Economy: Contemporary Theories*. London: Routledge.

Parsons, W. (1995) *An Introduction to the Theory and Practice of Policy Analysis*. Cheltenham: Edward Elgar.

Pateman, C. (1988) 'The Fraternal Social Contract', in J. Keane (ed.), *Civil Society and the State: New European Perspectives*. London: Verso.

Paterson, M. (1996) 'Neorealism, Neoinstitutionalism and the Climate Change Convention', in J. Vogler and M. Imber (eds), *The Environment and International Relations*. London: Routledge.

Paterson, M., Doran, P. and Barry, J. (2006) 'Green Theory', in C. Hay, M. Lister and D. Marsh (eds), *The State: Theories and Issues*. Basingstoke: Palgrave Macmillan.

Pavelec, S. (ed.) (2010) *The Military Industrial Complex and American Society*. Santa Barbara, CA: ABC-CLIO LLC.

Perejra, C. (2002) 'Configuring "Global", "National" and "Local" in Governance Agendas and Women's Struggles in Nigeria', *Social Research*, 69(3), 781–804.

Peters, G. (1999) *Institutional Theory in Political Science: 'The New Institutionalism'*. London: Continuum.

Peterson, V. (2002) 'Rewriting (Global) Political Economy as Reproductive, Productive and Virtual (Foucauldian) Economies', *International Feminist Journal of Politics*, 4(1), 1–30.

PEW Research Center (2007) 'Private Security Companies in Iraq – A PEJ Study', *PEW Research Center's Project for Excellence in Journalism*, 21 June, http://www.journalism.org/node/6153 (accessed 18 May 2010).

Polanyi, K. (1944) *The Great Transformation*. Boston, MA: Beacon.

Polsby, N. (1970 *Community Power and Political Theory*. New Haven, CT: Yale University Press.

Poulantzas, N. (1969) 'The Problems of the Capitalist State', *New Left Review*, 58, 67–78, reprinted in R. Blackburn (ed.) (1972) *Ideology in Social Science*. London: Fontana.

—— (1973a) 'On Social Class', *New Left Review*, 78 (March–April), 27–54.

— (1973b) *Political Power and Social Classes*. London: New Left.

— - (1975) *Classes in Contemporary Capitalism*. London: New Left.

—— (1976) 'The Capitalist State: A Reply to Miliband and Laclau', *New Left Review*, 95 (January–February), 63–83.

Pressman, J. and Wildavsky, A. (1973) *Implementation*. Berkeley, CA: University of California Press.

Price, R. and Tannenwald, N. (1996) 'Norms and Deterrence: The Nuclear and Chemical Weapons Taboos', in P. Katzenstein (ed.), *The Culture of National Security: Norms and Identity in World Politics*. New York, NY: Columbia University Press.

Pringle, R. (1996) 'Women's Struggles Unity and Diversity', in L. McDowell and R. Pringle (eds), *Defining Women: Social Institutions and Gender Divisions*. Cambridge: Polity Press.

Prudham, S. (2009) 'Pimping Climate Change: Richard Branson, Global Warming and the Performance of Green Capitalism', *Environmental Planning A*, 41, 1594–613.

Przeworski, A. (1977) 'Proletariat into a Class: The Process of Class Formation from Karl Kautsky's "The Class Struggle" to Recent Controversies', *Politics and Society*, 7(4), 343–401.

—— (1980) 'Social Democracy as a Historical Phenomenon', *New Left Review*, 122.

—— (1985) *Capitalism and Social Democracy*. Cambridge: Cambridge University Press.

Rai, S. (2008) 'Institutional Mechanisms for the Advancement of Women: Mainstreaming Gender, Democratizing the State?', in S. Rai (ed.), *Mainstreaming Gender, Democratizing the State? Institutional Mechanisms for the Advancement of Women*. Manchester: Manchester University Press, 15–39.

Randall, V. (2010) 'Feminism', in D. Marsh and G. Stoker (eds), *Theory and Methods in Political Science*. Basingstoke: Palgrave Macmillan.

Redclift, M. (1986) 'Redefining the Environmental "Crisis" in the South', in J. Weston (ed.), *Red and Green: The New Politics of the Environment*. London: Pluto Press.

—— (1987) *Sustainable Development*. London: Routledge.

Rheingold, H. (1995) *The Virtual Community*. London: Mandarin Paperback.

Rhodes, R. (1995) 'The Institutional Approach', in D. Marsh and G. Stoker (eds), *Theory and Methods in Political Science*. London: Macmillan.

Richardson, J. (1993) 'Pressure Groups and Government', in J. Richardson (ed.), *Pressure Groups*. Oxford: Oxford University Press.

Ritchie, N. (2010) 'Relinquishing Nuclear Weapons: Identities, Networks and the British Bomb', *International Affairs*, 86(2), 465–87.

Robertson, G. (2003) 'NATO and the Transatlantic Community: The "Continuous Creation"', *Journal of Transatlantic Studies*, 1(1), 1–7.

Robinson, P. (1999) 'The CNN Effect: Can the News Media Drive Foreign Policy?', *Review of International Studies*, 25, 301–9.

—— (2001) 'Theorizing the Influence of Media on World Politics', *European Journal of Communication*, 16(4), 523–44.

—— (2002) *The CNN Effect: The Myth of News, Foreign Policy and Intervention*. London: Routledge.

Ropke, I. (1994) 'Trade Development and Sustainability: A Critical Assessment of the "Free Trade" Dogma', *Ecological Economics*, 9(1), 13–22.

Ross, K. (2005) 'Women in the Boyzone, Gender, News and *Herstory*', *Journalism: Critical Issues*. Maidenhead: Open University Press, 287–98.

Rosser, A. (2006) 'The Political Economy of the Resource Curse: A Literature Review', *IDS Working Paper* No. 268, cited in Olarinmoye, 2008.

Ruggie, J (1983) 'Continuity and Transformation in the World Polity: Toward a Neorealist Synthesis', *World Politics*, 35 (Jan) 261–85.

Ruggie, J. (1992) 'Multilateralism: The Anatomy of an Institution', *International Organization*, 46(3) (Summer), 561–98.

Russett, B. (1994) *Grasping the Democratic Peace*. Princeton, NJ: Princeton University Press.

Sabatier, P. (2007) *Theories of the Policy Process*. Colorado, CO: Westview Press.

Sabatier, P. and Jenkins-Smith, H. (eds) (1993) *Policy Change and Learning: Advocacy Coalition Approach (Theoretical Lenses on Public Policy)*. Tennessee, TN: Westview Press.

Sagan, S. and Waltz K. (1995) *The Spread of Nuclear Weapons: A Debate*. New York, NY: W. W. Norton.

Salleh, A. (1997) *Ecofeminism as Politics: Nature, Marx and the Postmodern*. London: Zed.

Samuelsohn, D. (2009) 'Obama Negotiates 'Copenhagen Accord' with Senate Climate Fight in Mind', *New York Times*, 21 December.

Sandel, M. (1982/1998) *Liberalism and the Limits of Justice*. Cambridge: Cambridge University Press.

Sanders, D. (1995) 'Behavioural Analysis', in D. Marsh and G. Sboker (eds), *Theory and Methods in Political Science*. London: Macmillan.

Sanders, ? (1995) reference to follow on proof.

Sanders, D. (2002/2010) 'Behaviouralism', in D. Marsh and G. Stoker (eds), *Theory and Methods in Political Science*. Basingstoke: Palgrave Macmillan.

Sanderson, J. (1961) 'The National Smoke Abatement Society and the Clean Air Act (1956)', *Political Studies*, 9, 236–53.

Savigny, H. (2007) 'Ontology and Epistemology in Political Marketing: Keeping it Real', special issue of *Journal of Political Marketing*, 6(2/3), 33–47.

—— (2010) 'Looking Back to Move Forward: Historicising the Social Construction of Disciplinary Narratives in Politics and International Relations', *European Political Science*, forthcoming.

Saville, M., Hoyt, W. and Toohey, J. (2010) *Report of the Bloody Sunday Enquiry*, http://www.bloody-sunday-inquiry-org (accessed 25 August 2010).

Schattschneider, E. (1960) *The Semi-Sovereign People: A Realist's View of Democracy in America*. New York, NY: Holt, Rinehart & Winston.

Scheffer, J. (2009) 'NATO at 60', *NATO Review*. Brussels: NATO.

Schiller, H. (1991) 'Not Yet the Post-Imperialist Era', *Critical Studies in Mass Communication*, 8, 13–28.

Schmidt, B. (2008) 'On the History and Historiography of International Relations', in W. Carlsnaes, T. Risse and B. Simmons (eds), *Handbook of International Relations*. London: Sage.

Schnaiberg, A. (1980) *The Environment: From Surplus to Scarcity.* New York, NY: Oxford University Press.

Scholte, J. (2001) 'Global Trade and Finance' in J. Baylis and S. Smith (eds) *The Globalization of World Politics: An Introduction to International Relations* (Oxford: Oxford University Press)

Schorr, D. (1991) 'Ten Days that Shook the White House', *Columbia Journalism Review*, July–August, 21–3.

Scott, J. (1988) 'Deconstructing Equality-Versus-Difference: Or, the Uses of Poststructuralist Theory for Feminism', *Feminist Studies*, 14(1), 32–50.

Seyfang, G. (2003) 'Environmental Mega-Conferences from Stockholm to Johannesburg and Beyond', *Global Environmental Change*, 13, 223–8.

Shaw, M. (1996) *Civil Society and Media in Global Crises: Representing Distant Violence.* London: Pinter.

Sheehan, M. (2005) *International Security: An Analytical Survey.* Boulder, CO: Lynne Rienner.

Simon, H. (1957) *Administrative Behaviour.* Glencoe: Free Press.

—— (1985) 'Human Nature and Politics The Dialogue of Psychology with Political Science', *American Political Science Review*, 79, 293–304.

Sinclair, J., Jacka, E. and Cunningham, S. (1996) 'Peripheral Vision', in J. Sinclair, E. Jacka and S. Cunningham (eds), *New Patterns in Global Television Peripheral Vision.* Oxford: Oxford University Press.

Skocpol, T. (1985) 'Bringing the State Back In: Strategies of Analysis in Current Research', in P. Evans, D. Rueschemeyer, and T. Skocpol (eds), *Bringing the State Back In.* Cambridge: Cambridge University Press.

Smith, A. (1776/1993) *Wealth of Nations.* Oxford: Oxford University Press.

Smith, M. (2006) 'Pluralism', in C. Hay, M. Lister and D. Marsh (eds), *The State: Theories and Issues.* Basingstoke: Palgrave Macmillan.

—— (2009) *Power and the State.* Basingstoke: Macmillan.

Smith, S. (1987) 'Paradigm Dominance in International Relations: The Development of International Relations as a Social Science', *Millennium: Journal of International Studies*, 16(2), 189–206.

Smith, S. and Owens, P. (2008) 'Alternative Approaches in International Theory', in J. Baylis, S. Smith and P. Owens (eds), *The Globalization of World Politics: An Introduction to International Relations.* Oxford: Oxford University Press.

Smits, K. (2009) *Applying Political Theory: Issues and Debates.* Basingstoke: Palgrave Macmillan.

Snidal, D. (2002) 'Rational Choice and International Relations' in W. Carlsnaes, T. Risse and B. Simmons (eds) *Handbook of International Relations.* London: Sage, 73–94.

Sorkin, A. S. (2009) *Too Big to Fail: Inside the Battle to Save Wall Street.* London: Allen Lane.

Spretnak, C. (1987) 'Ecofeminism: Our Roots and Flowering', *EcoSpirit*, 3(2), 2–9.

Squires, J. (1999) *Gender in Political Theory.* Cambridge: Cambridge University Press.

Standage, T. (1998) *The Victorian Internet.* London: Weidenfeld & Nicolson.

Steans, J. (1998) *Gender and International Relations: An Introduction.* Cambridge: Polity.

—— (2000) 'The Gender Dimension', in D. Held (ed.), *A Globalizing World? Culture, Economics, Politics.* London: Routledge.

Stern Review (2006) *Stern Review: The Economics of Climate Change*, http://www. hm-treasury.gov.uk/stern_review_report.htm (accessed 18 May 2010).

Stern, N. (2008) 'The Economics of Climate Change', *American Economic Review: Papers and Proceedings*, 98(2), 1–37.

Stoker, G. (2006) *Why Politics Matter*. Basingstoke: Palgrave Macmillan.

Stoker, G. and Marsh, D. (2002) 'Introduction', in D. Marsh and G. Stoker (eds), *Theory and Methods in Political Science*. Basingstoke: Palgrave Macmillan.

Stone, D. (2002) *Policy Paradox: The Art of Political Decision Making*. New York, NY: W. W. Norton.

Strange, S. (1987) 'The Persistent Myth of Lost Hegemony', *International Organisation*, 41, 551–74.

Street, J. (1997) *Politics and Popular Culture*. Cambridge: Polity.

—— (2001) *Mass Media Politics and Democracy*. Basingstoke: Palgrave Macmillan.

Sutton, M. (2001) 'An Index of Deaths form the Conflict in Ireland', http://www. cain.ulst.ac.uk/sutton (accessed 25 August 2010).

Taggart, P. and Lees, C. (2006) 'Politics: The State of the Art', *Politics*, 26(1), 1–2.

Tannenwald, N. (1999) 'The Nuclear Taboo: The United States and the Normative Basis of Nuclear Non-Use', *International Organization*, 53(3), 433–68.

Tashakkori, A. and Teddlie, C (1998) *Mixed Methodology. Combining Qualitative and Quantitative Approaches*. Thousand Oaks, CA: Sage.

Taylor, C. (1995) *Philosophical Arguments*. Cambridge, MA: Harvard University Press.

Taylor, M. (2006) *Rationality and the Ideology of Disconnection*. Cambridge: Cambridge University Press.

Temple, M. (2006) 'Dumbing Down is Good for You', *British Politics*, 1(2), 257–73.

—— (2008) *The British Press*. Maidenhead: Open University Press.

Thelen, K. and Steinmo, S. (1992) 'Historical Institutionalism in Comparative Politics', in S. Steinmo, K. Thelen and F. Longstreth (eds), *Structuring Politics Historical Institutionalism in Comparative Analysis*. Cambridge: Cambridge University Press.

Therborn, G. (1982) 'What Does the Ruling Class Do When It Rules?', in A. Giddens and D. Held (eds), *Classes, Power and Conflict*. Berkeley, CA: University of California Press.

Thompson, G. (2000) 'Economic Globalization?, in D. Held (ed.), *A Globalizing World?: Culture, Economics, Politics*. Bath: Open University/Routledge.

Thucydides (1954) *The Peloponnesian War*, trans. Rex Warner. Harmondsworth: Penguin.

Tickner J (1988) 'Hans Morgenthau's Principles of Political Realism: A Feminist Reformulation', *Millennium*, 17(3), 429–40.

—— (1995) 'Revisioning Security', in K. Booth and S. Smith (eds), *International Relations Theory Today*. Cambridge: Polity Press.

—— (2008) 'Gender in World Politics', in J. Baylis, S. Smith and P. Owens (eds), *The Globalization of World Politics: An Introduction to International Relations*. Oxford: Oxford University Press.

Traynor, I. (2003) 'The Privatisation of War', *Guardian*, 10 December, http://www. sandline.com/hotlinks/Guardian_Privatisation-war.html (accessed 18 May 2010).

Tsebelis, G. (1990) *Nested Games: Rational Choice in Comparative Politics*. Berkeley, CA: University of California Press.

Turner T. and Brownhill, L. (2004) '"Why Women are at War with Chevron" Nigerian Subsistence Struggles Against the International Oil Industry', *Journal of African and Asian Studies*, 39(1–2), 63–93.

Turner, T. and Oshare, M. (1994) 'Women's Uprising Against the Nigerian Oil Industry in the 1980s', in T. Turner and B. Ferguson (eds), *Arise Ye Mighty People: Gender Class Race in Popular Struggle.* New Jersey, NJ: African World Press.

Ukeje, C. (2004) 'From Aba to Ugborodo: Gender Identity and Alternative Discourse of Social Protest Among Women in the Oil Delta of Nigeria', *Oxford Development Studies*, 32(4), 65–17.

UNDP (2006) *Human Development Report 2006: Beyond Security: Power, Poverty and the Global Water Crisis.* New York, NY: UNDP.

UNFCC (2009) *Copenhagen Accord*, Framework Convention on Climate Change, http://unfccc.int/resource/docs/2009/cop15/eng/l07.pdf (accessed 18 May 2008).

Vidal, J. (2010) 'Nigeria's Agony Dwarfs the Gulf Oil Spill. The US and Europe Ignore it', *The Observer*, 30 May.

Vidal, J., Stratton, A. and Goldenberg, S. (2009) 'Low Targets, Goals Dropped: Copenhagen Ends in Failure. Deal Thrashed Out at Talks Condemned as Climate Change Scepticism in Action', *The Guardian*, 18 December.

Villmoare, A. (1990) 'Politics and Research: Epistemological Moments', *Law and Social Inquiry*, 15(1), 149–54.

Viotti, P. and Kauppi, M. (eds) (2010) *International Relations Theory.* New York, NY: Longman.

Von Hayek, F. (1991) *The Road to Serfdom.* London: Routledge.

Waever, O. (1998) 'The Sociology of a Not So International Discipline: American and European Developments in International Relations', *International Organization*, 52(4), 687–727.

Wallerstein, I. (1974; 1980; 1989) *The Modern World System*, 3 vols. New York, NY: Academic Press.

—— (2010) 'The Modern World System as a Capitalist World-Economy', in P. Viotti and M. Kauppi (eds), *International Relations Theory.* New York, NY: Longman Pearson.

Walt, S. (1997) 'Why Alliances Endure or Collapse', *Survival*, 39(1), 156–79.

Walter, N. (2010) *Living Dolls: The Return of Sexism.* London: Virago Press.

Waltz, K (1959) *Man, the State and War: A Theoretical Analysis.* New York, NY: Columbia University Press.

—— (1979) *Theory of International Politics.* Reading, MA: Addison-Wesley.

—— (1989) 'The Origins of War in Neorealist Theory', in R. Rotbeg and T. Robb (eds), *The Origin and Prevention of Major Wars.* Cambridge: Cambridge University Press.

—— (1993) 'The Emerging Structure of International Politics', *International Security*, 25(1), 5–41.

Wamukonya, N. and Skutsch, M. (2001) *Is there a Gender Angle to the Climate Change Negotiations?* New York: Commission for Sustainable Development.

Wapner, P. (2003) 'World Summit on Sustainable Development: Toward a Post Jo'burg Environmentalism', *Global Environmental Politics*, 3(1), 1–10.

Watson, M. (2005) *Foundations of International Political Economy.* Basingstoke: Palgrave Macmillan.

Waylen, G. (1997) 'Gender, Feminism and Political Economy', *New Political Economy*, 2(2), 205–20.

Weale, A. (2010) 'Political Theory and Practical Public Reasoning', *Political Studies*, 58 (2) 266–81.

Webb, T. (2010) 'Clumsy Response Threatens to Make a Bad Situation Worse', *Guardian*, 2 June, 16.

Weber, M. (1932/1946) 'Bureaucracy', in H. Gerth and C. Wright Mills (eds), *From Max Weber: Essays in Sociology*. New York: Cambridge University Press.
—— (1964) *The Theory of Social and Economic Organization*. New York: Free Press.
Weedon, C. (2004) *Feminist Practices and Poststructuralist Theory*. Malden, MA: Blackwell.
Weingast, B. R. and Wittman, D. A. (2006) 'The Reach of Political Economy', in *The Oxford Handbook of Political Economy*, ed. B.R.Weingast and D.A.Wittman. Oxford: Oxford University Press.
Wendt, A. (1987) 'The Agent–Structure Problem in International Relations Theory', *International Organization*, 41, 335–70.
—— (1992) 'Anarchy is What States Make of It: The Social Construction of Power Politics', *International Organization*, 46(2) (Spring), 391–425.
—— (1995) 'Constructing International Politics', *International Security*, 20(1) (Summer), 71–81.
—— (1999) *The Social Theory of International Politics* Cambridge: Cambridge University Press
Wheeler, M. (1997) *Politics and the Mass Media*. Oxford: Blackwell.
Whitworth, S. (1994) *Feminism and International Relations Towards a Political Economy of Gender in Interstate and Non-Governmental Institutions*. New York, NY: St Martin's Press.
—— (2009) 'Feminist Perspectives', in P. Williams (ed.), *Security Studies: An Introduction*. Abingdon: Routledge.
Williams, C. and Millington, A. (2004) 'The Diverse and Contested Meanings of Sustainable Development', *The Geographical Journal*, 170(2), 99–104.
Williams, M. (1996) 'International Political Economy and Global Environmental Change', in J. Vogler and M. Imber (eds), *The Environment and International Relations*. London: Routledge.
Wilson, E. (1998) *Consilience*. London: Little, Brown.
Wollstonecraft, M. (1792/1993) *Vindication of the Rights of Women*. Harmondsworth: Penguin.
Women's Environment and Development Organization – (WEDO) (2009) *Gender and Climate Change at Copenhagen COP-15: WEDO's Perspective on a History-making Year*, http://www.gendercc.net/fileadmin/inhalte/Dokumente/Press/WEDO_COP15_Gender_Perspective_Feb2010.pdf (accessed 18 May 2010).
World Bank (2000) *Entering the 21st Century: World Development Report 1999/2000*. Oxford: Oxford University Press.
Wright, E. (1978) *Class, Crisis and the State*. London: New Left Books.
Wright, O., Levine, A. and Sober, E. (1992) *Reconstructing Marxism: Essays on Explanation and the Theory of History*. London: Verso.
Wright Mills, C. (1956) *The Power Elite*. New York, NY: Oxford University Press.
Yearley, S. (2002) 'The Social Construction of Environmental Problems: A Theoretical Review and Some Not-very-Herculean Labors', in R. Dunlap, F. Buttel, P. Dickens and A. Gijswijt (eds), *Sociological Theory and the Environment: Classical Foundations, Contemporary Insights*. Lanham, MD: Rowman & Littlefield.
Young, M. (1958/1973) *The Rise of the Meritocracy*. Harmondsworth: Penguin.
Zakaria, F. (2003) *The Future of Freedom: Illiberal Democracy at Home and Abroad*. New York, NY: W. W. Norton.

Index